An Encyclopaedic Dictionary of Indian Mythology

A SERIES OF AN ENCYCLOPAEDIC DICTIONARY OF INDIAN HISTORY AND CULTURE

AN ENCYCLOPAEDIC DICTIONARY OF INDIAN MYTHOLOGY

Editors
Dr. A.N. Kapoor
V.P. Gupta
Mohini Gupta

RADHA PUBLICATIONS
NEW DELHI 110 002

First Published 2004

ISBN 81-7487-284-1

Published by

RADHA PUBLICATIONS
4378/4-B, Ansari Road,
Daryaganj,
New Delhi 110002
Phones: 3261839, 3254306

PRINTED IN INDIA

Published by Nitin Garg for Radha Publications, Lasertypeset by Jitendra Kumar Singh, Delhi-94, and printed at Tarun Offset Press, Delhi.

Preface

An Encyclopaedic Dictionary of Indian Mythology is the first title in the series on *An Encyclopaedic Dictionary of Indian History and Culture*. The volume proposes to deal with Indian mythology in all its aspects. The Indian mythology is probably the most complicated and the oldest mythologies in the world. The origin of this mythology can be traced to the first book of mankind—the *Rigveda*.

The mythology was developed in the two epics—the *Ramāyāṇa* and the *Mahābharata* and found its culmination in the *Purāṇas*. The deeds of the gods and goddesses and also of ancient heroes have moulded the psyche of Indians.

The volume has three sections: (1) Historical Perspectives; (2) Encyclopaedic Entries from A to Z and (3) Bibliography.

The volume does not contain a section on chronology as it is well-nigh impossible to provide creditable data for the personalities or deeds related to the theme.

The first section Historical Perspectives has two chapters: The first chapter deals with the meaning and role of mythology in world civilizations. The second chapter deals with the sources and evolution of Indian mythology. There is a brief discussion of the Buddhist, Jain, Islamic, Sikh, Christian, and tribal mythologies besides a detailed exposition of the Hindu pantheon.

Editors

Contents

Section One

Historical Perspectives

1

Meaning and Role of Mythology

Meaning of Mythology

Mythology is the study or science of myths. A body or collection of myths is also known as mythology.

Myths are essentially stories. They originated in ancient times and deal with ideas or beliefs about the early history of a race. They give explanations of many natural events, such as the seasons. The myths are mostly imaginary, fictitious or impossible. However, they underlie a given culture and provide symbolic interpretation of its various aspects. The myths describe gods, creation, ancestral heroes and events which do not possess historical authenticity but are handed down from generation to generation, carrying with them some vital truths of the culture.

Mythology and Religion

Religion is a code of belief or philosophy, which often involves the worship of a God or gods. Belief in a supernatural power is not essential as is the case with Buddhism and Confucianism, but faithful adherence is usually considered to be rewarded. Among the organised religions of the world are: Bahai's Faith, Buddhism,

Christianity, Confucianism, Hinduism, Jainism, Judaism, Shintoism, Sikhism, Taoism and Zoroastrianism. In addition to these organized world religions, there are a large number of tribal religions and innumerable religious sects and Cults.[1] Mythology is often interwoven with religion and manifests certain intimate beliefs of mankind.

Components of Mythology

God is the basic component of mythology. It is used to mean the person who made and controls the universe. Pagan people[2] worshipped idols which they called gods. These gods were supposed to have power over the earth and the lives of the people. People have always yearned for a god. The nature and character of god has, however, varied in different cultures.

Some civilizations believe in one god. There are civilizations which have faith in several gods. Civilizations having faith in one god are called *monotheistic*. People believing in several gods are known as *polytheistic*. Judaism, Christianity and Islam are monotheistic religions. Most Christians believe that God is a Trinity. The Trinity is three aspects or persons—the *Father,* the *Son* and the *Holy Spirit* in one God. The Father is the God in heaven. The Son is Jesus Christ who came to earth in human form to redeem mankind. The Holy Spirit is the inner consciousness of man which guides people's thoughts and actions.

In the cosmic process there is a constant struggle between two principles—the *Divine* and the *Evil. Ahura Mazda,* the lord of the Zoroastrians is opposed to the evil principle. The nature of sin and its eradication has been discussed in all religions.

Several of the great religions of the world talk of the existence of angel beings are higher and wiser than men, but still lower than God and created by Him. Angels appear in the mythologies of the Hindus mainly as the messengers and servants of God. The same is the case with Persians, Jews and other religions.

In Jewish, Christian and Islamic religions the chief spirit of evil is called the Devil or Satan. The Devil is against God and tries to tempt people away from God. There are many examples of the struggles between good and evil in many mythologies.

Good or Truth is believed to triumph in the end.[3] Milton's *Paradise Lost* tells how Satan fell from heaven through pride, and then persuaded Adam and Eve[4] to turn away from God. He describes their pertinence and draws the lesson that through Christ God would eventually win people back.

The notion of *Heaven* and *Hell* constitute an important ingredient of mythologies. The ancient Egyptians believed that the sun, moon and sky were gods. They thought that all living things originally came from the *Heavens* and would in the end return there.

The ancient Greeks believed that after death they would go to *Hades,* an underworld ruled by the god Pluto and his wife, Persephone.

The ancient Hebrew idea of life after death was a dull underworld called *Sheol.*

Muslims look forward to the Heaven as described in their sacred text book *Quran*. It is the paradise which has all the pleasures of life.

The Christians believe that the resurrection, when Jesus Christ came back to life, is an inspiring message for the believers that death does not destroy the souls of the people. In the New Testament Heaven is the place where true believers will go after death.

The Role of Archaeology

Archaeology has played an important role in enhancing our knowledge about mythology. The archaeologists by digging in the ruins of ancient cities have thrown light on the nature and growth of various mythologies across the world. It is now established that the cave dwellers of southern Europe, the Celts[5] of England and Western Europe, the Sumerians[6], Hittites[7], and Babylonians[8] of the eastern Mediterranean region, had rich mythologies. The work of the archaeologists is also leading to a better appreciation of American Indian Civilization in Central and South America. Archaeologists, digging into 5,000 years old Villages have found carved figures resembling statutes of gods.

Man has always stood in awe before nature. He has not been able to control the forces of nature which have remained mysterious to him. He has considered these forces to be gods or manifestations of God's power.

Creation Mythology

The *creation mythology* attempts to answer the questions regarding the genesis of the world and mankind. All the major religions of the world have tried to solve the mystery. According to the Bible, the world and humanity were created by a supernatural creator, not more than 6,000 years ago. The modern science rejects this view and believes in Darwin's theory of evolution.

The Sumerians, around 3000 BC, thought that the god of the waters, Enki, told his old water mother, Nammu, to take bits of clay and mould the shapes of men and women. She made perfect men and women of every sort. Then Enki and his wife, the Earth goddess had a contest. Each created various sorts of deformed people. This explains why some people are not perfect.

Greek Mythology

Zeus was the most important god in Greek mythology. He ruled the Earth and the heavens. His brother Pluto ruled the underworld. Another brother Poseidon, ruled the sea. The Greeks believed that Zeus was the son of an earlier god, Cromus. Cromus, like his son Zeus, had come to power by conquering his father, Uranus.

Zeus and his brothers and sisters along with their sons and daughters were called the Olympian gods because they lived on Mount Olympus[9]. Here was Zeus' wife. One of their sons was Hephaestus, the smith god, who lived in a great cave under the mountain. The smoke and five from his forges caused Volcanoes. Some of the other Greek gods were: Apollo (sun-god), Artemis (moon goddess). Athena (goddess of war and wisdom), Aphrodite (goddess of beauty), Ares (god of war), Bacchus (wine god), and Hermes (the messenger). The *Illiad* tells much about the way the gods behaved. The Greeks thought that the gods lived and conducted themselves like ordinary human beings.

Roman Mythology

The Romans believed in sacred spirits which were called *nunuina.* These spirits lived in every object in nature and the home. The Romans developed their gods after coming into contact with the Greeks. Jupiter or Jove was the chief god of the Romans. He has been identified with the Greek god Zeus. He was god of the sky and was associated with lightning and thunderbolt. Jupiter was the protector in battle and bestowed victory. Jupiter is believed to be the son of Saturn. He married his sister Juno, and reigned on Mount Olympus as lord of heaven.

Horatius was one of the legendary heroes of ancient Rome who flourished in the 6th century BC and defended the city of Rome from foreign invaders. Hercules (in Greek mythology) was another Roman hero.

Romulus was the legendary founder and first king of Rome according to Roman mythology. Romus was his twin brother. Bachchus happened to be the god of fertility and wine. He was the Roman counterpart of the Greek god Dionysus.

Some of the leading Roman goddesses included Abnoba, Abindemita, Acca Larentia, Diana, Flora, Juno, Jineiva, Pales, Psyche and Venus.

Egyptian Mythology

Throughout ancient Egyptian history, beliefs about the gods changed many times. There were many local gods also. The most famous Egyptian gods were Osiris, his wife, Isis and their son Horus. Isis was considered to be the goddess of medicine, marriage and agriculture.

Scandinavian and Germanic Mythology

About the 1st century AD, the Germanic peoples of northern Europe worshipped their gods in sacred groves of trees. Certain trees were thought to be divine.

The Norsemen[10] believed in many gods. They also believed in other strange and powerful creatures, such as elves, frost giants and fire giants. The four most eminent Norse gods were Tiw, Woden, Thor and Freya.

American Indian Mythology

When the Spanish conquerors arrived in Central and South America, in the 16th century, they found well-developed Indian civilizations such as the Aztecs and Mayas in Mexico, the Chief-Chas in Colombia and the Incas in Peru. Quetzal-Coastl was the chief god of the Aztecs. The Mayas had Kukulcan as their principal deity. The sun was also an important god of the Incas of Peru. They believed their king descended from the sun itself. Therefore it was divine. The Incas also had gods of the sea, of the moon, and of important stars and planets.

Most of the Indians of North and South India lived as scattered tribes and did not develop large civilizations. They were not able to evolve their mythologies also. However they believed that some kind of magical, or supernatural power existed in animals and plants. Some of these tribes thought that they had a certain kind of brotherhood with some animals.

Mythologies of the Far East

The mythologies of China, Korea and Japan are related. But there are also many differences. The Chinese believed that the world was ruled by Heaven who was husband of Earth. Certain men and women who performed noteworthy deeds became gods.

The Koreans worshipped nature. Their chief god was Tankun whom they considered to be the founder of their kingdom.

The Japanese also claim to have descended from the sun. Izangi, Izanami and Amaterasu are their chief divinities. They believe that their emperors have descended from the sun-god.

Japan has been influenced by certain Buddhist mythologies also. Shintoism is the indigenous Japanese religion which was introduced in Japan in the 6th century AD. Ancient Shintoism was polytheistic. The chief god was Kami, who ruled seas and mountains. He was also manifested in outstanding men. The followers of Shinto also believed in *Kami* of ideas such as growth, creation and judgment. According to Shintoism all the deities are said to cooperate with one another. A life lived according to the teachings of Shintoism is believed to produce a mystical power that gains the protection of the gods.[11]

Sumerian Mythologies

The earliest mythologies are said to have developed in Sumeria whose civilization goes back more than 3,000 years BC. The Sumerians had a number of city gods. There are many myths and legends associaterd with the greatest of the Sumerian heroes *Gilgamesh*.[12]

Celtic Mythologies

The Celtic peoples of Western Europe were scattered

in several tribes. They developed their particular myths which were written down by Roman travellers. Their chief gods were Cernunnos and Dagda. Cuchulian was a great warrior hero. Morrigan was the Celtic goddess of war.

Slavic Mythology

The most important gods of the Slavic peoples[13] were Perun (god of thunder), Svarog (god of sky) and Duzbag (the sun god). The Slavs also believed in wicked gods and in nature gods.

Tribal Mythologies

In addition to the organized religions of the world, there are tribal religions found in all parts of the globe. *Shaman* is the priest of the earliest tribes who can talk to the spirits and obtain help from them. The tribal people have, down the ages, developed a number of cults such as The Cult of After Life, The Agriculture Cult, The Cult of Ancestor *Worship,* The Cult of Animal Worship, The Cult of Burial, The Cult of Chiefs, The Clan and Family Cult, The Community Cult, The Fire Cult, The Nature Cult, The Cult of Gurus and The Cult of the Mother Goddess.[14]

The Present Status

With the growth of science and technology, myths have lost their importance in actual life. They now mostly live in folk tales and traditions. They, however, continue to be a source of literary creations.

References

1. For a concise discussion of world religions see A.N. Kapoor and V.P. Gupta, *A Dictionary of World Religions,* Ajanta Publications, Delhi, 1998.

2. Pagan is a person who does not believe in any religion especially Christianity. He is similar to a heathen or an atheist.
3. *Satyameva Jayate Nanritam* are the words taken form *Mundak Upanishad*. They mean "Truth alone triumphs, not the falsehood." *Satyameva Jayate* is inscribed on the state emblem of India which is an adaption from the Sarnath Lion Capital of Ashoka. The emblem was adopted by the Government of India in January 1950.
4. In the Old Testament Adam and Eve are hailed as the founder of the human race. Adam was created by God from dust and given the breath of life. He was placed in the Garden of Eden, where Eve was created from his rib and given to him as companion. Eve tempted Adam who tasted the forbidden fruit of Tree of Knowledge of God and Evil. God expelled them from Heaven for this trespass.
5. The term "Celt" is derived from the Greek word "Keltoi". Celt was a member of an Indo-European people that originated in Alpine Europe and spread to Iberian peninsula. In the 1st century BC they were defeated by the Roman Empire and confined largely to Britain, Ireland and North France.
6. Sumerian Civilization was the world's earliest civilization. It is dated about 3500 BC, and located at the confluence of the Tigris and Euphrates rivers in lower Mesopotamia (present day Iraq).
7. Hittites were a group of people who inhabited Anatolia and North Syria from the 1st millennium BC. They were a great power between 1400-1200 BC.
8. Babylonia and Assur were two of the greatest cities of Mesopotamia. These cities became the centres of the empires of Babylonia and Assyria around 3000 BC.
9. The original olympic games were played at this place. They were abolished in AD 394. The present day games have been held every four years since 1896.
10. Norsemen were early inhabitants of Norway. The term Norsemen is also applied to Scandinavian people who, during the 8th-11th centuries, raided and settled in Britain, Ireland, France, Russia, Iceland and Greenland.
11. A.N. Kapoor and V.P. Gupta, *op. cit.*, pp. 219-224.
12. Gilgamesh is the best-known of all Mesopotamian heroes.

His adventures during his search for immortality are chronicled on 12 incomplete tablets. There is no historical evidence for his exploits.

13. The Slavs are an Indo-European people of Central and East Europe, the Balkans and parts of North Asia. They moved from Central Asia and settled in the East and South East Asia during the 2nd and 3rd millennium.
14. For a historical survey of different religious sects and cults, refer to A.N. Kapoor and V.P. Gupta, *op. cit.*, pp. 303-18.

2

Sources and Evolution of Indian Mythology

A Composite Phenomenon

Indian mythology is probably the most complicated, varied and the oldest mythology in the world. It has a long history of about 5000 years and has passed through different phases. Indian mythology, like Indian culture is a composite phenomenon and consists of many currents. While Hinduism continues to be at the core, Indian mythology, has been enriched by Buddhism, Jainism, Islam, Zoroastrianism, Sikhism and Christianity. The rich tribal life has also contributed to the shaping of Indian mythology.

Indus Valley Civilization

Like Indian history, Indian mythology starts with the Indus Valley Civilization popularly known as the *Harappan Culture* (2700-1500 BC). The Harappan Culture was essentially an urban culture which had plans of well-laid streets, elaborate drainage system, public baths, residential areas, granaries and fortified administrative-cum religious centres. Religious and social practices inferrred from Harappan artifacts demonstrate ritual bathing, phallus worship, ascetic practices, yogi discipline and feminine worship. Majority of scholars have concluded that some sort of goddess worship was practised in the Indus Valley. This Cult of the Mother Goddess was similar to its counterpart in Asia Minor and Mediterranean. On the basis of three scenes depicted on seals, we can surmise that the Indus Valley people had a goddess who was associated with vegetation and presided over plant and animal life. She was worshipped for her life-giving and life-sustaining attributes[1].

The Vedic Age

The *Vedas* are four in number—the *Rigveda*, the *Yajurveda*, the *Samaveda* and the *Atharvaveda*.

The *Rigveda* is the oldest of the four *Vedas*. It is dated sometime between 3000 BC and 1500 BC. It is credited to be the earliest respository of human experience. It refers specifically to the onke Reality, conceived of by sages in several ways and called by different names. The *Rig-Veda* is considered to mark the beginning of Hindu religious-philosophic thought including mythology. Some of the major general Vedic deities are *Dyaus* (Sky), *Prithvi* (Earth), *Aditi* (mother of gods), *Adityas* (descendents of Aditi), and *Agni* (Fire). Sun is an important Vedic deity and its manifestations are *Surya, Pushan, Mitra, Varuna, Asvins*, and *Ushas*. The significant storm deities include *Indra, Indrani, Parjanya, Vayu*, and *Maruti*. *Soma, Visevakarma* and *Yama* are other leading Vedic deities. According to W.J. Wilkins, Agni, Indra and Surya formed the Vedic Triad.[2] The will of the Vedic gods was sovereign. No mortal could thwart their design. In the numerous hymns of the *Rigveda* every single god is represented as supreme and absolute.[3]

Vedic mythology occupies a very important position in the study of the history of religions. Its oldest source presents to us the earliest stage in the evolution of the beliefs based on the personification and worship of natural phenomenon. To this oldest phase can be traced the germs of the religious beliefs of the great majority of the modern Indians.[4]

The Two Epics

After the Vedic age comes the age of the two epics—the *Ramayana* by Valmiki and the *Mahabharata* by Vyasa.

The *Ramayana* is the life-history of Lord Rama. The epic has exercised a deep influence throughout India and beyond in the countries of South East Asia. The story of the *Ramayana* has been told and retold in all the languages of India. Rama is hailed as an incarnation of God Vishnu and a major focus of ther Bhakti movement. Sugriva, Lakshman, Hanuman, Nala and Sushena are the demi-gods of the *Ramayana*. Sita, the consort of Rama is supposed to be goddess Lakshmi in human form. Other important female characters of the *Ramayana* like Kaushalya, Kaikeyi, Manthara, Urmila, Shabri, Sulochana and Mandodari have left their permanent impact on Indian mind.

The *Mahabharata* is the longest poem known to the literary history. It consists of 1,00,000 *slokas* and is equal to about eight times the *Illiad* and *Odyssey* put together. The main story of the *Mahabharata*, dealing with court of Hasthinapur, forms only one-fifth of the whole work. The remaining portion is in the nature of an encyclopaedia of Indian history, philosophy, social system, mythology and geography. The *Mahabharata* is revered as the fifth Veda and its author Krishna Dvaipayana Vyasa is looked upon as the God Narayan himself. Towards the end, the epic says of itself, what is found here is found everywhere, what is not present here, cannot be seen anywhere. The victory of the *Dharma* or righteousness is the message of the epic.[5]

The *Gita*—the celestial song—is a part of the *Mahabharata*. The teacher of the *Gita* is Lord Krishna himself who exhorts his disciple Arjuna, the hero of the *Mahabharata* to carry out his duties even if it involves the killing of the kith and the kin. The *Gita* repeats the essence of the *Vedas* and the *Upanishads* and expounds the theory of incarnations of God in different forms to combat the cosmic disorder.

The heroic characters of the *Mahabharata* including hundreds of kings, warriors, sages, men and women, provide a biographical dictionary of ancient India. Some of the well-known characters of the Mahabharata are Abhimanyu, Agastya, Ahalya, Amba, Ambalika, Anasuya, Angira, Aniruddha, Arjuna, Ashwathama, Atreyi, Bakasura, Balarama, Bhima, Bhishma, Chitrangada, Dadhichi, Damayanti, Devayani, Dhrishtadyumna, Dhritarashtra, Draupadi, Drona, Duryodhana, Ekalavya, Gandhari, Ganga, Jayadratha, Karna, Krishna, Kunti, Madri, Nakula, Pandu, Parikshit, Satyaki, Savitri, Shakuni, Shantanu, Shikhandi, Shishupala, Subhadra, Urvashi, Uttara, Vidura, and Yudhishthira.[6]

The Purāṇas

Purāṇa means old. Hence, a *Purana* is an ancient legend or tale of olden times. The *Puranas* celebrate the powers and achievements of gods and goddesses. They represent the development of Hinduism and are considered as scriptures. The *Puranas* are written in verse and are in the nature of a dialogue between an exponent and an inquirer. The major *Puranas* are eighteen in number. There are eighteen subordinate Puranas also.

Related to three broad categories: (1) *Vishnu,* (2) *Shiva* and (3) *Brahma,* some of the most important *Purāṇas* are (1) *Agni Purāṇa,* (2) *Bhāgvat Purāṇa,* (3) *Bhavishya Purāṇa,* (4) *Brahmāṇḍa Purāṇa,* (5) *Brahma Purāṇa,* (6) *Brahma Vaivarta Purāṇa,* (7) *Devi Bhagvata Purāṇa,* (8) *Garuḍa Purāṇa,* (9) *Kalika Purāṇa,* (10) *Kurma Purāṇa,* (11) *Linga Purāṇa,* (12) *Markandeya Purāṇa,* (13) *Matsya Purāṇa,*

(14) *Nāradiya Purāṇa*, (15) *Padma Purāṇa*, (16) *Shiva Purāṇa*, (17) *Skanda Purāṇa*, (18) *Varuṇa Purāṇa*, (19) *Varaha Purāṇa*, and (20) *Vishnu Purāṇa*.

Brahma, Vishnu and Shiva are the chief male deities of the *Purāṇas*. Lakshmi, Parvati and Durga are portrayed as principal female deities. The eight incarnations of Vishnu is a favourite theme of the *Purāṇas*. The divine *rishis* like Bhrigu, Pulastya, Angiras, Atri, Vashistha, Kubera and Narada are also described in the *Purāṇas*.[7]

The Two Reform Movements

The fifth century India produced two reform movements—Buddhism and Jainism. Both these religions were opposed to the Brahmanical sacrifices and rituals. They were led by Gautam Buddha (550-468 BC) and Mahavira Vardhamana (sixth century BC died 527 or 467 BC). These religions had their own texts, principles and rites. In course of time they developed their own mythologies.

The Buddhist Mythology

The Buddhist mythology consists of the numerous legends, myths and tales of the Buddha and his manifestations not only in India but also in other countries such as Sri Lanka, Tibet, Central Asia, Japan, Sian and Indo-China. The myths deal with the historical Buddha as well as the celestial *Buddhas* and *Bodhisattvas*. The doctrine of the Bodhisattva is peculiar to *Mahayan Buddhism*. The Boddhisattva is someone who seeks enlightenment in order to help other living beings. A Bodhisattva is free to enter Nirvana but voluntarily chooses to be reborn until all other beings have attained that state. Bodhisattvas are looked upon as intercessors to whom believers may pray for redemption. *Mar* in the Buddhist mythology is the devil who represents evil and is a tempter. He is considered as a supernatural being who attempted to distract the Buddha from meditations that led to his enlightenment. With the *Tantras* the Buddhist mythology parts company with the original Buddha myth and links up with the Hindu mythology. The Hindu god Bhairava is known as Vajrabhairava in Tantrik Buddhism.

Following are some of the Buddhist deities worshipped in India and abroad.

Abhimukhi (friendly disposed)—Minor goddess. (Vajrayena)

Abhijnarja—Physician god Lamaist.

Adhimukticarya—Minor goddess. (Vajrayana)

Acali (immovable)—Minor goddess (Vajrayana).

Adhimuktivasita (Control of Confidence)—Minor goddess. One of a group of twelve goddesses personifying the disciplines of spiritual regeneration.

Adibuddha (the primeval Buddha): The original Buddha, the primordial force in the cosmos from whom the five Dhyanbuddhas arose. He is considered to be the embodiment of the concept of emptiness.

Akasagarbha (Essence of the Sky): Astral god Buddhist (Mahayana) and Lamaist (Tibet), one of the Bodhisattvas or meditation Buddhas. He lives in the "womb of the sky". His colour is green and book, jewel, lotus, and sun disc are his attributes.

Aksobha (Imperturbable): He is one of the fiver mystic spiritual counterparts of a human Buddha in Vajrayana Buddhism. His *Sakli* is Locana and he is normally accompanied by two elephants. His attributes include bell, three monkish robes, staff, jewel, lotus, prayer wheel and sword.

Amitabha (Of immense splendour): He is one of the five mystic spiritual counterparts of a human Buddha in Vajrayan Buddhism. Amitabha is a product of Adibuddha who represents that branch of the cosmos which is concerned with consciousness. His *Sakti* is Pandara and he is normally accompanied by two peacocks. His attributes are lock of hair, lotus, monks robe and water jar. Amitabha is also taken as a tutelary god in Lamaism (Tibet). His emanations include Padmapani, Manjusri and many other minor names.

Amoghpāśa: He is a Buddhist god, a variety of Avalokitesvara. Amoghpāśa is depicted with one head and six, eight or twenty hands. His attributes are arrow, bell, lotus, noose, prayer wheel, rosary, staff and tiger skin.

Amoghasiddhi (Unfailing power): He is one of the five mystic spiritual counterparts of a human Buddha in Vajrayana Buddhism. He is a product of the Adibuddha who represents the branch of the cosmos concerned with consciousness. His attributes are staff and seven headed snake. Anoghasiddhi is also taken as a tutelary deity in Tibetan Lamaism.

Arya-Tara (The Honourable Tara): She is a Buddhist goddess, the Sakti of Amoghsiddhi. Her name is often abbrievated to Tara. Her attributes are green lotus and staff.

Avalokitesvar (Merciful Lord): He is one of the most important deities of the Mahayana sect of Buddhism. He equates with Vishnu in Hinduism. In cosmic mythology he is a creator deity. His *Sakti* is Pandara and his attendant animal is a lion. His attributes are lotus rosary, sword and water jar.

Balaparamita (Perfection of Strength): She is one of a group of ten-*paramitas*. Her attributes are book and banner with jewel.

Jain Mythology

The term Jain is derived from *Jin* meaning conqueror or Great Hero. The core of Jainism lies in "Three Jewels" of right faith, right knowledge and right conduct. Jainism entails vows of non-violence, truth, chastity, charity, and non-attachment. Jain scholars do not postulate any creator. They believe in eternal law according to which the Universe continually passes through cycles of progress and decline. According to Jain teachings all things are composed of matter and *Jiva,* or souls. The purpose of living is to purify the soul and secure release from the bondage of birth and death.

Jain mythology consists of a number of significant figures. They are—

Tirthankars 2
Chakravartins 12
Vasudevas 9
Baldevas 9
Naradas 9
Rudras 11
Kamadevas 24

Subordinated to these figures are the gods classified into four groups: *Bhavanvasis* (gods of the house), *Vyantaras* (intermediaries), *Jyotiskas* (luminaries) and *Vaimanuks* (astral gods).

The notable Jain saints called Tirthankaras are twenty-four in number. There are many myths associated with their lives. Vrishabha was the first *Tirthankar*. He was son of Nabhi and Manudev. Parshwanath was born at Benares (now Varanasi) and commenced his family life when he was thirty years of age. He continued his asceticism for seventy years and died at the age of hundred years. Mahavira is the last and best known of all the Jain saints. He was born in a royal family. His father was Siddhartha and mother Trishala. At twenty-eight he lost his father, became king and reigned for two years. Then resigning his royal state, he entered upon a life of asceticism. He died at the age of seventy-two.

Islam

Islam originated in Arabia in the early seventh century and rapidly spread to Africa, Middle East, and India. In India Islam gradually spread over the entire subcontinent and ruled over the country for about eight centuries.

Islam in India is a synthesis of diverse Indian groups with four major extra-subcontinental ethno-cultural streams—the Arab, Turkish, Persian and Afghan. Sufis were the most formative of Islamic influences.

Islam faced on ancient civilization in India. It could not conquer it. Nor could it be absorbed in it. It has maintained its own mythology derived from Quran and the Arab world.

Islam has borrowed a number of myths from Judaism and Christianity. It has some myths of its own which are woven around the Prophet Muhammad and the members of his family.

Some myths of Islam are listed in the paragraphs that follow:—

Abdal: "Substitute". They are certain persons through whom the God continues the world in existence. Their number is seventy—forty reside in Syria and thirty elsewhere. When one dies another takes his place, being so appointed by God.

Abel (Arabic Habil): In the Quran the two sons of Adam are called Habil and Qabul.

Abraham: One of the six great prophets to whom god delivered special laws. Abraham is very frequently mentioned in the Quran together with Ishmail and Isaac.

Adam: The first man. He is reckoned by the Muslim writers as the one, to whom ten portions of Quran were revealed. According to the Muhammadans, Adam fell on the isle of Ceylon (now Sri Lanka) and Eve near Makkah in Arabia after they were thrown from heaven. Later on, angel Gabriel took Adam to a mountain near Makkah where he found his wife. The mountain was named Arafat.

Adn: The Garden of Eden. It is said to be the garden of perpetual abode. The term is used both for the garden of Eden in which the founders of human race lived and also for a place in celestial bliss.

Al-Ahad: "The One". A title given to God.

Al-Ali: One of the ninety-nine special names of God,

it means "The Exalted One".

Al Araf: The partition between heaven and hell described in the Quran.

Arafat: The feast of sacrifice when the pilgrims proceed to Mount Arafat.

Arafat: The "Mount of Recognition" situated twelve miles from Makkah. It is the place where the pilgrims stay on the ninth day of the pilgrimage, and recite the mid-day and afternoon prayers. It is said that Adam found his wife Eve at this place.

Ashura: Literally it means "the tenth". It is a voluntary fast day, observed on the tenth of the month of Muharram. It is related that Muhaṃmad observed it, and said it was a day respected by Jews and Christians. It is hailed as the day on which God created Adam and Eve, heaven and hell, life and death. The Sunnis keep a fast, on this day.

Babel: Babel is regarded by the Muslims as the fountain-head of the science of magic. They suppose Harut and Marut to be two angels who, in consequence of their want of compassion for the frailties of mankind, were sent down to earth to be tempted. They both sinned. On being permitted to choose whether they would like to be punished now or hereafter they chose the former. They are still suspended by the feet at Babel in a rocky pit. They are the great teachers of magic.

David: Arabic Dawud. He was a king of Israel and a Prophet to whom the God revealed the Book of Psalms.

Eden: Arabic *Adn* which means a "fixed abode". It refers to Paradise where Adam and Eve lived before their expulsion from heaven.

Eve. Arabic Hawwa. She was the first woman, wife of Adam. She was tempted by Satan to taste the fruit of the Tree of Knowledge of Good and Evil. She then tempted Adam to eat the fruit as well. This brought about their expulsion from the Garden of Eden.

Gabriel: He is Jibrail in Quran. He is the angel who was the medium of the revealation of Quran to

Muhammad. In Muslim books as "The Supreme Spirit", "The Honoured Spirit," "The Holy Spirit" and "The Faithful Spirit".

God: The name of the creator of the Universe in the Quran is Allah. The title is given to the Supreme Being by Muhammadans of every race and language. There are 99 names or attributes of the God in Quran. Some of them are:—

Rahman: The Merciful
Rahim: The Compassionate
Malik: The King
Mumin: The Faithful
Aziz: The Mighty
Jabbar: The Repairer
Khaliq: The Creator
Bari: The Maker
Ghaffar: The Forgiver
Wahhab: The Bestower
Razzaq: The Provider
Alun: The Knower
Rafi: The Exalter

Paradise: The Muhammadan Paradise is called "the garden". It is *Jannat* in Arabic and *Bihisht* in Persian. There are eight paradises mentioned in the Quran:

1. *Jannatu-I-Khuld,* The Garden of Eternity.
2. *Darus-salam,* The Dwelling of Peace.
3. *Daru-Qarar,* The Dwelling with abideth.
4. *Jannatu-l-Adn,* The Garden of Eden.
5. *Jannatu-I-Mawa,* The Garden of Refuge.
6. *Jannatu-l-Naim,* The Garden of Delight.
7. *Illiyun,* The seventh stage of celestial bliss.
8. *Jannatu-l-Firdaus,* The Gardens of Paradise.

The sensual delights of Muhammad's Paradise are proverbial. They must have exercised a considerable influence upon the minds of the people to whom he made known his mission.[8]

Sikhism

Sikhism was founded by *Guru Nanak* in the fifteenth century. The Sikhs had the *gurus*. Many scholars consider Sikhism as a variation of Hinduism. The tenth and the lost Sikh guru—Guru Gobind Singh—set up the *Khalsa* or the Sikh fraternity. He also announced the end of personal guruship and passed the perpetual succession to the Holy Scripture *The Guru Granth Sahib*.

The mythology of Sikhism is largely drawn from Hinduism. *The Bachitar Natak* (Play Marvellous), *Chandi Charitra* (story of the Goddess Chandi), *Chandi di Var* (The Praise of Goddess Chandi) and *Gian Prabodh* (Consciousness of Knowledge) written by Guru Gobind Singh are mythological compositions.[9]

Christianity

The Christians number about 20 million or nearly 2 per cent of the total population of India. According to popular tradition the Apostle Thomas came to South India in the first century AD. Descendents of his followers form a respected community in Kerala. The Portuguese came in the sixteenth century and undertook mass conversions. Saint Francis Xavier came to Goa in 1542. The Christian missionaries had a strong impact on the rectification of religion among all communities—Hindus, Muslims and Sikhs. The Indian Christians subscribe to the traditional Christian mythology which includes the *Old Testament*, stories of Prophets, miracles of Christ and his apostles like Peter, James, John, Andrew, Philip, Bartholomew, Mathew, Thomas, Lebbaeus, Sunion and Judas Iscariot.

Parsis

Parsis constitute a small ethno-religious community in India. They have descended from Persian Zoroastrians and took refuge in India to save themselves from invading Arabs in the seventh century AD. The *Avesta* plays a central role as the holy book of the Parsis. The *Shah Namah* of Firdausi preserves the Iranian tradition of the Parsi community. The *Kissah-i-Samyan* chronicles their exodus from Iran. The Mughal Emperor Akbar had invited the Parsi priests to represent Zoroastrian doctrines in his religious discussions. Ahura Mazda is the one god worshipped by the Zoroastrians.

Tribal Mythologies

In addition to magic religions like Hinduism, Buddhism, Jainism, Islam and Sikhism, there are a number of tribal religions with their own distinct beliefs and customs. The tribal religions have their mythologies, gods and views about creation. The native population of the Andaman Islands is almost extinct. Their ancestors are given the names of animals. *Plug* was their most powerful mythological figure. The Christian missionaries gave its name as the name of god—*Tomo* was their first ancestor.

The following are a few of the tribal deities popular in South India.

Ammavaru: She is the Hindu-Dravidian primordial mother goddess. She is said to have generated the cosmic egg in the sea of milk from which the major gods *Brahma, Vishnu* and *Siva* were born.

Anna Kuari: She is a local vegetation goddess worshipped by the Oraon tribe of Chota Nagpur. She receives human sacrifice in the months of spring. She is believed to endow riches on the sacrificer and to ensure plentiful harvest.

Ayappan: She is the local goddess of growth in the Kerala region.

The Cult of Mother Goddess

The Cult of the Mother Goddess constitutes a belief in

the supremacy of female energy identical with the creative power in the cosmic process. While the traces of this cult may be found in many ancient civilizations—both eastern and western—the tradition has been quite marked in India down the ages from the times of the *Rigveda* to the present day. The most lucid exposition of the goddess cult is to be found in the *Devi Mahatmya* of *Markandeya Purana*. The manifestations of the mother goddess in Hinduism are *Aindri, Amba, Ambika, Amman, Ammavaru, Annapurna, Aparajita, Arya, Bhagvati, Bhavani, Brahmāṇi, Chamuṇḍa, Chaṇḍi, Chinnamasta, Devi, Durga, Ganga, Gauri, Gayatri, Indrani, Kali, Kamakhya, Lakshmi, Mahāmāya, Maheshwari, Nārayaṇi, Nitya, Parvati, Radha, Sati, Shakti, Sita, Tārā, Usha, Vaishnavi* etc.[10]

References

1. V.P. Gupta and Mohini Gupta, *Mother Goddess: A Global Perspective*, Ambe Books, Delhi, 1999, p. 17.
2. Wilkins, W.J., *Hindu Mythology*, Rupa & Co., New Delhi, 1997, p. 10.
3. *Ibid.*, p. 11.
4. A.A. Macdonell, *Vedic Mythology*, p. 2.
5. Vyasa says:
   "With uplifted hands, shout, Alas! None listens to me. From *Dharma* one can obtain his *Artha* and *Kama*. Why is that people do not follow *Dharma*? Not out of passion, not out of fear, not out of avarice, not even for the sake of life one should abandon *Dharma*. This is the essence, that is the *Bharat Savitri;* meditate upon this as you rise out of bed every morning". Quoted by V.P. Gupta and Mohini Gupta, *op. cit.*, p. 21.
6. Subhash Mazumdar, *Who Is Who in the Mahabharata*, Bhartiya Vidya Bhawan, Bombay, 1990.
7. Vettan Mani's *Puranic Encyclopaedia* is a comprehensive dictionary with special reference to Epic and Puranic literature. Motilal Banarasidass, Delhi, Reprint 1984.
8. Source, Thomas Patrick Hughes, *Dictionary of Islam*, Rupa & Co., Delhi, 1988.

9. For details refer to V.P. Gupta and Mohini Gupta, *An Encyclopaedia of Punjabi History and Culture,* Ambe Books, Delhi, 1999.
10. V.P. Gupta and Mohini Gupta in their recent work *Mother Goddess: A Global Perspective* (Ambe Books, Delhi, 1999) have presented the theology, historical evolution, manifestations and shrines of the Divine Mother.

for details refer to: N.P. Gupta and Mohini Gupta: *An Encyclopaedia of Hindu Writing and Culture*, Amar Books, Delhi, 1999.

11. S.P. Gupta and Mohini Gupta in their recent work *Mother Goddess: A Cultural Panorama* (Amar Books, Delhi, 1999) have presented the mythology, historical evolution, manifestations and shrines of the Divine Mother.

Section Two

Dictionary Entries from A to Z

A

ĀBHĀSWARAS. This is class of deities, sixty-four in number, about whose nature little is known.

ABHIDHĀNA. A dictionary or vocabulary. One of the oldest of such works is the *Abhidhāna ratna-mālā* of Halāyudha Bhaṭṭa (circa 7th cent.), and one of the best is the *Abhidhāna Chintā-maṇi* of Hema-chandra, a Jaina writer of celebrity (13th cent.). The former has been edited by Aufrecht; the latter by Colebrooke and Böhtlingk and Rieu.

ABHIMĀNĪ. Agni, the eldest son of Brahmā. Pāvaka, Pavamāna, and Śuchi were his three sons from his wife Swāhā. "They had forty-five sons, who, with the original son of Brahmā and his three descendants, constitute the forty-nine fires." *See* Agni.

ABHIMANYU. Son of Arjuna from his wife Subhadrā, known as the metronymic Saubhadra. He killed Lakshmaṇa, the son of Dur-yodhana, on the second day of the great battle of the Maha-bhārata but on the thirteenth day he himself fell fighting heroically against fearful odds. He is said to be very handsome. Uttarā, daughter of the Rāja of Virāta was his wife. His son, Parīkshit, succeeded to the throne of Hastināpura.

ABHĪRA, ĀBHĪRA. A cowherd, according to Manu, is offspring of a Brāhman from a woman of the Ambashṭha or medical tribe, found in the north of India along the Indus. There has been a good deal of misapprehension about these people. Hindu writers have described them as living in the north and in the west. Translators have mixed them up with the Sūdras. Sometimes called Sūras, they have been called Sūrābhīras. Perhaps there is something more than identity of locality in the association of the *Ahirs* of today with the Sūdras. It has been suggested that the country or city of the Abhīras is the *Ophir* of the Bibles.

ABHIRĀMA-MAṆI. A drama in seven acts on the history of Rāma, written by Sundara Misra in 1599 A.D., "the composition possesses little dramatic interest, although it has some literary merit."—*Wilson*.

ĀCHĀRA. 'Rule, custom usage', they are the rules of practice of castes, orders, or religion. There are many books of rules which have this word for the first member of their titles, as *Āchārachandrikā*, 'looking-glass of customs'; *Āchāra-dīpa*, 'lamp of customs,' etc.

ĀCHĀRYA. A spiritual teacher or guide. Droṇa, the teacher of the Pāndavas, had this title.

ACHYUTA. 'Unfallen;' a name of Vishṇu or Krishṇa, it has been variously interpreted as signifying "he who does not perish with created things,"; as "he who is not distinct from final emancipation," in the *Mahabharata* and in the *Skanda* Purāna as "he who never declines (or varies) from his proper nature."

ADBHUTA-BRĀHMAṆĀ. 'The Brāhmaṇa of miracles. A Brāhmaṇa of the Sāma-veda which treats of auguries and marvels, has been published by Weber.

ADHARMA. Unrighteousness, vice is personified as a son of Brahmā, and called "the destroyer of all beings."

ADHIRATHA. A charioteer, the foster-father of Karṇa. According to some he was king of Anga, and according to others the charioteer of King Dhṛitarāshṭra, perhaps he was both.

ADHWARYU. A priest whose business it is to recite the prayers of the *Yajur-veda*.

ADHYĀTMAN. The supreme spirit, the soul of the universe.

ADHYĀTMA RĀMĀYAṆA. A very popular work, considered to be a part of the Brahmaṇda Purāṇa, it has been printed in India. *See* Rāmāyaṇa.

ĀDI-PURAṆA. 'The first, Purāṇa,' a title generally conceded to the Brahma Purāṇa.

ADITI. 'Free, unbounded.' Infinity; the boundless heaven as compared with the finite earth. According to Max Muller, "the visible infinite, visible by the naked eye; the endless expanse beyond the earth, beyond the clouds, beyond the sky." In the *Rig-veda* she is frequently implored "for blessings on children and cattle, for protection and for forgiveness." Aditi is called Deva-mātṛi, 'mother of the gods,' and is represented as being the mother of Daksha and the daughter of Daksha. "Eight sons were born from the body of Aditi; she approached the gods with seven but cast away the eighth, Mārttaṇḍa (the sun)." These seven were the Ādityas. In the *Yajur-veda* Aditi is addressed as "Supporter of the sky, sustainer of the earth, sovereign of this world, wife of Vishṇu;" but in the *Mahābhārata* and *Rāmāyaṇa,* as well as in the Purāṇas, Vishṇu is called the son of Aditi. In the *Vishṇu Purāṇa* she is said to be the daughter of Daksha and wife of Kaśyapa, by whom she was mother of Vishṇu, in his dwarf incarnation (wherefore he is sometimes called Āditya), and also of Indra, and she is called "the mother of the gods" and "the mother of the world." According to the *Matsya Purāṇa* a pair of ear-rings was produced at the churning of the ocean, which Indra gave to Aditi, and several of the Purāṇas tell a story of these ear-rings being stolen and carried off to the city of Prāg-jyotisha by the Asura king Naraka, from whence they were brought back and restored to her by Krishṇa. Devakī, the mother of Krishṇa, is represented as being a manifestation of Aditi. *(See* Max Muller's *Rig Veda,* i. 230; Muir's *Texts,* iv. 11, v. 35.)

ĀDITYA. In the early Vedic times Ādityas were six, or more frequently seven celestial deities, of whom Varuṇa was the chief. Consequently he was the Aditya. Aditi, who had eight sons, approached the gods with only seven, having cast away the eighth, Mārttāṇḍa (the sun). In after-times the number was increased to twelve, as representing the sun in the twelve months of the year. Āditya is one of the names of the sun. Dr. Muir quotes the following from Professor Roth:—"There (in the highest heaven) dwell and reign those gods who bear in common the name of Ādityas. We must, however, if we would discover their earliest character, abandon the conceptions which in a later age, and even in that of the heroic poems, were entertained regarding these deities. According to this conception they were twelve sun-gods, bearing evident reference to the twelve months. But for the most ancient period we must hold fast the primary signification of their name. They are the inviolable, imperishable, eternal beings. Aditi, eternity, or the eternal, is the element which sustains or is sustained by them. . . . The eternal and inviolable element in which the Ādityas dwell, and which forms their essence, is the celestial light. The Ādityas, the gods of this light, do not therefore by any means coincide with any of the forms in which light is manifested in the universe. They are neither sun, nor moon, nor stars, nor dawn, but the eternal sustainers of this luminous life, which exists, as it were, behind all these phenomena."

Mitra, Aryaman, Bhaga, Varuṇa, Daksha, and Ansa are the six Ādityas. Daksha is frequently excluded, and Indra, Savitri (the sun), and Dhātri are added. Even though twelve Ādityas are variously given, but many of them are names of the sun.

ĀDITYA PURĀṆA. One of the eighteen Upa-purāṇas.

AGASTYA. A celebrated personage in Hindu mythology, he is a reputed author in the *Rigveda*. Lopamudra was his wife. Agastya holds a great place in Tamil literature also.

AGHĀSURA. (Agha the Asura.) An Asura, who was Kansa's general, assumed the form of a vast serpent, and Krishṇa's companions, the cowherds, entered its mouth, mistaking it for a mountain cavern but Krishṇa rescued them.

AGNĀYĪ. Wife of Agni, she is seldom referred to in the Vedas and is of no importance.

ĀGNEYA. Son of Agni, a name of Kārttikeya or Marsch is also an appellation of the Muni Agastya and others.

ĀGNEYĀSTRA. 'The weapon of fire' was given by Bharadwāja to Agnivesa, the son of Agni, and by him to Droṇa. A similar weapon was, according to the Vishnu Purāṇa, given by the sage Aurva to his pupil. King Sagara, and with its help "he conquered the tribes of barbarians who had invaded his patrimonial possessions."

ĀGNEYA PURĀṆA. See *Agni Purāṇa*.

AGNI Fire, one of the most ancient and most sacred objects of Hindu worship. He appears in three phases—in heaven as the sun, in mid-air as lightning, on earth as ordinary fire. Agni is one of the chief deities of the Vedas, and a great number of the hymns are addressed to him, indeed more than to any other god. He is one of the three great deities—Agni, Vāyu (or Indra), and Sūrya—who respectively preside over earth, air, and sky, and are all equal in dignity. "He is considered as the mediator between men and gods, as protector of men and their homes, and as witness of their actions; hence his invocation at all solemn occasions, at the nuptial ceremony, &c. Fire has ceased to be an object of worship, but is held in Vahni, Anala, Pāvak. Vaiśwānara, son of Viśwānara, the sun; Abja-hasta, 'lotus in hand;' Dhūma-ketu, 'whose sign is smoke:' Hutāsa or Huta-bhuj, 'devourer of offerings;' Śuchi or Śukra, 'the bright;' Rohitāśwa, 'having red horses;' Chhāga-ratha, 'ramrider;' Jāta vedas (q.v.); Sapta-jihva, 'seven-tongued;' Tomaradhara, 'javelin-bearer,' are the names and epitents of Agni.

AGNI-DAGDHAS. Pitris, or Manes, who when alive, kept up the household flame and presented oblations with fire. Those who did not do so were called *Anagni dagdhas.* See Pitris.

AGNI PURĀṆA. This Purāṇa derives its name from its having been communicated originally by Agni, the deity of fire, to Muni Vasishtha, for the purpose of equipping him with the twofold knowledge of Brahmā. Its contents are variously specified as "sixteen thousand, fifteen thousand, and fourteen thousand stanzas." This work is devoted to the glorification of Siva, but its contents are of a very varied and cyclopaedical character. It has portions on ritual and mystic worship, cosmic descriptions, the duties of kings and the art of war, which have the appearance of being extracted from some older work, in adding to a chapter on law from the text-book of Yājnawalkya, some chapters on medicine from the Susruta, and some treatises on rhetoric, prosody, and grammar according to the rules of Pingala and Pāṇini. Its motley contents "exclude it from any legitimate claims to be regarded as a Purāṇa, and prove that its origin cannot be very remote." The text of this Purāṇa is now being pursued in the *Bibliotheca Indica,* edited by Rājendra Lāl Mitra.

AGNISHWĀTTAS. Pitris or Manes of the gods who, when living upon earth, did not maintain their domestic fires or offer burnt-sacrifices. According to some authorities they were descendants *See* Pitris

AGNIVESA. A sage, the son of Agni, and an early writer on medicine.

AHALYĀ. Wife of the Rishi Gautama, and a very beautiful woman. In the Rāmāyana it is stated that she was the first woman made by Brahmā, and that he gave her to Gautama. She was seduced by Indra, who had to suffer for his adultery. One version of the Rāmāyana represents her as knowing the god and being flattered by his condescension; but anotther version states that the god assumed the form of her husband, and so deceived her. Another story is that Indra secured the help of the moon, who assumed the form of a cock and crowed at midnight. This roused Gautama to his morning's devotions, when Indra went in and took his place. Guatama expelled Ahalyā from his hermitage, and deprived her of her prerogative of being the most beautiful woman in the world, or, according to another statement, he rendered her invisible. She was restored to her natural state by Rāma and reconciled to her husband. This seduction is explained mythically by Kumārila Bhatta as Indra (the sun's) carrying away the shades of night—the name Ahalyā, by a strained etymology, being made to signify 'night.'

AHI. A serpent name of Vritra, the Vedic demon of drought: but Ahi and Vritra are sometimes "distinct, and mean, most probably, differently formed clouds."—*Wilson*.

AHI-CHHATRA, AHI-KSHETRA. A city mentioned in the *Mahābhārata* as lying north of the Ganges, and as being the capital of Northern Panchāla. It is apparently the Adisadra of Ptolemy, and its remains are visible near Rāmnaga.

AINDRI. 'Son of Indra.' An appellation of Arjuna.

AIRĀVATA. 'A fine elephant.' An elephant produced at the churning of the ocean, and appropriated by god Indra. The word Irāvat, signifying 'produced from water' is the derivation of this name. He is guardian of one of the points of the compass.

AITAREYA. The name of a Brāhmana, an Āranyaka, and an Upanishad of the *Rig-veda*. The Brāhman has been edited and translated by Dr. Haug. The text of Āranyaka has been published in the *Bibliotheca Indica* by Rājendra Lāl, and there is another edition. The upanishad has been translated by Dr. Roer in the same series. "The *Aitareya Āraṇyaka* consists of fivo books, each of which is called Āraṇyaka. The second and third books form a separate Upanishad, and a still further subdivision here takes place, inasmuch as the four last sections of the second book, which are particularly consonant with the doctrines of the Vedānta system, pass as the Aitareyopanishad."—*Weber.*

AJA. 'Unborn', epithet applied to many of the gods prince of the Solar race, sometimes said to be the son of Raghu, at others the son of Dilīpa, son of Raghu. He was the husband chosen at her swayam-vara by Indumatī, daughter of the Rāja of Vidarbha, and was the father of Dasaratha and grandfather of Rāma. The *Raghu-vansa* relates how on his way to the swayam-vara he was annoyed by a wild elephant and ordered it to be shot. When the elephant was mortally wounded, a beautiful figure issued from it. It declared itself a gandharva who had been transformed into a mad elephant for deriding a holy man. The gandharva was delivered, as it had been foretold to him, by Aja, and he gave the prince some arrows which enabled him to excel in the contest at the swayam-vara. When Dasaratha grew up, Aja ascended to Indra's heaven.

ĀJAGAVA. The 'primitive bow' of Siva, which fell from heaven at the birth of Prithu.

AJĀMILA. A Brāhman of Kanauj, who married a slave and had children.

AJĀTA-ŚATRU. 'One whose enemy is unborn.' 1. A king of Kāśī, mentioned in the Upanishads, who was very learned, and, although a Kshatriya, instructed the Brāhman Gārgya-bālāki. 2. A name of Siva. 3. Name of Yudhishthira. 4. A king of Mathurā who reigned in the time of Buddha.

AJAYA-PĀLA. Author of a Sanskrit vocabulary of some repute.

AJĪGARTTA. A Brāhman Rishi who sold his son Sunah-sephas to be a sacrifice.

AJIT. 'Unconquered.' A title given to Vishṇu, Siva, and many others. There were classes of gods bearing this name in several Manwantaras.

AKRŪRA. A. Yādava and uncle of Krishṇa. He was son of Swa-phalka and Gāndin. It was he who took Krishṇa and Rāma to Mathurā when the former broke the great bow. He is chiefly noted as being the holder of the Syamantaka gem.

AKSHA. The eldest son of Rāvaṇa, slain by Hanumān. Also a name of Garuḍa.

AKSHAMĀLĀ. A name of Arundhati.

ĀKULI. An Asura priest. *See* Kilātākuli.

AKŪPĀRA. A tortoise or turtle. The tortoise on which the earth rests.

ĀKŪTI. A daughter of Manu Swāyambhuva and Śatarūpā, whom he gave to the patriarch Ruchi. She bore twins, Yajna and Dakshinā, who became husband and wife and had twelve sons, the deities called Yāmas.

ALAKĀ. The capital of Kuvera and the abode of the gandharvas on Mount Meru. It is also called Vasudhārā, Vasu-sthalī, and Prabhā.

ALAKA-NANDĀ. One of the four branches of the river Gangā, which flows south to the country of Bhārata. According to Vaishnwas this is said to be the terrestrial Gangā which Siva received upon his head.

ALAMBUSHA. A great Rākshasa worsted by Sātyaki in the great war of the *Mahābhārata*, and finally killed by Ghatot-kacha. He is said to be a son of Rishyasringa.

ALĀYUDHA. A Rākshasa killed after a fierce combat by Ghatotkacha in the war of the *Mahābhārata* (Fauche, ix. 278).

AMARA-KANṬAKA. 'Peak of the immortals.' A place of pilgrimage in the table-land east of the Vindhyas.

AMARA-KOSHA. This title may be read in two ways—'the immortal vocabulary,' or, more appropriately, 'the vocabulary of Amara or Amara Sinha'—"The oldest vocabulary hitherto known, and one of the most celebrated vocabularies of the classical Sanskrit." It has been the subject of a great number of commentaries. The text has been often printed. There is an edition published in India with an English interpretation and annotations by Colebrooke. The text with a French translation has been printed by Deslongchamps.

AMARA SINHA. The author of the vocabulary called *Amara-kosha,* he was one of the nine gems of the court of Vikrama. (See Nava-ratna.) Wilson inclines to place him in the first century B.C. Lasson places him about the middle of the third century A.D., and others incline to bring him down later.

AMARĀVATĪ. The capital of Indra's heaven, renowned for its greatness and splendour, it is situated somewhere in the vicinity of Meru. It is sometimes called Deva-pura, 'city of the gods,' and Püsha-bhāsā, 'gun-splendour.'

AMAREŚWARA. 'Lord of the immortals.' A title of Vishṇu, Siva, and Indra. Name of one of the twelve great lingas. *See* Linga.

AMARU-ŚATAKA. A poem consisting of a hundred stanzas written by a king named Amaru, attributed by some to the philosopher Śankara, who assumed the dead form of that king for the purpose of conversing with his widow. The verses are of an erotic character, but, like many others of the same kind. A religions or philosophical interpretation has been found for them. There is a translation with the text in French by Apudy and a translation in German by Ruckert.

AMBĀ. 'Mother.' 1. A name of Durgā. 2. The eldest daughter of a king of Kāsī. She and her sisters Ambikā and Ambālikā were carried off by Bhīshma to be the wives of Vichitravīrya. Ambā had been previously betrothed to a Rāja of Salwa, and Bhīshma sent her to him, but the Rāja rejected her because she had been in another man's house. She retired to the forest and got engaged in devotion to obtain revenge of Bhīshma. Siva promised her the desired vengeance in another birth. Then she ascended the pile and was born again as Śikhandin, who slew Bhīshma.

AMBĀLIKĀ. The younger widow of Vichitra-vīrya and mother of Pāṇḍu by Vyāsa. See *Mahābhārata*.

AMBARĪSHA. 1. A king of Ayodhyā, twenty-eighth in descent from Ikshwāku. (See Sunahsephas.) 2. An appellation of Siva. 3. Name of one of the eighteen hells.

AMBASHTHA. 1. A militant people inhabiting a country of the same name in the middle of the Panjāb; 2. the medical tribe in Manu.

AMBIKĀ. 1. A sister of Rudra, but in later times identified with Umā. 2. Elder widow of Vichitra-vīrya and mother of Dhrita-rāshtra by Vyāsa. See *Mahābhārata*.

AMBIKEYA. A metronymic applicable to Ganesa, Skanda, and Dhrita-rāshtra.

ĀMNĀYA. Sacred tradition. The Vedas in the aggregate.

AMRITA. 'Immortal.' A god. The water of life. The term was known to the Vedas, and seems to have been applied to various things offered in sacrifice, but more especially to the Soma juice. It is also called Nir-jara and Pīyūsha. In later times it was the water of life produced at the churning of the ocean by the gods and demons, the legend of which is told with some variations in the *Rāmāyaṇa,* the *Mahābhārata,* and the *Purāṇas.* The gods, feeling their weakness, having been worsted by the demons, and being, according to one authority, under the ban of a holy sage, repaired to Vishṇu, beseeching him for renewed vigour and the gift of immortality. He directed them to churn the ocean for the Amrita and other precious things which had been lost.

ANĀDHRISHTI. A son of Ugrasena and general of the Yādavas.

ĀNAKA-DUNDUBHI. 'Drums', a name of Vasudeva, who was so called because the drums of heaven resounded at his birth.

ĀNANDA. 'Joy, happiness.' An appellation of Siva, also of Bala-rāma.

ĀNANDA GIRI. A follower of Śankarāchārya, and a teacher and expositor of his doctrines, he was the author of a *Śankara-vijaya,* and lived about the tenth century.

ĀNANDA-LAHARI. 'The wave of joy,' poem attributed to Śankarāchārya. It is a hymn of praise addressed to Pārvatī, consort of Siva, mixed up with mystical doctrine. It has been translated into French by Troyer as *L'Onde de Beatitude.*

ANANGA. 'The bodiless', name of Kāma, god of love.

ANANTA. 'The infinite', name of the serpent Sesha. The term is also applied to Vishnu and other deities.

ANARANYA. A descendant of Ikshwāku and king of Ayodhyā. According to the *Rāmāyṇa,* many kings submitted to Rāvana without fighting, but when Anaranya was summoned to fight or surrender, he preferred to fight. His army was over-powered and he was thrown off from his chariot. Rāvana triumphed over his prostrate foe, who retorted that he had been beaten by fate, not by Rāvana, and predicted the death of Rāvana at the hands of Rāma, a descendant of Anaranya.

ANARGHA RĀGHAVA. A drama in seven acts by Murāri Misra, possibly written in the thirteenth or fourteenth century. Rāghava or Rāma is the hero of the piece. "It has no dramatic merit, being deficient in character, action, situation, and interest. As poem it presents occasionally poetic thoughts, but they are very few, and are lost amid pages of flat commonplace, quaint conceit, hyperbolical extravagance, and obscure mythology."—Wilson. It is also called, after its author, *Murāri Nātaka.*

AN-ĀRYA. 'Unworthy, vile,' refers to people who were not Aryans, but barbarians of other races and religion.

ANASŪYĀ. 'Charity.' In *Rāmāyaṇa* as wife of Rishi Atri, appears living with her husband in a hermitage in the forest south of Chitra-kūta. She was very pious and given to austere devotion, through which she had obtained miraculous powers. When Sītā visited her and her husband, she was very attentive and kind, and gave Sītā an ointment which was to keep her beautiful for ever. She was mother of the irascible sage Durvāsas and a friend of Śakuntalā.

ANDHAKA. 1. A demon, son of Kaśyapa and Diti, with a thousand arms and heads, two thousand eyes and feet, and called Andhaka because he walked like a blind man, although he saw very well. He was slain by Siva when he attempted to carry off the Pārijāta tree from Swarga. This non for Siva the appellation Andhaka-ripu, 'foe of Andhaka.' 2. A grand son of Kroshtri and son of Yudhājit, of the Yādava race, who, together with his brother Vrishni, is the ancestor of the celebrated family of Andhaka-Vrishnis. 3. The name was borne by many others of less note.

ANDHRA, ĀNDHRA. Name of a country and people in the south of India, the country of Telengana. It was the seat of a powerful dynasty, and the people were known to Pliny as *gens Andarae.*

ANDHRA-BHRITYA. A dynasty of kings that reigned in Magadha somewhere about the beginning of the Christian era. The name seems to indicate that its founder was a native of Andhra, now Telengana.

ANGA. 1. The country of Bengal proper about Bhāgalpur. Its capital was Champā, or Champā-purī. 2. A supplement to the Vedas. *See* Vedānga.

ANGADA. 1. Son of Lakshmana and king of Āngadi, capital of a country near the Himālaya. 2. Son of Gada (brother of Krishṇa) by Vrihatī. 3. Son of Bali, the monkey king of Kishkindhyā, he was protected by Rāma and fought on his side against Rāvaṇa.

ANGIRAS. A Rishi to whom many hymns of the Rig-veda are attributed, he was one of the seven Maharshis or great Rishis, and also one of the ten Prajāpatis or progenitors of mankind. In later times Angiras was one of the inspired lawgivers, and also a writer on astronomy. As an astronomical personification he is Brihaspati, the regent of the planet Jupiter, or the planet itself. He was also called "the priest of the gods," and "the lord of sacrifice." There is much ambiguity about the name. It comes from the same root as agni, 'fire,' and resembles that word in sound. This may be the reason why the name Angiras is used as an epithet or synonym of Agni. The name is also employed as an epithet for the father of Agni, and it is found more especially connected with the hymns addressed to Agni, Indra, and the luminous deities. According to one statement, Angiras was the son of Uru by Āgenyī, the daughter of Agni, although, as stated above, the name is sometimes given to the father of Agni. Another account represents that he was born from the mouth of Brahmā. His wives were Smriti, 'memory,' daughter of Daksha; Śradhā, 'faith,' daughter of Karkama; and Swandhā 'oblation,' and Sati, 'truth,' two other daughters of Daksha. His daughters were the Richas or Vaidik hymns, and his sons were the Manes called Havishmats. But he had other sons and daughters, and among the former were Utathya, Brihaspati, and Mārkaṇḍeya. According to the *Bhāgavata Purāṇa* "he begot sons possessing Brahmanical glory by the wife of Rathī-tara, a Kshatriya. who was childless, and these persons were afterwards called descendants of Angiras."

ANGIRASAS, ANGIRASES. Descendants of Angiras. "They share in the nature of the legends attributed to Angiras. Angiras, being the father of Agni, they are considered as descendants of Agni himself, who is also called the first of the Angirasas. Like Angiras, they occur in hymns addressed to the luminous deities, and, at a later point of time they become for the most part personifications of light, of luminous bodies, of divisions of time, of celestial phenomena, and fires adapted to peculiar occasions, as the full and change of the moon, or to particular rites, as the Aswa-medha, Rāja-sūya, etc."—Goldstucker. In the *Śatapatha Brāhmana* they and the Ādityas are said to have descended from Prajāpati, and that "they strove together for the priority in ascending to heaven."

Some descendents of Angiras by the Kshatriya wife of a childless king are mentioned in the Purāṇas as two tribes of Angirasas who were Brāhamans as well as Kshatriyas.

The hymns of the *Atharva-veda* are called Angirasas, and the descendants of Angiras were specially charged with the protection of sacrifies performed in accordance with the Atharva-veda. Because of this or from their being associated with the descendents of Atharvan, they were called distinctively Atharvāngirasas.

ĀNGIRASAS. A class of Pitris.

ANILA. 'The wind.' *See* Vāyu.

ANILAS. A gana or class of deities, forty-nine in number, connected with Anila, the wind.

ANIRUDDHA. 'Uncontrolled.' son of Pradyumna and grandson of Krishṇa, he married his cousin, Su-bhadrā. A Daitya princess named Ushā, daughter of Bāṇa, fell in love with him, and had him brought by magic influence to her apartments in her father's city of Sonita-pura. Bāṇa sent some guards to seize him, but the valiant youth, taking an iron club, slew his assailants. Bāna then invoked his magic powers and secured him. On discovering whither Aniruddha had been carried, Krishṇa, Bala-rāma, and Pradyumna went to rescue him. A great battle was fought; Bāna was aided by Siva and by Skanda, god of war. The former was overcome by Krishṇa, and the latter was wounded by Garuḍa and Pradyumna. Bāṇa was defeated, but his life was spared at the intercession of Shiva, and Aniruddha was carried home to Dwārakā with Ushā as his wife. He is also called Jhashānka and Ushā-pati. He had a son named Vajra.

ANJANA. 1. The elephant of the west or south-west quarter. 2. A serpent with many heads descended from Kadru.

ANJANĀ. Mother of Hanumān by Vāyu, god of the wind.

ANNA-PŪRṆA. 'Full of food.' A form of Durgā,

worshipped for her power of providing food Cf. the roman Anna Perenna.

ANSUMAT, ANSUMĀN. Son of Asamanjas and grandson of Sagara, he brought back to earth the horse which had been carried off from Sagara's Aśwa-medha sacrifice, and he discovered the remains of that king's sixty thousand sons, who had been killed by the fire of the wrath of Kapila.

ANTAKA. 'The ender.' A name of Yama, judge of the dead.

ANTARĪKSHA. The atmosphere or firmament between heaven and earth, the sphere of the Gandharvas, Apsarases, and Yakshas.

ANTARVEDĪ. The Doab or country between the Ganges and the Jumna.

ANU. Son of King Yayāti by his wife Śarmishthā, a Daitya princess. He refused to exchange his youthful vigour for the curse of decrepitude passed upon his father, and in consequence his father cursed him that his posterity should not possess dominion. Notwithstanding this, he had a long series of descendants, and among them were Anga, Banga, Kalinga, etc., who gave their names to the countries they dwelt in.

ANUKRAMAṆI, ANUKRAMAṆIKĀ. A index or table of contents, particularly of a Veda. The Anukramanis of the Vedas follow the order of each Saṁhitā, and assign a poet, a metre, and a deity to each hymn or prayer.

ANUMATI. The moon on its fifteenth day, just short of its full. In this stage it is personified and worshipped as a goddess.

ANUSARA. A rākshasa or other demon.

ANUVINDA. A king of Ujjayinī. See Vinda.

APARĀNTA. 'On the western border.' A country which is named in the Vishnu Purāna in association with countries in the north, the Vāya Purāna reads the name as Aparita, which Wilson says is a northern nation.

The *Hari-vanśa,* however, mentions it as "a country conquered by Paraśurāma, from the ocean," and upon this the translator Langlois observes: "Tradition records that Parsu-rāma besought Varuna, god of the sea, to grant him a land which he might bestow upon the Brāhmans in expiation of the blood of the Kshatriyas. Varuna withdrew his waves from the heights of Gokarna near Mangalore) down to Cape Comorin" (As. Researches, v 1). This agrees with the traditions concerning Paraśu-rāma and Malabar, but it is not at all clear how a gift of territory to Brāhmans could expiate the slaughter of the Kshatriyas by a Brahman and on behalf of Brāhmans.

APARṆĀ. According to the Harivansa, the eldest daughter of Himavat and Menā. She and two sisters, Eka-parṇā and Eka-pātalā, gave themselves up to austerity and practised extraordinary abstinence; but while her sisters lived, as their names denote, upon one leaf or on one pātalā (Bignonia) respectively, Aparṇā managed to subsist upon nothing, and even lived without a leaf (a-parnā). This so distressed her mother that she cried out, 'U-mā,' 'Oh, don't'. Aparṇā thus became the beautiful Umā, the wife of Siva.

ĀPASTAMBA. An ancient writer on ritual and law, author of Sūtras connected with the Black Yajur-veda and of a Dhurma-sāstra, he is often quoted in law-books. Two versions of the *Taittirīya Sanhitā* are ascribed to him or his school. The Sūtras have been translated by Buhler, and are reprinted in the Sacred Books of the East by Max Muller.

ĀPAVA. 'Who sports in the waters.' A name of the same import as Nārāyaṇa, and having a similar though not an identical application. According to the *Brahma Purāṇa* and the *Hari-vanśa,* Āpava performed the office of the creator Brahmā, and divided himself into two parts, male and remale, the former from begetting offspring—the latter. The result was the production of Vishnu, who created Virāj, who brought the first man into the world. According to the *Mahābhārata,* Āpava is a name of the Prajāpati Vaśishtha. The name of Āpava is of late introduction and has been vaguely used. Wilson says: "According to the Prajāpati Vaśishtha, the name of Āpava is of late introduction and has been vaguely used. Wilson says: "According to the commentator, the first stage was the creation of Āpava cr Vaśishtha or Virāj by Vishnu, through the agency of Brahmā, and the next was that of the creation of Manu by Virāj."

APSARAS. The Apsaras are the celebrated nymphs of Indra's heaven. The name, which signifies 'moving in the water, has some analogy to Aphrodite. They are not prominent in the Vedas, but Urvaśī and a few others are mentiond. In Manu they are said to be the creations of the seven Manus. In the epic poems they become prominent, and the Rāmāyaṇa and the Purāṇas attribute their origin to the churning of the ocean. (*See* Amrita.) It is said that when they came forth from the waters neither the gods nor the Asuras would have them for wives, so they became common to all. They have the appellations of Surānganās, 'wives of the gods,' and Sumad-ātmajās 'daughters of pleasure.'

ĀRAṆYAKA. 'Belonging to the forest.' Certain religious and philosophical writings which expound the mystical sense of the ceremonies, discuss the nature of God. They are attached to the Brāhmanas, and are intended for study in the forest by Brāhmans who have retired from the distractions of the world. There are four of them: 1. Brīhad; 2. Taittirīya; 3. Aitareya; and 4. Kaushītaki Āraṇyaka. The Āraṇyakas are closely connected with the Upanishads, and the names are occassionally used interchangeably. Thus the Brihad is called indifferently *Brihad Āraṇyaka* or *Brihad Āraṇyaka Upanishad*. It is attached to the *Śatapatha Brāhmaṇa*. The *Aitareya Upanishad* is a part of the *Aitareya Brāhmaṇa,* and the *Kaushītaki Āraṇyaka* consists of three chapters, of which the third is the *Kaushītaki Upanishad*. "Traces of modern idea (says Max Muller) are not wanting in the Āraṇyakas, and the very fact that they are destined for a class of men who had retired from the world in order to give themselves up to the contemplation of the highest problems, shows an advanced and already declining and decaying society, not unlike the monastic age of the Christian world." "In one sense the Āraṇyakas are old, for they reflect the very dawn of thought; in another they are modern, for they speak of that dawn with all the experience of a past day. There are passages in these works unequalled in any language for grandeur, boldness, and simplicity. These passages are the relies of a better age. But the generation which became the chronicler of those Titanic wars of thought was a small race; they were dwarfs, measuring the footsteps of departed gaints."

ARBUDA. Mount Ābu. Name of the people living in the vicinity of that mountain.

ARBUDA. 'A serpent.' Name of an Asura slain by Indra.

ARDHA-NĀRĪ. 'Half-woman.' A form in which Siva is represented as half-male and half-female, typifying the male and female energies. There are several stories accounting for this form. It is called also Ardhanāriśa and Parāngada.

ARJUNA. 'White', is the name of the third Pāndu prince. All the five brothers were of divine paternity, and Arjuna's father was Indra, hence he is called Aindri. A brave warrior, high-minded, generous, upright, and handsome, he was the most prominent and the most amiable and interesting of the five brothers. He was taught the use of arms by Drona, and was his favourite pupil. By his skill in arms he won Draupadi at her Swayamvara. For an involuntary transgression he imposed upon himself twelve year's exile from his family, and during that time he visited Paraśu-rāma, who gave him instruction in the use of arms. During this period he developed a connection with Ulūpī, a

Nāga princess, and from her had a son named Irāvat. He also married Chitrāngadā, the daughter of the king of Manipura, from whom he had a son named Babhru-vāhana. He visited Krishṇa at Dwārakā, and there he married Su-bhadrā, the sister of Krishna. (*See* Su-bhadrā.) From her he had a son named Abhimanyu. Arjuna obtained the personal assistance of Krishṇa, who acted as his charioteer, and, before the great battle began, related to him the *Bhagavad-gītā*. Arjuna has many appellations: Bībhatsu, Guḍa-kesa, Dhananjaya, Jishnu, Kirītin, Pāka-sāsani, Phālguna, Savya-sāchin, Śweta-vāhana, and Pārtha.

ARJUNA. Son of Krita-vīrya, king of the Haihayas. He ·is better known under his patronymic Kārta-vīrya.

ARTHA-SĀSTRA. The useful arts. Mechanical science.

ARUṆA. 'Red, rosy.' The dawn, personified as the charioteer of the sun. This is of later origin than the vedic Ushas (q.v.). He is said to be the son of Kaśyapa and Kadru. He is also called Rumra, 'tawny,' An-uru, 'thighless,' and Āsmana, 'stony.'

ARUNDHATĪ. The morning star, personified as the wife of the Rishi Vaśishtha, and a model of conjugal excellence.

ARUSHA, ARUSHĪ. 'Red.' 'A red horse.' In the *Rig-veda* the red horses or mares of the sun or of fire. The rising sun.

ARVAN, ARVĀ. 'A horse.' One of the horses of the moon. A fabulons animal-half-horse, half-bird on which the Daityas are supposed to ride.

ARVĀVASU. See Raibhya.

ĀRYA, ĀRYAN. 'Loyal, faithful.' The name of the immigrant race from which all that is Hindu originated. The name by which the people of the *Rig-veda* "called men of their own stock and religion, in contradistinction to the Dasyus (or Dasas), a term by which we either understand hostile demons or the rude aboriginal tribes" of India, who were An-āryas.

ĀRYA-BHAṬA. The earliest known Hindu writer on algebra, and, according to Colebrooke, "if not the inventor, the improver of that analysis," which has made but little advance in India since. He was born, according to his own account, at Kusuma-pura (Patna), in A.D. 476, and composed his first astronomical work at the early age of twenty-three. His larger work, the *Ārya Siddhānta,* was produced at a riper age. He is probably the Andubarius (Ardubarius?) of the Chronichon Paschale, and the Arjabahr of the Arabs. Two of his works, the *Dasāgītisūtra* and *Āryāshtasata,* have been edited by Kern under the title of *Āryabhatīya*. See Whitney in *Jour. Amer. Or. Society* for 1860, Dr. Bhau Dājī in *J. R. A. S.* for 1865, and Barth in *Revue Critique* for 1875. There is another and later astronomer of the same name, distinguished as *Laghu Ārya-bhaṭa,* i.e. Āryabhaṭa the Less.

ARYAMAN. 'A bosom friend.' 1. Chief of the Pitris. 2. One of the Ādityas. 3. One of the Viswe-devas.

ĀRYA SIDDHĀNTA. The system of astronomy founded by Ārya-bhaṭa in his work bearing this name.

ĀRYĀVARTA. 'The land of the Āryas.' The tract between the Himālaya and the Vindhya ranges, from the eastern to the western sea.—Manu.

ASAMANJAS. Son of Sagara and Kesinī. He was a wild and wicked young man, and was abandoned by his father, but he succeeded him as king, and, according to the *Hari-vansa,* he was afterwards famous for valour under the name of Panchajana.

ĀSANGA. Author of some verses in the *Rig-veda.* He was son of Playoga, but was changed into a woman by the curse of the gods. He recovered his male form by repentance and the favour of the Rishi Medhātithi, to whom he gave abundant wealth, and addressed the verses preserved in the Veda.

ĀSARA. A rākshasa or other demon.

ASHṬĀVAKRA. A Brāhman, the son of Kahoda, whose story is told in the *Mahābhārata.* Kahoda married a daughter of his preceptor, Uddālaka, but he was so devoted to study that he neglected his wife. When she was far advanced in her pregnancy, the unborn son was provoked at his father's neglect of her, and rebuked him for it, Kahoda, was angry at the child's impertinence, and condemned him to be born crooked. So he came forth with his eight *(ashta)* limbs crooked *(vakra);* hence his name Kahoda went through a great sacrifice at the court of Janaka, king of Mithilā. Present there was a great Buddhist sage, who challenged disputations, upon the understanding that whoever was overcome in argument should be thrown into the river. This was the fate of many, and among them of Khoda, who was drowned. In his twelfth year Ashṭāvakra learnt the manner of his father's death, and set out to avenge him. The lad had great ability and wisdom. He got the better of the sage who had worsted his father, and insisted that the sage should be thrown into the water. The sage then declared himself to be a son of Varuna, god of the waters, who had sent him to obtain Brāhmans for officiating at a sacrifice by overpowering them in argument and throwing them into the water. When all had been explained and set right, Kahoda directed his son to bathe in the Samangā river. The lad became perfectly straight after the bath. A story is told in the *Vishṇu Purāṇa* that Ashṭāvakra was standing in water performing penances when he was seen by some celestial nymphs and worshipped by them. He was pleased, and asked them to seek a boon. They asked for the best of men as a husband. He came out of the water and offered himself. When they saw him, ugly and crooked at eight places, they laughed in derision. He was angry, and as he could not recall his blessing, he said that, after obtaining it, they should fall into the hands of thieves.

ASIKNĪ. The Vedic name of the Chināb, and probably the origin of the classic Akesines.

A-SIRAS. 'Headless.' Spirits or beings without heads.

ASMAKA. Son of Madayantī, the wife of Kalmāsha-pāda or Saudāsa. *See* Kalmāsha-pāda.

AŚOKA. A celebrated king of the Maurya dynasty of Magadha, and grandson of its founder, Chandra-gupta, he reigned for thirty-six years, from about 234 to 19 B.C., and exercised authority more or less direct from Afghānistān to Ceylon. This fact is attested by a number of very curious Pāli inscriptions found engraved upon rocks and pillars, all of them of the same purport, and some of them almost identical in words, the variations showing little more than dialectic differences. Ashoka embraced Buddhism after Kalinga war and did much to spread the religion beyond India.

ĀŚRAMA. Name of the four stages in the life of a Brāhman See Brāhman.

ĀSTĪKA. An ancient sage, son of Jarat-kāru and the sister of the great serpent Vāsuki, he saved the life of the serpent Takshaka when Janamejaya made his great sacrifice or serpents, and induced that king to forego his persecution of the serpent race.

ASURA. 'Spiritual, divine.' In the oldest parts of the Riv-veda this term is used for the supreme spirit, and is the same as the Ahura of the Zoroastrians. In the sense of 'god' it was applied to several of the chief deities, like Indra, Agni, and Varuṇa. It afterwards acquired an entirely opposite meaning, and came to signify, as now, a demon or enemy of the gods. The word is found with this signification in the later parts of the *Rig-veda,* particularly in the last book, and also in the *Athar-veda*. The Brāhmaṇas attach the same meaning to it, and record many contests between the Asuras and the gods. According to the *Taittirīya Brāhmaṇa,* the breath *(asu)* of Prajāpati became alive, and "with that breath he created the Asuras." In another part of the same work it is said that Prajāpati "became pregnant. He created Asuras from his abdomen." The *Śatapatha Brāhmana* agrees with the former statement, and states that "he created Asuras from his lower breath." The *Taittirīya Āraṇyaka* points out that Prajāpati created "gods, men, fathers, Gandharvas, and Apsaras" from water, and that the Asuras, Rākshasas, and Pisāchas sprang from the drops which were spilt. Manu's statement is that they were created by the Prajāpatis. According to the *Vishnu Purāna,* they were produced from the groin of Brahmā (Prajāpati). The account of the *Vāyu Purāṇa* is: "Asuras were first produced as sons from his *(Prajāpati's)* groin. Asu is declared by Brāhmans to mean breath. These beings were produced from it. Hence they are Asuras." The word has long been used as a general name for the enemies of the gods, including the Daityas and Dānavas and other descendants of Kaśyapa, but not all including the Rākshasas descended from Pulastya. In this sense a different derivation has been found for it: the source is no longer asu, 'breath,' but the initial a is taken as the negative prefix, and *a-sura* signifies 'not a god,' hence, according to some, arose the word sura, commonly used for 'a god.' *See* Sura.

ĀSURĪ. One of the earliest professors of the Sānkhya philosophy.

ĀŚWALĀYANA. A celebrated writer of antiquity. He was pupil of Saunaka, and was author of *Srauta-sūtras, Grihyasūtras,* and other works upon ritual, as well as founder of a Śākhā of the *Rig-veda*. The Sūtras have been published by Dr. Stenzler, and are there in the *Bibliotheca Indica.*

AŚWA-MEDHA. 'The sacrifice of a horse.' This is a sacrifice which, in Vedic times, was performed by kings desirous of offspring. The horse was killed with certain ceremonies, and the wives of the king had to pass the night by its carcass. Upon the chief wife fell the duty of going through a revolting formality which can only be hinted at. Subsequently, as in the time of the *Mahābhārata,* the sacrifice obtained a high importance and significance. It was performed only by kings, and implied that he who instituted it was the conqueror and king of kings. It was believed that the performance of one hundred such sacrifices would enable a mortal king to overthrow the throne of Indra, and to become the ruler of the universe and sovereign of the gods. A horse of a particular colour was consecrated by the performance of certain ceremonies, and was then turned loose to wander at will for a year. The king, or his representative, followed the horse with an army, and when the animal entered a foreign country, the ruler of that country was bound either to fight or to submit. If the liberator of the horse succeeded in obtaining or enforcing the submission of all the countries over which it passed, he returned in triumph with the vanquished Rājas in his train; but if he failed, he was disgraced and his pretensions ridiculed. After the successful return a great festival was held, at which the horse was sacrificed, either really or figuratively.

AŚWA-MUKHA. 'Horse faced.' *See* Kinnara.

AŚWA-PATI. 'Lord of horses.' An appellation of many kings.

AŚWATTHĀMAN. Son of Droṇa and Kripā, and one of the generals of the Kauravas; also called by his patronymic Drauṇāyana. After the last great battle, in which Duryodhana was mortally wounded, Aśwatthāman with two other warriors, Kripa and Krita-varman, were the sole survivors of the Kaurava host that were left effective. Aśwatthāman was made the commander. He was fierce in his hostility to the Pāndavas, and craved for revenge upon Dhrishta-dyumna, who had slain his father, Droṇa. These three surviving Kauravas entered the Pāndava camp at night. They found Dhrishta-dyumna asleep, and Aśwatthāman stamped him to death as he lay. He then killed Śikhandin, the other son of Drupada, and he also killed the five young sons of the Pāndavas and carried their heads to the dying Duryodhana. He killed Parīkshit, while yet unborn in the womb of his mother, with his celestial weapon Brahmāstra, by which he incurred the curse of Krishṇa, who restored Parīkshit to life. On the next morning he and his comrades fled, but Draupadī clamoured for revenge upon the murderer of her children. Yudhishthira represented that Aśwatthāman was a Brāhman, and pleaded for his life. She then consented to forego her demand for his blood if the precious and protective jewel which he wore on his head were brought to her. Bhīma, Arjuna, and Krishṇa then went in his pursuit. Arjuna and Krishna overtook him, and compelled him to give up the jewel. They carried it to Draupadī, and she gave it to Yudhishthira, who afterwards wore it on his head.

AŚWINS, AŚWINAU (dual), AŚWINĪ KUMĀRAS. 'Horsemen.' Dioskouroi. Two Vedic deities, twin sons of the sun or the sky. They are ever young and handsome, bright, and of golden brilliancy, agile, swift as falcons, and possessed of many forms; and they ride in a golden car drawn by horses or birds, as harbingers of Usha, the dawn. "They are the earliest bringers of light in the morning sky, who in their chariot hasten onwards before the dawn and prepare the way for her."—Roth. As personifications of the morning twilight, they are said to be children of the sun from a nymph who concealed herself in the form of a mare; hence she was called Aświnī and her sons Aświns. But inasmuch as they precede the sun rise, they are called his parents in his form Pūshan. Mythically they are the parents of the Pāndu princes Nakula and Sahadeva. Their attributes are numerous, but relate mostly to youth and beauty, light and speed, duality, the curative power, and active benevolence. The number of hymns addressed to them testify to the enthusiastic worship they received. They were the physicians of Swarga, and in this character are called Dasras and Nāsatyas, Gadāgadau and Swar-vaidyau; or one was Dasra and the other Nāsatya. Their appellations are Abdhijau, 'ocean born;' Pushkara-srajau, 'wreathed with lotuses;' Bādaveyau, sons of the submarine fire, Bādava. Many instances are recorded of their benevolence and their power of healing. They restored the sage Chyavana to youth, and prolonged his life when he had become old and decrepit, and through this they were admitted to partake of the libations of soma, like the other gods, although Indra strongly opposed them. (See Chyavana.)

ATHARVA, ATHARVAN. The fourth Veda.

ATHARVAN. Name of a priest mentioned in the Rigveda, where he is represented as having "drawn forth" fire and to have "offered sacrifice in early times." He is mythologically represented as the eldest son of Brahmā, to whom that god revealed the Brahma-vidyā (knowledge of God), as a Prajāpati, and as the inspired author of the fourth Veda. At a later period he is identified with Angiras. His descendants are called Atharvanas, and are often associated with the Angirasas.

ATHARVĀNGIRASAS. This name relates to the descendants of Atharvan and Angiras, or to the Angirasas alone, who are especially connected with the *Atharva-veda,* and these names are probably given to the hymns of that Veda so as to confer on them greater authority and holiness.

ĀTMA-BODHA. 'Knowledge of the soul,' short work attributed to Śankarāchārya. It has been printed, and a translation by Taylor was published in 1812. There is a French version by Neve and an English translation by Kearns in the *Indian Antiquary,* vol v.

ĀTMAN, ĀTMA. The soul. The principle of life. The supreme soul.

ĀTREYA. A patronymic from Atri. A son or descendant of Atri; a people so called.

ATRI. 'An eather.' A Rishi, and author of many Vedic hymns. "A Maharshi or great saint, who in the Vedas occurs especially in hymns composed for the praise of Agni, Indra, the Aświns, and the Viśwa-devas. In the epic period he is considered as one of the ten Prajāpatis or lords of creation engendered by Manu for the purpose of creating the universe; at a later period he appears as a mind-born son of Brahmā, and as one of the seven Rishis who preside over the reign of Swāyambhuva, the first Manu, or, according to others, of Swārochisha, the second, or of Vaivaswata, the seventh. He married Anasūyā, daughter of Daksha, and their son was Durvāsas."—Goldstucker. In the Rāmāyana an account is given of the visit paid by Rāma and Sītā to Atri and Anasūya in their hermitage south of Chitrakūta. In the Purānas he was also father of Soma, the moon, and the ascetic Dattātreya from his wife Anasūyā. As a Rishi he is one of the stars of the Great Bear.

AURVA. A Rishi, son of Urva and grandson of Bhrigu, he is described in the *Mahābhārata* as son of the sage Chyavana and Ārushī. From his race he is called Bhārgava.

AUSANA, or AUSANASA PURĀṆA. See Purāṇa.

AUTTAMI. The third Manu. See Manu.

AVANTĪ, AVANTIKĀ. A name of Ujjayinī, one of the seven sacred cities.

AVATARS. It refers to the in carnation of a deity, particularly of Vishnu, who is suffered to appear on earth in 10 major forms (1) Matsya (The Fish); (2) Kurma (The Tortoise); (3) Varaha (The Boar); (4) Narsinha (The Man-Lion); (5) Vamana (The Dwarf); (6) Paraśurāma (Rāma with the Axe); (7) Rāma (The hero of *Rāmāyaṇa);* Krishṇa (The celebrated author of *Gita*); (9) Buddha (Founder of Buddhism); and (10) Kalki (The future incarnation).

While, the above are the usually required incarnations, the *Bhagvata Purāṇa* enumerates twenty-two incarnations.

AVATĀRANA. An abode of the Rākshasas.

AYODHYĀ. The modern Oude. The capital of Ikshwāku, the founder of the Solar race, and afterwards the capital of Rāma. It is one of the seven sacred cities, even though the exact site has not been discovered.

ĀYUR-VEDA. 'The Veda of life,' a work on medicine, attributed to Dhanwantari, and sometimes regarded as a supplement to the *Atharva-veda*.

AYUS. The first-born son of Purūravas and Urvasī, and the father of Nahusha, Kshattra-vriddha, Rambha, Raji, and Anenas.

B

BABHRU-VĀHANA. Son of Arjuna and Chitrāngadā. He was adopted as the son of his maternal grandfather, and reigned at Manipura as his successor. When Arjuna went to Manipura with the horse of the Aśwa-medha, there was a quarrel between Arjuna and King Babhrū-vāhana, the latter killing his father with an arrow. In repentance for his deed, he determined to kill himself, but he obtained from his step-mother, the Nāga princess Ulūpī, a gem which restored Arjuna to life. He returned with his father to Hastināpura. The description of this combat has been translated from the *Mahā-bhārata* by Troyer in his *Rāja Taranginī,* tome i. p. 578.

BĀDARĀYAṆA. A name of Veda Vyāsa, especially used for him as the reputed author of the Vedānta philosophy. He was the author of the *Brahma Sūtras,* published in the *Bibliotheca Indica.*

BADARĪ, BADARĪKĀŚRAMA. A place sacred to Vishṇu, near the Ganges in the Himālayas, particularly in Vishṇu's dual form of Nara-Nārāyaṇa. Thus, in the *Mahābhārata,* Siva, addressing Arjuna, says, "Thou wast Nara in a former body, and, with Nārāyaṇa for thy companion, didst perform dreadful austerity at Badarī for many myriads of years." It is now known as Badarī-nātha, though this is properly a title of Vishnu as lord of Badarī.

BADAVĀ. 'A mare, the submarine fire.' In mythology it is a flame with the head of a horse, called also Haya-siras, 'horse-head.' *See* Aurva.

BĀHĪKAS. People of the Panjāb, so called in Pāṇini and the *Mahābhārata.* They are spoken of as being impure and out of the law.

BĀHU, BĀHUKA. A king of the Solar race who was vanquished and driven out of his country by the tribes of Haihaya and Tālajanghas. He was father of Sagara.

BĀHUKA. The name of Nala after he had been transformed into a dwarf.

BAHULĀS. The Krittikās or Pleides.

BAHVRICHA. A priest or theologian of the *Rig-veda*.

BALA-BHADRA. *See* Bala-rāma.

BĀLA-GOPĀLA. The Krishna.

BALA-RĀMA. Also Bala-bhadra, was the elder brother of Krishṇa. Bala-rāma is recognised as the seventh Avatāra or incarnation in place of Krishṇa who is regarded as a full manifestation of Vishṇu. According to this view of Vaishṇavas, Krishṇa is full divinity while Bala-rāma an incarnation; but the story of their birth, as told in the *Mahābhārata*, places them on equality. According to *Mahābhārata*, Vishnu took two hairs, a white and a black one, and that these became the children of Devaki—Bala-rāma of fair complexion, Krishṇa very dark. As soon as Bala-rāma was born, he was carried away to Gokula to preserve his life from the tyrant Kansa, and he was there nurtured by Nanda as a child of Rohinī. He and Krishṇa grew up together, and he took part in many of Krishṇa's boyish freaks and adventures. The killing of the great Asura Dhenuka, who had the form of an ass, was his earliest exploit. Another Asura attempted to carry off Bala-rāma on his shoulders, but the boy beat out the demon's brains with his fists. Bala-rāma accompanied Krishṇa when he went to Mathurā, and manfully supported him killing Kansa. Once, Bala-rāma called upon the Yamunā river to come to him, that he might bathe. But his command was not obeyed so he plunged his ploughshare into the river, and dragged the waters wherever he went, until they were obliged to assume a human form and beseech his forgiveness. This is why he is called Yamunā-bhid and Kālindī-karshana, breaker or dragger of the Yamunā. He killed Rukmin in a gambling brawl. Sāmba, son of Krishṇa, was detained as a prisoner at Hastināpur by Duryodhana, Bala-rāma demanded his release; when the Kauravas refused, he thrust his ploughshare under the ramparts of the city, and drew them towards him, thus compelling the Kauravas to give up their prisoner. The killing of the great ape Dwivida, who had stolen his weapons and derided him, was his last exploit.

BĀLA-RĀMĀYAṆA. A drama by Rāja-sekhara, which has been printed.

BĀLEYA. A descendant of Bāli, a Daitya.

BĀLHI. A northern country, Balkh famous for its horses, according to the *Mahābhārata*.

BĀLHĪKAS, BĀHLĪKAS. "Always associated with the people of the north, west, and ultra-Indian provinces, and usually considered to represent the Bactrians or people of Balkh."—Wilson.

BALI. A good and virtuous Daitya king, son of Virochana, Prahlād and Hiraṇya-kaśipu. Vindhyāvalī was his wife, defeated Indra, humbled the gods, and extended his authority over the three worlds. The gods sought Vishnu's protection, who took his Dwarf Avatāra for the purpose of restraining Bali. Having obtained from Bali the boon of three steps of ground, he stepped over heaven and earth in two strides; but then, out of regard for Bali's kindness and his grandson Prahlāda's virtues, left to him Pātāla, the infernal regions. According to *Rig-veda,* Vishṇu is represented as three steps over earth, heaven, and the lower regions, typifying perhaps the rising, culmination, and setting of the sun.

BĀLĪ, BĀLIN. He was supposed to be the son of Indra, and to have been born from the hair (bāla) of his mother. This monkey king of Kishkindhā, was slain by Rāma, and kingdom was given to his brother Sugrīva, the friend and ally of Rāma. Tārā was his wife and Angada and Tāra was his sons.

BĀṆA. Eldest son of Bali, this Daitya had a thousand arms. He was a friend of Śiva and enemy of Vishṇu. His daughter Ushā fell in love with Aniruddha, the grandson of Krishna, and had him conveyed to her by magic art. Krishna, Bala-rāma, and Pradyumna went to the rescue, and were resisted by Bāṇa, who was assisted by Śiva and Skanda, god of war. Śiva was overpowered by Krishna; Skanda was wounded; and the many arms of Bāṇa were cut off by the missile weapons of Krishna. Śiva then interceded for the life of Bāna, and Krishna granted it. He is also called Vairochi.

BANGA. Banga meant the districts north of the Bhāgīrathi—Jessore, Krishnagar, etc. *See* Anu.

BARBARAS. Name of a people. "The analogy to 'barbarians' is not in sound only, but in all the authorities these are classed with borderers and foreigners and nations not Hindu.—Wilson.

BARHISHADS. A class of Pitris, who live in Vaibhraja-loka. When alive, they kept up to the household flame, and presented offerings to the fire. They are also the months. *See* Pitris.

BAUDHĀYANA. A writer on Dharma-sāstra or law. The author of a Sūtra work.

BHADRĀ. Wife of Utathya.

BHADRACHĀRU. A son of Krishna and Rukminī.

BHADRA-KĀLĪ. Name of goddes Durgā.

BHADRĀŚWA. 1. A region lying to the east of Meru. 2. A celebrated horse, son of Uchchaih-śravas.

BHAGA. A Vedic deity of very indistinct personality and powers, supposed to bestow wealth and preside over marriage, is classed among the Ādityas and Viswedevas.

BHAGA-NETRA-GHANA (or-HAN). 'Destroyer of the eyes of Bhaga.' An appellation of Siva.

BHAGAVAD-GĪTĀ. 'The song of the Divine One,' a celebrated episode of the *Mahābhārata*, in the form of a metrical dialogue, in which the chief speaker, divine Krishṇa expounds to Arjuna his philosophical doctrines. Krishṇa, as a god, is a manifestation of Vishnu; but in this song, and in other places, he is held to be the supreme being. As man, he was related to both the Pāndavas and the Kauravas, and in the great war between these two families he refused to take up arms on either side. But he consented to act as the Pāndava Arjuna's charioteer. When the opposing hosts were drawn up in array against each other, Arjuna, touched with compunction for the approaching slaughtor of kindred and friends, appeals to Krishṇa for guidance. This gives the occasion for the philosophical teaching. "The poem is divided into three sections, each containing six chapters, the philosophical teaching in each being somewhat distinct," but "undoubtedly the main design of the poem, the sentiments expressed in which have exerted a powerful influence throughout India for the last 1600 years, is to inculcate the doctrine of Bhakti (faith), and to exalt the duties of caste above all other obligations, including those of friendship and kindred." So Arjuna is told to do his duty as a soldier without heeding the slaughter of friends. "In the second division of the poem the Pantheistic doctrines of the Vedānta are more directly inculcated than in the other sections. Krishṇa. here, in the plainest language, claims adoration as one with the great universal spirit pervading and constituting the universe." The language of this poem is exceedingly beautiful, and its tone and sentiment of a very lofty character, so that they have a striking effect even in the prose translation. It was one fo the earliest Sanskrit works translated into English by Wilkins; but a much more perfect translation, with an excellent introduction, has since been published by Mr. J. Cockburn Thompson. There are several other translations in French, German, etc. This composition is Dwarf to have been interpreted in the *Mahābhārata* because it is of a much later date—later than the six Darsna or philosophical Schools, having record imposition from Sankhya, Yoga and Vedanta. It is said to have appeared in 2nd or 3rd century AD.

BHĀGAVATA PURĀṆA. The Purāṇa "in which ample details of duty are described, and which opens with (an extract from) the Gāyatrī; that in which the death of the Asura Vritra is told, and in which the mortals and immortals of the Sāraswata Kalpa, with the events that then happened to them in the world, are related, that is celebrated as the Bhāgavata, and consists of 18,000 verses." "The Bhāgavats," says Wilson, "is a work of great celebrity in India, and exercises a more direct and powerful influence upon the opinions and feelings of the people than perhaps any other of the Purānas. It is placed fifth in all the lists, but the Padma ranks it as the eighteenth, the extracted substance of all the rest. According to the usual specification, it consists of 18,000 slokas, distributed amongst 332 chapters, divided into twelve skandhas or books. It is known as Bhāgavata from its being dedicated to the glorification of Bhāgavata or Vishṇu." The most popular and characteristic part of his Purāṇa is the tenth book, which narrates in detail the history of Krishṇa, and has been translated into perhaps all the vernacular languages of India. Colebrooke concurs with the opinion of many learned Hindus that this Purāṇa is the composition of the grammarian Vopadeva, who lived about six or seven centuries ago at the court of Hemādri, Rāja of Deva-giri (Deogurh or Daulatābād), and Wilson sees no reason for calling in question the tradition which assigns the work to this writer. This Purāna has been translated into French by Burnoui.

BHĀGĪRATHĪ. The Ganges. The name is derived from Bhagīratha, a descendant of Sagara, whose austerities induced Siva to allow the sacred river to descend to the earth for the purpose of bathing the ashes of Sagara's sons, who had been consumed by the wrath of the sage Kapila. Bhagīratha named the river Sāgara, and after leading it over the earth to the sea, he conducted it to Pātāla, where the ashes of his ancestors were purified with its waters.

BHAIRAVA (mas.), BHAIRAVĪ (fem.). 'The terrible.' Names of Śiva and his wife Devī. The Bhairavas are eight inferior forms or manifestations of Śiva, all of them of a terrible character:—(1) Asitānga, black limbed; (2) Sanhāra, destruction; (3) Ruru, a dog; (4) Kāla, black; (5) Krodha, anger; (6) Tāmra-chūdā, red crested; (7) Chandra-chūdā, moon crested; (8) Mahā, great. Other names met with as variants are Kapāla, Rudra, Bhīshana, Un-metta, Ku-pati, etc. In these forms Śiva often rides upon a dog, wherefore he is called Swāśwa, 'whose horse is a dog.'

BHĀMATĪ. A gloss on Śankara's commentary upon the Brahma Sūtras by Vāchaspati Misra. It is a course of publication in the *Bibliotheca Indica.*

BHĀNUMATĪ. Daughter of Bhānu, a Yādava chief, who was abducted from her home in Dwārakā by the demon Nikumbha during the absence of her father.

BHARDWĀJA. A Rishi to whom many Vedic hymns are attributed. He was son of Brihaspati and father of Droṇa, the preceptor of the Pāndavas. The *Taittirīya Brāhmaṇa* says that "he lived through three lives" (probably meaning a life of great length), and that "he became immortal and ascended to the heavenly world, to have union with the sun." In the *Mahābhārata* he is represented as living at Hardwār. In the *Rāmāyaṇa* he received Rāma and Sītā in his hermitage at Prayāga, which was then and afterwards much celebrated. According to some of the Purāṇas and the *Hari-vanśa,* he became by adoption the son of King Bharata.

BHĀRADWĀJA. 1. Droṇa. 2. Any descendant of Bharadwāja or follower of his teaching. 3. Name of a grammarian and author of Sūtras.

BHARATA. 1. A hero and king from whom the warlike people called Bhāratas, frequently mentioned in the *Rig-veda,* had descended.

2. An ancient king of the first Manwantara, he was devoted to Vishṇu, and abdicated his throne that he might continue in constant meditation upon him.

3. Son of Dasaratha by his wife Kaikeyī, and half-brother of Rāma-chandra.

4. A prince of the Puru branch of the Lunar race. Bharata was son of Dushyanta and Śakuntalā.

5. A sage who invented dramatic entertainments.

BHĀRATA. A descendant of Bharata, especially one of the Pāndu princes.

BHĀRATA-VARSHA. India, as having been the kingdom of Bharata, comprising nine Khandas or parts: Indra-dwipa, Kaserumat, Tāmara-varna, Gabhastimat, Nāga-dwīpa, Saumya, Gāndharva, Vāruna.

BHĀRATĪ. A name of Saraswatī.

BHĀRGAVA. A descendant of Bhrigu, as Chyavana, Saunaka, Jamad-agni, but more especially used for the latter and Paraśu-rāma.

BHARTRI-HARI. A celebrated poet and grammarian, who is said to have been the brother of Vikramāditya. He wrote three Śatakas or Centuries of verses, called—(1) *Sringāra-śataka,* on amatory matters; (2) *Nīti-śataka,* on polity and ethics; (3) *Vairāgya-śataka,* on religious austerity. These maxims are said to have been written when he had taken to a religious life after a licentious youth. He was also author of a grammatical work of high repute called *Vākya-padīya,* and the poem called Bhaṭṭikāvya is by some attributed to him.

BHĀSHA-PARICHCHHEDA. An exposition of the Nyāya philosophy. There are several editions.

BHĀSKARĀCHĀRYA. (Bhāskara + Āchārya.) A celebrated mathematician and astronomer, who was born early in the eleventh century A.D. He was author of the *Bīja-gaṇita* on arithmetic, the *Līlāvatī* on algebra, and the *Siddhānta Siromaṇi* on astronomy. Bhāskara "was fully acquainted with the principle of the Differential Calculus."

BHAṬṬĀCHĀRYA. *See* Kumārila Bhaṭṭa.

BHAṬṬI-KĀVYA. A poem on the action of Rāma by Bhaṭṭi. It is of a very artificial character, and is designed to illustrate the laws of grammar and the figures of poetry and rhetoric. The text has been printed with a commentary, and part has been translated into German by Schultz.

BHAUMA. Son of Bhūmi (the earth), metronymic of the Daitya Nāraka.

BHAUTYA. The fourteenth Manu. *See* Manu.

BHAVA. 1. A Vedic deity often mentioned in connection with Sarva the destroyer. 2. A name of Rudra or Siva, or of a manifestation of that god. *See* Rudra.

BHAVA-BHUTI. A celebrated dramatist, the author of three of the best extant Sanskrit dramas, the *Mahāvīra Charita, Uttara Rāma Charita,* and *Mālatī Mādhava.* He was also known as Srī-kantha, or 'throat of eloquence.' A Brāhman, and a native either of Beder or Berar, he flourished in eighth century. Wilson the translator of his three plays in blank verse, says of *Mālatī Mādhava,* "The author is fond of an unreasonable display of learning, and occasionally substitutes the phraseology of logic or metaphysics for the language of poetry and nature. At the same time the beauties predominate over the defects, and the language of the drama is in general of extraordinary beauty and power."

BHAVISHYA PURĀṆA. "This Purāṇa, as its name implies, should be a book of prophecies foretelling what will be." The copies discovered contain about 7000 stanzas and unlike the Purāṇas, is principally a manual of rites and ceremonies, for its deity Śiva. There is another work, containing also about 7000 verses, called the *Bhavishyottara Purāṇa,* seemingly a continuation or supplement of the former," while its contents ring of a similar character.

BHAVISHYOTTARA PURĀṆA. See *Bhavishya Purāṇa.*

BHAWĀNĪ. One of the names of the wife of Śiva. *See* Devī.

BHELA. An ancient sage who, wrote upon medicine.

BHIKSHU. A mendicant; the Brāhman in the fourth and last stage of his religious life. *See* Brāhman.

Any mendicant, especially, in its Pāli form, Bhikkhu, a Buddhist mendicant.

BHIMA, BHĪMA-SENA. 'The terrible.' The second of the five Pāndu princes, and mythically son of Vāyu, 'the god of the wind,' he was a man of vast size, and had great strength. He was wrathful in temper, and given to abuse, a brave warrior, but a fierce and cruel foe, coarse in taste and manners, and a great eater. That is why he was called Vrikodara, 'wolf's belly'. Bhīma took a very prominent part in the great battle between the Kauravas and Pāndavas. He fought against Bhīshma; on the second day he slew the two sons of the Rāja of Magadha, and after them their father, killing him and his elephant at a single blow. In the night between the fourteenth and fifteenth day of the battle, Bhīma fought with Droṇa until the rising of the sun. On the seventeenth day he killed Duh-sāsana, and drank his blood, as he had vowed to do, in retribution of Duh-sāsana's insults to Draupadī. On the eighteenth and last day of the battle Dur-yodhana fled and hid himself in a lake. Ultimately Bhīma and Dur-yodhana fought as usual with clubs. The battle was long and furious; the parties were equally matched, and Bhīma was getting the worst of it, when he struck an unfair blow which smashed Dur-yodhana's thigh, and brought him to the ground. Thus he fulfilled his vow and avenged Draupadī.

He had a son named Ghatotkacha from his Asura wife Hidimbā and he also had a son named Sarvatraga or Sarvaga. from his wife Balandhara, princess of Kāśī. Bhīma-sena, Bāhu-sālin, 'the large armed,' Jarāsandha-jit, 'vanquisher of Jarāsandha,' are the other appellations of Bhīma .

BHĪMA. Name of the father of Damayantī. A name of Rudra or of one of his personifications. *See* Rudra.

BHĪMA SANKARA, BHĪMESWARA. Name of one of the twelve great Lingas. *See* Linga.

BHĪMA-SENA. A name of Bhīma.

BHĪSHMA. 'The terrible.' Son of King Śāntanu and the holy river goddess Gangā, he was called Śāntanava, Gāngeya, and Nadi-ja, 'the river-born.' When King Śantanu was very old he desired to marry a young and beautiful wife. His son Śāntanava or Bhīshma found a suitable damsel, but her parents objected to the marriage because Bhīshma was heir to the throne, and if she bore sons they could not succeed. To gratify his father's desires, he made a vow to the girl's parents that he would never accept the throne, nor would ever marry so that he does not become the father of children. Śāntanu then married the damsel, whose name was Satyavatī, and she bore him two sons. When the war began he took the side of the Kauravas, the sons of Dhrita-rāshtra, and he was made commander-in-chief of their army. He laid down some rules for mitigating the horrors of war, and he stipulated that he should not be called upon to fight against Arjuna. Goaded by the reproaches of Dur-yodhana, he attacked Arjuna on the tenth day of the battle. He was unfairly wounded by Śikhandin, and was pierced with innumerable arrows from the hands of Arjuna, so that there was not a space of even two fingers' breadth left without a wound in his whole body, and when he fell from his chariot he was upheld from the ground by the arrows and lay as on a couch of darts. He was mortally wounded, but he had obtained the power of determining the time of his death. So he survived fifty-eight days, after delivering several long didactic discourses.

BHĪSHMAKA. 1. An appellation of Siva. 2. King of Vidarbha, father of Rukmin and of Rukminī, the chief wife of Krishna.

BHOGAVATĪ. 'The voluptuous.' The subterranean capital of the Nāgas in the Nāga-loka portion of Pātāla. Another name is Pūt-kārī.

BHOJA. A name borne by many kings. Most conspicuous among them was Bhoja or Bhoja-deva, king of Dhār, who is said to have been a great patron of literature, and probably died before 1082 A.D. 2. A prince of the Yādava race who reigned at Mrittikavatī on the Parnāsa river in Mālwa; he is called also Mahābhoja. 3. A tribe living the Vindhya mountains. 4. A country; the modern Bhojpur, Bhāgalpur, etc.

BHOJA-PRABANDHA. A collection of literary anecdotes relating to King Bhoja of Dhār, written by Ballāla, the text has been lithographed by Pavie.

BHRIGU. A Vedic sage. He is one of the Prajāpatis and great Rishis, and is regarded as the founder of the race of the Bhrigus or Bhārgavas, in which was born Jamadagni and Paraśurāma. Manu calls him son, and says that he confides to him his Institutes. According to the Mahābhārata, he officiated at Daksha's celebrated sacrifice, and had his beard pulled out by Śiva. It is also part of Bhrigu that he rescued the sage Agastya from the tyrannyof King Nahusha, who had obtained superhuman power. Bhrigu crept into Agastya's hair to avoid the glance of Nahusha, and when that tyrant fixed Agastya to his chariot and kicked him on the head to make him move, Bhrigu cursed Nahusha, and he was turned into a serpent. However, Bhrigu, on Nahusha's supplication, limited the duration of his curse.

BHRIGUS. 'Roasters, consumers'. "A class of mythical beings who belonged to the middle or aerial class of gods."—Roth. They are connected with Agni, and are spoken of as producers and nourishers of fire, and as makers of chariots. They are associated with the Angirasas, the Atharvans, Ribhus, etc.

BHU, BHUMI. The earth. See Prithivī.

BHUR. See Vyāhriti.

BHURI-SRAVAS. A prince of the Bālhikas and an ally of the Kauravas, who was killed in the great battle of the *Mahābhārata*.

BHUR-LOKA. *See* Loka.

BHUTA. A ghost, imp, goblin These malignant spirits haunt cemeteries, lurk in trees, animate dead bodies, and delude and devour human beings. According to

Vishnu Purāṇa they are "fierce beings and eaters of flesh," who were created by the Creator when he was incensed. According to the *Vāyu Purāṇa* Krodhā, 'anger' is said to have been their mother'.

BHUTEŚA, BHUTEŚWARA. 'Lord of beings or of created things.' A name applied to Vishṇu, Brahmā, and Krishna; as 'lord of the Bhūtas or goblins,' it is applied to Siva.

BHUVANEŚWARA. A ruined city in Orissa, sacred to the worship of Śiva, and containing the remains of several temples. It was formerly called Ekāmra-kānana.

BHUVAR. *See* Vyāhriti.

BHUVAR-LOKA. *See* Loka.

BĪBHATSU. 'loathing,' An appellation of Arjuna.

BINDUSĀRA. The son and successor of Chandragupta.

BRAHMA, BRAHMAN (neuter). The supreme soul of the universe, self-existent, absolute, and eternal, from which all things emanate, and to which all return. This divine essence is incorporeal, immaterial, invisible, unborn, uncreated, without beginning and without end, illimitable, and inappreciable by the sense until the nature both animate and inanimate, in the highest god and in the meanest creature. This supreme soul receives no worship, but it is the object of that abstract meditation which Hindu sages practise in order to obtain absorption into it. It is sometimes called Kala-hansa.

There is a passage in the *Satapatha Brāhmaṇa* which represents Brahma (neut.) as the active creator. *See* Brahmā.

The Veda is sometimes called Brahma.

BRAHMĀ (masculine). The first member of the Hindu triad; the supreme spirit manifested as the active creator of the universe. Brahma was the father of Daksha, who is said to have sprung from his thumb, and he was present at the sacrifice of that patriarch, which was rudely disturbed by Rudra. The four Kumāras, the chief of whom was called Sanat-kumāra or by the patronymic Vaidhātra, were later creations or sons of Brahmā.

BRAHMACHĀRĪ. The Brāhman student. *See* Brāhman.

BRAHMĀDIKAS. The Prajāpatis (q.v.).

BRAHMA-GUPTA. An astronomer who composed the *Brahma-gupta Siddhānta* in A.D. 628.

BRAHMA-LOKA. *See* Loka.

BRĀHMAN. The first of the four castes; the sacerdotal class, the members of which may be, but are not necessarily, priests. A Brāhman is the chief of all created beings; his person is inviolate; he is entitled to all honour, and enjoys many rights and privileges in the caste system. The *Śatapatha Brāhmaṇa* declares that "there are two kinds of gods; first the gods, then those who are Brāhmanas, and have learnt the Veda and repeat it: they are huṃan gods." The chief duty of a Brāhman is the study and teaching of the Vedas, and the performance of sacrifices and other religious ceremonies; but in modern times many Brāhmans entirely neglect these duties, and they engage in most of the occupations of secular life. Under the law of Manu, the life of a Brāhman was divided into four āsramas or stages:—

1. *Brahmachārī*.—The student, whose duty was to pass his days in humble and obedient attendance upon his spiritual preceptor in the study of the Vedas.

2. *Grihastha*.—The householder; the married man living with his wife as head of family engaged in the ordinary duties of reading and teaching the Vedas, sacrificing, assisting to sacrifice, bestowing alms and receiving alms.

3. *Vānaprastha*.—The anchorite, or "dweller in the woods," who, having discharged his duties as a man of the world, has retired into the forest to devote himself to self-denial in food and raiment, to mortifications of various kinds, to religious meditation and to the strict performance of all ceremonial duties.

4. *Sannyāsī*.—The religious mendicant, who, freed from all forms and observances, wanders about subsisting on alms, practising or striving for that condition of mind which, heedless of the joys and pains, cares and troubles of the flesh, is intent only upon the deity and final absorption.

BRĀHMAṆA. 'Belonging to Brāhmans.' Works composed by and for Brāhmans. That part of the Veda which was intended for the use and guidance of Brāhmans in the use of the hymns of the Mantra, and therefore of later production; but the Brāhmana, equally with the Mantra, is held to be Śruti or revealed word. Excepting its claim to revelation, it is a Hindu Talmud. The Brāhmaṇa collectively is made up of the different ritualistic and liturgical writings in prose. They contain the details of the Vedic ceremonies, with long explanations of their origin and meaning; they give instructions as to the use of particular verses and metres; and they abound with curious legends, divine and human, in illustration. "The oldest rituals we have, the oldest linguistic explanations, the oldest traditional narratives, and the oldest philosophical speculations" are found is there. As literary productions they are not of a high order, but some "striking thoughts, bold expressions, sound reasoning, and curious traditions are found among the mass of pedantry and grandiloquence." Each of the Sanhitās or collection of hymns has its Brāhmaṇas, and these generally maintain the essential character of the Veda to which they belong. Thus the Brāhmanas of the Rig are specially devoted to the duties of the Hotri, who recites the richas or verses; those of the Yajur to the performance of the sacrifices by the Adhwaryu, and those of the Sāman to the chaunting by the Udgātri. The Rig has the *Aitareya Brāhmaṇa*, which is perhaps the oldest, and many date as far back as the seventh century B.C. This is sometimes called *Āśwalāyana*. It has another called *Kaushitaki* or *Sānkhāyana*. The *Taittiriya Sanhitā* of the *Yajur-veda* has the *Taittiriya*

Brāhmaṇa, and the *Vājasaneyī Sanhitā* has the *Satapatha Brāhmaṇa,* one of the most important of all Brāhmanas. The *Sāma-veda* has eight Brāhmanas, of which the best known are the Praudha or *Pancha-vinsa,* the *Tāndya,* and the *Shad-vinsa.* The Atharva has only one, the *Gopatha Brāhmaṇa.* In their fullest extent, the Brāhmanas embrace also the treatises called Āraṇyakas and Upanishads.

BRAHMANASPATI. A Vedic equivalent of the name Brihaspati.

BRAHMANDA PURĀṆA. "That which has declared, in 12,200 verses, the magnificence of the egg of Brahmā, and in which an account of the future kalpas is contained, is called the *Brahmāṇḍa Purāṇa,* and was revealed by Brahmā." This Purāna, like the *Skanda,* is "no longer procurable in a collective body," but is represented by a variety of Khandas and Māhātmyas professing to be derived from it. The *Adhyātma Rāmāyaṇa,* a very popular work, is considered to be a part of this Purāṇa.

BRAHMĀṆĪ. The female form, or the daughter of Brahmā, also called Śata-rūpā.

BRAHMĀ-PURA. The city of Brahmā, the heaven of Brahmā, on the summit of Mount Meru, and enclosed by the river Gangā.

BRAHMA PURĀṆA. It is sometimes entitled the Ādi or "First" Purāṇa, because in all the lists of the Purāṇas the Brahma stands first. It was repeated by Brahmā to Marīchi, and is said to contian 10,000 stanzas, but the actual number is between 7000 and 8000. It is also called the Saura Purāṇa, because "it is, in great part, appropriated to the worship of Sūrya, the sun". "The early chapters give a description of the creation, an account of the Manwantaras, and the history of the solar and Lunar dynasties to the time of Krishṇa in a summary manner, and in words which are common to it and several other Purāṇas. A brief description of the universe succeeds; and then come a number of chapters relating to the holiness of Orissa, with its temples and sacred groves, dedicated to the Sun, to Śiva, and Jagannātha, the latter especially. These chapters are characteristic of this Purāṇa, and show its main object to be the promotion of the worship of Krishṇa as Jagannātha. To these particulars succeeds a life of Krishṇa, which is word for word the same as that of the *Vishṇu Purāṇa;* and the compilation terminates with a particular detail of the mode in which Yoga or contemplative devotion, the object of which is still Vishṇu, is to be performed. There is little in this which corresponds with the definition of a Pancha-lakshaṇa Purāṇa, and the mention of the temples of Orissa, the date of the original construction of which is recorded, shows that it could not have been compiled earlier than the thirteenth or fourteenth century."

BRAHMARSHI-DEŚA. "Kurukshetra, the Matsyas, the Panchālas, and the Surasenas. This land, which comes to Brahmāvartta, is the land of brahmarshis."—*Manu.*

BRAHMARSHIS. Rishis of the Brāhman caste, who were the founders of the gotras of Brāhmans, and dwell in the sphere of Brahmā. *See* Rishi.

BRAHMA-SĀVARNI. The tenth Manu. *See* Manu.

BRAHMA SŪTRAS. Aphorisms on the Vedānta philosophy by Bādarāyaṇa or Vyāsa, they are also called Brahma Mimānsā Sūtrās.

BRAHMA VAIVRTA PURĀṆA. "The Purāṇa which is related by Sāvarni to Nārada, and contains the account of the greatness of Krishṇa, with the occurrences of the Rthantra Kapla, where also the story of Brahmavarāha is repeatedly told, is called the Brahma Vaivarta Purāṇa, and contains 18,000 stanzas." The copies known rather exceed this number of stanzas, but the contents do not correspond to this description. "The character of the work is so decidedly sectarial, and the sect to which it belongs so distinctly marked—that of the worshippers of the juvenile Krishna and Rādhā, a form of belief of known modern origin."—that it must be a production of a comparatively later date. A specimen of the text and translation has been published by Stenzler.

BRAHMĀVARTTA. "Between the two divine rivers, Saraswatī and Drishadwatī, lies the tract of land which the sages have named Brahmāvartta, because it was frequented by the gods."—Manu, ii. 17.

BRAHMA-VEDA. A name given to the Atharvan or fourth Veda, the Veda of prayers and charms.

BRAHMA-YUGA. 'The age of Brāhmans.' The first or Krita-yuga. *See* Yuga.

BRAHAD ĀRAṆYAKA, BRIHAD UPANISHAD. The *Brihad Āraṇyaka Upanishad* belongs to the *Śatapatha Brāhmaṇa,* and is ascribed to the sage Yājnawalkya.

BRIHAD-DEVATĀ. An ancient work in slokas by the sage Śaunaka, which enumerates and describes the deity or deities to which each hymn and verse of the *Rig-veda* is addressed. It frequently recites legends in support of its attributions.

BRIHAD-RATHA. The tenth and last king of the Maurya dynasty, founded by Chandragupta.

BHIHAN NĀRADĪYA PURĀṆA. See *Nārada Purāṇa.*

BRIHASPATI. In the *Rig-veda* the names Brihaspati and Brahmanaspati alternate, and are equivalent to each other. They are names "of a deity in whom the action of the worshipper upon the gods is personified. He is the suppliant, the sacrificer, the priest, who intercedes with gods on behalf of men and protects mankind against the wicked. Hence he appears as the prototype of the priests and priestly order; and is also designated as the *Purohita* (family priest) of the divine community. He is called in one place 'the father of the gods,' and a widely extended creative power is ascribed to him. He is also designated as 'the shining' and 'the gold-coloured,' and as 'having the thunder for his voice."

In later times he is a rishi. He is also regent of the planet Jupiter, and the name is commonly used for the planet itself.

BRIHAT-KATHĀ. A large collection of tales, the original of the *Kathā-sarit-sāgara* (q.v.).

BRIHAT-SANHITĀ. A celebrated work on astronomy by Varāha Mihira, it has been printed by Kern in the *Bibliotheca Indica,* who has also published a translation in *Jour. R.A.S.* for 1970 and following years.

BUDDHA. Gautama Buddha, the founder of Buddhism. Vishnu's ninth incarnation. *See* Avatāra.

BUDHA. 'Wise intelligent.' The planet Mercury, son of Soma, the moon, by Rohinī, or by Tārā, wife of Brihaspati. He married Ilā, daughter of Manu Vaivaswata, and had a son, Purūravas, Budha was author of a hymn in the *Rig-veda.* He is called Saumya and Rauhineya after his parents. He is also called Praharshana, Rodhana, Tunga, and Syāmānga, 'black-bodies'. The intrigue of Soma with Tārā was the cause of a great quarrel, in which the gods and the Asuras fought against each other. Brahmā compelled Some to give up Tārā, and after she returned to her husband Brihaspati, refused to tell his paternity, but finally upon the command of Brahmā, she declared Soma to be the father, and he gave the boy the name of Budha, which is distinct from Buddha.

C

CHAITANYA-CHANDRODAYA. 'The rise of the moon of Chaitanya,' a drama in ten acts by Kavi-karna-pura. It has been published in the *Bibliotheca India*. Chaitanya was a modern Vaishṇava reformer, who was an incarnation of Krishṇa.

CHAITRA-RATHA. The grove or forest of Kuvera on Mandara, one of the spurs of Meru. It is so called because it is cultivated by the gandharva Chitra-ratha.

CHAKORA. A kind of partridge, a fabulous bird, supposed to live upon the beams of the moon.

CHAKRA-VARTĪ. A universal emperor, described by the *Vishṇu Purāṇa* as one who is born with the mark of Vishṇu's discus visible in his hand. According to Wilson, "the grammatical etymology is, 'He who abides in or rules over an extensive territory called a Chakra.'"

CHĀKSHUSHA. The sixth Manu. See Manu.

CHAMPA. Son of Prithu-lāksha, a descendant of Yayāti, through his fourth son, Anu, and founder of the city of Champā.

CHAMPĀ, CHAMPĀVATĪ, CHAMPA-MĀLINĪ, CHAMPĀ-PURI. The capital city of the country of Anga. Its traces still remain in the neighbourhood of Bhāgalpur. It was also called Mālinī, because it was surrounded with champaka trees as with a garland (mālā). Although it is said to have derived its name from Champa, its founder, the abundant Champaka trees may also be responsible for its designation.

CHĀMUNDĀ. An emanation of the goddess Durgā, sent forth from her forehead to encounter the demons Chanda and Munda. According to the *Mārkandeya Purāṇa*, "From the forehead of Ambikā (Durgā), contracted with wrathful frowns, sprang swiftly forth a goddess of black and formidable aspect, armed with a scimitar and noose, bearing a ponderous mace, decorated with a garland of dead corpses, robed in the hide of an elephant, dry and withered and hideous, with yawning mouth, and lolling tongue, and bloodshot eyes, and filling the regions with her shouts." When she had killed the two demons, she took their heads to Durgā, who told her that she should henceforth be known, by a contraction of their names, as Chāmundā.

CHĀṆAKYA. A celebrated Brāhman, who took a leading part in the destruction of the Nandas, and in the elevation of Chandra-gupta to their throne. He was a great master of finesse and artifice, and has been called the Machiavelli of India. A work upon morals and polity called *Chāṇakya Sūtra* is ascribed to him. He is the chief character in the drama called *Mudrārākshasa,* and is known also by the names Vishṇu-gupta and Kauṭilya. His maxims have been translated by Weber.

CHANDĀ, CHANDĪ. The goddess Durgā, especially in the form she assumed for the destruction of the asura called Mahisha.

CHANDĪPĀṬ, CHANDĪPĀṬHA. A poem of 700 verses, forming an episode of the *Mārkandeya Purāṇa,* it celebrates Durgā's victories over the Asuras, and is recited daily in the temples of that goddess. The work is also called *Devī-māhātmya.*

CHANDRA. The moon, as a planet or a deity. *See* Soma.

CHANDRA-GUPTA. This name was identified by Sir W. Jones with the Sandracottus or Sandrocyptus mentioned by Arrian and the other classical historians of Alexander's campaign; and somewhat later as having entered into a treaty with Seleucus Nicator through the ambassador Megasthenes. Even though this identification has been contested, the chief writers on Indian antiquities have admitted it as an established fact, and have added confirmatory evidence from various sources, so that the identity admits of no reasonable doubt. This identification is of the utmost importance to Indian chronology. It is the only link by which Indian history is connected with that of Greece, and everything in Indian chronology depends upon the date of Chandra-gupta as ascertained from that assigned to Sandracottus by the classical writers. He ruled for twenty-four years, from 315 B.C. to 291 B.C. Chandra-gupta is a prominent name in both Brāhmanical and Buddhist writings, and his accession to the throne is the subject of the drama *Mudrārākshasa*.

When Alexander was in India, he learned that a king named Xandrames reigned over the Prasii (Prāchyas) at the city of Palibothra, situated at the confluence of the Ganges and another river called Erranaboas (the Sone). At this time, Sandracottus was young, but he waged war against Alexander's captains, and he raised bands of fighters, with whose help he succeeded in establishing freedom in India.

Hindu and Buddhist writers are entirely silent to Alexander's appearance in India, but they show that Chandra-gupta overthrew the dynasty of the Nandas, which reigned over Magadha, and "established freedom in India with he help of bands of fighters." He established himself at Pātali-putra, the capital of the Nandas, which is indentical with the Greek Palibothra, and has been shown as the modern Patna.

The dynasty of the Nandas that reigned over Magadha are frequently spoken of as "nine Nandas," meaning apparently nine despots; the last Nanda, named Mahā-padma, and his eight sons. Mahā-padma Nanda was the son of a Sūdra, and so by law he was a Sūdra himself. He was powerful and ambitious, cruel and avaricious. His people were disaffected; but his fall is represented as having been brought about by the Brāhman Chāṇakya. Chandra-gupta was then raised to the throne and founded the Mauryan dynasty, the third king of which was the great Aśoka, grandson of Chandra-gupta.

CHANDRA-HĀSA. A prince of the south, who lost his parents soon after his birth, and fell into a state of destitution, but after going through a variety of adventures came to the throne. *See* Wheeler, vol. i. p. 522.

CHANDRA-KĀNTA. 'The moon-stone.' A gem or stone or a crystal supposed to be formed by the congelation of the rays of the moon. It is supposed to exercise a cooling influence.

CHANDRA-KETU. 1. A son of Lakshmaṇa. 2. A king of the city of Chakora. 3. A country near the Himālayas.

CHANDRA-VANSA. The Lunar race. Divided into the two great branches, the Yādavas and Pauravas, respectively descended from Yadu and Puru. Krishṇa belonged to the line of Yadu, and Dushyanta with the Kuru and Pāndu princes to the line of Puru.

CHĀṆURA. A wrestler in the service of Kansa, who was killed by Krishṇa.

CHARAKA. A writer on medicine who lived in Vedic times. He received the materials of his work from Agniveśa, to whom they were delivered by Ātreya. A legend represents him as an incarnation of the serpent Sesha. The work was translated into Arabic before the end of the eight century. The text has been printed in India.

CHARAKA. One of the chief schools of the Yajur-veda.

CHARAKA-BRĀHMAṆA. A Brāhmana of the Black Yajur-veda.

CHARAṆA. A Vedic school or society. It is explained by a commentator as "a number of men who are pledged to the reading of a certain Sākhā of the Veda, and who have in this manner become one body."

CHĀRAṆAS. Panegyrists. The panegyrists of the gods.

CHARMANVĀTĪ. The river Chambal.

CHĀRU, CHĀRU-DEHA, CHĀRU-DESHNA, CHĀRU-GUPTA. Sons of Krishṇa and Rukminī.

CHĀRU-DATTA. The Brāhman hero of the drama *Mrichchhakatī*.

CHĀRU HĀSINĪ. 'Sweet smiler,' an epithet used for Rukminī and Lakshmanā, and perhaps for other wives of Krishna.

CHĀRU-MATĪ. Daughter of Krishṇa and Rukminī.

CHĀRVĀKA. 1. A Rākshasa, and friend of Duryodhana, who disguished himself as a Brāhman and reproached Yudhishthira for his crimes, when he entered Hastināpura in triumph after the great battle. The Brāhmans discovered the imposture and reduced Chārvāka to ashes with the fire of their eyes. 2. A sceptical philosopher who advocated materialistic doctrines. He probably lived before the composition of the *Rāmāyaṇa,* and is perhaps identical with the Chārvāka of the *Mahābhārata.* His followers are known by his name.

CHATUR-VARṆA. The four castes. *See* Varṇa.

CHEDI. Name of a people and of their country, the modern Chandial and Boglekhand. The capital was Sukti-matī, and among the kings of this country were Dama-ghosha and Śiśu-pāla.

CHEKITĀNA. A son of Dhrishta-ketu, Rāja of the Kekayas, and an ally of the pāndavas.

CHERA. A kingdom in the south of the Indian peninsula, which was absorbed by its rival the Chola kingdom.

CHHANDAS, CHHANDO. Metre, one of the Vedāngas. The oldest known work on the subject is "the Chhandah-sāstra, ascribed to Pingala, which may be as old as the second century B.C." It has been published in the *Bibliotheca Indica.* The subject is one to which great attention has given by the Hindus from the earliest times.

CHHANDOGA. A priest or chanter of the *Sāma-veda.*

CHHĀNDOGYA. Name of a Upanīshad of the Sāma-veda. (See Upanishad.) It has been printed by Dr. Roer, and it has been the *Bibliotheca Indica*. There is also another printed edition of the text. The *Chhāndogya Upanishad* consists of eight out of ten chapters of the *Chhāndogya Brāhmana*. It is remembered for its rich store of legends regarding the gradual development of Brahmanical theology.

CHHĀYĀ. 'Shade.' A handmaid of the sun. Sanjna, wife of the sun, being unable to bear the fervour of her lord, put her handmaid Chhāyā in her place. The sun, believing Chhāya to be his wife, had three children by her: Śani, the planet Saturn; the Manu Sāvarni; and a daughter, the Tapatī river. As mother of Saturn, Chhāyā is known as Śani-prasū. The partiality which she showed for these children provoked Yama, the son of Sanjnā, and he lifted his foot to kick her. She cursed him that his leg be affected with sores and worms. This made it clear that she was not Sanjnā and mother of Yama. So the sun went in search of Sanjnā and brought her back. According to one Purāna, Chhāyā was a daughter of Viśwakarma, and sister of Sanjnā, the wife of the sun.

CHINTĀ-MAṆI. 'The wish-gem,' a jewel which is supposed to have the power of granting all desires. Also known as the philosopher's stone, it is said to have belonged to Brahmā, who is himself called by this name. It is also called Divya-ratna.

CHIRA-JĪVIN. 'Long-lived.' Gods or deified mortals, who live for long periods.

CHITRA-GUPTA. A scribe in the abodes of the dead, who records the virtues and vices of men. The recorder of Yama.

CHITRA-KUṬA. 'Bright-peak.' The seat of Vālmiki's hermitage, in which Rāma and Sītā both found refuge at different times. It is the modern Chitrakote, on the river Pisuni, about fifty miles south-east of Banda. In Bundelkhand. It is a very holy place, and abounds with temples and shrines, hinted by thousands every year. "The whole neighbourhood is Rāma's country. Every headland has some legend, every cavern is connected with his name."—Cust in *Calcutta Review.*

CHITRA-LEKHĀ. A picture. Also name of a nymph who was skilled in painting and in the magic art. She was the friend and confidante of Ushā. *See* Ushā.

CHITRĀNGADA. The elder son of King Śāntanu, and brother of Bhīshma. He was arrogant and proud, and was killed in earlylife in a conflict with a Gandharva of the same name.

CHITRĀNGADĀ. Daughter of King Chitra-vāhana of Mani-pura, wife of Arjuna and mother of Babhru-vāhana.

CHITRA-RATHA. 'Having a fine car.' The king of the Gandharvas. There are many others known by this name.

CHITRA-SENA. 1. One of the hundred sons of Dhrita-rāshtra. 2. A chief of the Yakshas.

CHITRA-YAJNA. A modern drama in five acts upon the legend of Daksha. It is the work of a Pandit named Vaidyanātha Vāchaspati.

CHOLA. A country and kingdom of the south of India about Tanjore. The country was called Chola-mandala, whence comes the name Coromandel.

CHYAVANA, CHYAVĀNA. A sage, son of the Rishi Bhrigu, and author of some hymns. According to the *Mahā-bhārata,* Chyavana was husband of Ārushī or Su-kanyā and father of Aurva. He is also considered to be the father of Hārita. The name is Chyavāna in the *Rig-veda,* but Chyavana in the Brāhmana and later writings.

D

DADHYANCH, DADHĪCHA. (Dadhīcha is a later form.) A Vedic Rishi, son of Atharvan, whose name frequently occurs. The legend about him, as it appears in the *Rig-veda,* is that India taught him certain sciences, but threatened to cut off his head if he taught them to any one else. The Aświns prevailed upon Dadhyanch to communicate his knowledge to them, and, to preserve him from the wrath of Indra, they took off his own head and replaced it with that of a horse. When Indra struck off the sage's equine head, the Aświns restored his own to him. A verse of the *Rig-veda* says, "Indra, with the bones of Dadhy-anch, slew ninetytimes nine Vritras;" and the story told by the scholiast in explanation is, that while Dadhyanch was living on earth the Asuras were controlled and tranquillised by his appearance; but when he had gone to heaven, they overspread the whole earth. Indra inquired for Dadhyanch, or any relic of him. He was told of the horse's head, and when this was found in a lake near Kurukshetra, Indra used the bones as weapons, and with them slew the Asuras, or, in the words of the Vedic verse, he "foiled the nine times ninety stratagems of the Asuras or *Vritras*". The story, as subsequently told in the *Mahābhārata* and Purāṇas, is that the sage devoted himself to death that Indra and the gods might be armed with bis bones as more effective weapons than thunderbolts for the destruction of Vritra and the Asuras. According to one account he was instrumental in bringing about the destruction of "Daksha's sacrifice." *See* Daksha.

DAITYAS. Titans. Descendants from Diti by Kaśyapa, they are a race of demons and giants, who warred against the gods and interfered with sacrifices. They were in turn victorious and vanquished. They and the

Dānava are hardly distinguishable. As enemies of sacrifices they are called Kratu-dwishas.

DĀKINĪ. A kind of female imp or fiend attendant upon Kālī and feeding on human flesh. The Dākinīs are also called Asra-pas, 'blook drinkers.'

DAKSHA. 'Able, competent, intelligent.' The name Daksha generally carries with it the idea of a creative power. Time is regarded as their chief. There is a great deal of doubt and confusion about him, which the old sage Parāsara could only account for by saying that "in every age Daksha and the rest are born and are again destroyed." In the *Rig-veda* it is said that "Daksha sprang from Aditi, and Aditi from Daksha." Upon this marvellous mutual generation Yāska in the Nirukta remarks, "How can this be possible? They may have had the same origin; or, according to the nature of the gods, they may have been born from each other, and have derived their substance from each ther." Roth's view is that Aditi is eternity, and that Daksha (spiritual power) is the male energy which generates the gods in eternity. In the *Śatapatha Brāhmaṇa,* Daksha is identified with Prajāpati, the creator. As son of Aditi, he is one of the Ādityas, and he is also reckoned among the Viśwadevas.

"Daksha's sacrifice," is an important event in the life of Daksha which was violently interrupted and broken up by Śiva. The germ of this story is found in the *Taittirīya Sanhitā,* where it is related that the gods, having excluded Rudra from a sacrifice, he pierced the sacrifice with an arrow, and that Pūshan, attempting to eat a portion of the oblation, broke his teeth. The story is found both in the *Rāmāyaṇa* and *Mahābhārata.* According to the latter, Daksha was engaged in sacrifice, when Siva in a rage, and shouting loudly, pierced the offering with an arrow. The gods and Asuras were alarmed and the whole universe shook. The Rishis endeavoured to appease the angry god, but in vain. "He ran up to the gods, and in his rage knocked out the eyes of Bhaga with a blow, and, incensed, assaulted Pūshan with his foot and knocked out his teeth as he was eating the offering." The gods and Rishis humbly propitiated him, and when he was appeased "they apportioned to him a distinguished share in the sacrifice, and through fear resorted him to their refuse." In another part of the same work the story is again told with considerable variation.

Daksha was a lawgiver, and is reckoned among the eighteen writers of Dharma-sāstras.

The name Daksha was borne by several other persons.

DAKSHA-SĀVARNA. The ninth Manu. *See* Manu.

DĀKSHĀYANA. Connected with Daksha. A son or descendant of that sage.

DĀKSHĀYANĪ. A name of Aditi as daughter of Daksha.

DAKSHIṆĀ. A present made to Brāhmans; the honorarium for the performance of a sacrifice. This is personified as a goddess, to whom various origins are assigned.

DAKSHIṆĀCHĀRĪS. Followers of the right-hand form of Śākta worship. *See* Tantra.

DAMA. A son, or, according to the vishnu Purāna, a grand son of King Marutta of the Solar race. He rescued his bride Su-anā from his rivals, and one of them, named Vapushmat, subsequently killed Marutta, who had retired into the woods after relinquishing his crown to his son. Dama, in retaliation, killed Vapushmat and offered his block in the funeral rites of Marutta, while he made an oblation of part of the flesh, and with the rest fed the Brāhmans who were of Rākshasa descent.

DAMA-GHOSHA. King of Chedi and father of Śisupāla.

DAMAYANTĪ. Wife of Nala and heroine of the tale of Nala and Damayantī. She is also known by her patronymic Bhaimī. *See* Nala.

DAMBHODBHAVA. A king whose story is related in the *Mahābhārata* as an antidote to pride. He had an overweening conceit of his own prowess, and when told by his Brāhmans that he was no match for Nara and Nārāyaṇa, who were living as ascetics on the Gandha-mādana mountain, he proceeded thither with his army and challenged them. They endeavoured to dissuade him, but he insisted on fighting. Nara then took a handful of straws, and used them as missiles, which whitened all the air, and penetrated the eyes, ears, and noses of the assailants, until Dambhodbhava fell at Nara's feet and begged for peace.

DĀMODARA. A name given to Krishṇa because his foster-mother tried to tie him up with a rope *(dāma)* round his belly *(udara)*.

DĀNAVAS. Descendants from Danu of the sage Kaśyapa, they were giants who warred against the gods. *See* Daityas.

DANDA-DHARA. 'The rod-bearer.' A title of Yama, the god of death.

DANDAKA. The *araṇya* or forest of Dandaka, lying between the Godāvarī and Narmadā. It was of vast extent, and some passages of the *Rāmāyaṇa* represent it as beginning immediately south of the Yamunā. This forest is the scene of many of Rāma and Sītā's adventures, and is described as "a wilderness over which separate hermitages are scattered, while wild beasts and Rākshasas everywhere abound."

DANTA-VAKTRA. A Dānava king of Karāsha and son of Vriddha-śarma. He took a side against Krishna, and was eventually killed by him.

DANU. A Dānava. Also the mother of the Dānavas. The demon Kabandha.

DARADA. A country in the Hindu Kush, bordering on Kashmīr. The people of that country, "the Durds, are still where they were at the date of the text (of the Vishnu Purāna) and in the days of Strabo and Ptolemy; not exactly, indeed, at the sources of the Indus, but along its course above the Himālaya, just before it descends to India."—Wilson.

DARBAS. 'Tearers.' Rākshasas and other destructive demons.

DARDURA. Name of a mountain in the south, it is associated with the Malaya mountain in the *Mahābhārata*.

DARŚANA. 'Demonstration.' The Shad-darśanas or six demonstrations, are the six schools of Hindu philosophy. All these schools have one starting-point, *ex nihilo nihil fit;* and all have one and the same final object, the emancipation of the soul from future birth and existence, and its absorption into the supreme soul of the universe. These schools are:—

1. *Nyāya*. Founded by the sage Gotama. The word *nyāya* means propriety or fitness, the proper method of arriving at a conclusion by analysis. This school has been called the Logical School, but the term is applicable to its method rather than to its aims. It is also said to represent "the sensational aspect of Hindu philosophy," because it has "a more pointed regard to the fact of the five senses than the others have, and treats the external more frankly as a solid reality." It is the exoteric school, because the Vedāna is the esoteric.

2. *Vaiśeshika*. Founded by a sage named Kanāda, who lived about the same time as Gotama. It is supplementary to the Nyāya, and these two schools are classed together. It is called the Atomic School, because it teaches the existence of a transient world composed of aggregations of eternal atoms.

Both the Nyāya and Vaiśeshika recognise a Supreme Being.

3. *Sānkhya*. The Sānkhya and Yoga are classed together because they have much in common, but the Sānkhya is atheistical, while the Yoga is theistical. The Sānkhya was founded by the sage Kapila, and takes its name from its numeral or discriminative tendencies. The *Sānkhya-Kārikā,* the text-book of this school, has been translated by Colebrooke and Wilson, and part of

the aphorisms of Kapila were translated for the *Bibliotheca Indica* by the late Dr. Ballantyne.

4. *Yoga*. This school was founded by Patanjali, and from his name is also called Pātanjala. It pursues the method of the Sānkhya and holds with many of its dogmas, but it asserts the existence not only of individual souls, but of one all-pervading spirit, which is free from the influences which affect other souls.

5. *Pūrva-mīmānsā*. 6. *Uttara-mīmānsā*. The prior and later Mīmānsās. These are both included in the general term Vedānta, but the Pūrva-mīmānsā is commonly known as the Mīmānsā and the Uttara-mīmānsā as the Vedānta, 'the end or object of the Vedas.' The Pārva-mīmānsā was founded by Jaimini, and the Uttara-mīmānsā is attributed to Vyāsa, the arranger of the Vedas. "The object of both these schools is to teach the art of reasoning with the express purpose of aiding the interpretation of the Vedas, not only in the speculative but the practical portion." The principal doctrines of the Vedānta (Uttara) are that "God is the omniscient and omnipotent cause of the existence, continuance, and dissolution of the universe. Creation is an act of his will; he is both the efficient and the material cause of the world." At the consummation of all things all are resolved into him. He is "the sole-existent and universal soul," and besides him there is no second principle; he is *adwaita*, 'Without a second.' Sankarāchārya was the great apostle of this school.

The period of the rise of these schools of philosophy is uncertain, and is entirely a matter of inference, but they are probably late than the fifth century B.C.

Sāmkhya is the latest of all Indian philosophy and according to Cockburn, "Its doctrines have been expounded in *Bhagwat-gita*".

Colebrooke's Essays are the great authorities on Hindu philosophy. Ballantyne has translated many of the original aphorisms, and he, Cockburn, Thomson, Hall, Banerjea, and others have written on the subject.

DĀRUKA. Krishṇa's charioteer, and his attendant in his last days.

DAŚA-KUMĀRA-CHARITA. 'Tales of the ten princes,' by Srī Dandī. It is one of the few Sanskrit works written in prose, but its style is so studied and elaborate that it is classed as a Kāvya or poem. The tales are stories of common life, and display a low condition of morals and a corrupt state of society. The text has been printed with a long analytical introduction by H.H. Wilson, and again in Mumori by Buhler. There is an abridged translation by Jacobs, also a translation in French by Fauche, and a longer analysis in vol. iv. of Wilson's works.

DAŚĀNANA. 'Ten faced,' a name of Rāvaṇa.

DAŚA-RATHA. A prince of the Solar race, son of Aja, a descendant of Ikshwāku, and king of Ayodhyā. He had three wives, but being childless, he performed the sacrifice of a horse, and, according to the Rāmāyaṇa, the chief queen, Kauśalyā, remained in close contact with the slaughtered horse for a night, and the other two queens beside her. Four sons were then born to him from his three wives. Kauśalyā bore Rāma, Kaikeyī gave birth to Bharata, and Sumitrā bore Lakshmaṇa and Śatru-ghna. Rāma partook of half the nature of Vishṇu, Bharata of a quarter, and the other two shared the remaining fourth. The Rāmāyaṇa, the explanation of this manifestation of Vishṇu, says that he had promised the gods to become incarnate as man for the destruction of Rāvana. He chose Daśa-ratha for his human parent; and when that king was performing a second sacrifice to obtain progeny, he came to him out of the fire as a glorious being, and gave im a vessel full of nectar to administer to his wives. Daśa-ratha gave half of it to Kauśalyā, and a fourth each to Sumitrā and Kaikeyī. In consequence they all became pregnant, and their offspring partook of the divine nature according to the portion of the nectar each had drunk.

See *Rāma-chandra*.

DAŚĀRHA, DĀŚĀRHA. Prince of the Daśārhas, a title of Krishna. The Dasārhas were a tribe of Yādavas.

DAŚA-RUPAKA. An early treatise on dramatic composition, it has been published by Hall in the *Bibliotheca Indica*.

DĀSAS. 'Slaves.' Tribes and people of India who opposed the progress of the intrusive Āryans.

DASRAS. 'Beautiful.' The elder of the two Aświns, or in the dual (Dasrau), the two Aświns.

DASYUS. In the Vedas they are evil beings, enemies of the gods and men. They are represented as beings of a dark colour, and probably were the natives of India who contended with the immigrant Āryans. It has, however, been maintained that they were hermits and ascetics of Āryan race. In later times they are represented as barbarians, robbers, outcastes, who, according to some authorities, descended from Viśwāmitra.

DATTAKA-CHANDRIKĀ. A treatise on the law of adoption by Devana Bhaṭṭa, translated by Sutherland.

DATTAKA-ŚIROMAṆI. A digest of the principal treatises on the law of adoption, printed at Calcutta.

DATTĀTREYA. Son of Atri and Anasūyā, a Brāhman saint in whom a portion of Brahmā, Vishṇu, and Śiva, or more particularly Vishṇu, was incarnate. He had three sons, Soma, Datta, and Durvāsas, to whom also a portion of the divine essence was transmitted. He was the patron of Kārta-vīrya, and gave him a thousand arms.

DĀYA-BHĀGA. 'Law of inheritance.' This title belongs especially to the treatise of Jīmūta Vāhana, current in Bengal, and translated by Colebrooke.

DĀYA-KRAMA-SANGRAHA. A treatise by Srī Krishna Tarkālakāra on the law of inheritance as current in Bengal. Translated by Wynch.

DĀYA-TATWA. A treatise by Raghunandana Bhattāchārya on the law of inheritance as current in Bengal.

DEVA. (Nom. Devas = Deus, from the root Div, to shine.) God. A deity. The gods are spoken of as thirty-three in number, eleven for each of the three worlds.

DEVAKA. Father of Devakī and brother of Ugrasena.

DEVAKĪ. Wife of Vasu-deva, mother of Krishṇa and cousin of Kansa. She is sometimes called an incarnation of Aditi, and is said to have been born again as Priśnī, the wife of King Su-tapas.

DEVALA. A Vedic Rishi, to whom some hymns are attributed. There are several men of this name; one was author of a code of law, another was an astronomer, and philosopher, the grandfather of Pānini.

DEVĀLĀ. Music, personified as a female.

DEVA-LOKA. The world of the gods, i.e. Swarga, Indra's heaven.

DEVA-MĀTRI. 'Mother of the gods,' an appellation of Aditi.

DEVA-RĀTA. 1. A royal Rishi of the Solar race, who dwelt among the Videhas, and had charge of Śiva's bow, which descended to Janaka and was broken by Rāma. 2. A name given to Sunah-sephas.

DEVARSHIS. (Deva-rishis.) Rishis or saints of the celestial class, who dwell in the regions of the gods, such as Nārada. Sages who have attained perfection upon earth and have been exalted as demigods to heaven.

DEVATĀ. A divine being or god. The name Devatās includes the gods in general, or, as most frequently used, the whole body of inferior gods.

DEVATĀDHYĀYA-BRĀHMAṆA. The fifth Brāhmaṇa of the Sāma-veda, the text has been edited by Burnell.

DEVAYĀNĪ. Daughter of Śukra, priest of the Daityas. She fell in love with her father's pupil Kacha, son of Brihaspati, but he rejected her advances. She cursed him, and in return he cursed her, that she, a Brāhman's daughter, should marry a Kshatriya. Devayānī was companion to Śarmishthā, daughter of the king of the

Daityas. One day they went to bathe, and the god Vāyu changed their clothes. When they were dressed, they began to quarrel about the change, and Devayānī spoke "with a scowl so bitter that Śarmishthā slapped her face, and pushed her into a dry well." She was rescued by King Yayāti, who took her home to her father. Śukra, at his daughter's vehement persuasion, demanded satisfaction from Śarmishthāa's father, the Daitya king. He conceded Devayānī's demand, that upon her marriage Śarmishthā should be given to her for a servant. Devayānī married King Yayāti, a Kshatriya, and Śarmishthā became her servant. Subsequently Yayāti became enamoured of Śarmishthā, and she bore him a son, the discovery of which so enraged Devayānī that she parted from her husband, and went home to her father, having borne two sons, Yadu and Turvasa or Turvasu. Her father, Sukra, cursed Yayāti with the infirmity of old age, but afterwards offered to transfer it to any one of Yayāti's sons who would submit to receive it. Yadu, the eldest, and progenitor of the Yādavas, refused, and so did all the other sons, with the exception of Śarmishthā's youngest son, Puru, who bore his father's curse for a thousand years, but succeeded his father as monarch, and was the ancestor of the Pandavas and Kauravas.

DEVA-YONI. 'Of divine birth.' A general name for the inferior gods, the Ādityas, Vasus, Viśwadevas, and others.

DEVĪ. 'The goddess,' or Mahā-devī, 'the great goddess,' wife of the god Śiva, and daughter of Himavat, i.e., the Himālaya mountains. In her milder form she is Umā, 'light,' and a type of beauty; Gaurī, 'the yellow or brilliant;' Pārvati, 'the mountaineer;' and Haimavatī, from her parentage' Jagan-mātā, 'the mother of the world,' and Bhavānī. In her terrible form she is Durgā, 'the inaccessible;' Kālī and Śyāmā, 'the black;' Chandī and Chandikā, 'the fierce;' and Bhairavī, 'the terrible.' It is in this character that sacrifices are offered to her, that the barbarities of the Durgā-pūjā and Charak-pūjā are perpetrated in her honour, and that the indecent orgies of the Tāntrikas are held to propitiate her favours and celebrate her powers. She has ten arms, and in most of her hands there are weapons. As Durgā she is a beautiful yellow woman, riding on a tiger in a fierce and menacing attitude. As Kālī or Kālikā, 'the black,' "she is represented with a black skin, a hideous and terrible countenance, dripping with blood, encircled with snakes, hung round with skulls and human heads, and in all respects resembling a fury rather than a goddess." As Vindhya-vāsinī, 'the dweller in the Vindhyas,' she is worshipped at a place of that name where the Vindhyas approach the Ganges, near Mirzapur, and it is said that there the blood before her image is never allowed to get dry. As Mahā-māyā she is the great illusion.

DEVĪ BHĀGAVATA PURĀṆA. A Śaiva Purāṇa, devoted to the worship of the Śaktis, which is by some placed among the eighteen Purāṇas instead of the Srī Bhāgavata, which is devoted to Vishṇu.

DEVĪ MĀHĀTMYA. 'The greatness of Devī,' a poem of 700 verses, which celebrates the triumphs of Devī over various Asuras. It is the text-book of the worshippers of Devī, and is read daily in her temples. It represents an episode of the *Mārkandeya Purāṇa,* and is also called Chandipātha.

DHANA-DA. 'Giver of wealth,' Kuvera, the god of riches.

DHANAN-JAYA. 'Conqueror of riches,' a title of Arjuna and of several others.

DHANANJAYA VIJAYA. 'victories of Dhananjaya (Arjuna). A drama in one act on the exploits of Arjuna when in the service of the Rāja Virāta.

DHĀNA-PATI. 'Lord of wealth.' Kuvera.

DHANUR-VEDA. The science of archery, the military art.

DHANWANTARI. 1. Name of a Vedic deity to whom offerings at twilight were made in the north-east quarter. 2. The physician of the gods, who was produced at the churning of the ocean. He was a teacher of medical science, and the Āyur-veda is attributed to him. In another birth he was son of Dīrghatamas, and his "nature was exempt from human infirmities, and in every existence he had been master of universal knowledge." He is called also Sudhā-pāni, 'carrying nectar in his hands,' and Amrita, 'the immortal.' Other physicians seem to have had the name applied to them, as Bhela, Divo-dāsa, and Pālakāpya. 3. A celebrated physician, who was one of "the nine gems" of the court of Vikrama. *See* Nava-ratna.

DHARAṆĪ. The earth. The wife of Paraśu-rāma.

DHARMA, DHARMA-RĀJA. 'Justice.' A name of Yama, the judge of the dead.

DHARMA. An ancient sage, sometimes classed among the Prajāpatis. He married thirteen (or ten) of the daughters of Daksha, and had a large number of children; but all his children "are manifestly allegorical, being personifications of intelligences and virtues and religious rites, and being therefore appropriately wedded to the probable authors of the Hindu code of religion and morals, or the equally allegorical representation of that code, Dharma, moral and religious duty."—Wilson.

DHARMA-PUTRA. 'Son of Dharma.' A name of Yudhishthira.

DHARMĀRAṆYA. A sacred grove. 1. A forest in Madhyadesa into which Dharma retired. 2. a city mentioned in the Rāmāyaṇa as founded by Amūrta-rajas, son of Kusa.

DHARMA-RĀJA. 1. Yama, king of the ded. 2. a title of Yudhi-shthira, who was mythically a son of Yama.

DHARMA-ŚĀSTRA. A law-book or code of laws. This term includes the whole body of Hindu law, but it is more especially applicable to the laws of Manu,

Yājnawalkya, and other inspired sages who first recorded the Smriti or "recollections" of what they had received from a divine source. These works are generally in three parts:—(1) Āchāra, rules of conduct and practice; (2) Vyavahāra, judicature; (3) Prāyaschitta, penance.

The inspired lawgivers are spoken of as being eighteen in number, but the names of forty-two old authorities are mentioned. Manu and Yājnawalkya stand apart by themselves at the head of these writers. After them the eighteen other inspired sages are recognised as the great authorities on law, and the works ascribed to them are still extant, either wholly or partially, or in an abridged form :—(1) Atri; (2) Vishnu; (3) Hārāta; (4) Usanas; (5) Angiras; (6) Yama; (7) Āpastamba; (8) Samvarta; (9) Kātyāyana; (10) Brihaspati; (11) Parāsara; (12) Vyāsa; (13, 14) Sankha and Likhita, whose joint treatise is frequently quoted; (15) Daksha; (16) Gotama; (17) Śātātapa; (18) Vaśishtha. But others like Nārada, Bhrigu, Marīchi, Kaśyapa, Viśwamitra, and Baudhāyana are more frequently cited than many of these. Other names that are met with are Pulastya, Gārgya, Paithīnasi, Sumantu, Lokākshi, Kuthui, and Dhaumya. The writings of some of these lawgivers have appeared in different forms, and are referred to with the descriptive epithets of Vriddha, 'old;' Brihat, 'great;' and Laghu, 'light or small.'

A general collection of the Smritis or Dharma-śāstras has been printed in Calcutta under the title of Dharma-śāstra-sangraha, by Jīvānanda.

DHARMA-SĀVARNI. The eleventh Manu. *See* Manu.

DHARMA-SŪTRAS. The Sāmayāchārika Sūtras are so called because they had among them maxims of a legal nature.

DHARMA-VYĀDHA. 'The pious huntsman.' This man is represented in the *Mahābhārata* as living by selling the flesh of boars and buffaloes, and yet as being learned in the Vedas and in all the knowledge of a Brāhman. Having been a Brāhman in a former birth, he was cursed to this vile occupation for having wounded a Brāhman when hunting.

DHĀTRI. 'Maker, creator.' In the later hymns of the *Rig-veda,* Dhātri is a deity of no very defined powers and functions, but he is described as operating in the production of life and the preservation of health. He promotes generation, brings about matrimony, presides over domestic life, cures diseases, heals broken bones, etc. He is said to "have formed the sun, moon, sky, earth, air, and heaven as before." He appears also as one of the Ādityas, and this character he still retains. In the later mythology he is identified with Prajāpati or Brahmā the creator; and in this sense of "maker" the term is used as an epithet of Vishṇu and Krishṇa. Sometimes he is a son of Brahmā.

DHAUMYA. 1. The younger brother of Devala and family priest of the Pāndavs. There are several others of the same name. 2. Author of a work on law.

DHENUKA. A demon killed by Bala-rāma. Krishṇa and Bala-rāma, as boys, picked some fruit in a grove belonging to Dhenuka, when he took the form of an ass, and while running to the spot began to kick Bala-rāma. The young boys seized him by the heals, whirled him round till, he was dead, and cast his carcass on the top of a palm-tree. Several of his companions who ran to his assistance were treated in the same way, so that "the tree were laden with dead asses."

DHRISHTA-DYUMNA. Brother of Draupadī, and commander-in-chief of the Pāndava armies. He killed, somewhat unfairly in combat, Droṇa, who had beheaded his father, and he in his turn was killed by Droṇa's son, Aśwatthāman, who stamped him to death with his feet as he lay asleep.

DHRISHTA-KETU. 1. A son of Dhrishta-dyumna. 2. A son of Śiśu-pāla, king of Chedi, and an ally o the Pāndavas. 3. A king of the Kekayas, also an ally of the Pāndavas. 4. Son of Satyadhriti. 5. Son of Nriga.

DHRITARĀSHTRA. 1. The eldest son of Vichitravīrya or Vyāsa, he was the brother of Pāndu. He married Gāndhārī, and by her had a hundred sons, the eldest of whom was Duryodhana. Dhritarāshtra was blind, and Pāndu was affected with a disease supposed, from his name, "the pale," to be a leprous infection. The two brothers in turn remounced the throne, and the great war recorded in the *Mahābhārata* was fought between their sons, Kauravas. and the Pāndavas. Dhritarāshtra and his wife were burnt in a forest fire. (See *Mahābhārata*.) 2. An enormous serpent of many heads and immense strength.

DHRUVA. The polar star. According to the Vishnu Purāna, the sons of Manu Swāyam-bhuva were Priyavrata and Uttānapāda. The latter had two wives; the favourite, Suruchi, was proud and haughty; the second, Sunīti or Sūnritā, was humble and gentle. Suruchi had a son named Uttama, and Sunīti gave birth to Dhruva. While quite a child Dhruva was contemptuously treated by Suruchi, and she told him that her own son Uttama would alone succeed to the throne. Dhruva and his mother submitted, but he declared that he wished for honours as his own actions should acquire. He was a Kshatriya, but he joined a society of rishis, and becoming a Rishi himself, he went through a rigid course of austerities, notwithstanding the efforts of Indra to distract him. At the end he obtained the favour of Vishnu, who raised him to the skies as the pole-star. He has the patronymic Auttānapādi, and he is called Grahādhāra, 'the stay or pivot of the planets.'

DHŪMA-VARṆA. 'Smoke coloured.' A king of the serpents. A legend in the *Hari-vanśa Purāṇa* relates that Yadu, the founder of the Yādava family, went for a pleasure trip on the sea, where he was carried off by Dhūma-varṇa to the capital of the serpents. Dhūmavarna married his five daughters to him, and from them sprang seven distinct families.

DHUNDHU. An Asura who harassed the sage Uttanka in his devotions. The demon hid himself beneath a sea of sand, but was dug out and killed by King Kuvalayāświa and his 21,000 sons, who were undeterred by the flames which checked their progress. On the basis of this exploit Kuvalayāśwa got the name of Dhundhumāra, 'slayer of Dhundhu.'

DHUNDHU-MĀRA. See Dhundhu and Kuvalayāśwa.

DHŪR-JAṬI. 'Having heavy matted locks.' A name of Rudra or śiva.

DHŪRTA-NARTAKA. 'The rogue actors.' A farce in two parts by Sāma Rāja Dīkshita. "The chief object of this piece is the ridicule of the Saiva ascetics."

DHŪRTA-SAMĀGAMA. 'Assemblage of rogues.' A comedy by Sekhara or Jyotir Īśwara. "It is somewhat indelicate, but not devoid of humour." It has been translated into French by Schoebel.

DIG-AMBARA. 'Clothed with space.' A naked mendicant. A title of Śiva.

DIG-GAJAS. The elephants who protect the eight points of the compass:—(1) Airāvata; (2) Pundarīka; (3) Vāmana; (4) Kumuda; (5) Anjana; (6) Pushpa-danta; (7) Sarva-bhauma; (8) Su-pratīka.

DIG-VIJAYA. 'Conquest of the regions (of the world).' 1. A part of the *Mahābhārata* which commemorates the conquests effected by the four younger Pāndava princes, and n virtue of which Yudhi-shthira maintained his claim to universal sovereignty. 2. A work by Sankarāchārya in support of the Vedānta philosophy, generally distinguished as *Śankara Dig-vijaya*.

DIK-PĀLA. 'Supporters of the regions.' The supporters of the eight points of the compass. *See* Dig-gaja.

DILĪPA. Son of Ansumat and father of Bhagīratha. He was of the Solar race and the ancestor of Rāma. On one occasion he failed to pay due respect to Surabhi, the 'cow of fortune,' and she passed a curse upon him that he should have no offspring until he and his wife

Su-dakshinā had carefully tended Surabhi's daughter Nandinī. They obediently waited on this calf Nandinī and in due time the curse was removed, and a son, Raghu, was born to them.

DĪRGHA-ŚRAVAS. Son of Dīrgha-tamas, and therefore a Rishi, but he took to trade for a livelihood during famine; the Rig-veda calls him "the merchant."

DĪRGHA-TAMAS, DĪRGHA-TAPAS. 'Long darkness.' A son of Kāśī-rāja, according to the *Mahābhārata;* of Uchāthya, according to the *Rig-veda;* and of Utathya and Mamatā in the Purānas. His appellations of Auchathya and Māmateya favour the latter parentage. He was born blind, but is said to have obtained sight by worshipping Agni (*R.V.* iii. 128). He was father of Kakshīvat and Dhanwntari; and he is said (in the *V. P.)* to have had five children by Su-deshnā, wife of Bali, viz., the countries Anga, Banga, Kalinga, Pundra, and Suhma.

DITI. A goddess or personification in the Vedas who is associated with Aditi, and seems to be intended as an antithesis or as a complement to her.

In the Rāmāyaṇa and in the Purāṇas she is daughter of Daksha, wife of Kaśyapa, and mother of the Daityas. The *Vishnu Purāṇa* relates that having lost her children, she begged of Kaśyapa a son of irresistible prowess, who should destroy Indra. The boon was granted, but with this condition: "If, with thoughts wholly pious and person entirely pure, you can fully carry the babe in your womb for a hundred years." She assiduously observed the condition; but Indra knew what was preparing for him. So he went to Diti and attended upon her with the utmost humility, watching for his opportunity. In the last year of the century, Diti retired one night to rest without washing her feet. Indra then with his thunderbolt divided the embryo in her womb into seven portions. Thus mutilated, the child cried bitterly, and Indra being unable to pacify it, became angry, and divided each of the seven portions into seven thus forming the swift-moving deities called Maruts, from the words, 'Mā-rodīh,' 'Weep not,' which Indra used to quiet them.

DIVO-DĀSA. 1. A pious liberal king mentioned in the Rig-veda, for whom it is said that Indra demolished a hundred stone cities, meaning perhaps the mythological aerial cities of the Asuras. 2. A Brāhman who was the twin-brother of Ahalyā, he is represented in the Veda as a "very liberal sacrificer," and as being delivered by the gods from the oppressor Sambara. He is also called Atithi-gwa, 'he to whom guests should go.' 3. A king of Kāśī, son of Bhima-ratha and father of Pratardana. he was attacked by the sons of King Vīta-havya and all his sons were slain. His son Pratardana was born to him through a sacrifice performed by Bharadwāja. He was celebrated as a physician and was called Dhanwantari.

DRAUPADI: She was also called "Krishna", "Panchal", "Yajna-seni", "Sain" and "Nitya Yauvana." She was the daughter of King Drupad of Panchala. Although Arjuna won her in a swayamvara, she was shared by all the five Pāndavas. She was humiliated in the court of Kauravas, Lord Krishṇa protected her however.

DRUHYU. Son of Yayāti, by Śarmishthā, daughter of the Daitya king Vrisha-parvan. He refused to exchange his youth for the curse of decrepitude passed upon his father, and in consequence Yayāti cursed him that his posterity should not possess dominion. His father gave him a part of his kingdom, but his descendants became "princes of the lawless barbarians of the north."

DRUPADA. King of Panchāla and son of Prishats, also called Yajna-sena. He was schoolfellow of Droṇa, the preceptor of the Kaurava and Pāndava princes, and he mortally offended his former friend by repudiating his acquaintance. Drona, in payment of his services as preceptor, required his puils to make Drupada prisoner. The Kauravas attacked him and failed, but the Pāndavas took Drupada captive and occupied his territory. Drona spared his life and restored the southern half of his kingdom to him. Drupada returned home burning for revenge, and, to procure it, he prevailed upon two Brāhmans to perform a sacrifice, by the efficacy of which he obtained two children, a son and a daughter, who were called "the alter-born," because they came forth from the sacrificial fire. These children were named Dhrishta-dyumna and Krishṇā, but the latter is better known by her patronymic Draupadī. After she had chosen Arjuna for her husband at her swayam-vara, and she had become, with Drupada's consent, the wife of the five Pāndavas, he naturally became the ally of his sons-in-law. He took an active part in the great battle, and on the fourteenth day he was killed and beheaded by Droṇa, who on the following day was killed by Dhrishta-dyumna, the son whom Drupada had obtained for wreaking his vengeance on Droṇa. Besides the two children mentioned, Drupada had a younger son named Śikhandin and a daughter Śikhandinī.

DUH-ŚALĀ. The only daughter of Dhrita-rāshtra and wife of Jayadratha.

DUH-ŚĀSANA. 'Hard to rule.' One of the hundred sons of Dhrita-rāshtra. When the Pāndavas lost their wife Draupadī in gambling with Duryodhana, Duhśāsana dragged her forward by the hair and otherwise ill treated her. For this outrage Bhīma vowed to drink his blood, a vow which he afterwards fulfilled on the sixteenth day of the great battle.

DRĀVIDA. The country extending from Chennai to Cape Comorin, where Tamil language is spoken. According to Manu, the people of this country were originally Kshatriyas, but sank to the level of Sūdras due to the extinction of sacred rites and the absence of Brāhmans. As applied to the classification of Brāhmans it has a much wider application, embracing Gujarāt, Mahārāshtra, and all the south.

DRISHADWATĪ. A common female name. 1. The wife of King Divo-dāsa. 2. A river forming one of the boundaries of Brahmāvarta, perhaps the Kāgar before its junction with the Sarsuti.

DROṆA. 'A bucket.' A Brāhman so named because he was generated by his father, Bharadwāja, in a bucket. He married Kripā, half-sister of Bhīshma, and became father of Aśwatthāman. He was āchārya, or teacher of the military art, both to the Kaurava and Pāndava princes, and so he was called Droṇāchārya. He had been slighted by Drupada, king of Panchāla, and became his enemy. Through the Pāndavas he made Drupada prisoner, and took from him half of his kingdom; but he spared his life and gave him back the other half of his country. In the great war Droṇa sided with the Kauravas, and after the death of Bhīshma he became their commander-in-chief. On the fourth day of his command he killed Drupada, and in his turn he was unfairly slain in combat by Dhrishta-dyumna, who had sworn to avenge his father's death. In the midst of this combat Droṇa was told that his son was dead, which so unnerved him that he laid down his arms and his opponent beheaded him.

DUR-GA. A commentator on the Nirukta.

DUR-GĀ. 'Inaccessible.' The wife of Siva.

DUR-MUKHA. 'Bad face.' Name of one of the sons of Dhritarāshtra; one of Rāma's monkey allies, and of several others.

DUR-VĀSAS. 'Ill-clothed.' A sage, the son of Atri and Anasūyā but, according to some authorities, he was a son or emanation of Śiva. He was noted for his temper, and many fell under his curse. It was he who cursed Śakuntalā for keeping him waiting at the door, and so caused her separation from King Dushyanta. But it was he who blessed Kuntī, so that she became a mother by the Sun. In the *Vishnu Purāṇa* he is represented as cursing Indra for showing disrespect to a garland presented by the sage. The curse was that "his sovereignty over the three worlds should be subverted," and under it Indra and the gods grew weak and were overpowered by the Asuras. According to *Mahābhārata* on one occasion Krishṇa entertained him hospitably, but omitted to wipe the fragments of food from the foot of the sage. At this the latter grew angry and foretold how Krishṇa would be killed. The *Vishṇu Purāṇa* states that Krishṇa fell according to "the imprecation of Dur-vāsas," and in the same work Dur-vāsas is made to describe himself as on "whose nature is stranger to remorse."

DUR-VĀSASA PURĀṆA. One of the eighteen upa Purāṇas. *See* Purāṇa.

DUR-YODHANĀ. He was the eldest son of King Dhritrāshtra, and brother of the Kauravas. It was his enmity towards the Pandavas that led to the war of *Mahābhāratā*. He was killed by Bhīma by unfair means.

DŪSHANA. A Rākshasa who fought as one of the generals of Rāvaṇa, and was killed by Rāma. He was generally associated with Rāvaṇa's brother, Khara.

DUSHMANTA, DUSHYANTA. A valiant king of the Lunar race, and descendant from Puru. He was husband of Śakuntalā, and father of Bharata. The love of Dushyanta and Śakuntalā, her separation from him, and her restoration through the discovery of his token-ring in the belly of a fish, form the plot of Kāli-dāsa's celebrated play Śakuntalā.

DŪTĀNGADA. 'The ambassador Angada.' A short play by Subhata, it is based on the mission of Angada to demand from Rāvaṇa the restoration of Sītā.

DWAIPĀYANA. *See* Vyāsa.

DWĀPARA YUGA. The third age of the world, extending to 864,000 years. *See* Yuga.

DWĀRAKĀ, DWĀRAVATĪ. 'The city of gates.' Krishṇa's capital, in Gujarat, which is said to have been submerged by the ocean seven days after his death. One of the seven sacred cities, also called Abdhi-nagarī.

DWIJARSHIS. (Dwija-rishis.) *See* Brahmarshis.

DWĪPA. An insular continent, the Dwīpas stretch out from the mountain Meru as their common centre, like the leaves of a lotus, and are separated from each other by distinct circumambient oceans. They are generally seven in number: 1. Jambu, 2. Plaksha or Go-medaka, 3. Sālmala, 4. Kusa, 5. Krauncha, 6. Śāka, 7. Pushkara; and the seas which surround them are—1. Lavana, salt water; 2. Ikshu, sugar-cane juice; 3. Surā, wine; 4. Sarpis or Ghrita, clarified butter; 5. Dadhi, curds; 6. Dugdha or Kshīra, milk; 7. Jala, fresh water. In the *Mahābhārata* four Dwīpas are named:—1. Bhadrāśwa, 2. Ketu-māla, 3. Jambu-dwīpa, 4. Uttara Kuru. Jambu-dwīpa has nine varshas or subdivision:—1. Bhārata, 2. Kim-purusha, Kin-nara, 3. Hari-varsha, 4. Ilā-vrita, which contains Meru; 5. Ramyaka, 6. Hiranmaya, 7. Uttara Kuru, 8. Bhadrāśwa, 9. Ketu-māla. According to the *Vishṇu Purāṇa*, Bhārata-varsha or India is divided into nine Dwīpas or portions:—1. Indra-dwīpa, 2. Kaserumat, 3. Tāmra-varna, 4. Gabhastimat, 5. Nāga-dwīpa, 6. Saumya, 7. Gāndharva, 8. Vāruna; 9. is generally left without a name in the books, but Bhāskara Āchārya calls it Kumāraka.

DWIVIDA. 1. An Asura in the form of a great ape, who was an implacable foe of the gods. He stole Balarāma's plough-share and derided him. This was the beginning of a terrific fight, in which Dwivida was felled to the earth, and "the crest of the mountain on which he fell was splintered into a hundred pieces by the weight of his body, as if the Thunderer had shivered it with his thunderbolt." 2. A monkey ally of Rāma.

DYAUS. The sky, heaven. In the Vedas he is a masculine deity, and is called occasionally Dyaus-pitri, 'heavenly father,' the earth being regarded as the mother. He is father of Ushas, the dawn. Fc. Zeug, Deus, Jovis, Ju-piter, Dyāvā-prithivī, 'heaven and earth,' are represented as the universal parents, not only men but also of gods. In other places they are spoken of as having been themselves created; and then, again, there are speculations as to their origin and priority. In one hymn it is asked, "Which of these two was the first and which the last? How have they been produced? Who knows?" The *Śatapatha Brāhmaṇa* declares in favour of the earth, saying, "This earth is the first of created beings."

E

EKA-CHAKRĀ. A city in the country of the Kīchakas, where, on the advice of Vyāsa, the Pandavas dwelt for a time during their exile. General Cunningham has identified it with the modern Ara or Arrah.

EKA-DANSHTRA, EKA-DANTA. 'Having one tusk.' A name of Ganesa.

EKALAVYA. Grandson of Deva-sravas, the brother of Vasudeva, he was brother of Satru-ghna. He was exposed in infancy, and was brought up among the Nishādas, of whom he became king. He assisted in a night attack upon Dwārakā, and was eventually killed by Krishna, who hurled a rock at him.

EKĀMRA, EKĀMRA KĀNANA. A forest in Utkala or Orissa, which was the favourite haunt of Siva, and became a great seat of his worship as the city of Bhuvaneswara, where some temples—sacred to him still remain. They have been described by Bābu Rājendra Lāla in his great work on Orissa.

EKA-PĀDA. 'One-footed,' a fabulous race of men spoken of in the Purānas.

EKA-PARṆĀ, EKA-PĀTALĀ. These, with their sister Aparnā, were, according to the Hari-vansa, daughters of Himavat and Menā. They performed austerities surpassing the powers of gods and Dānavas, and alarmed both worlds. Eka-parnā took only one leaf for food, and Eka-pātalā only one pātalā (Bigonia). Aparnā took no sustenance at all and lived *a-parṇa,* 'without a leaf.' Her mother being distressed at her abstinence, exclaimed in her anxiety, "U-mā"—"O don't." Through this she became manifest as the lovely goddess Umā, the wife of Śiva.

EKĀSHTAKĀ. A deity mentioned in the *Atharva-veda* as having practised austere devotion, and being the daughter of Prajāpati and mother of Indra and Soma.

EMŪSHA. In the Brāhmana, a black boar with a hundred arms which raised up the earth. This is probably the germ of the Varāha or boar incarnation. *See* Avatāra.

G

GADA. A younger brother of Krishṇa.

GĀDHI, GĀTHIN. A king of the Kuśika race, and father of Viśwāmitra. He was son of Kuśāmba, or, according to the *Vishṇu Purāṇa,* he was Indra, who took upon himself that form.

GĀIAVA. A pupil of Viśwāmitra.

Also there was a teacher of the White Yajur-veda named Gālava, and also an old grammarian named by Pāṇini.

GAṆA-DEVATAS. 'Troops of deities,' who generally appear, or are spoken of, in classes. Nine such classes are:—(1) Ādityas; (2) Viśwas or Viśwe-devas; (3) Vasus; (4) Tushitas; (5) Ābhāśwaras; (6) Anilas; (7) Mahārājikas; (8) Sādhyas; (9) Rudras. These inferior deities are attendant upon Siva, and under the command of Gaṇesa. They dwell on Gaṇa-parvata, *i.e.* Gaṇesa.

GĀṆAPATYA. A small sect who worship Gaṇa-pati or Gaṇesa as their chief deity.

GAṆAS. *See* Gaṇa-devatas.

GANDAKĪ. The river Gandak (vulg. Gunduk), in U.P.

GANDHA-MĀDANA. 'Intoxicating with fragrance.' 1. mountain and forest in Ilāvrita, the central region of the world, which also contains the moutain Meru. The authorities are not agreed as to its position in relation to Meru. 2. A general of the monkey allies of Rāma, he was killed by Rāvaṇa's son Indra-jit, but was restored to life with the help of the medicinal herbs brought by Hanumān from Mount Kailāsa.

GANDHĀRA, GĀNDHĀRA. A country and city on the west bank of the Indus around Attock. Mahomedan geographers call it Kandahār, but it must not be confounded with the modern town of that name. It is the Gandaritis of the ancients, and it people are the Gandarii of Herodotus. The *Vāyu Purāṇa* says it was famous for its breed of horses.

GĀNDHĀRĪ. Princess of Gandhāra, the daughter of Subala, king of Gandhāra, wife of Dhrit-rāshtra, and mother of his hundred sons and an only daughter, Duh-śalā. As her husband was blind, she always wore a bandage over her eyes. Her husband and she, both perished in a forest fire. She is also called by the patronymics Saubalī and Saubaleyī. She is said to have owed her hundred sons to the blessing of Vyāsa, who, in acknowledgment of her kind hospitality, offered her a boon.

GANDHARVA. The 'heavenly Gandharva' of the Veda was a deity who knew and revealed the secrets of heaven and divine truths in general. The Gandharvas generally had their dwelling in the sky or atmosphere, and one of their assignments was to prepare the heavenly soma juice for the gods. A great partiality for women, they had a mystic power over them.

GANDHARVA-LOKA. *See* Loka.

GĀNDHARVA-VEDA. The science of music and song, which is considered to include drama and dancing. It is an appendix of the Sāma-veda, and its invention is ascribed to the Muni Bharata.

GĀNDINĪ. 1. Daughter of Kāśī-rāja; she had been twelve years in her mother's womb who was born after her father presented to the Brāhmans a cow every day for three years. The child, on being born, received the name of Gāndinī, 'cow daily.' She continued the gift as long as she lived. She was wife of Swa-phalka and mother of Akrūra. ā. The Gangā or Ganges.

GĀNDĪVA. The bow of Arjuna, said to have been given by Soma to Varuna, by Varuna to Agni, and by Agni to Arjuna.

GAṆEŚA (Gana + Īsa), GAṆA-PATI. Lord of the Ganas or troops of inferior deities, especially those attendant upon Siva. Son of Śiva and Pārvatī, or of

Pārvatī only. One legend represents that he sprang from the scurf of Pārvatī's body. Regarded as the god of wisdom and remover of obstacles, he is invariably propitiated at the beginning of any important undertaking, and is invoked at the commencement of books. He is said to have written down the *Mahābhārata* from the dictation of Vyāsa. He is represented as a short fat man of yellow colour, with a protuberant belly, four hands, and the head of an elephant, which has only one tusk. In one hand he holds a shell, in another a discus, in the third a club or goad, and in the fourth a water-lily. Sometimes he is depicted riding upon a rat or attended by one; hence his appellation Akhu ratha.

GAṆEŚA-GĪTĀ. The Bhagavad-gītā, but with the name of Gaṇeśa substituted for that of Krishṇa. It is used by the Gāṇapatyas or worshippers of Gaṇeśa.

GAṆEŚA PURĀṆA. An Upa Purāṇa having especial reference to the glory and greatness of Gaṇeśa.

GANGĀ. The sacred river Ganges, which is said to be mentioned only twice in the *Rig-vedā*. According to the Purānas the Viyadgangā, or heavenly Gangas, is said to flow from the toe of Vishnu, and to have been brought down from heaven, by theprayers of the saint Bhagīratha, to purify the ashes of the sixty thousand sons of King Sagara, who had been burnt by the angry glance of the sage Kapila. The river is also called Bhāgīrathī. Gangā was angry at being brought down from heaven, and Śiva, to save the earth from the shock of her fall, caught the river on his brow, and checked its course with his matted. Therefore, he is called Gangādhara, 'upholder of the Ganges.' The river descended from Śiva's brow in several streams, four according to some, and ten according to others, but the number generally accepted is seven, being the Sapta-sindhava, the seven sindhus or rivers. The Ganges proper is one of the number. The descent of the Ganges disturbed the sage Jahnu as he was performing a sacrifice, and in his anger he drank up the waters, but he relented and allowed the river to flow from his ear, hence the Ganges has the name of Jāhnvī. Personified as a goddess, Gangā is the eldest daughter of Himavat and Menā, and sister of Umā. She became the wife of King Śāntanu and bore a son, Bhīshma; who is also known by the metronymic Gāngeya. Being also, in a peculiar way, known by the metronymic Gāngeya. Being also, in a peculiar way, the mother of Kārtikeya, she is called Kumāra-sū.

GANGĀ-DHARA. A name of Śiva.

GANGĀ-DWĀRA. The gate of the Ganges. The opening in the Himālaya mountains through which the river descends into the plains, now known as Hardwār.

GANGĀ-SĀGARA. The mouth of the Ganges, a holy bathing-place sacred to Vishṇu.

GĀNGEYA. 1. A name of Bhīshma, from his reputed mother, the river goddess Gangā. 2. Also of Kārttikeya.

GARGA. An ancient sage, a son of Vitatha and one of the oldest writers on astronomy. According to Vishṇu Purāṇa, "From Garga sprang Sina (or Sini); from them were descended the Gārgyas and Sainyas, Brāhmans of Kshatriya race." But as for the Bhāgavata, "From Garga sprang Sina; from them Gārgya, who from a Kshatriya became a Brāhman." Of the many Gargas, one was a priest of Krishṇa and the Yādavas.

GĀRGAS, GĀRGYAS. Descendants of Garga, who, "although Kshatriyas by brith, became Brāhmans and great Rishis."

GĀRGYA, GĀRGYABĀLĀKI. Son of Bālāki and a Brāhman, is renowned as a teacher and as a teacher and as a grammarian, who dealt especially with etymology. Even though well read in the Veda, he still agreed to receive instruction from the Kshatriya Ajāta-śatru.

GARUḌA. A mythical bird or vulture, half-man half-bird, on which Vishṇu rides. The king of birds, he is descended from Kaśyapa and Vinatā, one of the daughters of Daksha. He is the great enemy of serpents, having inherited his hated from his mother, who had quarrelled with her co-wife and superior, Kadru, the mother of serpents. His lustre was so brilliant that soon after his birth the gods mistook him for Agni and worshipped him. He is represented as having the head, wings, talons, and beak of an eagle, and the body and limbs of a man. His face is white, his wings red, and his body golden. He had a son named Sampāti, and his wife was Unnati or Vināyakā. According to the *Mahābhārata,* his parents gave him liberty to devour bad men, but he was not to touch Brāhmans. Once, however, he swallowed a Brāhman and his wife, but the Brāhman so burnt his throat that he was glad to disgorge both of them.

Grauḍa is said to have stolen the Amrita from the gods in order to bargain with it the freedom of his mother from Kadru. Indra discovered the theft and fought a fierce battle with Garuḍa. The Amrita was recovered, but Indra was worsted in the fight, and his thunderbolt was smashed.

Garuḍa has many names and epithets. He is called Kāśyapi and Vainteya. He is the Suparna and the Garutmān, or chief of birds. He is also called Dakshāya, Sālmalin, Tārkshya, and Vināyaka. Sitānana, 'white faced;' Rakta-paksha, 'red winged;' Śweta-rohita, 'the white and red;' Suvarṇa-kāya, 'golden bodies;' Gaganeśwara, ' lord of the sky;' Khageśwara, 'king of birds;' Nāgāntaka, and Pannaga-nāsana, 'destroyer of serpents;' Sarpārāri, 'enemy of serpents;' Taraswin, 'the swift;' Rasāyana, 'who moves like quicksilver;' Kāma-chārin, 'who goes where he will;' Kāmāyus, 'who lives at pleasure;' Chirād, 'eating long;' Vishṇu-ratha, 'vehicle of Vishṇu;' Amritāharana and Sudhā-hara, 'stealer of the Amrita;' Surendra-jit, 'vanquisher of Indra;' Vajra-jit, 'subduer of the thunderbolt,' etc. are some other epithets related to him.

GRAUḌA PURĀṆA. This Purāna is, "That which Vishṇu recited in the Gāruḍa kalpa, relating chiefly to the birth of Garuda from Vinatā, is called the *Garuḍa Purāṇa,* and in it there are read 19,000 stanzas." The works bearing this name were examined by Wilson who formed that they did not correspond in any respect with this description, so he considered it doubtful if a genuine *Garuḍa Purāṇa* is in existence.

GĀTHĀ. A song, a verse, a religious verse, but one not taken from the Vedas. Verses interspersed in the Sanskrit Buddhist work called *Lalita-vistara,* which are composed in a dialect between the Sanskrit and the Prākrit, the Gāthā dialect.

GĀTU. A singer, a Gandharva.

GAUṆA, GAURA. The ancient name of Central Bengal; also the name of the capital of the country, the ruins of which city are still visible. The great northern nation of Brāhmans. *See* Brāhman.

GAUPĀYANAS. Sons or descendants of Gopa. Four Rishis, who were the authors of four remarkable hymns in the Rig-veda. One of them named Su-bandhu, was killed and miraculously brought to life again. The hymns have been translated by Max Muller in the *Journal R. A. S.,* vol. ii. 1866.

GAURĪ. The 'yellow' or 'brilliant,' a name of the consort of Śiva. (*See* Devī.) Varuṇa's wife also is called Gaurī.

GAUTAMA. 1. A name of the sage Saradwat, as son of Gotama. He was husband of Ahalyā, who was seduced by Indra. This seduction has been explained mythologically as signifying the carrying away of night by the morning sun, Indra being the sun, and Ahalyā being explained as meaning night. 2. Author of a Dharma-sāstra, which has been edited by Stenzler.

3. A name common to many men.

GAUTAMEŚĀ. 'Lord of Gautama.' Name of one of the twelve great Lingas. *See* Linga.

GAUTAMĪ. 1. An epithet of Durgā. 2. Name of a fierce Rākshasī or female demon.

GAYĀ. A city in Bihār, it is one of the seven sacred cities, and is still a place of pilgrimage, though its glory has departed.

GĀYATRĪ. A most sacred verse of the *Rig-veda,* which it is the duty of every Brāhman to repeat mentally in his morning and evening devotions. It is addressed to the sun as Savitri, the generator, and so it is called also Sāvitrī. Personified as a goddess, Sāvitrī is the wife of Brahmā, mother f the four Vedas, and also of the twice-born or three superior castes. Colebrooke's translation of the Gāyatrī is "Earth, sky, heaven. Let us meditate on (these, and on) the most excellent light and power of that generous, sportive, and resplendent sun, (praying that) it may guide our intellects."

GHATA-KARPARA. A poet, who was one of the "nine gems" of the court of Vikramāditya. There is a short artificial poem, descriptive of the rainy season, bearing this name, which has been translated into German by Dursch. The words mean 'potsherds,' and form probably an assumed literary name.

GHATOTKACHA. A son of Bhīma by the Rākshasī Hidimbā, he was killed in the great battle by Karṇa with the fatal lance that he had obtained from Indra.

GHOSHĀ. It is said in the Veda that the Aświns "bestowed a husband upon Ghoshā growing old," and the explanatory legend is that she was a daughter of Kakshīvat, but being a leper, was incapable of marriage. When she was advanced in age the Aświns gave her health, youth, and beauty, so that she obtained a husband.

GHRITĀCHĪ. An Apsara or celestial nymph, who had many affairs with great sages and mortal men. She was mother of ten sons by Raudrāśwa of Kuśa-nābha, a descendant of Puru, and the Brahma. *Vaivartta Purāṇa* attributes the origin of some of the mixed castes to her issue by the sage Viśwa-karman. The *Hari-vanśa* asserts that she had ten daughters as well as ten sons by Raudrāśwa. Another legend represents her as mother by Kuśa-nābha of a hundred daughters, whom Vāyu wished to accompany to the sky. They refused, and in his rage he cursed them to become deformed; but they recovered their natural shape and beauty, and were married to Brahma-datta, king of Kāmpila.

GIRI-JĀ. 'Mountain born,' a name of Pārvatī or Devī.

GIRI-VRAJA. A royal city in Magadha, identified with Rāja-griha in Bihar.

GĪTĀ. The Bhagavad-gītā.

GĪTĀ-GOVINDA. A lyrical poem supposed to have been around 12th or 13th century by Jaya-deva on the early life of Krishna as Govinda the cowherd. It is an erotic work, and sings of the loves of Krishna with Rādhā, and other but a mystical interpretation has been put upon it.

GOBHILA. An ancient writer of the Sūtra period, he was author of some Grihya Sūtras, and of some Sūtras on grammar. The Grihya Sūtras, have been published in the *Bibliotheca Indica*.

GO-KARṆA. 'Cow's ear.' A place of pilgrimage sacred to Śiva, on the west coast, near Mangalore.

GO-KULA. A pastoral district on the Yamunā, about Mathurā, where Krishna passed his boyhood with the cowherds.

GO-LOKA. 'The place of cows.' Krishna's heaven; a modern addition to the original series of seven Lokas.

GO-MANTA. A great mountain in the Western Ghāts. According to the *Hari-vanśa* it was the scene of a defeat of Jarā-sandha by Krishna.

GO-PĀTĪ. The Gomtī river but there are others which bore the name. One fell into the Sindhu or Indus.

GO-PĀLA, GO-VINDA. 'Cow-keeper,' a name of the youthful Krishṇa, who lived among the cowherds in Vrindā-vana.

GOPĀLA-TĀPANI. An Upanishad in honour of Krishṇa. Printed in the *Bibliotheca Indica.*

GO-PATHA BRĀHMAṆA. The Brāhmana of the Atharva or fourth Veda. It has been published by Rājendra Lāla in the *Bibliotheca Indica.*

GOPATI-RISHABHA. 'Chief of herdsmen.' 1. A title of Śiva. 2. A demon mentioned in the *Mahābhārata* as slain by Krishṇa.

GOPĪS. The cowherd damsels and wives with whom Krishna sported in his youth.

GOTAMA. The founder of the Nyāya school of philosophy, is also called Sutānanda, and is author of a Dharma-sāstra or law-book, which has been edited by Stenzler. He is frequently called Gautama.

GO-VARDHANA. A mountain in Vrindāvana, which Krishṇa induced the cowherds and cowherdesses to worship instead of Indra. This enraged the god, who sent a deluge of rain to wash away the mountain and all the people of the country, but Krishṇa held up the mountain on his little finger for seven days to shelter the people of Vrindāvana. Indra retired baffled, and afterwards paid homage to Krishṇa.

GOVARDHANA-DHARA. 'Upholder of Govardhana,' a title of Krishna.

GO-VINDA. 'Cow-keeper,' a name of Krishṇa.

GRAHA. 'Seizing.' 1. The power that seizes and obscures the sun and moon, causing eclipses; the ascending node, Rāhu. 2. Evil spirits which possess people, especially children, and which cause sickness and death. They are supposed to be amenable to medicine and exorcism.

GRIHA-STHA. 'Householder.' A Brāhman in the second stage of his religious life. *See* Brāhman.

GRIHYA SŪTRAS. Rules for the conduct of domestic rites and the personal sacraments, extending from the birth to the marriage of a man. (*See* Sūtra.) The Grihya Sūtras of Āśwalāyana have been printed Rishi of many hymns in the second Mandala of the *Rig-veda*. According to *Vishṇu Purāṇa* he was a Kshatriya and son of Suna-hotra, being descended from Purūravas of the Lunar race. From him sprang Śaunaka, the eminent sage versed in the *Rig-veda* "who originated the system of four castes." The *Vāyu Purāṇa* declares Śaunaka to be the son of Gritsa-mada, and Śaunaka the son of Śunaka: this seems probable. "It is related of him by Sāyana that he was first a member of the family of Angiras, being the son of Suna-hotra. He was carried off by the Asuras whilst performing a sacrifice, but was rescued by Indra, under whose authority he was henceforth designated as Gritsa-mada, the son of Śunaka or Śaunaka of the race of Bhrigu. Thus the Anukramaṇikā says of him: He who was an Āngirasa, the son of Suna-hotra, became Saunaka of the race of Bhrigu." According to the *Mahābhārata,* he was son of Vīta-havya, a king of the Haihayas, a Kshatriya, who became a Brāhman. (*See* Vītahavya.) The *Mahābhārata* alludes to a legend of his having assumed the semblance of Indra, and so enabled that deity to escape from the Asuras, who were lying in wait to destroy him. There are several versions of the story, but they all agree that after Indra had escaped, Gritsa-mada saved himself by reciting a hymn in which he showed that Indra was a different person.

GUḌĀ-KESA. 'Whose hair is in tufts.' An epithet of Arjuna.

GUHA. 'Secret.' 1. A name of the god of war. (*See* Kārttikeya.) 2. A king of the Nishādas or Bhils, who was a friend of Rāma. 3. A people near Kalinga, who possibly got their name from him.

GUHYAKAS. 'Hidden beings.' Inferior divinities attendant upon Kuvera, and guardians of his hidden treasures.

GUPTAS. A dynasty of kings who reigned in Magadha. The period of their ascendancy has been a subject of great contention, and cannot be said to be settled.

GURJJARA. The region of Gujarat.

H

HAIHAYA. This name is supposed to be derived from haya, 'a horse.' 1. A prince of the Lunar race, and great-grandson of Yadu. 2. A race or tribe of people to whom a Scythian origin has been ascribed. The *Vishṇu Purāṇa* represents them as descendants of Haihaya of the Yadu race, but they are generally associated with outlying tribes on the borders. In the Vāyu and other purānas, five great divisions of the tribe named are Tālajanghas, Vīti-hotras, Avantis, Tundikeras, and Jātas, or rather Su-jātas.

HALA-BHRIT. 'Bearing a plough.' Bala-rāma.

HALĀYUDHA. 'Who has a ploughshare for his weapon,' *i.e.* Bala-rāma.

HANSA. 1. This, according to the Bhāgavata Purāna, was the name of the "one caste," when, in olden times, there was only "one Veda, one god, and one caste." 2. A name used in the *Mahābhārata* for Krishṇa. 3. A mountain range north of Meru.

HANSA. Hansa and Dimbhaka were two great warrior brothers mentioned in the *Mahābhārata* as friends of Jarā-sandha. A certain king also named Hansa was killed by Bala-rāma. Hearing that "Hansa was killed," Dimbhaka, unable to live without him, committed suicide, and when Hansa heard of this he drowned himself in the Yamunā.

HANUMĀN, HANUMAT, HANŪMAT. A celebrated monkey chief, he was son of Pavana, 'the wind,' by Anjanā, wife of a monkey named Kesarī. He was able to fly, and is a conspicuous figure in the Rāmāyana. He and the other monkeys who assisted Rāma in his war against Rāvana were of divine origin, and their powers were superhuman. Hanumān jumped from India to Srilanka in one bound; he tore up trees, carried away the Himālayas, seized the clouds, and performed many other wonderful exploits. (*See* Surasā.) His form is "as vast as a mountain and as tall as a gigantic tower. His complexion is yellow and glowing like molten gold. His face is as red as the brightest ruby; while his enormous tail spreads out to an interminable length. He stands on a lofty rock and roars like thunder. He leaps into the air, and flies among the clouds with a rushing noise, whilst the ocean waves are roaring and splashing below." In one of his fights with Rāvaṇa and the Rākshasas, they greased his tail and set it on fire, but with it he burnt down their capital city, Lankā. This exploit obtained for him the name Lankā-dāhī. His services to Rāma were great and many. He acted as his spy, and fought most valiantly. He flew to the Himālayas, from whence he brought medicinal herbs with which he restored the wounded, and he killed the monster Kāla-nemi, and thousands of Gandharvas who assailed him. He accompanied Rāma on his return to Ayodhyā, and there he received from his the reward of perpetual life and youth. The exploits of Hanumān are favourite among Hindus from childhood to age, and paintings of them are common. He is called Marut-puta, and he has the patronymics Ānili, Māruti, etc., and the metronymic Ānjaneya.

HANUMĀN-NĀTAKA. A long drama by various hands upon the adventures of the monkey chief Hanumān. This drama is fabled to have been composed by Hanumān, and inscribed by him on rocks. Vālmīki, the author of the Rāmāyana, saw it and feared that it would throw his own poem into the shade. He complained to the author, who told him to cast the verses into the sea. He did so, and they remained concealed there for ages. Portions were discovered and brought to King Bhoja, who directed Dāmodara Mishra to arrange them and fill up the lacunae. He did so, and the result was this drama. "It is probable," says Wilson, "that the fragments of an ancient drama were connected in the manner described. Some of the ideas are poetical, and the sentiments just and forcible; the language is generally very harmonious, but the work itself is, after all, a most disjointed and nondescript composition, and the patchwork is very glaringly and clumsily put together." It is a work of the tenth or eleventh century. It has been printed in India.

HARA. A name of Śiva.

HARI. A name which commonly designates Vishṇu, but it is exceptionally used for other gods.

HARI-DWĀRA. 'The gate of Hari.' The modern Hardwār. The place where the Ganges finally breaks through the mountains into the plains of Hindustan. It is a great place of pilgrimage.

HARI-HARA. A combination of the names of Vishnu and Śiva, representing the union of the two deities in one.

HARISCHANDRA. He was a king of the Solar race and was known for his piety and justice. The sage Viśwamitra clouded the sacrificial gift due to him and stripped him of his wealth and kingdom. Harischandra sold his wife, his son and himself for completing of the gift. It was at the intervention of Lord Vishṇu that he was saved.

HARITA, HĀRĪTA. 1. A son of Yuvanāswa of the solar race, descendant of Ikshwāku. From him descended the Hārita Angirasas. In the *Linga Purāṇa* it is said, "The son of Yuvanāśwa was Harita, of whom the Hāritas were sons. They were, on the side of Angiras, twice-born men (Brāhmans) of Kshatriya lineage;" or according to the Vāyu, "they were the sons of Angiras, twice-born men (Brāhmans), of Kshatriya race," possibly meaning that they were sons raised up to Harita by Angiras. According to some he was a son of Chyavana. 2. Author of a Dharma-śāstra or law-book.

HĀRITAS, HĀRITA-ĀNGIRASES. *See* Harita.

HARITS, HARITAS. 'Green.' In the *Rig-veda* the horses, or rather mares, of the sun, seven or ten in number, and typical of his rays. "The prototype of the

Grecian Charities."—Max Muller.

HARI-VANŚA. The genealogy of Hari or Vishṇu, a long poem of 16,374 verses, it purports to be a part of the *Mahābhārata,* but it is of much later date, and "may more accurately be ranked with the Paurāṇik compilations of least authenticity and latest date." It is in three parts; the first is introductory, and gives particulars of the creation and of the patriarchal and regal dynasties; the second contains the life and adventures of Krishṇa: and the last and the third treats of the future of the world and the corruptions of the Kali age. It contains many indications of its having been written in the south of India.

HARSHANA. A deity who presides over the Śrāddha offerings.

HARYAŚWA. A grandson of the Kuvalayāśwa who killed the demon Dhundhu. The country of Panchāla is said to have been named from his five (*pancha*) sons. There were several others of this name.

HARYAŚWAS. Five thousand sons of the patriarch Daksha, begotten by him for the purpose of peopling the earth. The sage Nārada dissuaded them from producing offspring, and they "dispersed themselves through the regions and have not returned."

HASTINĀ-PURA. The capital city of the Kauravas, for which the great war of the *Mahābhārata* was waged. It was founded by Hastin, son of the first Bharata, and hence, as some say, its name; but the Mahā-bhārata and the Vishṇu Purāṇa call it the "elephant city," from *hastin*, an elephant. The ruins are traceable near an old bed of the Ganges, about 57 miles N.E. of Delhi and local tradition has preserved the name. It is said to have been washed away by the Ganges.

HĀSYĀRṆAVA. 'Ocean of laughter,' a modern comic piece in two acts, by a Pandit named Jagadīśa. "It is a severe but grossly indelicate satire upon the licentiousness of Brāhmans assuming the character of religious mendicants."—*Wilson*.

HAVIR-BHUJ, HAVISH-MATA. Pitris or Manes of the Kshatriyas, and inhabitants of the solar sphere. *See* Pitris.

HAYA-GRĪVA. 'Horse-necked.' According to one legend, he was a Daitya who stole the Veda as it slipped out of the mouth of Brahmā while he was sleeping at the end of a Kalpa, and was killed by Vishṇu in the fish Avatāra. According to another, Vishṇu himself assumed this form to recover the Veda, which had been carried off by two Daityas.

HAYA-SIRAS, HAYA-SĪRSHA. 'Horse-head.' In the *Mahā-bhārata* it is recorded that the sage Aurva "cast the fire of his anger into the sea," and that there it "became the great Haya-siras, known to those acquainted with the Veda, which vomits forth that fire and drinks up the waters." A form of Vishṇu.

In the *Bhāgavata Purāṇa* Brahmā is represented as saying, "In my sacrifice Bhagavat himself was Haya-sīrsha, the male of the sacrifice, whose colour is that of gold, of whom the Vedas and the sacrifices are the substance and the gods the soul; when he respired, charming words came forth from his nostrils."

HEMA-CHANDRA. Author of a good Sanskrit vocabulary, printed under the superintendence of Colebrooke.

HEMĀDRI. 'The golden peak.' A chain of mountains represented as lying north of the Himālayas, between them and Mount Meru.

HIDIMBA (mas.), HIDIMBĀ (fem.). A powerful Asura, who had yellow eyes and a horrible aspect. He was a cannibal, and dwelt in the forest to which the Pāndavas retired after the burning of their house. He had a sister named Hidimbā, whom he sent to lure the Pāndavas; but on meeting Bhīma, she fell in love with him, and offered to carry him away to safety on her back. Bhīma refused, and while they were parleying, Hidimba came up, and a terrible fight ensued, in which Bhīma killed the monster. Hidimbā was at first much terrified and fled, but she returned and claimed Bhīma for her husband. In response to his mother's desire Bhīma married her, and by her had a son named Ghatotkaccha. She has a temple in Manali.

HIMĀCHALA, HIMĀDRI. The Himālaya mountains.

HIMAVAT. The personification of the Himālaya mountains, husband of Menā or Menakā, and father of Umā and Gangā.

HIRAṆYA-GARBHA. 'Golden egg' or 'golden womb.' In the *Rig-veda* Hiraṇya-garbha "is said to have arisen in the beginning, the one lord of all beings, who upholds heaven and earth, who gives life and breath, whose command even the gods obey, who is the god over all gods, and the one animating principle of their being." According to Manu, Hiranya-garbha was Brahmā, the first male, formed by the undiscernible eternal first cause in a golden egg resplendent as the sun. "Having continued a year in the egg, Brahmā divided it into two parts by his mere thought, and with these two shells he formed the heavens and the earth; and in the middle he placed the sky, the eight regions, and the eternal abode of the waters." See Brahmā.

HIRAṆYĀKSHA. 'Golden eye,' a Daitya who dragged the earth to the depths of the ocean. He was twin-brother of Hiranyakasipu, and was killed by Vishṇu in the Boar incarnation.

HIRANYA-KAŚIPU. 'Golden dress.' A Daitya who, according to the *Mahābhārata* and the Purāṇas, obtained from Siva the sovereignty of the three worlds for a million years, and persecuted his son Prahlāda for worshipping Vishnu. He was slain by Vishṇu in the Nara-sinha, or man-lion incarnation. He and Hiraṇyāksha were twin-brothers and chiefs of the Daityas.

HITOPADEŚA. 'Good advice.' The well-known collection of ethical tales and fables compiled from the larger and older work called *Pancha-tantra*, it has been often printed, and there are several translations. Among them is an edition by Johnson of text, vocabulary, and translation.

HOTRI. A priest who recites the prayers from the *Rig-veda*.

HRISHĪKESA. A name of Krishṇa or Vishṇu

HŪṆAS. According to Wilson, "the White Huns or Indo-Scythians, who were established in the Panjāb and along the Indus at the commencement of our era, as we know from Arrian, Strabo, and Ptolemy, confirmed by recent discoveries of their coins," and still further confirmed by inscriptions and additional coins.

HŪN-DESA. The country round Lake Mānasarovara.

HUSHKA HUVISHKA. A Tushkara or Turki king, whose name is mentioned in the *Rāja Taraṅgiṇi* as Hushka, which has been found in inscriptions as Huvishka, and upon the corrupt Greek coins as Oerki. He is supposed to have reigned just at the commencement of the Christian era.

I

IDĀ. In the *Rig-veda* is primarily food, refreshment, or a libation of milk. It represents a stream of praise, personified as the goddess of speech. She is called the instructress of Manu, and frequent passages ascribe to her the first institution of the rules of performing sacrifices. According to Sāyaṇa, she is the goddess presiding over the earth. A legend in the Śatapatha Brāhmaṇa represents her as springing from a sacrifice which Manu performed for the purpose of obtaining offspring. She was claimed by Mitra-Varuṇa, but remained faithful to him who had produced her. Manu lived with her, and praying and fasting to obtain offspring, he begot the race of Manu.

IDĀVIDĀ. Daughter of Trinabindu and the Apsaras Alambushā. There are different statements in the Purānas regarding her. She is represented to be the wife of Viśravas and mother of Kuvera, or the wife of Pulastya and mother of Viśravas.

IKSHWĀKU. Son of the Manu Vaivaswat, who was son of Vivaswat, the sun, "He was born from the nostril of the Manu as he happened to sneeze." Ikshwāku was founder of the Solar race of kings, and reigned in Ayodhyā at the beginning of the second yuga or age. He had a hundred sons, the eldest of whom was Vikukshi. Another son, named Nimi, founded the Mithilā dynasty. According to Max Muller the name is mentioned once, and only once, in the *Rig-veda*. Respecting this he adds: "I take it, not as the name of a king, but as the name of a people, probably the people who inhabited Bhājeratha, the country washed by the northern Gangā or Bhāgīrathī." Other place is the Ikshwākus in the north-west.

INDRA. He is the god of the firmanent. In the Vedas he stands in the first rank among the gods. More hymns are addressed to Indra than any other deity is the Vedas. His wife is Indrani. His weapon is thunderbolt. He frequently sends celestial nymphs to excite the passion of the holy men; to distract them from the potent penances. He is represented as the king of gods who had to fight the demons quite often.

INDRA-DYUMNA. Son of Su-mati and grandson of Bharata. There were several others of the name, the most important among them being ,a king of Avantī, by whom the temple of Vishnu was built, and the image of Jagan-nātha was set up in Orissa.

INDRA-JIT. Megha-nāda, son of Rāvana. When Rāvana went against Indrā's forces in Swarga, his son Megha-nāda accompanied him, and fought most valiantly. Indra himself was obliged to interfere, when Megha-nāda, availing himself of the magical power of becoming invisible, which he had obtained from Śiva, bound Indra and carried him off to Lankā. The gods, headed by Brahmā, went thither to obtain the release of Indra, and Brahmā gave to Megha-nāda the name Indra-jit, conqueror of Indra.'

INDRA-KĪLA. The mountain Mandara.

INDRA-LOKA. Indra's heaven, Swarga.

INDRĀṆĪ. Wife of Indra, and mother of Jayanta and Jayantī. She is also called Śachī and Aindrī. She is mentioned a few times in the *Rig-veda,* and is said to be the most fortunate of females, "for her husband shall never die of old age." The *Taittirīya Brāhmaṇa* states that Indra chose her for his wife from a number of competing goddesses, because she surpassed them all in voluptuous attractions.

INDRA-PRAMATI. An early teacher of the *Rig-veda,* who received one Sanhitā direct from Paila.

INDRA-PRASTHA. The capital city of the Pāndu princess. The name is still known, and is used for a part of the city of Delhi.

INDRA-SENA (mas.), INDRA-SENĀ (fem.). Names of the son and daughter of Nala and Damayantī.

INDU. The moon.

INDU-MATĪ. Sister of Bhoja, king of Vidarbha, who chose Prince Aja for her husband at her swayam-vara. She was killed by Nārada's garland falling upon her while asleep.

INDU-MANI. The moon gem. *See* Chandra-kānta.

IRĀVAT. A son of Arjuna by his Nāga wife Ulupī.

IRĀVATĪ. The river Rāvī or Hydraotes.

ĪŚA. 'Lord.' (1) A title of Śiva. (2) Name of a Upanishad.

ĪŚANA. A name of Siva or Rudra, or of one of his manifestation. He is guardian of the north-east quarter.

ISHTI-PAŚAS. 'Stealers of offerings.' Rākshasas and other enemies of the gods, who steal the oblations.

ĪŚWARA. 'Lord.' A title given of Śiva.

ISWARA KRISHNA. Author of the philosophical treatise called ITIHĀSAS. Legendary poems. Heroic history. "Stories like those of Urvaśī and Purūravas." The term is especially applied to the *Mahābhārata*.

J

JĀBĀLI, JĀVĀLI. A Brāhman who was priest of King Daśa-ratha, and held sceptical philosophical opinions. He is represented in the *Rāmāyana* as enforcing his views upon Rāma, who decidedly repudiated them. Thereupon he asserted that his atheistical arguments had been used only for a purpose, and that he was really imbued with sentiments of piety and religion. He is said to have been a logician and so probably he belonged to the Nyāya school.

JAGAD-DHĀTRI (DHĀTĀ). 'Sustainer of the world.' An epithet given to both Saraswatī and Durgā.

JAGAN-MĀTRI (MĀTĀ). 'Mother of the world.' One of the names of Siva's wife.

JAGAN-NĀTHA. 'Lord of the world.' A particular form of Vishnu, or rather of Krishna, who is worshipped in Bengal and other parts of India. Puri, near the town of Cuttack, in Orissa, is the great seat of his worship, and crowds of pilgrims resort there from all parts, especially on the two great festivals of the Snāna-yātra and Rath-yātra, in the months of Jyaishtha and Āshādha. The first the image is bathed, and in the second, or car festival, the image is brought out upon a car along with the images of his brother Bala-rāma and sister Su-bhadra, and is drawn by the devotees. The legend of the origin of Jagan-nātha is peculiar. Krishna was killed by a hunter, and his body was left to rot under a tree, but some pious persons found the bones and placed them in a box. A devout king named Indra-dyumna was directed by Vishnu to form an image of Jagan-nātha and to place the bones of Krishna inside it. Viswa-karma, the architect of the gods, undertook to make the image, on condition of being left quite undisturbed till the work was complete. After fifteen days the king was impatient and went to Viśwa-karma, who was angry, and left off work before he had made either hands or feet, so that the image has only stumps. Indra-dyumna prayed to Brahmā, who promised to make the image famous, and he did so by giving to it eyes and a soul, and by acting as high priest at its consecration.

JĀHNAVĪ. The Ganges. *See* Jahnu.

JAHNU. A sage descended from Purūravas, he was disturbed in his devotions by the passage of the river Gangā, and consequently drank up its waters. He afterwards relented, and allowed the stream to issue from his ear. Hence Gangā is called Jāhnavī, daughter of Jahnu.

JAIMINI. A celebrated sage, a disciple of Vyāsa, he is said to have received the Sāma-veda from his master, and to have been its publisher or teacher. He was also the founder of the Pūrva-mīmānsā philosophy. The text of Jaimini is printed in the *Bibliotheca Indica*.

JAIMINīYA-NYĀYA-MĀLA-VISTARA. A work on the philosophy by Mādhava, which has been edited by Goldstucher and Cowell.

JĀJALI. A Brāhman mentioned in the Mahā-bhārata as having by ascetism acquired a supernatural power of locomotion, of which he was so proud that he deemed himself perfect in virtue and superior to all men. A voice from the sky told him that he was inferior to Tulādhāra, a Vaiśya and a trader. He went to this Tulādhāra and learnt wisdom from him.

JALA-RŪPA. The fish or the Makara on the banner of Kāma.

JALA-SĀYIN. 'Sleeping on the waters,' an appellation of Vishnu, as he is supposed to sleep upon his serpent couch on the waters during the rainy season, or during the submersion of the world.

JAMAD-AGNI. A Brāhman and a descendant of Bhrigu, he was the son of Richīka and Satya-vatī, and was the father of five sons.

Jamad-Agni suspected the fidelity of his wife Renuka who was killed at his latest by his son Paraśu-rāma. Jamad-Agni was murdered by the king krita-viriya. Parasu-rāma, in revenge slew all the sons of the Kata-virias and dared the earth of the Kshatriya caste.

JĀMADAGNYA. The patronymic of Paraśu-rāma.

JĀMBAVAT. King of the bears. A celebrated gem called Syamantaka had been given by the Sun to Satrā-jit. Fearing that Krishṇa would take it from him he gave it to his brother, Prasena. One property of this jewel was to protect its wearer when good, to ruin him when bad. Prasena was wicked and was killed by a lion, which was carrying off the gem in its mouth. This lion was encountered and slain by Jāmbavat. After Prasena's disappearance, Krishṇa was suspected of having killed him for the sake of the jewel. Krishṇa with a large party tracked the steps of Prasena, till it was ascertained that he had been killed by a lion, and that the lion had been killed by a bear. Krishṇa then tracked the bear, Jāmbavat, into his cave, and a great fight ensued between them. After waiting outside for seven or eight days, Krishṇa's followers went home and performed his funeral ceremonies. On the twenty-first day of the fight, Jāmbavat submitted to his adversary, gave up the gem, and presented to him his daughter, Jāmbavatī, as an offering. Jāmbavat with his army of bears aided Rāma in his invasion of Lankā, and always played the role of a sage counsellor.

JĀMBAVATĪ. Daughter of Jāmbavat, king of the bears, wife of Krishṇa, and mother of Sāmba.

JAMBHA. Name of several demons. One who fought against the gods and was slain by Indra. For this deed he was called Jambha-bhedin. Also of one who fought against Arjuna and was killed by Krishna.

JAMBU-DWĪPA. One of the seven islands or continents of which the world is made up. The great mountain, Meru, stands at its centre, and Bhārata-varsha or India is its best part. It has mine Varshas or divisions:—(1) Bhārata, south of the Himālayas and southernmost of all, (2) Kim-purusha, (3) Hari-varsha, (4) Ilā-vrita, containing Meru, (5) Ramyaka, (6) Hiranmaya, (7) Uttara-Kuru, each to the north of the preceding one, (8) Bhadrāśwa, and (9) Ketu-māla lie respectively to the east and west of Ilā-vrita, the central region.

JAMBU-MĀLI. A Rākshasa general of Rāvaṇa, he was killed by Hanumān.

JANAKA. 1. King of Mithilā, of the Solar race. When Nimi, his predecessor, died without leaving a successor, the sages subjected the body of Nimi to attrition, and produced from it a prince "who was called Janaka, being born without a progenitor". He was the first Janaka to be born twenty generations earlier than Janaka the father of Sītā.

2. King of Videha and father of Sītā, remarkable for his great knowledge and good works and sanctity. He is called Sīra-dhvaja, 'he of the plough banner,' because his daughter Sītā sprang up fully formed from the furrow when he was ploughing the ground and preparing for a sacrifice to obtain offspring. The sage Yājnawalkya was his priest and adviser. The Brāhmanas relate that he "refused to submit to the hierarchical pretensions of the Brāhmans, and asserted his right of performing sacrifices without the intervention of priests." He succeeded in his contention, for it is said that through his pure and righteous life he became a Brāhman and one of he Rājarshis. He and his priest Yājnawalkya are thought to have prepared the way for Buddha.

JĀNAKĪ. A patronymic of Sītā.

JANAMEJAYA. A great king, who was son of Parikshit, and great-grandson of Arjuna. It was to this king that the *Mahā-bhārata* was recited by Vaiśampāyana, and the king listened to it is expiation of the sin of killing a Brāhman. His father, Parikshit, died from the bite of a serpent, and Janemajaya is said to have performed a great sacrifice of serpents (Nāgas) and to have conquered the Nāga people of Taksha-silā. Hence he is called Sarpa-sattrin, 'serpent-sacrificer.' There were several others of the same name.

JANĀRDDANA. 'The adored of mankind.' A name of Krishna.

JANA-STHĀNA. A place in the Dandaka forest where Rāma stayed for a while in his exile.

JARAS. 'Old age.' The hunter who unwittingly killed Krishna.

JARĀ-SANDHA. Son of Brihad-ratha, and king of Magadha. Brihad-ratha had two wives, who after being long barren brought forth two halves of a boy. These abortions were regarded with horror and thrown away. A female man-eating demon named Jarā picked them up and put them together to carry them off. On their coming in contact a boy was formed, who cried out so lustily that he brought out the king and his two queens. The Rākshasī explained what had happened, resigned the child, and retired. The father gave the boy the name of Jarā-sandha, because he had been put together by Jarā. Future greatness was prophesied for the boy, and he became an ardent worshipper of Śiva. Through the favour of this god he prevailed over many kings, and he especially fought against Krishna, who had killed Kansa, the husband of two of Jarāsandha's daughters. He besieged Mathurā, and attacked Krishna eighteen times, and was as always defeated; but Krishna was so weakened that he retired to Dwārakā. Jarā-sandha had many kings in captivity, and when Krishna returned from Dwārakā, he, with Bhīma and Arjuna, went to Jarā-sandha's capital for the purpose of slaying their enemy and liberating the kings. Jarā-sandha refused to release the kings, and accepted the alternative of a combat, in which he was killed by Bhīma.

JARAT-KĀRU. An ancient sage who married a sister of the great serpent Vāsukī, and was father of the sage Āstīka.

JARITĀ. A certain female bird of the species called Sārngikā, whose story is told in the *Mahābhārata*. The saint Manda-pāla, who returned from the shades because he had no son, assumed the form of a male bird, and made her give birth to four sons. He then abandoned her. In the conflagration of the Khāndava forest she showed great devotion in the protection of her children, who were eventually saved through the influence of Manda-pāla over the god of fire. Their names were Jaritāri, Sārisrikta, Stamba-mitra, and Drona. They were "interpreters of the Vedas;" and some hymns of the Rig-veda bear the names of the second and the third.

JATĀSURA. A Rākshasa who disguised himself as a Brāhman and carried off Yudhi-shthira, Saha-deva, Nakula, and Draupadī. He was overtaken and killed by Bhīma.

JĀTA-VEDAS. A Vedic epithet for fire. "The meaning is explained in five ways:—(1) Knowing all created beings; (2) Possessing all creatures or everything existent; (3) Known by created beings; (4) Possessing Vedas, riches; (5) Possessing Vedas, wisdom. Other derivations and explanations are found in Brāhmanas, but the exact sense of the word seems to have been very early lost, and of the five explanations given, only the first two would seem to be admissible for the Vedic texts. In one passage a form, Jāta-veda, seems to occur."—*Williams.* This form of the term, and the statement of Manu that the Vedas were formed out from fire, air, and the sun, may perhaps justify the explanation, 'producer of the Vedas.'

JATĀYU, JATĀYUS. A bird according the Rāmāyaṇa, he was son of Vishṇu's bird Garuḍa, and king of the vultures. Others say he was a son of Aruna. As an ally of Rāma he fought furiously against Rāvaṇa to prevent the carrying away of Sītā. Rāvaṇa overpowered him and left him mortally wounded. Rāma found him in time to hear his dying words, and to learn what had become of Sītā. Rāma and Lakshmaṇa performed his funeral rites to "secure his soul in the enjoyments of heaven," whither he ascended in a chariot of fire.

In the Purāṇas he is the friend of Daśa-ratha. Jatāyu caught the falling king and saved him, when that king went to the eciliptic to recovere Sītā from Śani (Saturn), his carriage was consumed by a glance from the eye of the latter.

JATILĀ. A daughter of Gotama, who is mentioned in the Mahā-bhārata as a virtuous woman and the wife of seven husbands.

JAYA-DEVA. A poet, author of the *Gītā-govinda* (q.v.).

JAYAD-RATHA. A prince of the Lunar race, son of Brihanmanas. He was king of Sindhu and was "indifferently termed Rāja of the Sindhus or Saindhavas, and Rāja of the Saindhavas and Sauvīras both being tribes living along the Indus. Jayad-ratha married Duhsalā, daughter of Dhrita-rāshtra, and was an ally of the Kauravas. When the Pāndavas were in exile he called at their forest abode while they were out hunting and Draupadī was at home alone. Jayad-ratha was captivated by the charms of Draupadī, and tried to induce her to elope with him. When he was indignantly refused he carried her off by force. On the return of the Pāndavas they pursued the ravisher, defeated his forces, and made him prisoner. His life was spared on the command of Yudhi-shthira, but Bhīma kicked and beat him terribly, cut off his hair, and made him go before the assembled Pāndavas and acknowledge himself to be their slave. However, on the intercession of Draupadī he was allowed to depart. He was killed, after a desperate conflict, by Arjuna on the fourteenth day of the great battle.

JAYANTA. Son of Indra, also called Jaya.

JAYANTĪ. Daughter of Indra. She is called also Jayanī, Deva-senā, and Tāvīhī.

JĪMŪTA. A great wrestler, who was overcome and killed by Bhīma at the court of Virāṭa.

JĪMŪTA-VĀHANA. 'Whose vehicle is the clouds,' it is a title of Indra. This name is borne by several persons, including among them by the author of the Dāya-bhāga.

JISHNU. A name of Arjuna.

JUSHKA. A Turushka or Turki king, who ruled in Kashmir and in Northern India. *See* Kanishka.

JWĀLĀ-MUKHĪ. 'Mouth of fire.' A volcano. A celebrated place of pilgrimage in the Lower Himālayas, north of the Panjāb, where fire issues from the ground. According to the legend, it is the fire created by Satī, the wife of Siva, in which she burnt herself.

JYĀMAGHA. A king of the Lunar race, proverbial, "most eminent among husbands submissive to their wives." Śaibyā, his wife, was barren, but he was afraid to take and her wife till, having overcome an enemy and driven him from his country, the beautiful daughter of the vanquished king became his captive and Jyāmagha desired to marry her with the assent of his queen. When Saibyā saw the maiden, she was filled with jealousy, and angrily demanded who the "light-hearted damsel" was. The king was disconcerted, and humbly replied, "She is the young bride of the future son whom thou shalt bring forth;" bore a son who was named Vidarbha, and he married the captive princess.

JYOTISHA. Astronomy. One of the Vedāngas. The object of this Vedānga is to fix the most auspicious days and seasons for the performance of sacrifices. There has been little that is ancient on this subject; only one "short tract, consisting of thirty-six verses, in a comparatively modern style, to which scholars cannot assign an earlier date than 300 years B.C."

K

KABANDHA. 1. A disciple of Su-mantu, the earliest teacher of the *Atharva-veda.* 2. A monstrous Rākshasa slain by Rāma. He is said to have been a son of the goddess Srī. He is described as "covered with hair, vast as a mountain, without head or neck, having a mouth armed with immense teeth in the middle of his belly, arms a league long, and one enormous eye in his breast." He was originally a Gandharva, and his hideous deformity arose, according to one legend, from Indra, whom he challenged, and who struck him with his thunderbolt, and drove his head and thigh into his body. According to another legend, his deformity arose from the curse of a sage. When mortally wounded, he requested Rāma to burn his body, and when that was done he came out of the fire in his real shape as a Gandharva, and counselled—Rāma has to conduct the war against Rāvaṇa. He was also called Danu.

KACHA. A son of Brihaspati. According to the *Mahābhārata* he became a disciple of Śukra or Uṣanas, the priest of the Asuras, with the object of obtaining from him the mystic power of restoring the dead to life, a charm which Sukra alone possessed. To prevent this the Asuras Killed Kacha again and again, but on both occasions he was restored to life by the sage at the intercession of Devayānī, his daughter, who had fallen in love with Kacha. They killed him a third time, burnt his body, and mixed his ashes with Śukra's wine, but Devayānī again implored her father to bring back to eye the young man. Unable to resist his daughter's importunity, Śukra once more performed the charm, and to his surprise heard the voice of Kacha come out from his own belly. To save his own life, Śukra taught his pupil the great charm. He then allowed himself to be ripped open, and upon coming out Kacha perfomed the charm, and restored his master to life. This incident is said to have caused Śukra to prohibit the use of wine to Brāhmans. Kacha resisted the proposals of Devayānī, and refused to make her his wife. She then cursed him, that the charms he had learnt from her father should become powerless. He in return condemned her to be sought by no Brahman, and to become the wife of a Kshatriya.

KĀDAMBARĪ. A daughter of Chitra-ratha and Madirā. Her name is the title of a well-known prose work, a king of novel, written by Vāṇa or Bāṇa-bhaṭṭa, in the seventh century.

KADRŪ. A daughter of Daksha, and one of the thirteen that were married to Kaśyapa. She was mother of "a thousand powerful many-headed serpents, the chief amongst whom were Śesha, Vāsuki, ... and many other fierce and venomous serpents." The *Vishṇu Purāṇa,* names twelve, the *Vāyu Purāṇa* forty. Her offspring bear the metronymic Kādraveya.

KAHODA. A learned Brāhman, father of Ashtāvakra. He with many others was defeated in argument at the court of Janaka by a Buddhist sage, and as a penalty was thrown into the river. Some years afterwards he was recovered by his son, who overcame the supposed Buddhist sage, and thus brought about a restoration. *See* Ashṭāvakra.

KAIKASĪ. Daughter of the Rākshasa Su-mālī and his wife Ketu-matī, wife of Viśravas and mother of Rāvaṇa.

KAIKEYA. Name of a country and its king. He was father-in-law of Krishṇa, and his five sons were allies of thc Pāndavas. His real name appears to have been Dhrishta-ketu.

KAIKEYAS, KEKAYAS. The people of Kaikeya, one of the chief nations in the war of the *Mahābhārata.* The *Rāmāyaṇa* places them in the west, beyond the Saraswatī and Vyās.

KAIKEYĪ. A princess of Kaikeya, wife of King Dasa-ratha, and mother of Bharata, his third son. She carefully tended Dasa-ratha when he was wounded in battle, and in gratitude he promised to grant any two requests she might make. Urged by the malignant counsels of Mantharā, a female attendant, she made use of this promise to procure the exile of Rāma, and to promote the advancement of her own son, Bharata, in his place.

KAILĀŚA. A mountain in the Himālayas, north of the Mānasa lake. Siva's paradise as well as Kuvera's abode is said to be on Mount Kailāsa. It is called also Gana-parvata and Rajatāgiri, 'silver mountain.'

KAIṬABHA. Kaiṭabha and Madhu were two horrible demons, who, according to the *Mahābhārata* and the Purāṇas, sprang from the ear of Vishṇu while he was asleep at the end of a kalpa, and were about to kill Brahmā, who was lying on the lotus springing from Vishṇu's navel. Vishṇu killed them, and hence he obtained the names of Kaiṭabha-jit and Madhu-sūdana. The Mārkandeya Purāṇa attributes the death of Kaiṭabha to Umā, and gives her the title of Kaiṭabhā. The Hari-vansa states that the earth received its name of Medinī from the marrow (*medas*) of these demons. In one passage it says that their bodies, being thrown into the sea, produced an immense quantity of marrow or fat, which Nārāyana used in forming the earth. In another place it says that the *medas* quite covered the earth, and so gave it the name of Medinī.

KAKSHĪVAT, KAKSHĪVĀN. A Vedic sage, particularly connected with the worship of the Aswins, he was the son of several hymns in the Rig-veda. He was also called Pajriya, because he belonged to the race of Pajra. In one of his hymns he lauds the liberality of King Swanaya.

KAKUDMIN. A name of Raivata.

KĀLA. 'Time.' A name of Yama, the judge of the dead. In the *Atharva-veda* Time is addressed as the source and ruler of all things. "It is he who drew forth the worlds and encompassed them. Being their father, he became their son. There is no other power superior to him." The *Vishṇu Bhāgavata*, and *Padma Purāṇas* state that Brahmā existed in the form of Time, "but the Purāṇas do not generally recognise Time as an element of the first cause."

KĀLAKĀ. A wife of Kaśyapa. According to the *Rāmāyaṇa* and *Mahābhārata* she was a daughter of Daksha, but the *Vishṇu Purāṇa* states that she and her sister Pulomā were daughters of the Dānava Vaiśwanara, "who were both married to Kaśyapa, and bore him 60,000 distinguished Dānavas, called Paulomas and Kālakanjas, who were powerful, ferocious, and cruel."

KĀLAKANJAS, KĀLAKEYAS. Sons of Kaśyapa by his wife Kālakā. There were many thousands of them, and they were "distinguished Dānavas, who were powerful, ferocious, and cruel."

KĀLA-MUKHAS. 'Black faces.' People who sprang from men and Rākshasa females.

KĀLA-NEMI. 1. In the *Rāmāyaṇa* a Rākshasa, uncle of Rāvana. At the solicitation of Rāvana, and with the promise of half his kingdom, he endeavoured to kill Hanumān. Assuming the form of a hermit-devotee, he went to the Gandha-mādana mountain, and when Hanumān proceeded there in search of medicinal herbs, the disguised Rākshasa invited him to his hermitage and offered him food. Hanumān refused, but went to bathe in a neighbouring pond. Upon his placing his foot in the water it was seized by a crocodile, but he dragged the creature out and killed it. From the dead body there arose a lovely Apsara, who had been cursed by Daksha to live as a crocodile till she should be released by Hanumān. She told her deliverer to be beware of Kāla-nemi. So Hanumān went back to that deceiver, told him that he knew him, and, taking him by the feet, sent him whirling through the air to Lankā, where he fell before the throne of Rāvana in the council-room. 2. In the

Purāṇas a great Asura, son of Virochana, the grandson of Hiraṇya-kaśipu, he was killed by Vishṇu, but was said to live again in Kansa and in Kāliya.

KĀLA-YAVANA. A Yavana or foreign king who led an army of barbarians to Mathurā against Krishna. That hero lured him into the cave of the mighty Muchukunda, who, being disturbed from sleep by a kick from Kāla-yavana, cast a fiery glance upon him and reduced him to ashes. This legend appears to indicate an invasion from the Himālayas. According to the *Vishṇu Purāṇa* and *Hari-vanśa,* Kāla-Yavana was the son of a Brāhman named Garga, who had an especial spite against the Yādavas, and was begotten by the wife of a childless Yavana king.

KALHAṆA PANDIT. Author of the *Rāja Tarangiṇī,* a history of Kashmīr, he is supposed to have lived about 1148 A.D.

KALI. The Kali-yuga, personified as the spirit of evil. In playing dice Kali is the ace and so is a personification of ill luck.

KĀLĪ. 'The black.' In Vedic days this name was associated with Agni (fire), who had seven flickering tongues of flame for devouring oblations of butter. Of these seven, Kālī was the black or terrific tongue. It has developed into the goddess Kālī, the fierce and bloody consort of Siva. *See* Devī.

KĀLI-DĀSA. The greatest poet and dramatist of India, he was one of "the nine gems" that adorned the court of King Vikramāditya at Ujjayinī. Wilson inclines to the beliėf that this was the Vikramādiya whose era begins in 56 B.C., but Dr. Bhāu Dājī argues in favour of Harsha Vikramāditya who lived in the middle of the sixth century, so the date of Kāli-dāsa is unsettled. Williams thinks that Kāli-dāsa wrote about the beginning of the third century. Lessen places him half a century earlier. Some believe that there was more than one poet who bore this name as an honorary title. Kāli-dāsa was author of the dramas *Śakuntalam* and *Vikramorvaśī,* and a third drama

Mālavikāgnimitra is attributed to him. *Śakuntalā* was translated by Sir W. Jones, and first brought Sanskrit literature to the notice of Europe. Wilson has translated *Vikramorvaśī,* and given a sketch of *Mālavikāgnimitra*. *Raghu-vanśa, Kumāra-sambhava, Megha-dūta, Ritu-sanhāra, Nalodaya* are said to have been utterly Kali-dāsa. He was also author of the Sruta-bodha, a work on prosody. The merits of Kāli-dāsa as a poet are well compressed by his great popularity in India, as well as by the great favour with which *Śakuntalā* was received in Europe.

KĀLIKĀ. The goddess Kālī.

KĀLIKĀ PURĀṆA. One of the eighteen upa Purāṇas, "it contains about 9000 stanzas in 98 chapters, and is the only work of the series dedicated to recommend the worship of the bride of Siva, in one or other of her manifold forms as Giri-jā, Devī, Bhadra-kālī, Mahā-māyā. It belongs, therefore, to the Śākta modification of Hindu belief, or the worship of the female powers of the deities. The influence of this worship shows itself in the very first pages of the work, which relate the incestuous passion of Brahmā for his daughter, Sandhyā, in a strain that has nothing analogous to it in the Vāyu, Linga, or Śiva Purāṇas. The marriage of Śiva and Pārvatī is a subject earlier described, with the sacrifice of Daksha and the death of Satī. And this work is authority for Śiva's carrying the dead body about the world, and the origin of the Pīthasthānas, or places where the different members of it were scattered, and where Lingas were consequently erected. A legend follows the births of Bhairava and Vetāla, whose devotion to the different forms of Devī furnishes occasion to describe, in great detail, the rites and formulae of which her worship consists, including the chapters on sanguinary sacrifices translated in the *Asiatic Researches* (vol. v.). Another peculiarity in this work is afforded by very prolific descriptions of a number of rivers and mountains at Kāmarūpa Tīrtha, in Assam, and rendered holy ground by the celebrated temple of Durgā in that country, as Kāmākshī or Kāmākshyā. It is a singular and yet uninvestigated circumstance, that Assam, or at least the north-east of Bengal, seems to have been, in a great degree, the source from which the Tāntrika and Śākta corruptions of the religion of the Vedas and Purāṇas proceeded."—*Wilson*.

KĀLINDĪ. A name of the river Yamunā, as daughter of Kalinda (the sun).

KALINGA. The region along the Coromandel coast, north of Tamilnadu. The Purāṇas absurdly make it one of the sons of Bali.

KĀLIYA. A serpent king who had five heads, and dwelt in a deep pool of the Yamunā, with numerous attendant serpents. His mouths vomitted fire and smoke, and he laid waste all the country round. Krishṇa, while yet a child, jumped into this pool, when he was quickly laced and entwined in the coils of the snakes. His companions and friends were horrified, but Bala-rāma called upon him to exercise his divine power. He did so, and the serpents were soon overcome. Placing his foot on the middle head of Kāliya, he compelled him and his followers to implore mercy. He spared them, but bade Kāliya and his followers to free the earth from their presence, and to move to the ocean. The Asura Kāla-nemi is said to have been animate in him.

KALI YUGA. The fourth or present age of the world, which is to endure for 432,000 years. It commenced in 3102 B.C. *See* Yuga.

KALKĪ. KALKIN. 'The white horse.' Vishṇu's tenth incarnation, which is yet to come. *See* Avatāra.

KALMĀSHA-PĀDA. A king of the Solar race, son of Su-dāsa and a descendant of Ikshwāku. His legend, as told in the *Mahābhārata,* relates that while hunting in the forest he encountered Saktri, the eldest son of Vaśishtha. As this sage refused to get out of his way, he struck him with his whip. The incensed sage cursed him to become a cannibal. This curse was heard by Viśwāmitra, the rival of Vaśishtha, and he so contrived that the body of the king became possessed by a man-eating Rākshasa. In this condition he caused human flesh to be served up to a Brāhman named Mitrasaha, who discovered what it was, and intensified the curse of Saktri by a new imprecation. One of Kalmāsha-pada's first victims was Saktri himself, and all the hundred sons of Vaśistha fell a prey to his disordered appetite.

It was after great persuasion that Vaśishtha surrendered his curse.

KALPA. A day and night of Brahmā, 4,320,000,000 years. See Yuga.

KALPA, KALPA SŪTRAS. Ceremonial; one of the Vedāngas. A ceremonial directory or rubric expressed in the form of Sūtras, short technical rules.

KĀMA, KĀMA-DEVA. The god of love. Eros, Cupid. In the *Rig-veda* (x. 129) desire is said to have been the first movement that arose in the One after it come into life through thepower of fervour or abstraction. Rati or Revā, the goddess of desire is his wife. He inspired Śiva with amorous thoughts of Pārvatī while he was engaged in penitential devotion, and for this offence the angry god reduced him to ashes by fire from his central eye. Śiva afterwards relented and allowed Kāma to be born again as Pradyumna, son of Krishṇa and Rukminī or Māyā, 'delusion.'

KĀMA-DHENU. The cow belonging to the sage Vasistha, which grants desires. She was produced out of the churning of the ocean. Among the examples of her supernatural powers was the creation of a host of warriors who aided Vaśishtha against Kārtavīrya. She is also called Kāma-duh, Saval, and Surabhi.

KĀMĀKSHĪ. A form of Devī worshipped at Kāmarūpa-tīrtha in Assam. See *Kālikā Purāṇa*.

KĀMANDAKI. Author of a work known by his name on "The Elements of Polity." The text has been printed in the *Bibliotheca Indica* by Rājendra Lāla Mittra.

KĀMARŪPA. The north-eastern part of Bengal and the western portion of Assam. The name still survives as Kāmrūp.

KĀMBOJAS. A race or tribe living to the north-west, and famous for their horses. They were among the races conquered by King Sagara.

KĀMPILYA. The city of King Drupada in the country of the Pānchāla, where the swayam-vara of Draupadī was held. It corresponds with the Kāmpila of modern times, situated in the Doāb on the old Ganges, between Badāūn and Farrukhābād.

KĀMYAKA. The forest in which the Pāndavas passed their exile on the banks of the Saraswatī.

KANĀDA. The sage who founded the Vaiśeshika school of philosophy.

KĀNCHĪ. One of the seven sacred cities, *holy* Conjeveram.

KANDARPA. The Hindu Cupid. *See* Kāma.

KĀNDARSHI. A Rishi who teaches one particular Kānda or part of the Vedas.

KANDU. A sage who beguiled from long and severe austerities by Pramlochā, a nymph sent from heaven by Indra for this purpose. He lived with her for some hundreds of years, which seemed to him only as a day, but he at length repudiated her and "went to the region of Vishṇu." Pramlochā gave birth, in an extraordinary manner, to his daughter Mārishā.

KANISHKA. "Hushka, Jushka, Kanishka." These are the names recorded in the *Rāja Taranginī* of three great Turushka, Turk or Tatar kings who belong to the Buddhist religion. The names of Kanishka and Hushka (or Huvishka) have been found in inscriptions and upon coins, showing that their dominions were of considerable extent in Northern India, and that they were, as the *Rāja Taranginī* represents, great supporters of the Buddhist religion. The name of Kanishka has been found in inscriptions at Mathurā, Manikyāla, Bhāwalpur, and Zeda, while his name appears on the corrupt Greek coins as Kanerki. Huvishka's name has been found at Mathurā and on a metal vase from Wardak in Afghanistan. On the coins his name is represented as Oerki. While

Kanishka preceded Huvishka, it is certain that their reigns covered a period of fifty-one years, and probably more just before the Christian era. A Roman coin of the data 33 B.C. has been found in the tope of Mankāla, which was built by Kanishka.

KANSA. The tyrannical king of Mathurā. Son of Ugrasena and cousin of Devakī the mother of Krishṇa, he was the cousin, not the uncle, of Krishṇa, as he is often called. He married two daughters of Jarā-sandha, king of Magadha. He deposed his father. It was foretold that a son born of Devakī should kill him, so he endeavoured to destroy all her children. But Bala-rāma, her seventh son, was smuggled away to Gokula, and was brought up by Rohiṇī. When Krishna the eighth was born his parents fled with him. The tyrant then gave orders for a general massacre of all vigorous male infants. Kansa became the great persecutor of Krishṇa, 'crane.' He is looked upon as an Asura, and is in some way identified with the Asura Kāla-nemi.

KANSA-BADHA. A drama in seven acts upon the destruction of Kansa by Krishṇa. The author is called Krishṇa Kavi, and the play was probably written about three centuries ago.

KĀṆWA. *See* Śatapatha Brāhmaṇa.

KAṆWA. Name of a Rishi to whom some hymns of the seven great Rishis are assigned. The sage who brought up Śakuntalā as his daughter. There are several others of the same name.

KĀṆWAS. The descendants or followers of Kaṇwa.

KANYĀ-KUBJA. The modern form of the name is Kanauj or Kinnauj, spelt in a variety of ways: 1. An ancient city of Hindustan on the Kālī-nadi, an affluent of the Ganges, and lying a little to the west of the latter. It was once the capital of a powerful dynasty. It was known to classical geographers as "Canogyza." The name means "humpbacked damsel," and refers to a legend relating to the hundred daughters of King Kusa-nābha, who were all made crooked by Vāyu for refusing to comply with his licentious desires. 2. A great national division of the Brāhman caste. *See* Brāhman.

KANYĀ-KUMĀRĪ. 'The virgin-damsel.' A name of Durgā. Her worship extended to the southernmost extremity of India in the days of Pliny, and 'Kumārī' still appears in the name Cape Comorin.

KAPARDIN. 'Wearing the Kaparda,' a peculiar braid or knot of hair. This epithet is applied to Śiva, to one of the Rudras, and some others.

KAPI-DHWAJA. An epithet of Arjuna, because he bore an ape (*kapi*) on his standard (*dhwaja*).

KAPILA. A celebrated sage, the founder of the Sānkhya philosophy. The *Hari-vanśa* declares him to be the son of Vitatha. He is sometimes identified with Vishṇu and sometimes with Agni. His one glance is said to have destroyed the hundred thousand sons of King Sagara.

KAPILA, KAPILA-VASTU. A town on the river Rohiṇī, an affluent of the Rāptī, this was the capital of Śuddhodana, the father of Gotama Buddha.

KAPIŚĀ. Mother of the Piśāchas, who bear the metronymic Kāpiśeya.

KARĀLĪ. 'Dreadful, terrible.' In Vedic times one of the seven tongues of Agni (fire), but in later days a name of the terrible consort of Śiva.

KARDAMA. According to the *Mahābhārata* and *Rāmāyaṇa,* he is one of the Prajāpatis who sprang from Brahmā. According to other authorities, a sage of the same name, was a son of Daksha or a son of Pulaha.

KARMA-MĪMĀNSĀ. The Pūrva-mīmānsā. *See* Darśana.

KARMA-MĪMĀNSĀ-SŪTRA. A work on the Vedānta philosophy, ascribed to Jaimini.

KARṆA. Son of Prithā or Kuntī by Sūrya, the sun, before her marriage to Pāndu. Karṇa was thus half-brother of the Pāndavas, but this relationship was not known to them till after his death. Kuntī, on one occasion, paid such attention to the sage Durvāsas, that he gave her a charm by virtue of which she might have a child from any god she preferred to invoke. She chose the sun, and the result was Karṇa, who was born equipped with arms and armour. Afraid of censure and disgrace, Kuntī exposed the child on the banks of the Yamunā, where it was found by Nandana or Adhiratha, the sūtra or charioteer of Dhrita-rāshtra. The charioteer and his wife, Rādhā, brought him up as their own. When he grew up, Indra disguised himself as a Brāhman, and cajoled him out of his divine cuirass. He gave him in return great strength and a javelin chargd with certain death. Karṇa became king of Anga or Bengal. Some authorities represent his foster-father as having been ruler of that country, but others say that Karṇa was made king of Anga by Duryodhana, in order to qualify him for the swayam-vara of Draupadī. This princess haughtily rejected him, saying, "I wed not with the base-born." Karṇa knew that he was half-brother of the Pāndavas, but he took the side of their cousins, the Kauravas, and he had especial rivalry and animosity against Arjuna, whom he vowed to kill. In the great battle he killed Ghatotkacha, the son of Bhīma, with Indra's javelin. Afterwards there was a terrific combat between him and Arjuna, in which the latter was nearly overpowered, but he killed Karṇa with a crescent-shaped arrow. Karṇa's relationship to the Pāndavas became known to them after his death, and they showed their regret for his loss by great kindness to his widows, children and dependants.

KARṆA-PRĀVARANAS. Men whose ears served them for coverings. They are mentioned in the Mahā-bhārata, Rāmā-yana, and other works.

KARṆĀṬA, KARṆĀṬAKA. The region where the Kannada language is spoken in modern Karnatak. A state of the Indian republic.

KĀRTA-VĪRYA. Son of Krita-vīrya, king of the Haihayas. This is his patronymic, by which he is best known; his real name was Arjuna. "Having worshipped a portion of the divine being called Dattātreya, sprung from the race of Atri, he sought and obtained, a thousand arms and a golden chariot that went wheresoever he willed it to go; the power of restraining wrong by justice; the conquest of the earth and the disposition to rule it righteously; invincibility by enemies, and death at the hands of a man renowned over the whole world. "No other king shall ever equal Kārta-vīrya in regard to sacrifices, liberality, austerities, courtesy, and self-restraint. "Thus he ruled for 85,000 years with unbroken health, prosperity, strength, and valour."—*V.P.*

He visited the hermitage of Jamadagni, and was received by that sage's wife with all respect; but he made an ill return for her hospitality, and carried off by violence "the calf of the milch-cow of the sacred oblation." For this outrage Paraśu-rāma cut off his thousand arms and killed him. "He oppressed both men and gods," so that the latter appealed to Vishṇu for succour. That god then came down to the earth as Paraśurāma for the especial purpose of killing him. Kārtavīrya was the contemporary of Rāvaṇa, and when that demon monarch came "in the course of his campaign of conquest to Mahishmatī (the capital of Kārta-vīrya), he was captured without difficulty, and was confined like a wild beast in a corner of his city." The statement of the Vāyu Purāṇa is that Kārta-vīrya invaded Lankā, and took Rāvana prisoner there.

KĀRTTIKEYA. The god of war and the planet Mars, also called Skanda. In the *Mahā-bhārata* and *Rāmāyaṇa* he is said to be the son of Śiva or Rudra, and to have been produced without the help of a woman. Śiva cast his seed into fire, and it was afterwards received by the Ganges: Kārttikeya was the result; hence he is called Agnibhū and Gangāja. He was fostered by the Pleiades (Krittikā), and hence he has six heads and the name Kārttikeya. His paternity is sometimes assigned to Agni (fire); Gangā (the Ganges) and Pārvatī are variously represented to be his mother. He is saved to have been born for the purpose of destroying Tāraka, a Daitya whose austerities had made him formidable to the gods. He is represented riding on a peacock called Paravāni, holding a bow in one hand and an arrow in the other. Kaumārī or senā is his wife. As a warrior he is called Mahā-sena, Senā-pati; Sidha-sena, 'leader of the Siddhas' and Yudha-ranga; also Kumāra, the boy; Guha, 'the mysterious one;' Śakti-dhara, 'spear-holder;' and in the south he is called Su-brahmanya. He is Gangā-putra, 'son of the Ganges;' Śara-bhū, 'born in the thicket;' Tāraka-jit, 'vanquisher of Tāraka;' Dwādasa-kara and Dwādasāksha, 'twelve-handed' and 'twelve-eyed;' Rijukāya, 'straight-bodied.'

KĀRUSHAS. People of Mālwa, inhabiting the back of the Vindhya mountins, they are said to have descended from Karusha, one of the sons of the Manu Vaivaswata.

KĀŚĪ. Varanasī.

KĀŚĪ KHANDA. A long poem, forming part of the Skanda Purāna, it gives a very minute description of the temples of Siva in and around Varanasī, and is presumably before the Mahomedan conquest.

KAŚYAPA. A Vedic sage to whom some hymns are attributed. All authorities agree in assigning to him a large part in the work of creation. According to the *Mahābhā,ata,* the *Rāmāyana,* and the Purānas, he was the son of Marīchi, the son of Brahmā, and he was father of Vivaswat, the father of Manu, the progenitor of mankind. The *Śatapatha Brāhmana* gives a different and not very intelligible account of his origin "Having assumed the form of a tortoise, Prajāpati created offspring. That which he created he made (*akarat*); hence the word *kūrma* (tortoise). Kaśyapa means tortoise; hence men say, 'All creatures are descendants of Kaśyapa. This tortoise is the same as Āditya." The *Atharva-veda* says, "The self-born Kaśyapa sprang from Time," and Time is often identical with Vishṇu. The *Mahābhārata* and later authorities agree in representing that Kaśyapa married Aditi and twelve other daughters of Daksha. From Aditi he begot the Ādityas, headed by Indra, and also Vivaswat, and "to Vivaswat was born the wise and mighty Manu." The *Rāmāyaṇa* and *Vishnu Purāṇa* also state that "Vishnu was born as a dwarf, the son of Aditi and Kaśyapa." He had a numerous and very diversified offspring demons, nāgas, reptiles, birds, and all kinds of living things from his other twelve wives. He was thus the father of all, and as such is sometimes called Prajāpati. He is one of the seven great Rishis, who appears as the priest of Paraśurāma and Rāma-chandra.

KĀ-TANTRA. A Sanskrit grammar by Sarva-varman. Edited by Eggeling for the *Bibliotheca Indica.*

KATA-PRŪ. 'Worm.' A class of beings similar to or identical with the Vidyā-dharas.

KATHA. Name of a upanishad. It has been translated by Dr. Roer in the *Bibliotheca Indica.*

KĀTHAKA. A school of the Yajur-veda, occupying a position between the Black and the White. It is supposed to be lost.

KATHĀRṆAVA. 'Sea of stories.' A compilation of miscellaneous stories in four books; the first two are the originals of the Hindī *Baitāl Pachīsī* and *Singhāsan Battīsī.*

KATHĀ-SARIT-SĀGARA. 'The ocean of the rivers of stories.' A collection of popular stories by Soma-deva-bhatta of Kashmīr, made about the beginning of the twelfth century A.D. It is drawn from a larger work called *Brihat-kathā.* The text has been printed and in part translated by Brockhaus.

KĀTYĀYANA. An ancient writer of great celebrity, he came after Pānini. He completed and corrected the grammar of Pāṇīnī and called it Vārttikas, 'supplementary rules and annotations.' He is generally identified with Vararuchi, the author of the *Prākrita Prakāśa.* Max Muller places him in the second half of the fourth century B.C.; Goldstucker in the first half of the second century B.C.; Weber about twenty-five years B.C. Besides his additions to Pānini's Grammar his Sūtras which bear his name, and of the *Yajur-veda Prātisākhya.* His Sūtras have been edited by Weber. A story in the *Kathā-sarit-sagara* makes him the incarnation of a demigod named Pushpa-danta. Kātyāyana was author also of a Dharma-sāstra.

KĀTYĀYANĪ. A name of Durgā.

KAUMODAKĪ. The mace of Krishna, presented to him by Agni in the course of fighting against Indra and burning the Khāndava forest.

KAUṆDINYA. An ancient sage and garmmarian. He offended Śiva, but was saved from that god's wrath by Vishṇu: he was hence called Vishṇu-gupta, 'saved by Vishṇu'.

KAUNTEYA. Son of Kuntī. A metronymic applicable to Yudhi-shthira, Bhīma, and Arjuna, but commonly applied to Arjuna.

KAURAVAS. Descendants of Kuru. A patronymic especially applied to the sons of Dhritarāshtra. See *Mahābhārata*.

KAUŚALAYA (mas.), KAUŚALYĪ (fem.). Belonging to the Kosala nation. There are several women known by this name—the wife of Puru and mother of Janamejaya; the wife of Daśa-ratha and mother of Rāma. Both, the mother of Dhrita-rāshtra and the mother of Pāndu were known by this name, being daughters of a king of Kāśī.

KAUŚĀMBĪ. The capital of Vatsa, near the junction of the Ganges and Jumna. An inscription found at Karra on the ganges mentions that place as being situated in Kausāmbī-mandala, the circle of Kauśāmbī; but General Cunningham identifies the place with the village of Kosam, said to be still called Kosambi nagar on the Jamuna, about thirty miles beyond Allahabad. It is the scene of the drama *Ratnāvalī*.

KAUSHĪTAKĪ. 1. A sākhā of the *Rig-veda*. 2. (Kaushītaki) the name of a Brāhmaṇa, an Āraṇyaka, and a Upanishad. The Brāhmana has been published with a translation by professor Cowell in the *Bibliotheca Indica*.

KAUŚIKA. A devotee mentioned in the *Mahābhārata* as having gone through a hell of torment for having pointed out to robbers a road by following which they pursued and killed some persons who fled from them.

KAUŚIKAS. Descendants of Kuśika. In one of the

hymns of the *Rig-veda* the epithet is given to Indra.

KAUŚIKĪ. The river Kosī in Bihār, but there were more rivers bearing this name. Satyavatī, mother of Jamadagni is said to have been changed into a river of this name.

KAUSTUBHA. A celebrated jewel obtained at the churning of the ocean, and worn by Vishṇu or Krishṇa on his bosom.

KAUṬILYA. Another name of Chāṇakya, the minister of Chandra-gupta.

KAUTSA. A rationalistic philosopher, who lived before the days of Yāska the author of the Nirukta, regarded "the Veda as devoid of meaning, and the Brahmanas as false interpretatios." Yāska replied to his objections.

KAUTUKA-SARVASWA. A modern farce, in two acts, by a Pandit named Gopīnātha. "It is a satire upon princes who addict themselves to idleness and sensuality, and fail to patronise the Brāhmans."— *Wilson*.

KAVASHA, KAVASHA-AILŪSHA. Son of Ilūsha by a slave girl, he was author of several hymns in the tenth book of the *Rig-veda*. The *Aitareya Brāhmaṇa* relates that the Rishis were performing a sacrifice on the banks of the Saraswatī, and that Kavasha was with them; but they drove him from among them because he was the son of a slave, and therefore not entitled to drink the water of the Saraswatī. When he was alone in the desert, a prayer was revealed to him by which he prevailed over the Saraswatī, and its waters came and surrounded him. The Rishis saw this, and knowing that it was the special favour of the gods, they admitted him to their society.

KAVI-RĀJA. Author of a poem of studied ambiguity called Rāghava-Pāndaviyam.

KĀVYA-DARŚA. 'Mirror of poetry.' A work on the Ars Poetica by Śrī Dandī, it has been printed in the *Bibliotheca Indica*.

KĀVYA-PRAKĀSA. A work on poetry and rhetoric by Mammaṭa Bhaṭṭa of Kashmīr.

KAVYAS, KĀVYAS. A class of Pitris; according to some they are the names of men of the third caste.

KĀYAVYA. The son of a Kshatriya by a Nishāda female, who is related in the *Mahābharata* to have risen by virtue, knowledge, and devotion from the state of a Dasyu to perfection.

KEDĀREŚA, KEDĀRA-NĀTHA. A name of Śiva. Name of one of the twelve great Lingas. Shapeless mass of stone at Kedāra-nātha in the Himālayas.

KEKAYA. *See* Kaikeya.

KELI-KILA. A demigod attendant upon Śiva.

KENA, KENOPANISHAD. Name of a Upanishad translated by Dr. Roer for the *Bibliotheca Indica*.

KERAKAS. One-footed men who live in forests, according to the *Mahābhārata*.

KERALA. The country of Malabar proper on the western coast.

KEŚAVA. 'Having much or fine hair.' A name of Vishṇu or Krishṇa.

KEŚĪ, KEŚIN. In the *Mahābhārata*, a demon who fought with and was defeated by Indra. In the Purāṇas, a Daitya who took the form of a horse and attacked Krishṇa, but was killed by that hero thrusting his arm into his jaws and rending him asunder.

KEŚINĪ. Wife of Viśravas and mother of Rāvaṇa; also called Kaikasī.

KEŚI-DHWAJA. Son of Krita-dhwaja, Keśi-dhwaja "was endowed with spiritual knowledge," and he had a cousin, Khāndikya, who "was diligent in the way of works and was renowned for religious rites." There was contention and hostilities between them, and Khāndikya was driven from his dominions but they subsequently became useful to each other and friendly. Khāndikya by his practical religion enabled Keśi-dhwaja to make atonement for the killing of a cow, and Kesi-dhwaja initiated Khāndikya in the mysteries of spiritual meditation (*yoga*).

KETU. The descending node in astronomy, represented by a dragon's tail; also a comet or meteor, and the ninth of the planets. he is said to be a Dānava, and son of Viprachitti and Sinhikā, he is also called A-kacha, 'hairless;' Asleshā-bhava, 'cut off;' Munda, 'bald.' *See* Rāhu.

KHĀNDAVA, KHĀNDAVA-PRASTHA. A forest and country on the banks of the Yamunā, which the Pāndavas received as their share when Dhrita-rāshtra divided his kingdom. In it they built the city of Indra-prastha and made it their capital. The forest was consumed with fire by the god Agni assisted by Krishṇa and Arjuna.

KHĀNKIKYA. *See* Kesi-dhwaja.

KHARA. A man-eating Rākshasa, the younger brother of Rāvana. He was killed by Rāma-chandra.

KHARVA. A dwarf. *See* Vālakhilya.

KHASĀ. A daughter of Daksha, wife of Kaśyapa, and mother of the Yakshas and Rākshasas, called after her Khasāt-majas.

KHASAS, KHASĀKAS, KHASĪKAS. An outlying or border people classed with the Śakas and other northern tribes. Professor Wilson thought that traces of them might be sought among the barbarous tribes on the north-east of Bengal, the Khasiyas.

KHATWĀNGA (also called Dilīpa). A prince of the Solar race. In a battle between the gods and the demons he rendered great assistance to the former, who desired him to seek a boon. He wanted to know the duration of his life, and the answer was, "Only an hour." He hastened to the world of mortals, and by earnest prayer he hecame united with the supreme being, Vishnu.

KĪCHAKA. Brother-in-law of the king of Virāṭa, who was commander of the forces and general director of the state affairs. He made love to Draupadī, and was slain by Bhīma.

KĪKATA. A country inhabited by people who were not Āryans; it is identified with Magadha or South Bihār.

KILATĀKULI. (Kilata + Akuli.) Two priests of the Asuras, who, according to the *Śatapatha Brāhmaṇa*, exercised a special influence between Manu and an "Asura-slaying voice."

KIM-PURUSHA. 'What man?' An indescribable man; one of a low type, partaking of the nature and appearance of animals. In later times it is synonymous with Kinnara. Name of a region between Himavat and Hemakūta. Also of a king of the latter region.

KIN-NARAS. 'What men?' Mythical beings with the form of a man and the head of a horse. They are celestial choristers and musicians, dwelling in the paradise of Kuvera on Kailāsa. They sprang from the toe of Brahmā with the Yakshas, but according to others, they are sons of Kaśyapa. They are also called Aśwa-mukhas, Turanga-vaktras, 'horse-faced,' and Mayus.

KIRĀTĀRJUNĪYA. A poem descriptive of the combat between Siva in the guise of a Kirāta or mountaineer and the Pāndu prince Arjuna. The story is first told in the *Mahābhārata*, and has been worked up in a poem of eighteen cantos by Bhāravi. Part of it has been translated into German by Schutz. There are several editions of the text. *See* Arjuna.

KIRĀTAS. Foresters and mountaineers living in the mountains of the east. (There is a tribe in the Central Himālayas called Kirāntis). They are described in the *Ramāyaṇa* as "islanders, who eat raw fish, live in the waters, and are mentigers" (men below and tigers above, according to the commentator. Their females are described as "gold-coloured and pleasant to behold," and as having "sharp-pointed hair-knots." They are perhaps the Cirrhadae placed on the Coromandel coast by classic writers.

KIRĪṬIN. 'Crowned with a diadem.' A title of Indra and also of Arjuna.

KIRMĪRA. A monster Rākshasa, brother of Vaka. He opposed the entrance of the Pāndavas into the Kāmyaka forest, and threatened that he would eat Bhīma. A furious combat ensued, in which Bhīma and the demon hurled large trees at each other, but the demon was at length strangled, with all his bones broken by Bhīma.

KISHKINDHYA. A country in the peninsula, thought to be in Mysore, which was taken by Rāma from the monkey king Bālī, and given back to his brother Sugrīva, the friend and ally of Rāma.

KOHALA. An ancient sage, to whom the invention of the drama is attributed; also a writer on music.

KOSALA. A country on the Sarayu river, having Ayodhyā for its capital. The name is variously applied to other countries in the east, and in the south, and in the Vindhya mountains. It probably widened with the dominions of its rulers, and part of Bihar is called Dakshina-Kosala, the southern Kosala.

KOTAVĪ, KOTARĪ, KOTTAVĪ. 'A naked woman.' A mystical goddess, the tutelary deity of the Daityas, and mother of Bāna the demon. The name is sometimes applied to Durgā.

KRATU. One of the Prajāpatis, and sometimes reckoned among the great Rishis and mind-born sons of Brahmā. The *Vishnu Purāna* says that his wife Samnati brought forth the 60,000 Vālikhilyas, pigmy sages no bigger than a joint of the thumb.

KRAUNCHA. 1. A pass situated somewhere in the Himālayas, said to have been opened by Paraśu-rāma with his arrows to make a passage from Kailāsa to the south. The *Vāyu Purāna* attributes the splitting of the mountain to Kārttikeya. Indra and Kārttikeya had a dispute about their respective powers, and agreed to decide it by running a race round the mountain. They disagreed as to the result, and therefore appealed to the mountain, who decided in favour of Indra. "Kārttikeya hurled his lance at the mountain and at once pierced it and the demon Mahisha." 2. A confederate of the demon Tāraka, against whom Kārttikeya led the gods and triumphed. 3. One of the seven Dwīpa. *See* Dwīpa.

KRISHṆA. The moden deity Krishṇa is the most celebrated hand of Indian mythology. He is said to be the eighth incarnation of Vishnu. A vast number of legends and fables has gathered around him, his having sport with Radha and Gopis, the variations of his life and his recitation of the *Gita* in the battlefied to Arjuna are well known these is India's. The popular history of Krishṇa, especially of his childhood is given in the *Purāṇas.* The *Bhāgvata Purāṇa* is a great authority.

KRISHṆĀ. The personal name of Drupadī.

KRISHNA DWAIPĀYANA. A name of Vyāsa.

KRITĀNTA. A name of Yama, the god of death.

KRITA-VARMAN. A Kuru warrior, one of the last surviving three who made the murderous night attack upon the camp of the Pāndavas. He was killed in a drunken brawl at Dwārakā. He was also called Bhoja.

KRITA-VĪRYA. Son of Dhanaka and father of Arjuna who is better known by his patronymic Kārta-vīrya. Krita-vīrya was a great patron of the Bhrigus, and according to the Purānas, "he ruled over the whole earth with might and justice, and offered 10,000 sacrifices. Of him this verse is still recited, "The kings of the earth will assuredly never pursue his steps in sacrifice, in munificence, in devotion, in courtesy, and in self-control."

KRITA YUGA. The first age of the world, a period of 1,728,000 years.

KRITTIKĀS. The Pleiades. The six nurses of Kārttikeya the god of war. They were daughters of a king according to one legend, wives of Rishis according to another.

KRIYĀ-YOGA-SĀRA. A portion of the *Padma Purāṇa* treating of rites and ceremonies. See *Padma Purāṇa*.

KRODHA, KRODHA-VASĀ. One of the many daughters of Daksha and sister-wives of Kaśyapa. She was the mother "of all sharp-toothed monsters, whether on the earth, amongst the birds, or in the waters, that were devourers of flesh."

KSHAṆADĀ-CHARA. 'Night walkers.' Ghosts of evil character, goblins, Rākshasas.

KSHAPAṆAKA. An author who was one of "the nine gems" at the court of Vikramāditya.

KSHATRIYA. The second or regal and warrior caste.

KSHATTRI. A name by which Vidura was familiarly called. The term. as explained by Manu, means the son of a Sūdra father and Brāhman mother, but Vidura's father was a Brāhman and his mother a slave girl.

KSHEMAKA. Son of Nira-mitra or Nimi, and the last prince of the Lunar race. There is a memorial verse quoted in the *Vishnu Purāna* which says. "The race which gave origin to Brāhmans and Kshatriyas, and which was purified by regal sages, terminated with Kshemaka in the Kali age."

KSHEMA-VRIDDHI. A general of the Śālwas who was commander in the army which attacked Dwārakā, and was defeated by Krishna's son, Sāmba.

KULA-PARVATAS. 'Family mountains.' A series or system of seven chains of mountains in Southern India. They are Mahendra, Malaya, Sahya, Śuktimat, Riksha (for which Gandha-mādana is sometimes substituted), Vindhya and Pāripātra. Mahendra is the Orissa chain; Malaya, the hills of Malabar proper, the south part of the Western Ghāts; Sahya, the northern parts of the Western Ghāts; Śuktimat is doubtful; Riksha, the mountains of Gondwāna; Vindhya is here applied to the eastern division of the Vindhya mountains; and Pāripātra, or Pāriyātra as it is frequently written, applies to the northern and western portions of the same range. The classification seems to have been known to Ptolemy, for he specifies seven ranges of mountains, but his names are not in accord.

KULIKA. One of the eight serpent kings, described as a dusky brown colour and having a half-moon on his head.

KULINDAS. A people living in the north-west.

KULLŪKA-BHAṬṬA. The famous commentator on Manu, whose gloss was used by Sir W. Jones in making the translation of Manu.

KUMĀRA. A name of Skanda, god of war. In the Brāhmanas the term is applied to Agni.

KUMĀRAS. Mind-born sons of Brahmā, who, declining to create progeny, remained ever boys and ever pure and innocent. There are four of them, Sanat-kumāra, Sananda, Sanaka, and Sanātana; a fifth, Ribhu, is sometimes added. *See* Vishnu Purāna.

KUMĀRA-SAMBAVA. 'The birth of the war god (Kumāra).' A poem by Kāli-dāsa. The complete work consists of sixteen cantos, but only seven are usually given.

KUMĀRĪ. 'The damsel.' An epithet of Sītā, also of Durgā. Cape Comorin.

KUMĀRILA-BHATTA, KUMĀRILA-SWĀMĪ. A celebrated teacher of the Mīmānsā philosophy and opponent of the Buddhists, whom he is said to have extirpated by argument and by force. He was senior to Śankarāchārya, in whose presence he is recorded to have burnt himself.

KUMBHA-KARṆA. Son of Viśravas by his Rākshasa wife Keśinī, and brother of Rāvaṇa. A monster who, under the curse of Brahmā (or, as otherwise represented, as a boon), slept for six months at a time and remained awake for only a single day. When Rāvana was hard pressed by Rāma he sent to arouse Kumbha-karna. He was armoured with great difficulty. After drinking 2000 jars of liquor he went to consult with his brother, and then took the field against the monkey army. He beat down Su-grīva, the monkey chief, with a large stone, and carried him a prisoner into Lankā. When he returned to the battle he encountered Rāma, and after a stout fight he was defeated, and Rāma cut off his head.

KUMUDA. 'A lotus.' A Naga or serpent king whose sister, Kumudvatī, married Kusa, son of Rāma.

KUMUDVATĪ. A Nāga or serpent princess whose marriage to Kuśa, son of Rāma, is described in the *Raghuvanśa*.

KUṆDINA-PURA. The capital of Vidarbha. It survives as themodern Kundapur, situated about 40 miles east of Amarāvatī, in Berar.

KUNTALA. A country in the Dakhin, about Adoni; the Dakhin.

KUNTĪ. (also called Prithā and Pārshnī). 1. Daughter of the Yādava prince (Śūra, king of the Śūrasenas), whose capital was Mathurā on the Yamunā. She was sister of Vasu-deva, and was given by her father to his childless cousin Kunti-bhoja, by whom she was brought up. In her maidenhood she showed such respectful devotion to the sage Dur-vāsas, that he gave her a charm by means of which she might have a child by any god she pleased to invoke. She called upon the sun, and by him had a son named Karṇa, but without any detriment to her virginity; still, to keep the affair secret, the child was exposed on the banks of the Yamunā. Subsequently she married Pāndu, whom she chose at a swayam-vara, and bore three sons, Yudhishthira, Bhīma, and Arjuna, who were called Pāndavas although they were said to be the sons of the gods Dharma, Vāyu, and Indra respectively. This may have happened, as is stated, from the potency of the old charm, but if so, it is strange that Mādrī, the second wife of Pāndu, should have enjoyed the same privilege, having borne twin children to the Aświns. This difficulty, however, is got over by a statement that Kuntī imparted to her the charm. Kuntī was a discreet and devoted mother, and although rather jealous of Mādrī, she was a kind mother to her children after Mādrī was burnt on her husband's pyre. After the end of the great war she retired into the forest with Dhritarāshtra and his wife Gāndhārī, and there they all perished in a forest fire. 2. Name of a people and country in Upper India.

KUNTI-BHOJA. King of the people called Kuntis. The adoptive father of Kuntī.

KŪRMA-AVATĀR. The tortoise incarnation. *See* Avatāra.

KŪRMA PURĀṆA. "That in which Janārdana (Vishṇu), in the form of a tortoise, in the regions under the earth, explained the objects of life—duty, wealth, pleasure, and liberation,—in communication with Indradyumna and the Rishis in the proximity of Śakra, which refers to the Lakshmī kalpa, and contains 17,000 stanzas, is the Kūrma Purāṇa." The account given in the Purāṇa and its actual contents donot agree with this description. "The name being that of an Avatāra of Vishṇu, might lead us to expect a Vaishṇava work; but it is always and correctly classed with the Śaiva Purāṇas, the greater portion of it inculcating the worship of Śiva and Durgā. The date of this Purāṇa cannot be very remote."—*Wilson*.

KURU. A prince of the Lunar race, son of Samvaraṇa by Tapatī, a daughter of the sun. He ruled in the north-west of India over the country around Delhi. A people called Kurus, and dwelling about Kuru-kshetra in that part of India, are connected with him. He was ancestor both of Dhrita-rāshtra and Pāndu, but the patronymic Kaurava is generally applied to the sons of the former.

KURU-JĀNGALA. A forest country in the upper part of the Doāb.

KURU-KSHETRA. 'The field of the Kurus.' A plain in Haryana where the great battle between the Kauravas and Pandavas was fought. It lies south-east of Thānesar, not far from Pānipat, the scene of many battles in later days.

KUŚA. One of the twin sons of Rāma and Sītā. After the death of Rāma, his two sons Kuśa and Lava became kings of the Southern and Northern Kosalas. Kuśa built Kuśa-sthalī or Kuśāvatī in the Vindhyas, and made it his capital. *See* Rāma.

KUŚA-DHWAJA. A brother of Janaka, king of Mithilā, and consequently uncle of Sītā. His two daughters, Māndavī and Śruta-kīrtti, were married to Bharata and Śatru-ghna, the sons of Janaka. Some make him king of Sānkāśyā, and others king of Kāśī, and there are differences also as to his genealogy.

KUŚĀMBA. Son of Kuśa and a descendant of Purūravas. He undertook devout penance to obtain a son equal to Indra, and that god was so alarmed at his austerities, that he himself became incarnate as Gādhi, son of Kuśāmba.

KUŚA-STHALĪ. 1. A city identical with or standing on the same spot as Dwārakā, it was built by Raivata, and was the capital of his kingdom called Ānarta. When Raivata went on a visit to the region of Brahmā, his city was destroyed by Puṇya-janas, *i.e.*, Yakshas or Rākshasas. 2. A city built by Kuśa, son of Rāma, on the brow of the Vindhyas. It was the capital of Southern Kosalā. Also called Kuśā-vatī.

KUŚĀ-VATĪ. The capital of Southern Kosala, built upon the Vindhyas by Kusa, son of Rāma.

KUSHMĀNDAS. 'Gourds.' A class of demigods or demons in the service of Śiva.

KUŚIKA. A king who, according to some, was the father of Viśwāmitra, or, according to others, the first of the race of Kuśikas from whom Gādhi, the father of Viśwāmitra descended.

KUSUMA-PURA. 'The city of flowers.' Pāṭali-putra or Patra.

KUSUMĀYUDHA. A name of Kāma, or Cupid as the bearer of the bow (*āyudha*) or flowers (*kusuma*).

KUTSA. A Vedic Rishi and author of hymns, he is represented as being persecuted by Indra, but on one occasion he was defended by that god against the demon Sushna. It is said that Indra took him to his place, and that they were so much alike that even Śachī or Pushpothatā, Indra's wife, did not know which was her husband.

KUVALĀŚWA, KUVALAYĀŚWA. A prince of the Solar race, who, according to the *Vishnu Purāna*, had 21,000 sons, but the *Hari-vansa* numbers them only as 100. Attended by his sons he attacked the great Asura, Dhundhu, who lived in a sea of sand, and harassed the devotions of the pious sage Uttanka. They unearthed the demon and slew him. This exploit of Kuvalāswa got the title of Dhundhu-māra, slayer of Dhundhu, but all his sons except three perished by the fiery breath of the monster.

KUVALAYĀPĪḌA. An immense elephant, or a demon in elephantine form, belonging to Kansa, and employed by him to trample Krishṇa and Bala-rāma to death. The attempt failed and the elephant was killed.

KUVERA. The god of wealth.

L

LAGHU-KAUMUDĪ. A modern and very much simplified edition of Pāṇini's Grammar by Varada Rāja. It has been edited and translated by Dr. Ballantyne.

LAKSHMAṆA. 1. Son of King Daśa-ratha by his wife Sumitrā. He was the twin brother of Śatru-ghna, and the half-brother and especial friend of Rāma-chandra. Under the peculiar circumstances of his birth, one-eighth part of the divinity of Vishṇu became manifest in him. (*See* Daśa-ratha.) But according to the *Adhyātma Rāmāyaṇa,* he was an incarnation of Sesha. When Rāma left his father's court to go to the hermitage of Viśwāmitra, Lakshmaṇa accompanied him, and afterwards attended on him in his exile and in all his wanderings. He was also very attached to Rāma's wife Sītā, which gave rise to the reproach that the two brothers were husbands of one wife. On one occasion, indeed, Sītā reproached Lakshmaṇa that he did not hasten to rescue Rāma from danger, because he wished to obtain herself. His own wife was Ūrmilā, the sister of Sītā, and he had two sons, Angada and Chandra-ketu. While Rāma and Lakshmaṇa were living in the wilderness, a Rākshasī named Śūrpanakhā, sister of Rāvaṇa, fell in love with Rāma and made advances to him. He jestingly referred her to Lakshmaṇa, who in like manner sent her back to Rāma. When she was again repulsed she attacked Sītā, whom Rāma was obliged to defend. Rāma then called upon Lakshmaṇa to disfigure the Rākshasī, and accordingly he cut off her nose and ears. The mutilated female called upon her brother to avenge her, and a fierce war ensued. When Sītā was carried off by Rāvaṇa, Lakshmaṇa accompanied Rāma in his search, and he ably and bravely supported him in his war against Rāvaṇa. Rāma's earthly career was drawing to a close, and time was sent to inform him that he must elect whether to stay longer on earth, or to return to the place from whence he had come. While they were in conference, the irascible sage Durvāsas came and demanded to see Rāma instantly, threatening him with the most direful curses if any delay was allowed to occur. To save his brother Rāma from the threatened curse, but to himself from breaking in upon Rāma's interview with Time, he went in and brought Rāma out. Lakshmaṇa knowing his fate, retired to the river Sarayū and resigned himself. The gods then showered down flowers upon him and conveyed him bodily to heaven. 2 A son of Duryodhana, killed by Abhimanyu.

LAKSHMĪ. The word occurs in the *Rig-veda* with the sense of good fortune, and in the *Atharva-veda* the idea has become personified in females both of a lucky and unlucky character. The *Taittirīya Sanhitā*, as explained by the commentator, makes Lakshmī and Srī to be two wives of Āditya, and the *Śatapatha Brāmaṇa* describes Śrī as issuing forth from Prajāpati.

Lakshmī or Śrī in later times is the goddess of fortune, wife of Vishnu, and mother of Kāma. The origin ascribed to her by the Rāmāyaṇa is the one commonly received. According to this legend she sprang, like Aphrodite, from the froth of the ocean, in full beauty with a lotus in her hand, when it was churned by the gods and the Asuras. Another legend represents her as floating on the flower of a lotus at the creation. With reference to this origin, one of her names is Kshīrābdhi-tanayā, 'daughter of the sea of milk.' From her connection with the lotus she is called Padmā. According to the Purānas, she was the daughter of Bhrigu and Khyāti. The *Vishṇu Purāṇa* says, "Her first birth was the daughter of Bhrigu by Khyāti. It was at a subsequent period that she was produced from the sea at the chuning of the ocean... When Hari was born as a dwarf, Lakshmī appeared from a lotus (as Padmā or Kamalā). When he was born as Rāma of the race of Bhrigu (or Paraśu-rāma), she was Dharaṇī. When he was Rāghava (Rāma-chandra), she was Sītā.

And when he was Krishṇa she became Rukminī. In the other descents of Vishnu she is his associate." One version of the Rāmāyaṇa also affirms that "Lakshmī, the mistress of the world, was born by her own will, in a beautiful field opened up by the plough," and received from Janaka the name of Sītā.

Lakshmī is said to have four arms, but she is the type of beauty, and is generally depicted as having only two. In one hand she holds a lotus. "She has no temples, but being goddess of abundance and fortune, she continues to be assiduously courted, and is not likely to fall into neglect," Other names of Lakshmī are Hīrā, Indirā, Jaladhi-jā, 'ocean-born;' Chanchalā or Lolā, 'the fickle,' as goddess of fortune; Loka-mātā, 'mother of the world.'

LALITA-VISTARA. A work in Sanskrit verse on the life and doctrines of Buddha. It has been printed in the *Bibliotheca Indica*.

LĀNGALĪ. 'Armed with a ploughshare.' Bala-rāma.

LANKĀ. 1. The island of Sri Lanka. The city is described in the Rāmāyaṇa as of vast extent and of great magnificence, with seven broad moats and seven stupendous walls of stone and metal. It is said to have been built of gold by Viśwa-karma for the residence of Kuvera, from whom it was taken by Rāvana. The *Bhāgavata Purāṇa* represents that the island was originally the summit of Mount Meru, which was broken off by the god of the wind and hurled into the sea. 2. Name of one of the Śākinīs or evil spirits attendant on Śiva and Devī.

LĀṬA. A country comprising Kandesh and part of Guzerat about the Mhye river. It is also called Lār.

LĀTYĀYANA. Author of a Sūtra work.

LAVA. One of the twin sons of Rāma and Sītā, he reigned at Śrāvastī.

LAVANA. A Rākshasa, son of Madhu by Kumbhīnasī, the sister of Rāvaṇa and daughter of Viśravas, he inherited from his father an invincible trident which had been presented to him by Siva. He was without his weapon when he was attacked by surprise and killed by Śatru-ghna. Lavana was king of Mathurā and Śatru-ghna succeeded him.

LIKHITA. Author of a Dharma-sāstra or code of law.

LĪLĀVATĪ. 'Charming.' The fanciful title of that chapter of Bhāskara's *Siddhānta-śiromaṇi* which treats of arithmetic and geometry.

LINGA, LINGAM. The male organ. The phallus. The symbol under which Siva is universally worshipped. It is of comparatively modern introduction and is unknown to the Vedas, but it receives distinct notice in the *Mahābhārata*.

The following are the twelve great Lingas:—

1. *Soma-nātha*. 'Lord of the moon.' At Somnāth Pattan, a city which still remains in Gujarat. This was the celebrated "idol" destroyed by Mahmūd of Ghaznī.

2. *Mallikārjuna* or *Śrī-śaila*. 'The mountain of Śrī.' On a mountain near the river Krishṇā.

3. *Mahā-kāla, Mahā-kāleswara*. At Ujjain. Upon the capture of Ujjain in the reign of Altamsh, 1231 A.D., this deity of stone was carried to Delhi and there broken up.

4. *Omkāra*. This is also said to have been at Ujjain, but it is probably the shrine of Mahādeva at Omkāra Māndhāttā, on the Narmadā.

5. *Amareśwara*. 'God of gods.' This is also placed at Ujjain.

6. *Vaidya-nātha*. 'Lord of Physicians.' At Deoghar in Jharkhand. The temple is still in being, and is a celebrated place of pilgrimage.

6. *Rāmeśa* or *Rāmeśwara*. 'Lord of Rāma.' On the island of Ramisseram, between the continent and Ceylon. This Lingam, whose name signifes 'Rāma's lord,' is fabled to have been set up by Rāma. The temple is still in tolerable repair, and is one of the most magnificent in India.

8. *Bhīma Śankara*. In Dākinī. This is in all probability the same with Bhīmeśwara, a Lingam worshipped at Dracharam, in the Rājama Rājamahendrī (Rajamundry) district, and there venerated as one of the twelve.

9. *Viśweśwara*. 'Lord of all.' At Benares. It has been for many centuries the chief object of worship at Benares. Also called Jyotir-lingam.

10. *Tryambaka, Tryaksha*. 'Tri-ocular.' On the banks of the Gomatī.

11. *Gautameśa*. 'Lord of Gautama.'

12. *Kedāreśa, Kedāra-nātha*. In the Himālaya. The deity is represented as a shapeless mass of rock.

LINGA PURĀṆA. "Where Maheśwara (Śiva), present in the Agni Linga, explained (the objects of life), virtue, wealth, pleasure, and final liberation, at the end of the Agni Kalpa, that Purāṇa, consisting of 11,000 stanzas, was called the Linga by Brahmā himself." This Purāṇa, which dates to earlier than the 8th or 9th century, conforms accurately enough to this description. "Although the Linga holds a prominent place in this Purāṇa, the spirit of the worship is as little influenced by the character of the type as can well be imagined. There is nothing like the phallic orgies of antiquity: it is all mystical and spiritual. The work has preserved, apparently, some Śaiva legends of an early date, but the greater part is ritual and mysticism of comparatively recent introduction."—*Wilson*.

LOHA-MUKHAS. 'Iron-faced men.' Described in the *Mahā-bhārata* as swift, one-footed, undecaying, strong men-eaters.

LOKA. A world, a division of the universe. In general the tri-loka or three worlds are heaven, earth, and hell. Another classification enumerates seven, exclusive of the seven infernal regions, which are classed under Pātāla. The upper worlds are:—(1) Bhur-loka, the earth. (2) Bhuvar-loka, the space between the earth and the sun, the region of the Munis, Siddhas, etc. (3) Swar-loka, the heaven of Indra, between the sun and the polar star.

(4) Mahar-loka, the usual abode of Bhrigu and other saints, who are supposed to be co-existent with Brahmā. During the conflagration of these lower worlds the saints ascend to the next, or (5) Jana-loka, which is described as the abode of Brahmā's sons, Sanaka, Sānanda, and Sanat-kumāra. Above this is the (6) Tapar-loka, where the deities called Vairāgīs reside. (7) Satya-loka or Brahmā-loka, is the abode of Brahmā. The first three worlds are destroyed at the end of each kalpa, or day of Brahmā; the last three at the end of his life, or of a hundred of his years; the fourth loka is equally permanent, but is uninhabitable from heat at the time the first three are burning. The seventh exempts beings from further birth.

Another enumeration calls the seven worlds earth, sky, heaven, middle region, place of birth, mansion of the blest, and abode of truth; placing the sons of Brahmā in the sixth division, and stating the fifth, or Jana-loka, to be that where animals destroyed in the general conflagration are born again.

The Sānkhya and Vedānta schools of philosophy recognise eight lokas or regions of material existence:— (1) Brahmā-loka, the world of the superior deities; (2) Pitri-loka, that of the Pitris, Rishis, and Prajāpatis; (3) Soma-loka, of the moon and planets; (4) Indra-loka, of the inferior deities; (5) Gandharva-loka, of heavely spirits; (6) Rākshasa-loka, of the Rākshasas; (7) Yaksha-loka, of the Yakshas; (8) Pisācha-loka, of the Pisāchas or imps and fiends.

LOKĀLOKA. 'A world and no world,' A fabulous belt of mountains bounding the outermost of the seven seas and dividing the visible world from the regions of darkness. It is "ten thousand yojanas in breadth, and as many in height, and beyond it perpetual darkness invests the mountains all around, which darkness is again encompassed by the shell of an egg." It is called also Chakra-vāda or Chakra-vāla.

LOKA-PĀLAS. Supporters or guardians of the world. The guardian deities who preside over the eight points of the compass, *i.e*, the four cardinal and four intermediate points of the compass are:—(1) Indra, east; (2) Agni, south-east; (3) Yama, south; (4) Sūrya, south-west; (5) Varuṇa, west; (6) Vāyu, north-west; (7) Kuvera, north; (8) Soma, north-east. Nirriti is by some substituted for No. 8.

Each of these guardian deities has an elephant who takes part in the defence and protection of the quarter, and these eight elephants are themselves called Loka-pālas:—(1) Indra's elephant at the east is Airāvata. He is also called Abhra-mātanga, 'elephant of the clouds;' Arkasodara, 'brother of the sun;' Nāga-malla, 'the fighting elephant;' Sadā-dāna, 'always in rut;' Madāmbara, 'covered with ichor.' His wife's name is Abhramu. (2) Agni's elephant at the south-east is Pundarīka and his female Kapilā. (3) Yama's at the south is Vāmana and his female is Pingalā. (4) Sūrya's at the south-west is Kumuda and his female is Anupamā. (5) Varuṇa's at the west is Anjana, whose female is Anjanavatī. (6) Vāyu's at the north-west is Pushpa-danta, whose female is Śubha-dantī. (7) Kuvera's at the north is Sārva-bhauma; and (8) Soma's elephant at the north-east is Su-pratīka. The two other females are Anjanā and Tāmra-karṇī, whose spouses are doubtful. Anjanāvatī is sometimes asigned to Su-pratīka. In the Rāmāyaṇa (1) Indra's eastern elephant is called Virūpāksha; (2) Varuṇa's elephant at the west, Saumanasa; (3) Yama's at the south is Mahā-padma, and (4) Kuvera's at the north is Hima-pāndara.

LOMA-HARSHANA (or Roma-harshana). A bard or panegyrist who was the first to give forth the Purānas.

LOMA-PĀDA (or Roma-pāda). A king of Anga, chiefly remarkable for his connection with Rishya-sringa (q.v.).

LOPĀMUDRĀ. A girl whom the sage Agastya formed from the most graceful parts of different animals and secretly introduced into the place of the king of Vidarbha, where the child was believed to be the daughter of the king. Agastya had made this girl with the object of having a wife after his own heart, and when she was mariageable he demanded her hand. The king was unwilling to consent, but was obliged to yield, and she became the wife of Agastya. Her name is explained as signifying that the animals suffered loss (*lopa*) by her engrossing their distinctive beauties (*mudrā*), as the eyes of the deer, etc. She is also called Kaushītakī and Vara-pradā. A hymn in the Rig-veda is attributed to her.

M

MADA. 'Intoxication'. Described in the *Mahābhārata* as "a fearful open-mouthed monster, created by the sage Chyavana, having teeth and grinders of portentous length, and jaws one of which enclosed the earth and the other the sky," who got Indra and the other gods into his jaws "like fishes in the mouth of a sea monster."

MADAYANTĪ. Wife of King Saudāsa or Kalmāsha-pada, she was allowed to consort with the sage Vaśishtha. According to some this was a meritorious act on the king's part and a favour to Vaśishtha; according to others it was for the sake of obtaining progeny.

MĀDHAVA. A name of Krishna or Vishṇu.

MĀDHAVA, MĀDHAVĀCHĀRYA. A celebrated scholar and religious teacher, he was a native of Tuluva, who became prime minister of Vīra Bukka Rāya, king of the great Hindu state of Vijaya-nagara, in the fourteenth century. He was brother of Sāyaṇa, the author of the great commentary on the Veda. Wilson observes, "Both the brothers are celebrated as scholars, and many important works are attributed to them; not only scholia on the Sanhitās and Brāhmaṇas of the Vedas, but original works on grammar and law; the fact no doubt being, that they availed themselves of those means which their situation and influence secured them, and employed the most learned Brāhmans they could attract to Vijayanagara upon the works which bear their names, and to which they contributed their own labour and learning; their works were therefore compiled under peculiar advantages, and are deservedly held in the highest estimation." The *Sarva-darśana-sangraha* and the *Sankshepa Śankaravijaya* are the works of Mādhava. Mādhava was a worshipper of Vishṇu, and as a religious philosopher he held the doctrine of *dwaita* or dualism, according to which the supreme soul of the universe and the human soul are distinct. Thus he was opposed to the teaching of Śankarāc harya, who was a follower of Śiva, and upheld the Vedānta doctrine of *a-dwaita,* "no duality," according to which God and soul, spirit—and matter, are all one.

MĀDHAVĪ. A name of Lakshmī.

MADHU. 1. A demon slain by Krishṇa.

2. Another, or the same demon, said to have been killed by Śatru-ghna.

MADHU-CHHANDAS. A son of Viśwāmitra, who had fifty sons older and fifty younger than this one; but they are spoken of as "a hundred sons". He is the reputed author of some hymns of the *Rig-veda.*

MADHU-KAŚĀ. Describd in the *Atharva-veda* as "the brilliant grand-daughter of the Maruts, the mother of the Ādityas, the daughter of the Vasus, the life of creatures, and the centre of immortality," she "sprang from the sky, the earth, the air, the sea, fire, and wind"; and it is added, "all creatures, worshipping her who dwells in immortality, rejoice in their hearts".

MADHURĀNIRUDDHA. A drama in eight acts by Śayani Chandra Śekhara. It is quite a modern work. "The subject is the secret love of Ūshā, daughter of the Asura Bāṇa and Aniruddha, grandson of Krishṇa. The piece abounds too much with description to be a good play; the style has considerable merit."—*Wilson.*

MADHU-SŪDANA. 'Slayer of Madhu,' a name of Krishṇa.

MADHYA-DEŚA. The middle country, described by Manu as "the tract situated between the Himavat and the Vindhya ranges to the east of Vināśana and to the west of Prayāga (Allahabad)." Another authority makes it the Doab.

MĀDHYANDINA. A Vedic school, a subdivision of the Vājasaneyī school, and connected with the *Śatapatha Brāhmaṇa.* It had also its own system of astronomy, and obtained its name from making noon (*madhya-dina*) the starting-point of the planetary movements.

MAHĀ-BHĀRATA. It is one of the first great epics of India, the other being *Rāmā-yaṇa*. It is ascribed to the poet Vyāsa. It concerns a feud over kingdom of Hastināpur between two groups of cousins, the five Pāndavas and the 100 Kauravās. The final battle was fought at Kurukshetrā, north of Delhi. *Mahābhārata* has been hailed as "the story of mankind".

The *Mahābhārata* is the biggest poem in the world. It consists of over 100,000 verses arranged in eighteen chapters. The *Bhāgvad-gītā* forms a part of the *Mahābhārata*. There are a number of tales interwoven in the *Mahābhārata*. These tales and different characters of the *Mahābhārata* exhibit human anger, hunger, love, jealousy, greed, dearth, revenge, envy, fear, pride and arrogance.

MADIRĀ. A name of Vāruṇī, wife of Varuṇa, and goddess of wine.

MADRA. Name of a country and people to the north-west of Hindustan. its capital was Śakala, and the territory extended from the Biyās to the Chināb, or, according to others, as far as the Jhelum.

MĀDRĪ. A sister of the king of the Madras, and second wife of Pāndu, to whom she bore twin-sons, Nakula and Sahadeva; but the Aświns are alleged to have been their real father. She became a satī on the funeral pyre of her husband.

MAGADHA. The country of South Bihar, where the Pāli language was spoken.

MĀGHA. A poet, son of Dattaka, and author of one of the great artificial poems called, *Śiśupāla-badha*, or, *Māgha-kāvya*.

MAGHAVAT, MAGHAVĀN. A name of Indra.

MAHĀ-BALI. A title of the dwarf Bali, whose city is called Mahābalipura, which name is applied to the Tamil "Māmallai-pura," or Seven Pagodas near Chennai.

MAHĀ-BHĀSHYA. A commentary by Patanjali on the Grammar of Pāṇini, in answer to the criticisms of Kātyāyana.

MAHĀ-BHOJA. *See* Bhoja.

MAHĀ-DEVA. 'The great god,' a name of Śiva. One of the Rudras.

MAHĀ-DEVĪ. 'The great goddess,' a name of Devī, the wife of Śiva. See Devī.

MAHĀ-KĀLA. 'Great Time.' 1. A name of Śiva in his destructive character. 2. One of the twelve great Lingas. (See Linga.) 3. In the caves of Elephanta this form of Śiva is represented with eight arms. In one hand he holds a human figure; in another, a sword or sacrificial axe; in a third, a basin of blood; in a fourth, the sacrificial bell; with two he is drawing behind him the veil which extinguishes the sun; and two are broken off. 4. Chief of the Gaṇas or attendants on Śiva.

MAHĀ-KĀVYAS. 'Great poems.' The six classified under this title are (1) *Raghu-vanśa;* (2) *Kumāra-sambhava;* (3) *Meghadūta;* (4) *Kirātārjunīya;* (5) *Śiśupāla-badha;* (6) *Naishadha-charitra.*

MAHĀ-MĀYĀ. See Māyā.

MAHĀ-NĀṬAKA. 'The great drama.' The *Hanumānnāṭ aka.*

MAHĀ-PADMA NANDA. The last of the Nanda dynasty. See Chandra-gupta. Total dissolution of the universe at the end of a kalpa, when the seven lokas and their inhabitants, men, saints, gods, and Brahmā himself, are annihilated. Also called Jahānaka, Kshiti, and Sanhāra.

MAHĀ-PURĀṆAS. 'The great Purāṇas.' The Vishṇu and the Bhāgavata, are the two great Purāṇas of the Vaishṇavas.

MAHĀ-PURUSHA. 'The great or supreme male;' the supreme spirit. A name of Vishṇu.

MAHĀRĀJIKAS. A Gaṇa or class of inferior deities, 236 or 220 in number.

MAHĀ-RĀSHTRA. The land of the Mahrattas.

MAHARSHIS (Mahārishis). 'Great Rishis.' The great Rishis or Prajāpatis.

MAHĀ-SENA. 'The great captain,' a name of Kārtikeya, god of war.

MAHAT. The great intellect produced at the creation.

MĀHĀTMYA. 'Magnanimity'. A legend of a shrine or other holy place.

MAHĀ-VĪRA CHARITA. 'The exploits of the great hero (Rāma).' A drama by Bhavabhūti, translated into English by Pickford. There are several editions of the text. "The situations an sentiments of this drama are of a stirring and martial description, and the language is adapted with singular felicity to the subject from which it springs."—Wilson.

MAHĀ-YOGĪ. 'The great ascetic,' a name of Śiva.

MAHĀ-YUGA. A great Yuga or age, consisting of 4,320,000 years.

MAHENDRA. A name of Indra. One of the seven mountain ranges of India; these hills which run from Gondwāna to Orissa and the Northern Circars. *See* Kula-parvatas.

MAHEŚWARA. A name of Śiva.

MAHISHA, MAHISHĀSURA. 1. The great Asura or demon killed by Skanda in the *Mahābhārata.*

2. Also a demon killed by Chandā or Durgā.

MAHISHMATĪ, MĀHISHMATĪ. The capital of Kārtavīrya, king of the Tālajanghas, who had a thousand arms. It has been identified by Colonel Tod with the village of Chuli Maheswar, which, according to him, is still called "the village of the thousand-armed."

MAHODAYA. A name of the city of Kanauj.

MAHORAGA (Mahā + uraga). 'Great serpent.' The serpent Śesha, or any other great serpent.

MAINĀKA. A mountain stated in the *Mahābhārata* to be north of Kailāsa. It is so called because it was the son of Himavat and Menakā. When, as the poets sing, Indra clipped the wings of the mountain, this is said to have been the only one which escaped. This mountain, according to some, stands in Central India, and, according to others, near the extremity of the Peninsula.

MAITREYA. A Rishi, son of Kuśarava, and disciple of Parāśara, he is one of the interlocutors in the *Vishṇu* and *Bhāgavata Purāṇas.*

MAITREYĪ. Wife of the Rishi Yājnawalkya, who was indoctrinated by her husband in the mysteries of religion and philosophy.

MAITRI, MAITRĀYAṆI. An Upanishad of the Black Yajur-veda.

MĀKANDĪ. A city on the Ganges, the capital of Southern Panchala.

MAKARA. A huge sea animal, which has been taken to be the crocodile, the shark, the dolphin, etc., but is probably a fabulous animal. It represents the sign Capricorn in the zodiac, and is depicted as having the head and forelegs of an antelope and the body and tail of a fish. It is the vehicle of Varuṇa, the god of the ocean, and its figure can be seem on the banner of Kāmadeva, god of love. It is also called Kanṭaka, Asita-danshṭra, 'black teeth,' and Jala-rūpa, 'water form'.

MĀKĀRAS. The five m's. See Tantra.

MAKHAVAT. A name of Indra.

MĀLATĪ-MĀDHAVA (Mālatī and Mādhava). A drama by Bhava-bhūti, translated by Wilson. "This drama," says the translator, "offers nothing to offend the most fastidious delicacy, and may be compared in this respect advantageously with many of the drama of modern Europe which treat of the passion (of love) that constitutes its subject."

MĀLAVA. The country of Mālwa.

MĀLAVIKĀGNIMITRA. (Mālavika and Agnimitra). A drama ascribed to Kāli-dāsa.

MALAYA. The country of Malabar proper; the mountains bordering Malabar. *See* Kula-parvatas.

MALINA-MUKHA. 'Black faced'. Rākshasas and other demons are represented as having black faces.

MĀLINI. 'Surrounded with a garland (māla)' of Champsa tree. A name of the city of Champā.

MALLIKĀRJUNA. A name of Śiva. One of the twelve great Lingas. *See* Linga.

MALLINĀTHA. A poet, and author of commentaries of great repute on several of the great poems, as the *Raghu-vanśa, Megha-duta, Śiśupāla-badha,* etc.,

MĀNASA. 'The intellectual', a name of the supreme being which has been defined in the *Mahābhārata* as. "The primeval god, without beginning or dissolution, indivisible, undecaying, and immortal, who is known and called by great Rishi Mānasa."

MĀNASA, MĀNASA-SAROVARA. The lake Mānasa in the Himālayas. According to *Vāyu Purāṇa* when the ocean fell from heaven upon Mount Meru, it ran four times round the mountain, then it divided into four rivers which ran down the mountain and formed four great lakes, Aruṇoda on the east, Sitoda on the west, *Mahābhadra* on the north, and Mānasa on the south. According to the mythological account, the river Ganges flows out of it, but in reality no river issues from this lake, though the river Satlej flows from another and larger lake called Rāvaṇa-hrāda, which lies close to the west of Manasa.

MANASĀ, MANASĀ-DEVĪ. Sister of the serpent king Śesha, and wife of the sage Jarat-kāru, she is also called Jagad-gaurī, Nityā (eternal), and Padmāvatī. She had especial power in counteracting the venom of serpents, and was hence called Vishaharā.

MĀNASĀ-PUTRAS. 'Mind (born) sons'. The seven or ten mind-born sons of Brahmā. See Prajāpati.

MANSA-TĀLA. The lion on which Devī rides.

MĀNAVA DHARMA-SĀSTRA. The code of Manu. See *Manu Sanhitā*.

MĀNAVA KALPA-SŪTRA. Manu's work on Vedic rites, part of which has been published in facsimile by Goldstucker.

MĀNAVī. The wife of Manu, also called Manāvī.

MANDA-KARṆI. A sage who dwelt in the Dandaka forest, and according to Rāmāyaṇa is said to have formed a lake which was known by his name. His austerities alarmed the gods, and Indra sent five Apsaras to beguile him from his penance of "standing in a pool and feeding on nothing but air for 10,000 years." They succeeded, and became his wives, and inhabited a house concealed in the lake, which, was called Panchāpsaras.

MANDĀKINĪ. The heavenly Ganges. The Ganges. An arm of the Ganges which flows through Kedārànātha. A river near the mountain Chitra-kūṭa in Bundelkhand. It was near the abode of Rāma and Sītā, and is mentioned both in the *Rāmâyaṇa* and *Mahābhārata*. It would seem to be the modern Pisuni.

MAṆDALA. 'A circle, orb.' A circuit or territorial division, as Chola-mandala, i.e., Coromandel. According to one arrangement, the Sanhitā of the *Rig-veda* is divided into ten Maṇdalas.

MAṆDALA-NRITYA. A circular dance. The dance of the Gopīs round Krishṇa and Rādhā.

MANDA-PĀLA. A childless saint, who, according to the *Mahābhārata*, after long perseverance in devotion and asceticism, died and went to the abode of Yama. As his desires were still unsatisfied, he wanted to know the cause, and was told that all his devotions had failed because he had no son, no *putra* (*put*, 'hell,' *tra*, 'drawer'), to save him from hell. He then assumed the form of a bird called Śārngikā, and by a female of that species, called Jaritā, he had four sons.

MANDARA. The great mountain which the gods used for the churming of the ocean. It is supposed to be the sacred mountain in Bhāgaplpur. *See* Kūrma-avatāra, *under* Avatāra.

MĀNDAVĪ. Daughter of Kuśa-dhwaja, cousin of Sītā, and wife of Rāma's brother Bharata.

MANDEHAS. A class of terrific Rākshasas, who were hostile to the sun and endeavoured to devour him.

MĀNDHĀTRI. A king, son of Yuvanāśwa, of the race of Ikshwāku, and author of a hymn in the *Rig-veda*. The *Harivansa* and some of the Purāṇas make Māndhātri to have been born in a natural way from his mother Gauri, but the *Vishṇu* and *Bhāgavata Purāṇas* tell an extraordinary story about his birth. Yuvanāśwa had no son, which grieved him much. Some holy sages near whom he lived instituted a religious rite to procure progeny for him. One night they placed a consecrated vessel of water upon an altar as part of their ceremony, and the water became endowed with prolific energy. Yuvanāśwa woke up in the night thirsty, and finding the water, he drank it. So he conceived, and in due time a child came forth from his right side. The sages then asked who would suckle the child, whereupon Indra appeared, gave his finger to the child and said, "He shall suck me," *mām ayam dhāsyati*. These words were contracted, and the boy was named Māndhātri. When he grew up he had three sons and fifty daughters.

MANDODARĪ. Rāvaṇa's favourite wife and the mother of Indra-jit.

MĀNDUKEYA. A teacher of the *Rig-veda*, who derived his knowledge from his father, Indra-pramati.

MĀNDUKYA. Name of an Upanishad translated by Dr. Roer in the *Bibliotheca Indica*.

MANGALA. The planet Mars, identified with Kārtikeya, the god of war. He was son of Śiva and the Earth, and as son of the Earth is called Angāraka, Bhauma, Bhūmi-putra, Mahī-suta.

MAṆI-BHADRA. The chief of the Yakshas and guardian of travellers.

MAṆIMAT. A Rākshasa slain by Bhīma.

MAṆI-PURA. A city on the sea-coast of Kalinga, where Babhru-vāhana, the son of Arjuna, dwelt. Wheeler identifies it with the modern Munnipur or Muneepore, east of Bengal; but this is very questionable.

MANMATHA. A name of Kāma, god of love.

MANTHARĀ. An ugly deformed slave, maid of Queen Kaikeyī, who stirred up her mistress's jealousy against Rāma-chandra, and led her to persuade King Daśarathā to banish Rāma from court. Śatru-ghna beat her and threatened to kill her, but she was saved by his brother Bharata.

MANTRA. That portion of the Veda which consists of hymns, as distinct from the Brāhmaṇas. *See* Veda.

MANU. (From the root *man*, to think.) 'The man.' This name belongs to fourteen mythological progenitors of mankind and rulers of the earth, each of whom holds sway for the period called a Manwantara *(manu-antara)*, the age of a Manu, i.e. a period of no less than 4,320,000 years. The names of the fourteen Manus are—(1) Swāyambhuva, (2) Swārochisha, (3) Auttami, (4) Tāmasa, (5) Raivata, (6) Chākshusha, (7) Vaivaśwata or Satya-vrata, (8) Sāvarṇa, (9) Daksha-sāvarṇa, (10) Brahmasāvarṇa, (11) Dharma-sāvarṇa, (12) Sāvarṇa or Rudra-sāvarṇa, (13) Rauchya, (14) Bhautya.

Ikshwāku, Nabhaga or Nriga, Dhrishṭa, Śaryāti, Narishyanta, Prānśu, Nābhāganedishṭa or Nābhānedishṭa, Karūsha, and Prishadhra were the sons of Manu Vaivaswata.

A curious and interestng legend of the deluge is connected with the seventh Manu, Vaivaswata. The first account of this is found in the *Śatapatha Brāhmaṇa*.

MANU-SANHITĀ. The well-known law-book, the Code of Manu, or Institutes of Manu. It is attributed to the first Manu, Swāyam-bhuva, who existed nearly thirty million years ago, but it bears the marks of being the production of more than one mind. This is the first and chief of the works classified as Smritis, ans is a collection or digest of current laws and creeds rather than a planned systematic code. It is the foundation of Hindu law, and is held in great reverence. The work belongs to a period later than that of the Vedas. It is apparently anterior to the philosophical schools. The fifth century B.C. is supposed to be about the time when it was composed, but the rules and precepts it contains had probably existed as traditions long before. It is commonly called the Code of Manu, and was current among the Mānavas, a class or school of Brāhmans who were followers of the Black Yajur-veda; but it deals with many subjects besides law, and is a most important record of old Hindu society. It is said to have consisted originally of 100,000 verses, arranged in twenty-four chapters; that Nārada is said to have shortened the work to 12,000 verses; and that Sumati made a second abridgment, reducing it to 4000, but only 2685 are extant. There was more than one rendering of the laws of the Mānavas, for a Brihan or Vrihan Manu, 'great Manu,' and Vriddha manu, 'old Manu,' are often referred to. Sir W. Jones's translation, edited by Haughton, is excellent, and is the basis of all others in French, German, etc.

MANWANTARA. (Manu-antara). The life or period of a Manu, 4,320,000 years.

MĀRĪCHA. A Rākshasa, son of Tārakā. According to the *Rāmāyaṇa* he interfered with a sacrifice which was being performed by Vishwāmitra, but was encountered by Rāma, who discharged a weapon at him, which drove him one hundred yojanas out to sea. He was afterwards the minister of Rāvaṇa, and accompanied him to the hermitage where Rāma and Sītā stayed. There, to mislead Rāma, he assumed the shape of a golden deer, which Rāma pursued and killed. On receiving his fatal wound he resumed a Rākshasa form and spoke, Rāma discovered whom he had killed but, in the meanwhile Rāvaṇa had carried off Sītā.

MARĪCHI. Chief of the Maruts. Name of one of the Prajāpatis. (*See* Prajāpati.) He is sometimes represented as springing direct from Brahmā. He was father of Kaśyapa, and one of the seven great Rishis. *See* Rishi.

MĀRISHĀ. Daughter of the sage Kandu, and wife of the Prachetasas, but from the mode of her birth she is called "the nursling of the trees, and daughter of the wind and the moon." She was mother of Daksha. Her mother was a celestial nymph named Pramlochā, who beguiled the sage Kaṇdu from his devotions and lived with him for a long time. When the sage awoke from his voluptuous delusion, he drove her from his presence. "She, passing through the air, wiped the perspiration from her with the leaves of the trees," and "the child she had conceived by the Rishi came forth from the pores of her skin in drops of perspiration. The trees received the living dews, and the winds collected them into one mass. Soma matured this by his rays, and gradually it increased in size till the exhalations that had rested on the tree-tops became the lovely girl named Mārishā."—*Vishnu Purāṇa.*

MĀRKAṆDEYA. A sage, the son of Mrikaṇda, and reputed author of the *Mārkaṇḍeya Purāṇa.* He was remarkable for his austerities and great age, and is called Dīrghāyus, 'the long-lived'.

MĀRKAṆDEYA PURĀṆA. "That Purāṇa in which commencing with the story of the birds that were acquainted with right and wrong, everything is narrated fully by Mārkaṇḍeya as it was explained by holy sages in reply to the question of the Muni, is called the Mārkaṇḍeya, containing 9000 verses." This Purāṇa is narrated in the first place by Mārkaṇḍeya, and in the second by certain fabulous birds profoundly versed in the Vedas, who relate their knowledge in answer to the questions of the sage Jaimini. "It has a character different from all the other Purāṇas. It presents an uninterrupted succession of legends, most of which, when ancient, are embellished with new circumstances, and, when new, partake so far of the spirit of the old, that they are disinterested creations of the imagination, having no particular motive, being designed to recommend no special doctrine or observance. They are most probably, for the greater part at least, original; and the whole has been narrated in the compiler's own manner, a manner superior to that of the Purāṇas in general, with exception of the Bhāgavata." The popular Durgā Māhātmya or Chandipātha is an episode of this Purāna. It may conjecturally be placed in the ninth or tenth century although Professor Banerjea places it in the eighth century. This Purāṇa has been published in the *Bibliotheca Indica,* and translated by the Rev. Professor K.M. Banerjea.

MĀRTTĀNDA. In the Vedas the sun or sun god.

MARTYA-MUKHA. 'Human-faced'. Any being in

which the figures of a man and animal are combined.

MARUTS. The storm gods, who hold a very prominent place in the Vedas, and are represented as friends and allies of Indra. Various origins are assigned to them. They are sons of Rudra, sons and brothers of Indra, sons of the ocean, sons of heaven, sons of earth. They are armed with lighting and thunderbolt, and "ride on the whirlwind and direct the storm." At one place they have been sent at thrice sixty, and in another only twenty-seven. In the *Rāmāyaṇa* they are repre sented to have their origin in an unborn son of Diti, whom Indra dashed into forty-nine pieces with his thunderbolt, and in compassion converted into Maruts. This is also the story told in the Purāṇas, and they are said to have obtained their name from the words *mā rodīh,* 'weep not,' which Indra addressed to them. There are a number of legends about him and these legends have manifestly been invented to explain those passages of the Vedas which make the Maruts the sons of Rudra. The world of the Maruts, called Māruta, is the appointed heaven of Vaiśyas. 2. The god of the wind, and regent of the north-west quarter.

MARUTTA. 1. A descendant of Manu Vaivaswata, he was a Chakravartī, or universal monarch, and performed a celebrated sacrifice. "Never," says the Vishṇu Purāṇa, "was beheld on earth a sacrifice equal to the sacrifice of Marutta. All the implements and utensils were made of gold. Indra was intoxicated with the libations of some juice, and the Brāhmans were enraptured with the magnificent donation they received. The winds of heaven encompassed the rite as guards, and the assembled gods attended to behold it." According to the *Vāyu Purāṇa,* Marutta was taken to heaven with his kindred and friends by Samvarta, the officiating priest at this sacrifice. But the *Markaṇdeya Purāṇa* says he was killed after he had laid down his crown and retired to the woods. 2. A king of the Solar race, who was killed by Vapushmat, and fearfully avenged by his son Dama.

MĀTALI. Charioteer of Indra.

MATANGA. 'An elephant.' A man who was brought up as a Brāhman but was the son of a Chaṇḍāla. In order to obtain elevation to the position of a Brāhman, he went through such a course of austerities as alarmed the gods. Indra refused to admit him. He persevered again for a hundred years, but still Indra persistently refused such an impossible request, and advised him to seek some other boon. Nothing daunted, he went on a thousand years longer, with the same result. Though dejected he did not despair, but proceeded to balance himself on his great toe. He continued to do this for a hundred years, when he was reduced to mere skin and bone, and was on the point of falling. Indra went to support him, but inexorably refused his request, but, "gave him the power of moving about like a bird, and changing his shape at will, and of being honoured and renowned." In the *Rāmāyaṇa*, Rāma and Sītā visited the hermitage of Matanga near Rishya-mūka mountain.

MĀTARI-ŚWAN. An aerial being who is represented in the *Rig-veda* as bringing down or producing Agni (fire) for the Bhrigus. It is supposed to be the wind by one.

MATHURĀ. An ancient and celebratd city on the right bank of theYamunā, the modern Mathurā. It was the birth place of Krishṇa and one of the seven sacred cities. The *Vishṇu Purāṇa* states that it was originally called Madhu or Madhu-vana, from the demon Madhu, who reigned there, but that when Lavaṇa, his son and successor, were killed by Śatrughna, the conqueror set up his own rule there and built a city which he called Madhurā or Mathurā.

MĀTRIS. 'Mothers', the divine mothers. These appear to have been originally the female energies of the great gods, as Brahmāṇī of Brahmā, Maheśwarī of Śiva, Vaishṇavī of Vishṇu, Indrāṇi or Aindrī of Indra, etc. The number varies from seven or eight to sixteen. They are connected with the Tantra worship, and are represented as worshipped Siva and attending upon his son Kārtikeya.

MATSYA. 'A fish.' 1. The Fish Incarnation. (*See* Avatāra.) 2. Name of a country. Wilson says, "Dinajpoor, Rungpoor, and Cooch Behar;" but there was more than one region of this name, and one would appear to have been situated in Northern India. Manu places Matsya in Brahmarshi. According to the *Mahābhārata,* King Virāṭa's capital was called Matsya, his people also were called Matsyas, and he himself was styled Matsya. General Cunningham finds it in the neighbourhood of Jaipur, and says that the town of Virāt or Bairāt, 105 miles south of Delhi, was its capital.

MATSYA PURĀṆA. This Purāṇa is so called from its contents having been narrated to Manu by Vishṇu in the form of a fish (matsya). Comprising between 14,000 and 15,000 stanzas, this work is a miscellaneous compilation, but includes in its contents the elements of a genuine Purāṇa. However, it is of too mixed a character to be considered as a genuine work of the Paurāṇik class. Many of its chapters are the same as parts of the Vishṇu and Padma Purāṇas. It has also drawn largely from the *Mahābhārata*. "Although a Śaiva work, it is not exclusively so, and it has no such sectarial absurdities as the Kūrma and Linga."

MAUNEYAS. A class of Gandharvas, sons of Kaśyapa, who dwelt beneath the earth, and were sixty million in number. They overpowered the Nāgas, and compelled them to fleee to Vishṇu for help and he sent Purukutsa against them who destroyed them.

MAURYA. The dynasty founded by Chandra-gupta at Pāṭali-putra (Patna) in Magadha. According to the *Vishṇu Purāṇa,* the Maurya kings were ten in number (1) Chandra-gupta, (2) Bindu-sāra, (3) Aśoka-vardhana, (4) Su-yasas, (5) Daśa-ratha, (6) Sangata, (7) Śāli-śūka, (8) Soma-śarman, (9) Śaśa-dharman, (10) Brihad-ratha and ruled for 137 years.

MAYA. A Daitya who was the architect of the Asuras, as Viśwa-karma was the the architect of the Suras or gods. He was son of Viprachitti and father of Vajra-kāmā and Mandodarī, wife of Rāvaṇa. He dwelt in the Deva-giri mountains not very far from Delhi, and his chief works were in the neighbourhood of that city, where he worked for men as well as as Daityas. The *Mahābhārata* speaks of a palace he built for the Pāndavas.

MĀYĀ. 'Illusion, deception.' 1. Illusion personified as a female form of celestial origin, created for the purpose of beguiling some individual. Sometimes identified with Durgā as the source of spells, or as a personification of the unreality of worldly things. In this character she is caled Māyā-devī or Mahā-māya. 2. A name of Gayā, one of the seven sacred cities.

MĀYĀ-DEVĪ, MĀYĀ-VATĪ. Wife of the demon Sambara. She brought up Pradyumna, is represented as being a revived embodiment of Kāma, the god of love; and in accordance with this legend Māyā-vatī is identified with his wife Rati, the Hindu Venus. *See* Māyā.

MĀYU. 'Bleater, bellower.' The Kinnaras are called Māyus.

MEDHĀTITHI. Name of a Kāṇwa who was a Vedic Rishi. There is a legend in one of the Upanishads that he was carried up to heaven by Indra in the form of a ram, because the god had been pleased with his austerities. *Cf.* Ganymeda.

MEDINĪ. The earth.

MEDINĪ, MEDINĪ-KOSHA. A well-known Sanskrit vocabulary. There are printed editions.

MEGHA-DŪTA. 'Cloud messenger.' A celebrated poem by Kāli-dāsa, in which a banished Yaksha implores a cloud to convey his tidings to his wife. It has been translated into English verse by Wilson, and there are versions in French and German. The text has been printed with a vocabulary by Johnson.

MEGHA-NĀDA. A son of Rāvaṇa. *See* Indra-jit.

MEKALA. Name of a mountain from which the Narmadā river is said to rise, and from which it is called Mekalā and Mekala-kanyā, 'daughter of Mekala.' A people of this name probably lived in the vicinity of this mountain. Their kings were also calld Mekalas, and there also appears to have been a city Mekalā.

MENĀ, MENAKĀ. 1. In the *Rig-veda,* a daughter of Vrishan-aśwa. Brāhmaṇa tells a strange story of Indra having assumed the form of Menā and then fallen in love with her. In the Purāṇas, wife of Himavat and mother of Umā and Gangā, and of a son named Maninākа. 2. An Apsara sent to reduce the sage Viśwāmitra from his devotions, who succeeded in her aim and became the mother of the nymph Śakuntalā.

MERU. A fabulous mountain in the navel or centre of the earth, on which is situated Swarga, the heaven of Indra, containing the cities of the gods and the habitations of celestial spirits, the Olympus of the Hindus. Regarded as a terrestrial object, it would seem to be some mountain north of the Himālayas. It is also Sumeru, Hemādri, 'golden mountain;' Ratnsānu, 'jewel peak;' Karṇikāchala, 'lotus mountain;' and Amarādri and Deva-parvata, 'mountain of the gods.'

MERU-SĀVARṆAS. The ninth, tenth, eleventh, and twelfth Manus, said to be the "mind-engendered sons of a daughter of Daksha by himself and the three gods Brahmā, Dharma, and Rudra, to whom he presented her on Mount Meru." The signification of the appellation Meru is obvious. That of Sāvarṇa or Sāvarṇi signifies that they were all of one caste *(varṇa).*

MĪMĀNSĀ. A school of philosophy. *See* Darśana.

MĪMĀNSĀ-DARŚANA. A work on the Mīmānsā philosophy. Printed in the *Bibliotheca India.*

MĪMĀNSĀ-VĀRTTIKA. A work on the Mīmānsā philosophy by Kumārila Bhaṭṭa.

MINJIKA (mas.) and MINJIKĀ (fem.). Two beings who, according to the *Mahābhārata,* sprang from the seed of Rudra, which was spilt upon a mountain. They are to be worshipped by those who desire the welfare of children.

MITĀKSHARĀ. A commentary by Vijnāneśwara on the Smriti or text-book of Yājnawalkya. The authority of this book is admitted all over India, with the exception of Bengal proper. The portion on inheritance has been translated by Colebrooke, and into French by Orianne.

MITHILĀ. A city, the capital of Videha or North Bihār, which corresponds to the modern Tirhut and Puraniya, between the Gandakī and Kosī rivers. It has given its name to one of the five northern nations of Brāhmans (*See* Brāhman), and to a school of law. It was the country of King Janaka, and the name of his capital, Janaka-pura, still survives in "Janakpoor," on the northern frontier.

MITRA. Probably connected with the Persian Mithra, a form of the sun. In the Vedas he is generally associated with Varuṇa, he being the ruler of the day and Varuṇa the ruler of the night. They together uphold and rule the earth and sky, guard the world, encourage religion, and chastise sin. He is one of the Ādityas—sons of Aditi.

MITRA-SAHA. A king called also Kalmāsha-pāda.

MLECHHAS. Foreigners, barbarians, people not of Āryan race.

MOHA-MUDGARA. 'Hammers for ignorance.' A poem in explanation of the Vedānta philosophy. It has been printed and translated by Neve.

MRICHCHHAKAṬĪ. 'The toy-cart'. A drama in ten acts by King Śūdraka, supposed to be the oldest Sanskrit drama extant, and to have been written in the first or second century A.D. The country over which Śūdraka reigned is not known. This play, says Wilson, its translator, "is a curious and interesting picture of national manners ... free from all exterior influence or adulteration. It is a portrait purely Indian. It represents a state of society sufficiently advanced in civilsation to be luxurious and corrupt, and is certainly offering a flattering similitude, although not without some attractive features." Williams observes, "The dexterity with which the plot is arranged, the ingenuity with which the incidents are connected, the skill with which the characters are delineated and contrasted, the boldness and felicity of the diction, are scarcely unworthy of our own great dramatists." There are translations in French and several editions of the text.

MRIGĀNKA-LEKHĀ. A play in four acts, written by Viśwa-nātha at Varanasī. The piece takes its name from the heroine, a princess of Kāmarūpa. It is a comparatively modern work.

MRITYU. 'Death.' A name of Yama, the god of the dead.

MUCHUKUNDA. In the Purāṇas, son of Māndhātri, and called 'king of men.' He rendered assistance to the gods in their wars with the Asuras or demons, and he asked and obtained as a reward the boon of a long uninterrupted sleep. Whosoever disturbed him was to be burnt to ashes by fire issuing from his body. Kāla-yavana was lured into his cave by Krishṇa and woke the sleeper, who cast a fiery glance upon the intruder which destroyed him. Muchukunda then paid laud and honour to Krishṇa, who gave him power to go to whatever celestial region he wished, and to enjoy all heavenly pleasures. Muchukunda left his cave and went to Gandhamādana to perform penance. The *Mahābhārata* says he was reproved by Kuvera for depending on his priest more than on his own prowess for success in war, but he replied that the religious aid of Brāhmans was as necessary as the warlike powers of Kshatriyas.

MUDGALA. A Vedic Rishi from whom the Maudgalya Brāhmans sprang. There were several other Brāhmans named Mudgala. A sage of this name is recorded in the *Mahābhārata* to have "lived a life of poverty, piety, and self-restraint, offering hospitality to thousands of Brāhmans, according to his humble means, with the grain which he gleaned like a pigeon, and which (like the widow of Zarephath's oil) never underwent diminution, or rather increased again, when it was required." The choleric sage Dur-vāsas went to test the patience of Mudgala, and six times, devoured all the food which his host possessed without ruffing his temper. Dur-vāsas in his admiration declared that Mudgala would go bodily to heaven, and the messenger of the gods arrived with his heavenly car. The sage, before accepting the invitation, desired to be informed of the joys and ills of heaven. After getting a full explanation, he found that the enjoyments of heaven must come to a close, so he declared that he "had no desire for heaven, and would seek only that eternal abode where there is no sorrow, nor distress, nor change." He dismissed the messenger of the gods, and began to practise ascetic virtues, becoming indifferent to praise and blame. Pure knowledge led to fixed contemplation; and that again imparted strength and complete comprehension, whereby he obtained supreme eternal perfection in the nature of quietude *(nirvāṇa)*.

MUDRĀ-RĀKSHASA. 'The signet of the minister.' A drama by Viśākha-datta. This play has an historical interest, for Chandra-gupta, the Sandracottus of Greek writers, is a leading character in it. The date of its production is apparently the eleventh or twelfth century A.D.

MUGDHA-BODHA. A standard Grammar by Vopadeva, written towards the end of the thirteenth century. It has been edited by Bohtlingk, and there are several Indian editions.

MŪKA. A Dānava, son of Upasunda. He assumed the form of a wild boar in order to kill Arjuna, but was himself killed by Śiva in his form of the Kirāta or mountaineer.

MUKHĀGNI. 'Fiery-faced.' Spirits or goblin with faces of fire, perhaps meteors.

MUṆDA. 'Bald.' An appellation of Ketu. Name of a demon slain by Durgā.

MUṆDAKA. Name of a Upanishad translated by Dr. Roer in the *Bibliotheca Indica* and by Rammohun Roy. There are several editions of the text.

MUNI. "A holy sage, a pious and learned person, endowed with more or less of a divine nature, or having attained to it by rigid abstraction and mortification. The title is applied to the Rishis, and to a great number of persons distinguished for their writings considered as inspired, as Pāṇini, Vyāsa." Having super human forces of blessings or curses.

MURA, MURU. A great demon who had seven thousand sons. He was an ally of the demon Naraka, who ruled over Prāg-jyotisha, and assisted him in the defence of that city against Krishṇa. He placed in the envirous of the city "nooses the edges of which were as sharp as razors," but Krishṇa cut them to pieces with his discus, slew Muru, "and burnt his seven thousand sons like moths with the flame of the edge of his discus."

MURĀRI. 'The foe of Mura.' An appellation of Krishṇa.

MURĀRī MISRA. Author of the drama *Murāri Nāṭ aka* or *Anargha Rāghava*.

MUSALA. The pestle-shaped club carried by Bala-rāma. It was named Saunanda.

MUSALA-DHARA, MUSALĀYUDHA, MUSALIN. 'Armed with a pestle.' An appellation of Bala-rāma.

MUSHṬIKA. A celebrated boxer in the service of Kansa, who directed him to kill Krishṇa or Bala-rāma in a public encounter, but Bala-rāma overthrew him and killed him.

N

NĀBHĀGADISHṬA, NĀBHĀGANDEDISHṬHA, NĀBHĀNEDISHṬHA. A son of Manu, who, while he was living as a Brahmachārī, was deprived of his inheritance, by his father according to the *Yajur-veda* but by his brothers according to the *Aitareya Brāhmaṇa*. He subsequently acquired wealth by imparting spiritual knowledge.

NACHIKETAS. The story of Nachiketas is told in the *Taittirīya Brāhmaṇa* and *Kathā Upanishad*. Vāja-śravasa or Aruṇi, the father of Nachiketas, desirous of attaining heaven, performed great sacrifices, and was profuse in his gifts to the priests. The son told him that he had not given all, for that he, his son, was left, and said, "To whom shall I be given?" On repeating the question, the father angrily replied, "To death." So the son departed to the abodes of death, and, after staying there three nights, Yama was constrained to offer him a boon. He prayed to see his father again and be reconciled. This boon was granted and another offered. All kinds of blessings were proposed, but the youth refused to be contented with anything but a true knowledge of the soul. Yama then proceeded to instruct him.

NĀGA. A snake, especially the cobra-capella. A mythical semi-divine being, having a human face with the tail of a serpent, and the expanded neck of the cobra. The race of Nāgas is said to be a thousand in number, and to have sprung from Kadru, the wife of Kaśyapa, for the purpose of peopling Pātāla, or the regions below the earth, where they reign in great splendour. From the name of their mother they are called Kādraveyas. Their mother is sometimes called Su-rasā. This dominion was taken from them by the Gandharvas, but they recovered it through their sister, the Narmadā river, who induced Vishṇu to send Pratardana to their assistance. Their females were handsome, and some of them intermarried with men, as Ulupī with Arjuna.

The Nāgas, or a people bearing the same name, are historical, and have left many traces behind them. There were mountains so called, and Nāga-dwīpa was one of the seven divisions of Bhārata-varsha. Kings of this race reigned at Mathurā, Padmāvatī, etc., and the name survives in the modern Nāgpur. There are various speculations as to who and what they were, but it seems clear they were a race distinct from the Hindus. The mythological accounts are probably based upon the historical, but they have been mixed up and confused. The favourite theory is that they were a Scythic race, and probably obtained their name from worshipping serpents or holding them in awe and reverence.

NĀGA-LOKA. Pātāla, the residence of the Nāgas.

NĀGA-NANDANA. A Buddhist drama in five acts by Srī Harsha Deva. It has been translated by Boyd. The text has been printed.

NAGARA. A city. There are seven sacred cities which confer eternal happiness—(1) Ayodhyā, (2) Mathurā, (3) Māyā (Gaya), (4) Kāśī (Benares), (5) Kānchī (Conjeveram), (6) Avanti or Avantikā (Ujjayinī), (7) Dwārakā or Dwārāvatī.

NAHUSHA. Son of Āyus the eldest son of Purūravas, and father of Yayāti. This king is mentioned by Manu as having come into conflict with the Brāhmans, and his story is repeated several times with variations in different parts of the *Mahābhārata* as well as in the Purāṇas, the aim and object evidently being to exhibit the retribution awaiting any man who derogates from the power of Brāhmans and the respect due to them. "By sacrifices, austere fervour, sacred study, self-restraint, and valour, Nahusha acquired the undisturbed sovereignty of the three worlds.... Through want of virtuous humility the great king Nahusha was utterly ruined."—Manu. One version of the story says that he aspired to the possession of Indrānī, wife of Indra, when that god had concealed himself for having killed a Brāhman. A thousand great Rishis bore the car of Nahusha through the air, and on one occasion he touched with his foot the great Agastya, who was carrying him. The sage in his anger cried out, "Fall, thou serpent," and Nahusha fell from his glorious car and became a serpent. Agastya, at the supplication of Nahusha, put a limit to the curse; and according to one version, the doomed man was released from it by the instrumentality of *Yudhishthira,* when he threw off "his huge reptile form, became clothed in a celestial body, and ascended to heaven".

NAIKASHEYAS. Carnivorous imps descended from Nikashā, mother of Rāvaṇa. They are called also Nikashātmajas.

NAIMISHA, NAIMISHĀRANYA. A forest *(araṇya)* near the Gomatī (Gūmtī) river, in which the *Mahābhārata* was rehearsed by Sauti to the assembled Rishis.

NAIRRITA. Belonging to the south-west quarter; the regent of that quarter. An imp, goblin, or Rākshasa.

NAISHADHA-CHARITA, NAISHADHĪYA. A poem on the life of Nala, king of Nishadha, by Śrī Harsha, a great sceptical philosopher who lived in the eleventh or twelfth century A.D. It is one of the six Mahā-kāvyas. There are several printed editions.

NAKSHATRAS. Mansions of the moon, lunar asterisms. Twenty-seven in number, they were later increased to twenty-eight. They are said to be daughters of Daksha. *See* Daksha.

NAKULA. The fourth of the Pāndu princes. He was the twin son of Mādrī, the second wife of Pāndu, but mythologically be was son of the Aświns, or more specifically of the Aświn Nāsatya. He was taught the art of training and managing horses by Droṇa, and when he entered the service of the king of Virāṭa he was master of the horse. He had a son named Nir-amitra by his wife Kareṇu-matī, a princess of Chedi. See *Mahābhārata.*

NALA. 1. King of Nishadha and husband of Damayantī. The story of Nala and Damayantī is one of the episodes of the *Mahābhārata*.

2. A monkey chief, said to be a son of Viśwa-karma. According to the *Rāmāyaṇa,* he had the power of making stones float in water. He was in Rāma's army and built the bridge of stone called Rāma-setu, or Nala-setu, from the continent to Sri Lanka, over which Rāma passed with his army.

MALA-KŪVARA. A son of Kuvera.

NALODAYA (Nala + udaya). 'The rise of Nala.' A poem describing the restoration to power of King Nala after he had lost his all. It is ascribed to a Kālidāsa, but the composition is very artificial, and the ascription to the great Kālidāsa may well be doubted.

NALOPĀKHYĀNA. The story of Nala, an episode of the *Mahābhārata.*

NAMUCHI. A demon slain by Indra with the foam of water. The legend of Namuchi first appears in the *Rigveda,* where it is said that Indra ground "the head of the slave Namuchi like a sounding of the rolling cloud," but it is amplified by the commentator and also in the *Śatapatha Brāhmaṇa* and *Mahābhārata*. When Indra conquered the Asuras there was one Namuchi who resisted so strongly that he overpowered Indra and held him. Namuchi offered to let Indra go on promise not to kill him by day or by night, wet or dry. Indra gave the promise and was released, but he cut off Namuchi's head at twilight, between day and night, and with foam of water, which was, according to the authorities, neither wet nor dry. The *Mahābhārata* adds that the head followed Indra calling out "O wicked slayer of thy friend."

NANDA. 1. The cowherd by whom Krishna was brought up. 2. A king, or dynasty of kings, of Magadha, that reigned at Pāṭaliputra, and was overthrown by Chandragupta Maurya about 315 B.C. See Chandragupta.

NANDANA. The grove of Indra, lying to the north of Meru.

NANDI. The bull of Śiva. The *Vāyu Purāṇa* makes him the son of Kaśyapa and Surabhi. His image, of a milky white colour, is always conspicuous before the temples of Śiva. He is the chamberlain of Śiva, ċhief of his personal attendants *(gaṇas)*, and carries a staff of office. He is guardian of all quadrupeds. He is also called Śālankāyana, and he has the appellations of Nādideha and Tāndavatālika, because he accompanies with music the *tāndava* dance of his master.

NĀNDI-MUKHAS. A class of Pitris or Manes, concerning whose character there is a good deal of uncertainty.

NANDINĪ. The cow of plenty belonging to the sage Vaśishtha. Said to have been born of Surabhi, the cow of plenty that was produced at the churning of the ocean.

NANDI-PURĀṆA. *See* Purāṇa.

NANDĪŚA, NANDĪŚWARA. 'Lord of Nandi.' A title of Śiva. It is related in the *Rāmāyaṇa* that Rāvaṇa went to the Śara-vana, the birth place of Kārttikeya, and on his way through the mountains he beheld "a formidable, dark, tawny-coloured dwarf called Nandīśwara, who was a followr r of Mahādeva, or rather that deity himself in another body. This being desired Rāvaṇa to halt, as Śiva was sporting in the mountain, and no onė, not even a god, could pass. Rāvaṇa asked derisively who Śiva was, and laughed cotemptuously at Nandīśwara, who had the face of a monkey. Nandīśwara retorted that monkeys having the same shape as himself and of similar energy should be produced to destroy Rāvaṇa's race. In reply to this menace, Rāvana threatened to pull up the mountain by its roots and let Śiva know his own danger. So he threw his arms round the mountain and lifted it up, which made the hosts of Śiva tremble and Pārvatī quake and cling to her husband. Śiva then pressed down the mountain with his great toe, and crushed and held fast the arms of Rāvaṇa, who uttered a loud cry which shook all creation. Rāvaṇa's friends counselled him to propitiate Śiva, and he did so for a thousand years with hymns and weeping. Śiva then released him, and said that his name should be Rāvaṇa from the cry *(rāva)* which he had uttered.

NARA. 'Man.' The original eternal man.

NĀRADA. A Rishi to whom some hymns of the *Rig-veda* are ascribed. He is one of the Prajāpatis, and also one of the seven great Rishis. The various notices of him are somewhat inconsistent. The *Rig-veda* describes him as "of the Kanwa family." Another authority states that he sprang from the forehead of Brahmā, and the *Vishṇu Purāṇa* makes him a son of Kaśyapa and one of the Daksha's daughters. The *Mahābhārata* and some Purāṇas state that he frustrated the scheme which Daksha had formed for peopling the earth, and consequently incurred that patriarch's curse to enter again the womb of a woman and be born. Daksha, however, relented at the solicitation of Brahmā, and consented that Nārada should be born again of Brahmā and one of Daksha's daughters; he was hence called Brāhma and Deva-brahmā. In some respects he bears a resemblance to Orpheus. He is the inventor of the *Vīṇā* (lute), and was chief of the Gandharvas or heavenly musicians. He also went down to the infernal regions (Pātāla), and was delighted with what he saw there. In later times he is connected with the legend of Krishṇa. He warned Kansa of the imminent incarnation of Vishṇu, and he afterwards became the friend and associate of Krishṇa.

The *Nārada-pancha-rātra* relates that Brahmā advised his son Nārada to marry, but Nārada censured his father as a false teacher, because devotion to Krishṇa .was the only true. Brahmā then cursed Nārada to lead a life of sensuality, in subjection to women, and Nārada retorted the curse, condemning Brahmā to lust after his own daughter, and to be an object unworthy of adoration. Nārada has the appellations, Kali-kāraka, 'strife-maker;' Kapi-vaktra, 'monkey-faced;' Piśuna, 'messenger or spy.'

Nārada was also one of the great writers upon law. His text-book, called "Nāradīya Dharma-sāstra," has been translated into English by Dr. Jolly.

NĀRADA PANCHA-RĀTRA. A ritualistic work of the Vaishnavas, it has been printed in the *Bibliotheca Indica.*

NĀRADA-PURĀṆA, NĀRADĪYA-PURĀṆA. 'Where Nārada has described the duties which were observed in the Brihat Kalpa, that is called the *Nāradīya,* having 25,000 stanzas." But the only copy that Wilson analysed contained not more than 3000 stanzas. There is another work called the Brihan or Great Nāradīya, but this extends only to 3500 verses. These Purāṇas, says Wilson, bear "no conformity to the definition of a Purāṇa; both are sectarial and modern compilations, intended to support the doctrine of Bhakti or faith in Vishṇu." They are modern compositions, possibly even of so late a date as the sixteenth or seventeenth century. One of them refers to the "killers of cows" and "contemners of the gods", meaning, no doubt, the Mohammadans, so that the passage would seem to have been written after India was in their hands.

NARAKA. Hell; a place of torture to which the souls of the wicked are sent. Manu enumerates twenty-one hells Tāmisra, Andha-tāmisra, Mahā-raurava, Raurava, Naraka, Kāla-sūtra, Mahā-naraka, Sanjīvana, Mahā-vīchi, Tapana, Sampratā-pana, Sanhāta, Sakākola, Kudmala, Pūtāmrittika, Loha-śanku, Rijisha, Panthāna, Śālmali, Asi-patra-vana, and Loha-dāraka. Other authorities vary greatly as to the numbers and names of the hells. See *Vishṇu Purāṇa,* ii. 214.

NARAKA. An Asura, son of the Earth. In the *Mahābhārata* and *Vishṇu Purāṇa* he is said to have carried off the ear-rings of Aditi to the impregnable castle of Prāg-jyotisha, but Krishṇa, at the request of the gods, went there and killed him and recovered the jewels. In the *Hari-vanśa* the legend differs. According to this, Naraka, king of Prāg-jyotisha, was an implacable enemy of the gods. He assumed the form of an elephant, and having carried off the daughter of Viśwakarma, he subjected her to violation. He seized the daughters of the Gandharvas, and of gods and of men, as well as the Apsarasas themselves, and had more than 16,000 women, for whom he built a splendid residence. He also appropriated to himself jewels, garments, and valuables of all sorts, and no Asura before him had ever been so horrible in his actions.

NARA-NĀRĀYAṆA. Two ancient Rishis, sons of Dharma and Ahimsa. The names are sometimes applied to Krishṇa and Arjuna. The *Vāmana Purāṇa* has a legend about them which is alluded to in the drama of *Vikramorvaśī*. Their penances and austerities alarmed the gods, so Indra sent nymphs to inspire them with passion and disturb their devotions. Nārāyaṇa took a flower and placed it on his thigh. Immediately there sprang from it a beautiful nymph whose charms far excelled those of the celestial nymphs, and made them return to heaven filled with shame and vexation. Nārāyaṇa sent this nymph to Indra with them, and as she had been produced from the thigh *(uru)* of the sage, she was called Urvaśī.

NARA-VISHWANA. 'A man-devourer; a Rākshasa or other malignant being.

NĀRĀYAṆA. 1. The son of Nara, the original man, and often identified or coupled with Nara. 2. The creator Brahmā, who, according to Manu, was so called because the waters *(nara)* were his first *ayaṇa* or place of motion. The name is found for the first time in the *Śatapatha Brāhmaṇa*. The name as commonly used for Vishṇu, and under which he was first worshipped.

NARMADĀ. The Nerbudda river, which is regarded holy. The personified river is variously represented as being daughter of a Rishi named Mekala (from whom she is called Mekalā and Mekala-kanyā), as a daughter of the moon, as a 'mind-born daughter' of the Somapas, and as sister of the Nāgas. It was she who brought Purukutsa to the aid of the Nāgas against the Gandharvas, and the grateful snake-gods made her name a charm against the venom of snakes. According to the *Vishṇu Purāṇa*, she had a son by Purukutsa who was named Trasadasyu. The *Matsya Purāṇa* gives Duh-saha as the name of her husband. The *Hari-vanśa* is inconsistent At one place it makes her wife of Purukutsa and mother of Trasadasyu; at another it makes her the wife of Trasadasyu. She is also called Revā and Pūrva-gangā, and, as a daughter of the moon, Indu-jā and Somodbhavā.

NĀSATYA. Name of one of the Aświns, it is also used in the plural for both of them.

NAVA-RATNA. (1) The nine gems: pearl, ruby, topaz, diamond, emerald, lapis lazuli, coral, sapphire, and Gomeda. (2) The nine gems of the court of Vikrama, probably meaning Vikramāditya, whose era the Samvat begins in 56 B.C. A verse gives their names as Dhanwantari, Kshapanaka, Amara Sinha, Śanku, Vetālabhaṭṭa, Ghaṭa-karpara, Kāli-dāsa, Varāha-mihira, Vararuchi.

NIDĀGHA. A Brāhman, son of Pulastya, who dwelt "at Vīra-nagara, a large handsome city on the banks of the Devikā river" (the Gogra). He was a disciple of the sage Ribhu, and when Ribhu went to visit his disciple, Nidāgha entertained him reverentially. Ribhu instructed him in divine knowledge until he learned to "behold all things as the same with himself, and, perfect in holy knowledge, obtained final liberation."

NIDĀNA-SŪTRA. An old work upon the metres of the Veda.

NIDHI. 'A treasure,' one of the nine treasures belonging to the god Kuvera. Each of them is personified or has a guardian spirit, which is an object of worship among the Tāntrikas. The nature of these Nidhis is not clearly understood. According to a note by Wilson on verse 534 of the *Meghadūta, Collected Works,* iv. 379, their names are Kachchhapa, Mukunda, Nanda (or Kunda), Kharba, Makara, Nīla, Sankha, Padma, and Mahā-padma. The Nidhis are called also Nidhāna, Nikara, and Śevadhi.

NIDRĀ. 'Sleep,' sometimes said to be a female form of Brahmā, at others to have been produced at the churning of the ocean.

NIGHAṆṬU, NIGHAṆṬUKA. A glossary, especially of synonyms and obsolete and obscure Vedic terms. There was at least one work of this kind before the days of Yāska. *See* Nirukta.

NIKASHĀ. A female demon, the mother of Rāvaṇa. The mother of the carnivorous imps called Pisitāsanas, or by their metronymic Naikusheyas and Nikashātmajas.

NIKUMBHA. 1. A Rākshasa who fought against Rāma. He was son of Kumbha-karṇa. 2. An Asura who, according to the *Hari-vaśa,* received the boon from Brahmā that he should die only by the hands of Vishṇu. He was king of Shaṭ-pura and had great magical powers, so that he could multiply himself into many forms, though he commonly assumed only three. He carried off the daughters of Brahmā-datta, the friend of Krishṇa, and that hero attacked him and killed him under different forms more than once, but he was eventually slain outright by Krishṇa, and his city of Shaṭ-pura was given to Brahmā-datta.

NĪLA. 'Blue.' 1. A mythic range of mountains north of Meru. 2. A mountain range of Orissa. 3. A monkey ally of Rāma. 4. A Pandava warrior killed by Aswatthāman.

NĪLA-KANTHA. 'Blue throat,' an epithet of Siva.

NIMI. Son of Ikshwāku, and founder of the dynasty of Mithilā, he was cursed by the sage Vaśishtha to lose his corporeal form, and he retorted the imprecation upon the sage. Both abandoned the bodily form. Vaśishtha was born again as the issue of Mitra and Varuṇa, "but the corpse of Nimi was preserved from decay by being embalmed with fragrant oils and resins, and it remained as entire as if it were immortal." The gods were willing to restore him to bodily life, but Nimi declined, declaring that the separation of soul and body was so distressing that he would never resume a corporeal shape and become liable to it again. "To this desire the gods assented, and Nimi was placed by them in the eyes of all living creatures, in consequence of which their eyelids are ever opening and shutting."—*Vishnu Purāṇa.* A wink of the eye is called *nimisha,* and the legend was probably built upon the resemblance of the two words.

NIRṆAYA-SINDHU. A work on religious ceremonies and law by Kamalākara, it has been printed at Mumbai and Varanasī.

NIRITTI. 'Death, decay'. Death personified as a goddess; sometimes regarded as the wife and sometimes as the daughter of A-dharma. One of the Rudras.

NIRUKTA. 'Etymology, glossary.' One of the Vedāngas, the Nirukta is devoted to the explanation of difficult Vedic words. The only work of the kind now known to us is that of Yāska, who was a predecessor of Pāṇini; but such works were no doubt numerous, and the names of seventeen writers of Niruktas are mentioned as having preceded Yāska. The Niruktas consists of three parts:—(1) Naighaṇṭuka, a collection of synonymous words; (2) Naigama, a collection of words peculiar to the Vedas; (3) Daivata, words relating to deities and sacrifices. These are mere lists of words, and are of little value. The real Nirukta, the valuable portion of the work, is Yāska's commentary, in which he explains the meaning of words, enters into etymological investigations, and quotes passages of the Vedas in illustration. These are valuable as being the oldest known examples of a Vedic gloss, which also throw light upon the scientific and religious condition of their times, but the extreme brevity of their style makes them obscure and difficult to understand.

NISHĀDA. A mountain tribe dwelling in the Vindhya mountains, said to have been produced from the thigh of Veṇa; the Bhīls or foresters, and barbarians in general. (*See* Veṇa.) Any outcast, especially the offspring of a Brāhman father and Śūdra mother.

NISHADHA. 1. A mythic range of mountains lying south of Meru, but sometimes described as on the east. It is north of the Himālaya. 2. The country of Nala, probably the Bhīl country.

NISHṬIGRĪ. In the *Rig-veda,* the mother of Indra.

NIŚUMBHA. An Asura killed by Durgā. *See* Śumbha.

NĪTI-MANJARĪ. A work on ethics by Dyā Dwiveda, it is full of stories and legends with special reference to the Vedas. Some specimens are given in the *Indian Antiquary,* vol. v.

NĪTI-ŚĀSTRAS. Works on morals and polity, consisting either of proverbs and wise maxims in verse, or of stories and fables inculcating some moral precept and illustrating its effects. These fables are generally in prose interspersed with pithy maxims in verse.

NIVĀTA-KAVACHAS. 'Clothed in impenetrable armour.' A class of Daityas descended from Prahlāda, "whose spirits were purified by rigid austerity." According to the *Mahā-bhārata* they were 30,000,00 in number, and dwelt in the depths of the sea. There are said to have been destroyed by Arjuna.

NRI-SINHA. The Nara-sinha or man-lion incarnation. *See* Avatāra.

NRI-SINHA TĀPANI. An Upanishad in which Vishnu is worshipped under his form Nri-sinha, published with the commentary of Śankarāchārya in the *Bibliotheca Indica.*

NYĀYA. The logical school of philosophy. *See* Darśana.

NYĀYA-DARŚANA, NYĀYA-SŪTRA-VRITTI. Works of Gotama on the Nyāya philosophy.

O

ODRA. The country of Orissa. A man of that country.

OM. A word of solemn invocation, affirmation, benediction, and consent, so sacred that when it is uttered no one must hear it. The word is used at the commencement of prayers and religious ceremonies, and is generally placed at the beginning of books. It is a compound of the three letters *a, u, m,* which are typical of the three Vedas; and it is declared in the Upanishads, to have a mystic power and to be worthy of the deepest meditation. In later times the monosyllable called Udggītha, represents the Hindu triad or union of the three gods, *a* being Vishṇu, *u* Śiva, and *m* Brahmā.

OMKĀRA. The sacred monosyllable *Om*. Name of one of the twelve great lingas. *See* Linga.

OSHADHI-PRASTHA. 'The place of medicinal herbs.' A city in the Himālaya mentioned in the *Kumār-sambhava.*

OSHṬHA-KARṆAKAS. A people mentioned in the *Mahābhārata,* whose lips extended to their ears.

P

PADA. The Pada text of the Vedas, or of any other work, is one in which each word (*pada*) stands separate and distinct, not joined with the next according to the rules of *sandhi* (coalition). *See* Patha.

PADMĀ, PADMĀVATĪ. A name of Lakshmī.

PADMĀVATĪ. Name of a city. It would seem, from the mention made of it in the drama *Mālatī Mādhava,* to lie in the Vindhya mountain.

PADMA-KALPA. The last expired kalpa or year of Brahmā.

PADMA-PURĀṆA, PĀDMA-PURĀṆA. This Purāṇa generally stands second in the list of Purānas, and is that which contains an account of the period when the world was a golden lotus (*padma*), and of all the occurrences of that time, is, therefore, called Padma by the wise. It contains 55,000 stanzas." The work is divided into five books or Khaṇdas:—"(1) Srishti Khaṇda, or section of creation; (2) Bhūmi Khaṇda, on the earth; (3) Swarga Khaṇda, on heaven; (4) Pātāla Khaṇda, on the regions below the earth; (5) Uttara Khaṇda, last or supplementary chapter. There is also current a sixth division, the *Kriyā-yoga-sāra,* a treatise on the practice of devotion." There is no reason to consider any of them as older than the twelfth century. The tone of the whole Purāṇa is strongly Vaishṇava; that of the last section especially so. In it Śiva is represented as explaining to Pārvatī the nature and attributes of Vishnu, and in the end the two join in adoration of that deity. A few chapters have been printed and translated into Latin by Wollheim.

PAHLAVA. Name of a people. Manu places the Pahlavas among the northern nations, and perhaps the name is connected with the word Pahlavi, *i.e.,* Persian. They let their beards grow by command of King Sagara. According to Manu, they were Kshatriyas who had become outcasts, but the *Mahābhārata* says they were created from the tail of Vaśishtha's cow of fortune. The *Rāmāyaṇa* states that they sprang from her breath. They are also called Pahnavas.

PAIJAVANA. A name of the King Sudās, his patronymic, as son of Pījavana.

PAILA. A learned man who was appointed in ancient days to collect the hymns of the *Rig-veda*. He arranged it in two parts, and must have been a coadjutor of Veda Vyāsa.

PĀKA-ŚĀSANA. A name of Indra, and of Arjuna as descended from Indra.

PĀLAKĀPYA. An ancient sage who wrote upon medicine, and is supposed to have been an incarnation of Dhanwantari.

PAMPĀ. A river which rises in the Rishyamūka mountain and falls into the Tungabhadra below Anagundi. Also a lake in the same locality.

PANCHA-CHŪḌĀ. A name of Rambhā.

PANCHAJANA. 1. Name of a demon who lived in the sea in the form of a conch-shell. He seized the son of Sāndīpani, under whom Krishṇa learnt the use of arms. Krishṇa rescued the boy, killed the demon, and afterwards used the conch-shell or a horn. 2. A name of Asamanjas.

PĀNCHAJANYA. Krishṇa's conch, formed from the shell of the sea-demon Panchajana.

PANCHĀLA. Name of a country, which, according to the *Mahābhārata* seems to have occupied the Lower Doab while Manu places it near Kanauj. It has sometimes been identified with the Panjāb, and with "a little territory in the more immediate neighbourhood of Hastināpur." Wilson says, "A country extending north and west from Delhi, from the foot of the Himālayas to the Chambal." It was divided into Northern and Southern Panchālas, and the Ganges separated them. Cunningham considers north Panchāla to be Rohilkhand, and south Panchāla the Gangetic Doab. The capital of the former was Ahi-chhatra, whose ruins are found near Rāmnagar, and of the latter Kāmpilya, identical with the modern Kāmpila, on the old Ganges between Badāūn and Farrukhābād.

PĀNCHĀLĪ. Draupadī as princess of Panchāla.

PANCHĀNANA. 'Five-faced.' An epithet applied to Śiva.

PANCHĀPSARAS. Name of a lake. *See* Manda-karni.

PANCHA-ŚIKHA. One of the earliest professors of the Sānkhya philosophy.

PANCHA-TANTRA. A famous collection of tales and fables in five (*pancha*) books (*tantra*), which was compiled by a Brāhman named Vishnu-śarman, about the end of the fifth century A.D., and was the original of the better-known Hitopadeśa. This work has reappeared in many languages both of the East and West, and has been the source of many familiar and widely known stories. It was translated into Pahlavi or old Persian by order of Naushīrvān in the sixth century A.D. In the ninth century it appeared in Arabic as *Kalila o Damna*. It was also translated into Hebrew, Syriac, Turkish, and Greek; and from these, versions were made into all the languages of Europe, and it became familiar in England as Pilpay's Fables (Fables of Bidpai). In modern Persia it is the basis of the *Anwār-i Suhailī* and *Iyār-i Dānish,* which has reppeared in Hindustani as the *Khirad-afroz*. The stories are popular throughout Hindustan, and have found their way into most of the languages and dialects.

PANCHĀVATĪ. A place in the great southern forest near the sources of the Godāvarī, where Rāma passed a long period of his banishment. Efforts have been made to identify it with the modern Nāsik, because Lakshmana cut off Sūrpa-nakhā's nose (*nāsika*) at Panchāvatī.

PANCHAVINŚA. *See* Praudha Brāhmana.

PANCHA-VRIKSHA. 'Five trees.' The five trees of Swarga, are Mandāra, Pārijātaka, Santāna, Kalpa-vriksha, and Hari-chandana.

PANCHOPĀKHYĀNA. The Pancha-tantra.

PĀNDAVAS. The descendants of Pāndu.

PĀNDU. 'The pale.' Brother of Dhritarāshtra, king of Hastināpura and father of the Pāndavas or Pāndu princes. See *Mahābhārata*.

PĀNDYA. Pāndya, Chola, and Chera were three kingdoms in the south of the Peninsula for some centuries before and after the Christian era. Pāndya was well known to the Romans as the kingdom of King Pandion, who is said to have sent ambassadors on two different occasions to Augustus Caesar. Its capital was Madura, the Southern Mathurā. Pāndya seems to have fallen under the ascendancy of the Chola kings in the seventh or eighth century.

PĀṆINI. The celebrated grammarian, author of the work called *Pāṇinīyam*. This is the standard authority on Sanskrit grammar, and it is held in such respect and reverence that it is considered to have been written be inspiration. Pāṇini, who is placed among the Rishis, is represented to have received a large portion of his work by direct inspiration from the god Śiva. It is also said that he was so dull a child that he was expelled from school, but the favour of Śiva placed him foremost in knowledge. Pāṇini was a native of Śalātura, in the country of Gandhāra, west of the Indus, and so is known as Śālottarīya. He is described as a descendant of Paṇin and grandson of Devala. His mother's name was Dākshi, who probably belonged to the race of Daksha, and he bears the metronymic Dāksheya. He is also called Āhika. The time when he lived is uncertain, but it is supposed to have been about four centuries B.C. Goldstucker carries him back to the sixth century, but Weber is inclined to place him considerably later. "His work", says Professor Williams, "is perhaps the most original of all productions of the Hindu mind." The work is written in the form of Sūtras or aphorisms, of which it contains 3996, arranged in eight *(ashta)* chapters *(adhyāya)*, from which the work is sometimes called Ashtadhyāyī. These aphorisms are exceedingly terse and complicated. Special training and study are required to reach their meaning. Colebrooke remarks, that "the endless pursuit of exceptions and limitations so disjoins the general precepts, that the reader cannot keep in view their intended connection and mutual relations. He wanders in an intricate maze, and the key of the labyrinth is continually slipping from his hand." As Goldstucker says, "Pāṇini's work is indeed a kind of natural history of the Sanskrit language." Pāṇini's grammar has been printed by Bohtlingk, and also in India. *See* Goldstucker's *Pāṇinī, His Place in Literature.*

PAṆIS. 'Niggards.' In the *Rigveda,* "the senseless, false, evil-speaking, unbelieving, unpraising, unworshipping Paṇis were Dasyus or envious demons who used to steal cows and hide them in caverns." They are said to have stolen the cows recovered by Śaramā.

PANNAGA. A serpent, snake. *See* Nāga.

PĀPA-PURUSHA. 'Man of sin.' A personification of all wickedness in a human form, of which all the members are great sins. The head is brahmanicide, the arm cow-killing, the nose woman-murder, etc.

PĀRADAS. A barbarous people dwelling in the north-west. Manu says they were Kshatriyas degraded to be Sūdras.

PARAMARSHIS (Parma-rishis). The great Rishis. *See* Rishi.

PARMĀTMAN. The supreme soul of the universe.

PARAMESHTHIN. 'Who stands in some distinguished mortals. A name used in the Vedas for a son or a creation of Prajāpati.

PARĀŚARA. A Vedic Rishi to whom some hymns of the Rig-veda are .attributed. He was a disciple of Kapila, and he received the Vishṇu Purāṇa from Pulastya and taught it to Maitreya. He was also a writer on Dharma-śāstra, and his texts are often cited in books on law. Speculations as to his era differ widely, from 575 B.C. to 1391 B.C. The legend of his birth, as given in the *Mahābhārata* is that King Kalmāsha-pāda met with Śaktri in a narrow path, and desired him to get out of the way. The sage refused, and the Rāja struck him with his whip. Thereupon, the sage cursed the Rāja so that he became a man-eating Rākshasa. In this state he ate up Śaktri, whose wife, Adriśyantī, afterwards gave birth to Parāśara. When this child grew up and heard the particulars of his father's death, he instituted a sacrifice for the destruction of all the Rākshasas, but was dissuaded from its completion by Vaśishtha and other sages. As he desisted, he scattered the remaining sacrificial fire upon the northern face of the Himālaya, where it still blazes forth as the phases of the moon, consuming Rākshasas, forests, and mountains.

PĀRĀŚARA-PURĀṆA. *See* Purāṇa.

PĀRAŚIKAS. Pārsikas or Fārsikas, *i.e.*, Persians.

PARAŚURĀMA. "Rāma with the axe". He was the sixth incarnation of Vishṇu and was born a son to Jamadagni and Reṇukā. By the command of his father he cut off the head of his mother Reṇukā who had entertained impure thought. He cleared the earth of the Kshatriyas twenty one times. Tradition ascribes the origin of the region of Malabar to Paraśurāma.

PĀRIJĀTA. The tree produced at the churning of the ocean, "and the delight of the nymphs of heaven, perfuming the world with its blossoms," it was kept in Indra's heaven, and was the pride of his wife Śachī, but when Krishṇa visited Indra in Swarga, his wife Satyabhāmā induced him to carry the tree away, which led to a great fight between the two gods and their adherents, in which Indra was defeated. The tree was taken to Dwārakā and planted there, but after Krishṇa's death it returned to Indra's heaven.

PARIKSHIT. Son of Abhimanyu by his wife Uttarā, grandson of Arjuna, and father of Janamejaya. He was killed by Aśwatthāman in the womb of his mother and was born dead, but he was brought to life by Krishṇa, who blessed him and cursed Aśwatthāman. When Yudhishthira retired from the world, Parikshit succeeded him on the throne of Hastinā-pura. He died from the bite of a serpent, and the *Bhāgavata Purāṇa* is represented as having been rehearsed to him in the interval between the bite and his death.

PĀRIPĀTRA. The northern part of the Vindhya range of mountains. According to the *Harivanśa,* it was the scene of the combat between Krishṇa and Indra, and its heights sank down under the pressure of Krishṇa's feet.

PARISHAD. A college or community of Brāhmans associated for the study of the Vedas.

PARIŚISHṬA. A supplement or appendix. A series of works called Pariśishṭas belong to the Vedic period, but they are the last of the series, and indicate a transition state.

PARIVRĀJAKA. A religious mendicant. A Brāhman in the forth stage of his religious life. *See* Brāhman.

PARJANYA. 1. A Vedic deity, the rain-god or rain personified. Three hymns in the *Rigveda* are addressed to this deity, and one of them is very poetical and picturesque in describing rain and its effects. The name is sometimes combined with the word *vāta* (wind), *parjanya-vāta,* referring probably to the combined powers and effects of rain and wind. In later times he is regarded as the guardian deity of clouds and rain, and the name is applied to Indra. 2. One of the Ādityas.

PĀRSHADA. Any treatise on the Vedas produced in a Parishad or Vedic college.

PĀRTHA. A son of Prithā or Kuntī. A title applicable to the three elder Pandavas, but especially used for Arjuna.

PĀRVATĪ. 'The mountaineer.' A name of the wife of Siva. *See* Devī.

PĀŚU-PATI. 'Lord of creatures.' A name of Rudra or of one of his manifestations. *See* Rudra.

PĀTĀLA. The infernal regions, inhabited by Nāgas (serpents), Daityas, Dānavas, Yakshas, and others. Seven in number, their names, according to the *Vishṇu Purāṇa,* are Atala, Vitala, Nitala, Gabhastimat, Mahātala, Sutala, and Pātāla. However, the *Padma Purāṇa* gives the names of the seven regions and their respective rulers as (1) Atala, subject to Mahā-māya; (2) Vitala, ruled by a form of Śiva called Hātakeśwara; (3) Sutala, ruled by Bali; (4) Talātala, ruled by Māya; (5) Mahātala, where reside the great serpents; (6) Rasātala, where the Daityas and Dānavas dwell; (7) Pātāla, the lowermost, in which Vāsuki reigns over the chief Nāgas or snake-gods. In the *Śiva Purāṇa* there are eight Pātālas—Pātāla, Tala, Atala, Vitala, Tāla, Vidhi-pātāla, Śarkarā-bhūmi, and Vijaya. The sage Nārada is said to have declared them to be far more delightful than Indra's heaven, and abounding with every kind of luxury and sensual gratification.

PĀṬALI-PUTRA. The Palibothra of the Greek writers, and described by them as being situated at the confluence of the Erranaboas (the Sone river) with the Ganges; it was the capital of the Nandas, and of the Maurya dynasty, founded by Chandra-gupta, which succeeded them as rulers of Magadha. The city has been identified with the modern Patna; for although the Sone does not now fall into the Ganges there, the modern town is smaller in extent than the ancient one, and there is good reason for believing that the rivers have changed their course.

PĀTANJALA. The Yoga philosophy.

PATANJALI. The founder of the Yoga philosophy. (*See* Darśana.) The author of the *Māhabhāshya,* a celebrated commentary on the Grammar of Pāṇini, and a defence of that work against the criticisms of Kātyāyana. He is supposed to have written about 200 B.C. Weber, however, makes his date to be 25 A.D.

PAṬHA. 'Reading.' There are three forms, in which the Vedic text is read and written:—(1) Sanhitāpāṭha, the ordinary form, in which the words coalesce according to the rules of Sandhi; (2) Pāda-pāṭha, in which each word stands separate and independent; (3) Krama-pātha, in which each word is given twice, first joined with the word preceding and then with the word following.

PATTANA. 'City.' Several great places have been known as Pattan or 'the city.' Soma-nātha was Pattan;

Anhalwāra is still known as Pattan, and there is also Patna.

PAULOMAS. Kaśyapa by his wife Puloma had many thousand "distinguished Dānavas called Paulomas, who were powerful, ferocious, and cruel". They were killed by Arjuna.

PAUNDRA, PAUNDRAKA. Belonging to the country of Pundra. The conch-shell of Bhīshma.

PAUNDRAKA. A pretender who, on the strength of being a Vāsu-deva, or descendant of one named Vasu-deva, set himself up in opposition to Krishṇa, who was son of Vasu-deva, and assumed his style and insignia. He was supported by the king of Kāśī-Vārānasī, but he was defeated and killed by Krishṇa and Vārānasī was burnt.

PAURAVAS. Descendants of Puru of the Lunar race. *See* Puru.

PAVANA. 'Wind.' The god of the wind. *See* Vāyu.

PHĀLGUNA. 1. A name of Arjuna. 2. Name of a month.

PINDĀRAKA. A watering-place on the coast of Gujarat, near Dwārakā, resorted to occasionally by Krishṇa. It still survives as a village, and is held in veneration. It is about twenty miles from the north-west extremity of the peninsula.

PINGALA. 1. The great authority on the Chandas or prosody of the Vedas, he is supposed to have written about two centuries B.C. 2. Name of one of the serpent kings sometimes identified with the foregoing.

PIPPALĀDA. A school of the *Atharva-veda,* founded by a sage of that name.

PIŚĀCHAS (mas.), PIŚĀCHĪ (fem.). Fiends, evil spirits, placed by the Vedas as lower than Rākshasas. The Brāhmaṇa and the *Mahābhārata* say that they were created by Brahmā, together with the Asuras and Rākshasas, from the stray drops of water which fell apart from the drops out of which gods, men, Gandharvas, etc., had been produced. According to Manu they sprang from the

Prajāpatis. In the Purāṇas they are represented as the offspring of Kaśyapa by his wife Krodhavaśā, or Piśāchā, or Kapiśā.

PIŚĀCH-LOKA. *See* Loka.

PIŚITĀŚANAS, PIŚITĀŚINS. Carnivorous and cannibal imps descended from Nikashā.

PITĀ-MAHA. A paternal grandfather. A name of Brahmā as the great father of all.

PĪTĀMBARA. 'Clothed in yellow garments.' A name of Vishṇu.

PĪTHA-STHĀNA. 'Seat,' or lit. 'place of a seat.' "Fifty-one places where, according to the Tantras, the limbs of Satī fell when scattered by her husband Śiva, as he bore her dead body about and tore it to pieces after she had put an end to her existence at Daksha's sacrifice. It bears some analogy to the Egyptian fable of Isis and Osiris. At the Pītha-sthānas, of Jwāla-mukhi, Vindhya-vāsinī, Kālī-ghāt, and others, temples are erected to the different forms of Devī or Satī, and the chief object of worship is a figure of the goddess—a circumstance in which there is an essential difference between the temples of Durgā and the shrines of Osiris."—*Wilson*.

PITRIS. Patres; the fathers; the Manes. This name is applied to three different classes of beings:—1. The Manes of departed forefathers, to whom *pindas* (balls of rice and flour) and water are offered at stated periods. 2. The ten Prajāpatis or mythical progenitors of the human race. 3. "According to a legend in the *Hari-vanśa* and in the *Vāyu Purāṇa*, the first Pitris were the sons of the gods. The gods having offended Brahmā by neglecting to worship him, were cursed by him to become fools; but, upon their repentance, he directed them to apply to their sons for instruction. Being taught accordingly the rites of expiation and penance by their sons, they addressed them as fathers; whence the sons of the gods were the first Pitris."

PITRI-LOKA. *See* Loka.

PITRI-PATI. 'The lord of the Manes.' Yama, judge of the dead.

PIYADAŚI. *See* Aśoka.

PRABHĀSA. A place of pilgrimage on the coast of Gujarat, near Dwārakā, and also close the temple of Somanātha.

PRABHĀVATĪ. Wife of Pradyumna.

PRABODHA-CHANDRODAYA. 'The rise of the moon of knowledge.' A philosophical drama by Krishṇa Miśra, who is supposed to have lived about the twelfth century. It has been translated into English by Dr. Taylor, and into German by Rosenkranz and by Hirzel.

PRACHANDA-PĀNDAVA. 'The incensed Pandavas.' A drama in two acts by Rāja Śekhara, dealing with the outrage of Draupadī by the assembled Kaurava princes.

PRACHETAS. 1. One of the Prajāpatis. 2. An ancient sage and lawgiver. 3. The ten Prachetasas were sons of Prāchinabarhis and great-grandsons of Prithu, and, according to the *Vishṇu Purāṇa,* they passed ten thousand years in the great ocean, deep in meditation upon Vishṇu, and obtained from him the boon of becoming the progenitors of mankind. *See* Daksha.

PRĀCHYAS. The people of the east; those east of the Ganges; the Prasii of the Greeks.

PRADHĀNA. Matter, primary matter, or nature as opposed to spirit.

PRADYUMNA. A son of Krishṇa by Rukmiṇī. When a child only six days old, he was stolen by the demon Śambara and thrown into the ocean. There he was swallowed by a fish, which was afterwards caught and carried to the house of Śambara. When the fish was opened, a beautiful child was discovered, and Māyā-devī or Māyā-vatī, the mistress of Śambara's household, took him under her care. The sage Nārada informed her who the child was, and she reared him carefully. When he grew up she fell in love with him, and informed him who he was and how he had been carried off by Śambara. He defied the demon and after a long battle slew him.

Then he flew through the air with Māyāvatī, and alighted in the inner apartments of his father's palace. Krishṇa presented him to his mother Rukmiṇī "with the virtous Māyāvatī his wife," declaring her really to be the goddess Rati. Pradyumna also married Kakudmatī, the daughter of Rukmin, and had by her a son named Aniruddha. Pradyumna was killed at Dwārakā in the presence of his father during a drunken brawl. According to a legend Pradyumna is a revival or resuscitation of Kāma, the god of love, who was reduced to ashes by the fiery glance of Śiva, and so the name Pradyumna is used for Kāma. (*See* Kāma.) According to *Vishṇu Purāṇa*, "When Manmatha (the deity of love) had perished, the goddess of beauty (Rati), desirous to secure his revival, assumed a delusive form, and by her charms fascinated the demon Śambara, and exhibited herself to him in various illusory enjoyments. This thy son is the descended Kāma; and this is (the goddess) Rati, his wife. There is no occasion for any uncertainty; this is thy daughter-in-law." In the *Harivanśa* he has a wife named Prabhāvatī, daughter of King Vajranābha. When he went to see her for the first time, he changed himself into a bee and lived in a garland of flowers which had been prepared for her. According to the *Mahābhārata*, he was Sanat-kumāra, the son of Brahmā.

PRADYUMNA-VIJAYA. 'Pradyumna victorious.' A drama in seven acts upon the victory of Pradyumna over the Daitya Vajra-nābha, written by Sankara Dīkshita about the middle of the nineteenth century.

PRĀG-JYOTISHA. A city situated in the east, in Kāma-rūpa on the borders of Assam.

PRAHLĀDA, PRAHRĀDA. A Daitya, son of Hiraṇya-kaśipu and father of Bali. Hiraṇya-kaśipu, in his wars with the gods, had wrested the sovereignty of heaven from Indra and dwelt there in luxury. His son Prahlāda, while yet a boy, became an ardent devotee of Vishṇu, which so enraged his father that he ordered the boy to be killed; but not the weapons of the Daityas, the fangs of the serpents, the tusks of the celestial elephants, nor the flames of fire took any effect, and his father was constrained to send him back to his preceptor, where he continued so earnest in performing and promoting the worship of Vishṇu that he eventually obtained final exemption from existence. According to some accounts, it was to avenge Prahlāda, as well as to vindicate his own insulated majesty, that Vishnu became incarnate as the Nara-sinha, 'man-lion,' and slew Hiraṇya-kaśipu. After the death of his father, Prahlāda became king of the Daityas and dwelt in Pātāla; but, according to the *Pādma Purāṇa,* he was raised to the rank of Indra for life, and finally united with Vishnu. The *Pādma Purāṇa* carries the story farther back to a previous birth. In this previous existence Prahlāda was a Brāhman named Soma-śarman, fifth son of Śiva-śarman. His four brothers died and obtained union with Vishṇu, and he desired to follow them. To accomplish this he engaged in profound meditation, but he allowed himself to be disturbed by an alarm of the Daityas, and so was born again as one of them. He took the part of his race in the war between them and the gods, and was killed by the discus of Vishṇu; after that he was again born as son of Hiraṇya-kaśipu.

PRAJĀ-PATI. 'Lord of creatures,' a progenitor, creator. In the Veda the term is applied to Indra, Savitri, Soma, Hiraṇya-garbha, and other deities. In Manu the term is applied to Brahmā as the active creator and supporter of the universe; so Brahmā is the Prajā-pati. It is also given to Manu Swāyambhuva himself, as the son of Brahmā and as the secondary creator of the ten Rishis, or "mind-born sons" of Brahmā, from whom mankind has descended. The name Prajā-pati most commonly is given these ten sages who are said to be the fathers of great human race. They are Marīchi, Atri, Angiras, Pulastya, Pulaha, Kratu, Vasishtha, Prachetas or Daksha, Bhrigu, and Nārada. According to some authorities the Prajā-pathis are only seven in number, being identical with the seven great Rishis. (*See* Rishi). The *Mahābhārata* makes twenty-one.

PRAKĀŚAS. Messengers of Vishṇu, also called Vishṇu-dūtas.

PRĀKRITA. The Prākrits are provincial dialects of the Sanskrit, exhibiting more or less deterioration from the original language; and they occupy an intermediate position between that language and the modern vernaculars of India, very similar to that of the Romance languages between the Latin and the modern languages of Europe. They resemble the European languages also in another respect: they have in them a small proportion of words which are apparently remnants of a different tongue and an older race. The Prākrits are chiefly known from the dramas in which kings and Brāhmans speak Sanskrit, while characters of inferior position speak in different Prākrits. Sometimes these Prākrit passages are so very debased that it hardly seems possible for them to be specimens of really spoken vernaculars. Such passages may perhaps be comic exaggerations of provincial peculiarities. The Prākrits have received careful study, and the *Prākrita-prakāśa,* a Grammar by Vararuchi, translated by Professor Cowell, was probably written about the beginning of the Christian era. *See* Kātyāyana.

PRAKRITI. Nature; matter as opposed to spirit. The personified will of the Supreme in the creation, and the prototype of the female sex, identified with Māyā or illusion. The Śakti of female energy of any deity.

PRALAMBA. An Asura killed by Krishṇa, according to the *Mahābhārata*. His story as told in the *Vishṇu Purāṇa* is, that he was an Asura and a dependant of Kansa. With the object of devouring the boys Krishṇa and Bala-rāma, he joined them and their playmates in jumping. Pralambā was beaten by his opponent Bala-rāma, and by the rules of the game had to carry the victor back on his shoulders to the starting-place. He took up Bala-rāma and then expanded his form, and was making off with his rider when Bala-rāma called upon Krishṇa for assistance. Krishṇa made a long speech, and ended by telling him to suspend awhile his mortal character and do what was right. Bala-rāma laughed, squeezed Pralamba with his knees, and beat him on the head with his fists till his eyes were knocked out and and his brain forced through his skull, so that he fell to the ground dead.

PRALAYA. A dissolution of the world at the end of a kalpa.

PRAMATHAS. A class of demi-gods or fiends attendant upon Śiva.

PRAMLOCHĀ. A celestial nymph sent by Indra to beguile the sage Kandu from his devotion and austerities. She lived with him for some hundreds of years, which were but as a day to the sage. When he awoke from his delusion he drove the nymph from his presence. The child with which she was pregnant came forth from her body in drops of perspiration, left upon the leaves of the tres. These drops congealed and became eventually the lovely nymph Mārishā.

PRĀṆA. 'Breath or life.' In the *Atharva-veda* it is personified and a hymn is addressed to it.

PRASANNA-RĀGHAVA. A drama by Jayadeva in seven acts.

PRASENA. Son of Nighna and brother of Satrājit or Sattrājita. He was killed by a lion.

PRAŚNA. Name of an Upanishad.

PRASŪTI. A daughter of Manu and wife of Daksha.

PRATARDANA. Son of Divodāsa, king of Kāśī. The whole family of Divodāsa was slain by a king named Vīta-havya. The afflicted monarch through a sacrifice performed by Bhrigu obtained a son, Pratardana, who became a mighty warrior, and avenged the family wrongs upon his father's foe. Vītahavya then flew to the sage Bhrīgu for protection, and was by him raised to the dignity of a Brahmarshi.

PRĀTIŚĀKHYAS. Treatises on the phonetic laws of the language of the Vedas, dealing with the euphonic combination of letters and the peculiarities of their pronunciation as they prevailed in the different Śākhās or Vedic schools. These treatises are considerably later than the hymns. Four such treatises are.

Rig-veda—One which is considered to belong to the Śākhalā-śākhā of this Veda, and is ascribed to Śaunaka. It has been edited and translated into German by Max Muller, and into French by M. Regner.

Yajurveda.—Taittirīya-prātiśākhya, belonging to the Black Yajur, printed in the *Bibliotheca India* and also in the *Journal of the American Oriental Society,* with a translation by Professor Whitney.

Vājasaneyī-prātiśākhya.—Belonging to the White Yajur, it is attributed to Kātyāyana, and has been edited and translated by Weber.

Atharva-veda.—The Śanukakīya Chaturādhyāyika, *i.e.,* Śaunaka's treatise in four chapters. Edited and translated into English by Whitney.

PRATI-SHṬHĀNA. An ancient city, the capital of the early kings of the Lunar race, "it was situated on the eastern side of the Ganges and Yamuna," opposite to the modern Allāhābād. The capital of Śālivāhana on the Godāvarī is supposed to be the same as "Pattan" or "Pyetan."

PRAUDHA-BRĀHMANA. One of the eight Brāhmaṇas of the Sāma-veda. It contains twenty-five sections, and is, therefore, also called Pancha-vinśa.

PRAYĀGA. The modern Allāhābād. The place where the Ganges, Yamuna, and the fabled subterranean Saraswatī unite, called also Tri-veṇī, 'the triple braid.' It has always been a celebrated place of pilgrimage.

PRETA. A ghost; an evil spirit animating a dead carcass, and haunting cemeteries and other places.

PRISHADHRA. A son of Manu Vaivaswata, who, according to the *Harivanśa* and the Purāṇas, became a Sūdra because he killed the cow of his religious preceptor.

PRISHATA. Drupada's father.

PRIŚNI. The earth, the mother of the Maruts. The name is used in the Vedas also for a cow. There were several females of this name, and one of them is said to have been a new birth of Devakī.

PRITHĀ. A name of Kuntī.

PRITHĪ, PRITHU, PRITH-YAINA. The *Śatapatha Brāhmaṇa* refers to Prithī as "first of men who was installed as a king." These early allusions receive a consistent form in the Purāṇas. He was called the first king, and from him the earth received her name Prithvi.

PRITHIVĪ. 'The broad.' The earth or wide world. In the Vedas the earth is personified as the mother of all beings, and is invoked together with the sky. According to the Vedas there are three earths corresponding to the three heavens, and our earth is called Bhūmī. Another name of the earth is Urvū, 'wide'. In the *Vishṇu Purāṇa* she is represented as receiving her name from a mythical person named Prithu, who granted her life, and so was to her as a father.

PRITHU. A king of the Solar race, a descendant of Ikshwāku. There are many Prithus.

PRIYA-DARŚI. A name of emperor Aśoka.

PRIYAM-VADA. A Vidyā-dhara, son of the king of the Gandharvas.

PRIYA-VRATA. One of the two sons of Brahmā and Śata-rūpā; or, according to other statements, a son of Manu Swāyam-bhuva. "Priya-vrata being dissatisfied that only half the earth was illuminated at one time by the solar rays, followed the sun seven times round the earth in his own flaming car of equal velocity, like another celestial orb, resolved to turn night into day." He was stopped by Brahmā. "The ruts which were formed by the motion of his chariot wheels were the seven oceans. In this way the seven continents of the earth were made."—*Bhāgavata Purāṇa*. In the *Vishṇu Purāṇa* his wife is stated to be Kāmyā, daughter of Kardama, by whom he had ten sons and two daughters. Three of the seven continents among the others.

PULAHA. Name of one of the Prajā-patis and great Rishis. His wife was Kshamā, and he had three sons, Kardama, Arva-rīvat, and Sahishṇu. A Gandharva.

PULASTYA. One of the Prajā-patis or mind-born sons of Brahmā, and one of the great Rishis. He was the medium through which some of the Purāṇas were communicated to man. He received the *Vishṇu Purāṇa* from Brahmā and communicated it to Parāśara, who made it known to mankind. He was father of Viśravas, the father of Kuvera and Rāvaṇa, and all the Rākshasas are supposed to have sprung from him.

PULINDAS. Barbarians; barbarous tribes living in woods and mountains, especially in Central India; but there were some in the north and on the Indus.

PULOMAN. A Dānava and father of Śachī, wife of Indra. He was killed by Indra when he wished to curse that deity for having ravished his daughter.

PUNDARĪKĀKSHA. 'The lotus-eyed;' a name of Vishṇu.

PUNDRA. A country corresponding "to Bengal proper, with part of South Bihār and the Jungle Mahals." A fabulous city between the Hima-vat and Hema-kūṭa.

PUṆYA-ŚLOKA (mas.), PUṆYA-ŚLOKĀ. (fem.). 'Hymned in holy verse.' An appellation applied to Krishṇa, Yudhishthira, and Nala, also to Draupadī and Sītā.

PURĀṆA. 'Old,' hence an ancient legend or tale of olden times. The Purāṇas succeed the Itihāsas or epic poems, but at a considerable distance of time, and must be distinguished from them. The epics treat of the legendary actions of heroes as mortal men, the Purāṇas celebrate the powers and works of positive gods, and represent a later and more extravagant development of Hinduism, of which they are in fact the Scriptures. According to Amara Sinha, an ancient Sanskrit lexicographer, Puraṇa is a work "which has five distinguishing topics: (1) The creation of the universe; (2) Its destruction and renovation; (3) The genealogy of gods and patriarchs; (4) The reigns of the Manus, forming the periods called Manwantaras. (5) The history of the Solar and Lunar races of kings." There are eighteen Purānas and in addition to these there are eighteen Upa-purāṇas or subordinate works. The Purāṇas are classified in three categories, according to the qualities of purity, gloom, and passion prevalent in them. Purāṇas in which the quality of Sattwa or purity prevails are—(1) Vishṇu, (2) Nāradīya, (3) Bhāgavata, (4) Garuḍa, (5) Padma, (6) Varāha. These are Vaishṇava Purāṇas, in which the god Vishṇu holds the pre-eminence. The Purāṇas in which Tamas, the quality of gloom or ignorance, predominates are— (1) Matsya, (2) Kūrma, (3) Linga, (4) Śiva, (5) Skanda, (6) Agni. These are devoted to the god Śiva. Those in which *Rajas* or passion prevails relate chiefly to the god Brahmā. They are—(1) Brahma, (2) Brahmāṇda, (3) Brahma-vaivarta, (4) Mārkaṇdeya, (5) Bhavishya, (6) Vāmana.

The Upa Purāṇas are named—(1) Sanat-kumāra, (2) Nara-sinha or Nri-sinha, (3) Nāradīya or Vrihan (old) Nāradīya, (4) Siva, (5) Dur-vāsasa, (6) Kāpila, (7) Mānava, (8) Ausanasa, (9) Vāruṇa, (10) Kālikā, (11) Śāmba, (12) Nandi, (13) Saura, (14) Pārāśara, (15) Āditya, (16) Māheśwara, (17) Bhāgavata, (18) Vāśishtha. There are also some other modern works to which the term Purāṇa has been applied.

PURAN-JAYA. 'City-conqueror.' The *Bhagavata Purāṇa* says that he took the city of the Daityas situated in the west. A prince of the Solar race, son of Vikukshi. According to *Vishṇu Purāṇa,* there was war between the gods and the Asuras in the Tretā age in which the former were worsted. They had recourse to Vishṇu for assistance, and he directed them to obtain the aid of Puran-jaya, into whose person he promised to infuse a portion of himself. The prince complied with their wishes, and asked that their chief, Indra, would asume the form of a bull and carry him, and the prince, upon his hump. This was done, and thus seated Puran-jaya destroyed all the enemies of the gods. As he rode on the hump he obtained the cognomen of Kakutstha.

PUROCHANA. The emissary of Duryodhana who attempted to burn the Pāndavas in their house and was burnt in his own house by Bhīma. See *Mahābhārata*.

PURU. The sixth king of the Lunar race, youngest son of Yayāti and Śarmishthā. He and his brother yadu were founders of two great branches of the Lunar race. The descendants of puru were called Pauravas, and of this race came the Kauravas and Pāndavas. The descendants of Yadu were the Yadavas and Krishṇa, was the most remarkable. *See* Yayāti.

PURUKUTSA. A son of Māndhātri, into whose person Vishnu entered for the purpose of destroying the subterranean Gandharvas, called Mauneyas. He reigned on the banks of the Narmadā, and that river personified as one of the Nāgas was his wife. By her he had a son, Trasadasyu. The *Vishṇu Purāṇa* is said to have been narrated to him by "Daksha and other venerable sages".

PURŪ-RAVAS. In the Vedas, a mythical personage connected with the sun and the dawn and existing in the middle region of the universe. According to the *Rigveda* he was son of Ilā, and a beneficent pious prince; but his mother and his father, the parentage usually assigned to him is that he was son of Budha by Ilā, daughter of Manu, and grandson of the moon." Through his mother he received the city of Pratishthāna. (*See* Ilā.) He is the hero of the story and of the drama of Vikrama and Urvaśī.

PURUSHA. 'Man.' 1. The original eternal man, the Supreme Being, and soul of the universe. 2. A name of Brahmā.

PURUSHA-NĀRĀYAṆA. The original male. The divine creator Brahmā.

PURUSHA-SŪKTA. A hymn of the *Rigveda* in which the four castes are first mentioned. It is considered to be one of the latest.

PURUSHOTTAMA. Literally 'best of men;' but the word Purusha is here used in its mythic sense of soul of the universe, and so the compound means the "supreme soul." It is a title of Vishṇu, and asserts his right to be considered the Supreme God. According to *Hari-vanśa,* "Purushottama is whatever is declared to be the highest, Purusha the sacrifice, and everything else which is known by the name of Purusha."

PURUSHOTTAMA-KSHETRA. The sacred territory around the temple of Jagannātha in Orissa.

PURVA-MĪMĀNSĀ. A school of philosophy. *See* Darśana.

PŪSHAN. A deity frequently mentioned in the Vedas, but he is not of a distinctly defined character. Many hymns are addressed to him. The word comes from the the root *push,* and the primary idea is that of "nourisher" or Providence.

PUSHKARA. A blue lotus. A celebrated tank about 8 km. from Ajmer in Rajasthan.

PUSHKARĀVATĪ. A city of the Gāndhāras not far from the Indus.

PUSHPA-DANTA. 'Flower-teeth.' 1. One of the chief attendants of Śiva. He incurred his master's displeasure by listening to his private conversation with Pārvatī and talking of it afterwards. For this he was condemned to become a man, and so appeared in the form of the great grammarian Kātyāyana. 2. One of the guardian elephants.

PUSHPAKA. A self-moving aerial car of large dimension, which contained within it a palace or city. Kuvera obtained it as a gift from Brahmā, but it was carried off by Rāvaṇa, his half-brother, and constantly used by him. After Rāma-chandra had slain Rāvaṇa, he made use of this capacious car to convey himself and Śītā, with Lakshmaṇa and all his allies, back to Ayodhyā; after that he returned it to its owner, Kuvera. It is also called Ratna-varshuka, "that rains jewels".

PUSHPA-KARANDINI. A name of Ujjayinī.

PUSHPA-MITRA. The first of the Śunga kings, who succeeded the Mauryas, and reigned at Pāṭaliputra. The grammarian Patanjali is supposed to have lived at this very time.

PUSHPOTKAṬĀ. A Rākshasī, the wife of Viśravas and mother of Rāvaṇa and Kumbha-karṇa.

PUT. A hell to which childless men are said to be condemned. "A name invented to explain the word *puttra*, son (hell-saver)."

PŪTANĀ. A female demon, daughter of Bali. She attempted to kill the infant Krishṇa by suckling him, but was herself sucked to death by the child.

R

RĀDHĀ. 1. Wife of Adhiratha and foster-mother of Karṇa. 2. The favourite mistress and consort of Krishṇa while he lived as Gopāla among the cowherds in Vrindāvana. She was wife of Ayana-ghosha, a cowherd. Considered by some to be an incarnation of Lakshmī, and worshipped accordingly, some have discovered a mystical character in Rādhā, and consider her as the type of the human soul drawn to the ineffable god, Krishṇa, or as that pure divine love to which the fickle lover returns.

RĀDHEYA. A metronymic of Karṇa.

RĀDHIKĀ. A diminutive and endearing form of the name Rādhā.

RĀGA (mas.), RĀGINī (fem.). The Rāgas are the musical modes or melodies personified, six or more in number, and the Rāginīs are their consorts.

RĀGHAVA. Descendant of Raghu, a name of Rāma.

RĀGHAVA-PĀNDAVīYA. A well reputed modern poem by Kavi Rāja, it is an artificial work, exhibiting extraordinary ingenuity in the employment of words. As its name implies, the poem celebrates the actions of Rāghava, *i.e.* Rāma, the descendant of Raghu, and also those of the Pāndava princes. It thus recounts at once in the same words the story of the *Rāmāyaṇa* and that of the *Mahābhārata*. The composition is so managed that the words may be understood as applying either to Rāma or the Pāndavas.

RĀGHAVA-VILĀSA. A poem on the life of Rāma by Viśwa-nātha, the author of the *Sāhitya-darpaṇa*.

RAGHU. A king of the Solar race. According to the *Raghu-vanśa,* he was the son of Dilīpa and great-grandfather of Rāma, who from Raghu got the patronymic Rāghava and the title Raghu-pati, chief of the race of

Raghu. The authorities disagree as to the genealogy of Raghu, but all admit him to be an ancestor of Rāma.

RAGHU-PATI. *See* Raghu.

RAGHU-VANŚA. 'The race of Raghu.' The name of a celebrated poem in nineteen cantos by Kāli-dāsa on the ancestry and life of Rāma. It has been translated into Latin by Stenzler, and into English by Griffiths. There are other translations and many editions of the text.

RĀHU. Rāhu and Ketu are the ascending and descending nodes in astronomy. Rāhu is the cause of the eclipses, and the term is used to designate the eclipse itself. He is also considered one of the planets, king of meteors, and a guardian of the south-west quarter. Mythologially Rāhu is a Daitya who is supposed to seize the sun and moon and swallow them, thus obscuring their rays and causing eclipses. He was son of Viprachitti and Sinhikā, and is called by his metronymic Sainhikeya. He had four arms, and his lower part ended in a tail. He was a great mischief-maker, and when the gods had produced the Amrita by churning the ocean, he assumed a disguise, and insinuating himself amongst them, drank some of it. The sun and moon detected him and informed Vishṇu, who cut off his head and two of his arms, but, as he had secured immortality, his body was placed in the stellar sphere, the upper parts, represented by a dragon's head, being the ascending node, and the lower parts, represented by a dragon's tail, being Ketu the descending node. Rāhu wreaks his vengeance on the sun and moon by occasionally swallowing them. According to Vishṇu Purāṇa "Eight black horses draw the dusky chariot of Rāhu, and once harnessed are attached to it for ever. On the Parvans (nodes, or lunar and solar eclipses) Rāhu directs his course from the sun to the moon, and back again from the moon to the sun. The eight horses of the chariot of Ketu, swift as the wind, are of the dusky red colour of lac, or of the smoke of burning straw." Rāhu is called by several names as Abhra-pisācha, 'the demon of the sky;' Bhārānī-bhū, 'born from the asterism Bharanī;' Graha, 'the seizer;' Kabandha, 'the headless'.

RAIBHYA. A sage who was the friend of Bhāradwāja. He had two sons, Arvāvasu and Parāvasu. The latter, under the curse of Bharadwāja, killed his father, mistaking him for an antelope, as he was walking about at night covered with an antelope's skin, Arvāvasu retired into the forest to obtain by devotion a remission of his brother's guilt. When he returned, Parāvasu charged him with the crime, and he again retired to his devotions. These so pleased the gods that they drove away Parāvasu and restored Raibhya to life. *See* Yava-krīta.

RAIVATA, RAIVATAKA. The range that branches off from the western portion of the Vindhya towards the north, extending nearly to the Yamuna.

RĀJA-GRITHA. The capital of ancient Magadha, its site is still traceable in the hills between Patna and Gaya.

RĀJANYA. A Vedic designation of the Kshatriya caste.

RĀJARSHI (Rāja-rishi). A Rishi or saint of the regal caste; a Kshatriya who, through pure and holy life on earth, has been raised as a saint or demigod to Indra's heaven, as Viśwā-mitra, Purūravas, etc.

RĀJA SEKHARA. A dramatist who wrote of the dramas *Viddha-Sālabhanjikā* and *Prāchanda-Pāndava.* He was also the writer of *Karpūra-Manjarī,* a drama entirely in Prākrit. Another play, *Bāla-Rāmāyaṇa,* is also attributed to him. He appears to have lived about the beginning of the twelfth century.

RĀJA-SŪYA. 'A royal sacrifice.' A great sacrifice performed at the installation of a king. Religious in its nature but political in its operation, it implied that he who instituted the sacrifice was the supreme lord, a king over kings, and his tributary princes were required to be present at the rite.

RĀJA-TARANGIṆĪ. A Sanskrit metrical history of Kashmīr by Kalhaṇa Pandit. It commences with the days of fable and comes down to the year 1027 A.D. The author probably lived about 1148 A.D. This is the only known work in Sanskrit which deserves the name of a history.

RAJI. A son of Āyus and father of 500 sons of great valour. In one of the chronic wars between the gods and the Asuras it was declared by Brahmā that the victory should be gained by that side which Raji joined. The Asuras first sought him, and he undertook to aid them if they promised to make him their king. They declined. The heavenly hosts came to him and undertook to make him their Indra. After the Asuras were defeated he became king of the gods, and Indra paid him homage. When he returned to his own city, he left Indra as his deputy in heaven. On Raji's death Indra refused to acknowledge the succession of his sons, with the help of Brihaspati, who led them astray and effected their ruin, Indra recovered his sovereignty.

RĀKA. A Rākshasī, wife of Viśravas and mother of Khara and Śūrpa-nakhā.

RĀKSHASAS. Goblins or evil spirits. They have been classified as of three sorts—the Yakshas, Titans or enemies of the gods, and lastly, demons and fiends who haunt cemeteries, disturb sacrifices, harass devout men, animate dead bodies, devour human beings, and vex and afflict mankind in all sorts of ways. These last are the Rākshasas, whose chief was Rāvaṇa, and according to some authorities, they are descendants of the sage Pulastya. According to other authorities, they sprang from Brahmā's foot. The *Vishṇu Purāṇa* also makes them descendants of Kaśyapa and Khasā, a daughter of Daksha. The *Rāmāyaṇa* states that when Brahmā created the waters, he formed certain beings to guard them. These guards were called Rākshasas. The *Vishṇu Purāṇa* also gives a somewhat similar derivation. It is thought that the Rākshasas of the epic poems were the rude barbarian races of India who were subdued by the Āryans.

RAKTA-VĪJA. An Asura whose combat with the

goddess Chāmuṇḍā (Devī) is celebrated in *Devī-māhātmya*. Each drop of his blood as it fell on the ground produced a new Asura, but Chāmuṇḍā put an end to this by drinking his blood and devouring his flesh.

RĀMA. There are three Rāmas: Paraśu-rāma, Rāma-chandra, and Bala-rāma. The name is specially applied to the second of these.

RĀMA. He was the eldest son of Dashratha, a king of Ayodhyā. Rāma is considered an incarnation of God Vishṇu. He killed the demon king Rāvaṇa and other demons. His story is told and retold in all the languages of India. Vālmiki in his *Rāmāyaṇa* and Tulsīdas in his *Rāmacharitmānas* have narrated the adventures of Rāma. Rāma is the national hero of India. His reign *Rām Rājya* is cited as a model rule.

RĀMA-GIRI. 'The hill of Rāma,' it stands a short distance north of Nāgpur.

RĀMA-SETU. 'Rāma's bridge,' constructed for him by his general, Nala, son of Viśwa-karma, at the time of his invasion of Sri Lanka. This name is given to the line of rocks in the channel between the continent and Sri Lanka, named "Adam's bridge" in maps.

RĀMATĀPANĪYOPANISHAD. An Upanishad of the *Atharva-veda,* in which Rāma is worshipped as the supreme god and the sage Yājnawalkya is his glorifier.

RAMBHĀ. An Apsara or nymph, produced at the churning of the ocean, and popularly the type of female beauty, she was sent by Indra to seduce Viśwāmitra, but was cursed by that sage to become a stone, and remain so for a thousand years. According to the *Rāmāyaṇa,* she was seen by Rāvaṇa when he went to Kailāsa, and he was so smitten by her charms that he ravished her, although she told him that she was the wife of Nala-Kūvara, son of his brother Kuvera.

RĀMEŚWARA. 'Lord of Rāma.' One of the twelve great Lingas set up, as is said, by Rāma at Rāmeśwaram or Rāmisseram, which is a celebrated place and contains a most magnificent temple.

RĀMOPĀKHYĀNA. 'The story of Rāma,' as told in the Vana-parva of *Mahābhārata,* relates many incidents celebrated in *Rāmāyaṇa*. It makes no mention of Vālmīki, the author of that poem, and it represents Rāma as a human being and a great hero, but not a deity.

RANTIDEVA. A pious and benevolent king of the Lunar race, sixth in descent from Bharata. He is mentioned in the *Mahābhārata* and Purāṇas as being enormously rich, very religious, in his sacrifices. The former authority says that he had 200,000 cooks. He had 2000 head of cattle and as many other animals slaughtered daily for use in his kitchen. He fed innumerable beggars daily with beef.

RATI. 'Love, desire.' The Venus of the Hindus, the goddess of sexual pleasures, wife of Kāma the god of love, and daughter of Daksha, she is also called Revā, Kāmi, Prīti, Kāma-patni, 'wife of Kāma,' Kāma-kalā, 'part of Kāma;' Kāmapriyā, 'beloved of Kāma;' Rāga-latā, 'vine of love;' Māyāvatī, 'deceiver;' Kelikilā, 'wanton;' Śubhāngī, 'fair-limbed'.

RATNĀVALĪ. 'The necklace.' A drama ascribed to a king of Kashmīr named Śrī Harsha Deva. The play is about the love of Udayana or Vatsa. princc of Kauśāmbī, and Vāsavadattā, princess of Ujjayinī. It was written between 1113 and 1125 A.D., and has been translated by Wilson.

RAUCHYA. The thirteenth Manu.

RAUDRA. A descendant of Rudra. A name of Kārttikeya, the god of war.

RĀVANA. He was the demon-king of Lanka. During the exile of Rāma, Rāvaṇa carried Sītā. Rāma invaded Lanka and killed Rāvaṇa. Though the chief of the demons, Rāvaṇa was a Brahman in his father's side and a great scholar of the Vedas.

RAVI. The sun. *See* Sūrya.

REṆUKĀ. Daughter of King Prasenajit or Reṇu, wife of Jamad-agni, and mother of Paraśu-rāma. She was also called Konkaṇā. A sight of the connubial endearments of King Chitra-ratha and his wife inspired her with impure thoughts, and her husband, perceiving that she had "fallen from perfection," desired her sons to kill her. Rumanwat, Su-shena, and Vasu, the three seniors, declined, and their father cursed them to be idiots. Paraśu-rāma, the fourth son, cut off her head. This act so gratified his father that Jamad-agni promised him whatever blessings he desired. Among other things, Paraśu-rāma asked for his mother to be brought back to life with ignorance of her death and in perfect purity. He also desired that his brothers might be restored to their senses.

REVĀ. The Narmadā river.

REVĀ. 1. Wife of Karna. 2. A name of Rati.

REVANTA. A son of Sūrya and Sanjanā, he is chief of the Guhyakas, and is also called Haya-vāhana.

REVATĪ. Daughter of King Raivata and wife of Bala-rāma, she was so beautiful that her father, thinking no one upon earth worthy of her, went up to Brahmā to consult him about a suitable husband. Brahmā delivered a long discourse on the glories of Vishṇu, and directed Raivata to proceed to Dwārakā, where a portion of Vishṇu was incarnate in the person of Bala-rāma. He went to Bala-rāma and gave him Revatī, but that hero, "beholding the damsel of excessively lofty height, shortened her with the end of his ploughshare, and she became his wife." She had two sons. Revatī is said to have taken part in her husband's drinking bouts.

RIBHU. 'Clever, skilful,' an epithet used for Indra, Agni, and the Ādityas. In the Purāṇic mythology, Ribhu is a "son of the supreme Brahmā, who, from his innate disposition, was of a holy character and acquainted with true wisdom." He was one of the four kumāras. His pupil was Nidāgha, a son of Pulastya, and he took especial interest in his instruction, returning to him after two intervals of a thousand years "to instruct him further in true wisdom." The *Vishṇu Purāṇa,* "originally composed by the Rishi (Nārāyaṇa), was communicated by Brahmā to Ribhu."

RIBHUS. Three sons of Su-dhanwan, a descendant of Angiras, severally named Ribhu, Vibhu and Vāja. Through their assiduous performance of good deeds they obtained divinity, exercised superhuman powers, and became entitled to receive praise and adoration. They are supposed to dwell in the solar sphere, and ther is an indistinct identification of them with the rays of the sun; but, whether typical or not, they prove the admission, at an early date, of the doctrine that men might become divinities.—*Wilson*. They are celebrated in the *Rigveda* as skilful workmen, who fashioned Indra's chariot and horses, and made their parents young again. By command of the gods, and with a promise of exaltation to divine honours, they made a single new sacrificial cup into four. They are also spoken of as supporters of the sky.

RIBHUKSHAN. The first of the three Ribhus. In the plural, the three Ribhus.

RICHĪKA. A Rishi descended from Bhrigu and husband of Satyavatī, son of Ūrva and father of Jamad-agni. (*See* Viśwāmitra.) In the *Mahābhārata* and *Vishṇu Purāṇa* it is related that Richīka was an old man when he demanded in marriage Satyavatī, the daughter of Gādhi, king of Kanya-kubja. Unwilling to give her to such an old man, Gādhi demanded 1000 white horses, each of them having one black ear. Rishīka obtained these from god Varuṇa, and so gained his wife. According to *Rāmāyaṇa,* he sold his son Śunaḥ-śephas to be a sacrifice.

RIDDHI. 'Prosperity.' The wife of Kuvera, god of wealth; the name is also used for Pārvatī, the wife of Śiva.

RIG-VEDA. *See* Veda.

RIG-VIDHĀNA. Writings which treat of the mystic and magic efficacy of the recitation of hymns of the *Rig-veda,* or even of single verses. Some of them are attributed to Śaunaka, but probably belong only to the time of the Purāṇas.—*Weber.*

RISHABHA. Son of Nābhi and Meru, and father of a hundred sons, the eldest of whom was Bharata. He gave his kingdom to his son and retired to a hermitage, where he led a life of such severe austerity and abstinence, that he became a mere "collection of skin and fibres, and went the way of all flesh". The *Bhāgavata Purāṇa* speaks of his wanderings in the art of the Peninsula, and connects him with the establishment of the Jain religion in those parts. Rishabha was the name of the first Jain Tīrthankara or saint.

RISHI. An inspired poet or sage, to whom the hymns of the Vedas were revealed, and under whose names they stand. "The seven Rishis" (*Saptarshi*), or the Prajāpatis, "the mind-born sons" of Brahmā, are often referred to, in the *Śatapatha Brāhamaṇa,* Bharadwāja, Viswāmitra, Jamad-agni, Vasishtha, Kasyapa, and Atri. The *Mahābhārata* list them as Marīchi, Atri, Angiras, Pulaha, Kratu, Pulastya, and Vaśishtha. The *Vāyu Purāṇa* adds Bhrigu to this list, making eight, although it still calls them "seven". The *Vishṇu Purāṇa,* more consistently, adds Bhrigu and Daksha, and calls them the nine Brahmarshis (*Brahma-rishis*). The names of Gautama, Kaṇwa, Vālmīki, Vyāsa, Manu, and Vibhāndaka are also enumerated among the great Rishis by different authorities. Besides these great Rishis there are many other Rishis. The seven Rishis are represented in the sky by the seven stars of the Great Bear constellation and as such are called Riksha and Chitra-śikhandinas, 'having bright crests.'

RISHI-BRĀHMAṆA. An old Anukramaṇi, or Index of the *Sāma-veda.*

RISHYA-MŪKA. A mountain near the source of the Pampā river and the lake Pampā. Rāma lived there for a time with the monkeys.

RISHYA-SRINGA. 'The deer-horned,' a hermit, the son of Vibhāndaka, descended from Kaśyapa. According to the *Rāmāyaṇa* and *Mahābhārata* he was born of a doe and had a small horn on his forehead. He was brought up in the forest by his father, and saw no other human being till he was on the verge of manhood. There was great drought in the country of Anga, and the king,

Lomapāda, was advised by his Brāhmans to send for the youth Rishya-śringa, who should marry his daughter Śāntā, and be the means of obtaining rain. A number of fair damsels were sent to bring him. He accompanied them back to their city, the desired rain fell, and he married Śāntā. This Śāntā was the adopted daughter of Lomapāda while her real father was Daśaratha; it was Rishya-śringa who performed the sacrifice which brought about the birth of Rāma.

RITU-PARṆA. A king of Ayodhyā, and son of Sarvakāma, into whose service Nala entered after he had lost his kingdom. He was "skilled profoundly in dice".

RITU-SANHĀRA. 'The round of the seasons,' a poem attributed to Kāli-dāsa. This poem was published by Sir W. Jones, and was the first Sanskrit work ever printed. There are other editions. It has been translated into Latin by Bohlen.

ROHIṆĪ. 1. Daughter of Kaśyapa and Surabhi, and mother of horned cattle, including Kāma-dhenu, the cow which grants desires. 2. Daughter of Daksha and fourth of the lunar asterisms, the favourite wife of the moon. 3. One of the wives of Vasu-deva, the father of Krishṇa and mother of Bala-rāma. She was burned with her husband's corpse at Dwārakā. 4. Krishṇa himself also had a wife.

ROHITA. 'Red.' A red horse; a horse of the sun or fire. 1. A deity celebrated in the *Atharva-veda,* probably a form of fire or the sun. 2. Son of King Hariś-chandra. He is also called Rohitāśwa. The fort of Rohtas is said to derive its name from him. *See* Hariś-chandra.

ROMA-HARSHANA. *See* Loma-harshana.

RUDRA. 'A howler or roarer; terrible.' In the Vedas Rudra has many attributes and many names. He is the howling terrible god, the god of storms, the father of the Rudras or Maruts, and is sometimes identified with the god of fire. On the one hand he is a destructive deity who brings diseases upon men and cattle, and upon the other he is a beneficent deity supposed to have a healing influence. It is worthy of note that Rudra is first called Mahādeva in the White Yajur-veda. As applied to the god Śiva, the name of Rudra generally designates him in his destructive character. In the *Brihad-āraṇyaka Upanishad* the Rudras are "ten vital breaths (*prāṇa*) With the heart (*manas*) as eleventh." In the *Vishṇu Purāṇa* the god Rudra is said to have sprung from the forehead of Brahmā, and at the command of the god to have separated his nature into male and female, then to have multiplied each of these into eleven persons, some of whom were white and gentle, others black and furious. Elsewhere it is said that the eleven Rudras were sons of Kaśyapa and Surabhi, and in another chapter of the same Purāṇa it is represented that Brahmā desired to come into existence as a youth. He wept and asked for a name. Brahmā gave him the name of Rudra; but he wept seven times more, and so he obtained seven other names: Bhava, Śarva, Īsāna, Pasupati, Bhīma, Ugra, and Mahā-deva.

RUDRA-SĀVARṆA. The twelfth manu. *See* Manu.

RUKMIN. A son of King Bhīshmaka and king of Vidarbha, who offered his services to the Pāndavas and Kauravas in turn, but was rejected by both on account of his extravagant boastings and pretensions. He was brother of Rukmiṇī, with whom Krishṇa eloped. Rukmin pursued the fugitives and overtook them, but his army was defeated by Krishṇa, and he owed his life to the entreaties of his sister. He founded the city of Bhoja-kata, and was eventually killed by Bala-rāma.

RUKMIṆĪ. Daughter of Bhīshmaka, king of Vidarbha. According to the *Harivanśa* she was sought in marriage by Krishṇa, with whom she fell in love. But her brother Rukmin was a friend of Kansa, whom Krishṇa had killed. He therefore opposed him and thwarted the match. Rukmiṇi was then betrothed to Śiśu-pāla, king of Chedi, but on her wedding day, as she was going to the temple, "Krishṇa saw her, took her by the hand, and carried away in his chariot." They were pursued by her intended husband and by her brother Rukmin, but Krishṇa defeated them both, and took her safe to Dwārakā, where he married her. She was his principal wife and bore him a son, Pradyumna. She had nine other sons Chāru-deshṇa, Su-deshṇa, Chāru-deha, Su-sheṇa, Chāru-gupta, Bhadra-chāru, Chāru-vinda, Su-chāru, and the very mighty Chāru; and one daughter, Chāru-mati. At Krishṇa's death she and seven other of his wives immolated themselves on his funeral pyre.

RŪMĀ. Wife of the monkey king Sugrīva.

S

SABALĀŚWAS. Sons of Daksha, one thousand in number.

SAGARA. He was a king of Ayodhya and belonged to the Solar race. His notorious sixty-thousand sons were reduced to ashes by the sacred flame that darted from the enraged sage Kapila. The grandson of Sagar Bhagirath brought down the holy Ganga from heaven. Its waters cleanesed the ashes of the sons of Sagara. Accordingly, Ganga received the name of Bhagirathi.

SHASRĀKSHA. 'Thousand-eyed.' An epithet of Indra.

SĀHITYA-DARPAṆA. 'The mirror of composition.' A celebrated work by Viśwanātha Kavi Rāja, written about the fifteenth century. It has been translated into English for the *Bibliotheca Indica*. There are several editions of the text.

ŚAIBYĀ. Wife of Hariś-chandra; wife of Jyāmagh; wife of Śata-dhanu.

SAINDHAVAS. The people of Sindhu or Sindh, of the country between the Indus and the Jhelum.

ŚAIVA PURĀṆA. Same as Śiva Purāṇa.

ŚAKA. An era commencing 78 A.D., and called the era of Śālivāhana. Cunningham supposes its epoch to be connected with the defeat of the Śakas by Śālivāhana.

ŚĀKALA. The city of the Bāhīkas or Madras, in the Panjāb. It has been identified with the Sagala of Ptolemy on the Hyphasis (Byās), south-west of Lahore. Cunningham says it is the Sangala of Alexander.

ŚĀKALYA. An old grammarian and expositor of the Vedas who lived before the time of Yaska. He is said to have divided a Sangala of the Veda into five, and to have taught these portions to as many disciples. He was also called Veda-mitra and Deva-mitra.

ŚĀKAPŪṆI, SĀKAPŪRṆI. An author who arranged

a part of the *Rig-veda* and he appended a glossary. He lived before the time of Yāska.

ŚAKAS. A northern people, usually associated with the Yavanas. Wilson says, "These people, the Sakai and Sacae of classical writers, the Indo-Scythians of Ptolemy, extended, about the commencement of our era, along the West of India, from the Hindu Koh to the mouths of the Indus." They were probably Turk or Tatar tribes, and were among those recorded as conquered by King Sagara, who compelled them to shave the upper half of their heads. They seem to have been encountered and kept back by King Vikramāditya of Ujjayinī, who was called Śakāri, 'foe of the Śakas.'

ŚĀKAṬĀYANA. An ancient grammarian. Part of his work is said to have been lately discovered by Dr. Buhler.

ŚĀKHĀ. 'Branch, sect.' The Śākhās of the vedas are renderings of the same text as taught and handed down traditionally by different schools and teachers, showing some slight variations, the effect of long-continued oral tradition.

ŚĀKINĪS. Female demons attendant on Durgā.

ŚAKRA. A name of Indra.

ŚĀKRĀṆĪ. Wife of Indra.

SAKRA-PRASTHA. Same as Indra-prastha.

ŚĀKTA. A worshipper of the Śaktis.

ŚAKTI. The wife or the female energy of a deity, but especially of Śiva.

ŚAKTI, ŚAKTRI. A priest and eldest son of Vaśishtha. King Kalmāsha-pāda struck him with a whip, and he cursed the king to be under the control of a man-eating Rākshasa. He himself became the first victim of the monster he had evoked.

ŚAKUNI. Brother of Queen Gāndhārī, and so uncle of the Kaurava princes. He was a skilful gambler and a cheat, so he was selected to be the opponent of Yudhishthira in the match in which that prince was induced to stake and lose his all. He was also known by the patronymic Saubala, from Su-bala, his father.

ŚAKUNTALĀ. A nymph who was the daughter of Viśwā-mitra and Menakā. She was born and left in a forest, where she was nourished by birds until found by the sage Kaṇwa. She was brought up by this sage in his hermitage as his daughter, and is often called his daughter. The love, marriage, separation, and re-union of Śakuntalā and King Dushyanta are the subject of the celebrated drama Śakuntalā. She was mother of Bharata, the head of a long race of kings, after whose name India is called Bhārata-varsha. The wars of his descendants are sung in the *Mahābhārata*. Śakuntalā was living in the hermitage of Kaṇwa when she was seen in the forest by King Dushyanta, who fell in love with her. He induced her to contract with him a Gandharva marriage, that is, a simple declaration of mutual acceptance.

While leaving her to return to his city, he gave her a ring as a pledge of his love. When the nymph went back to the hermitage, she was so engrossed with thoughts of her husband that she heeded not the approach of the sage Dur-vāsas, who had come to visit Kaṇwa, and the choleric saint cursed her to be forgotten by her beloved. He afterwards relented, and promised that the curse would be removed as soon as Dushyanta should see the ring. Śakuntalā, finding herself with child, set off to her husband; but on her way she bathed in a sacred pool, and there lost the ring. On reaching the palace, the king did not recognise her and would not own her, so she was taken by her mother to the forest, where she gave birth to Bharata. Then it happened that a fisherman caught a large fish and in it found a ring which he carried to Dushyanta. The king recognised his own ring, and he soon afterwards accepted Śakuntalā and her son Bharata. Kālidāsa's drama of Śakuntalā was the first translation made from Sanskrit into English. It excited great curiosity and gained much admiration and there are many translations into the languages of Europe. Professor Williams has published a beautifully illustrated translation.

ŚĀLAGRĀMA. A stone held sacred and worshipped by the Vaishṇavas, because its spirals are supposed to contain or be typical of Vishṇu. It is an ammonite found in the river Gandak, and is valued more or less highly according to the number of its spirals and perforations.

ŚĀLIVĀHANA. A celebrated king of the south of India, who was the enemy of Vikramāditya, and whose era, the Śaka, dates from A.D. 78. His capital was Pratishthāna on the Godāvarī. He was killed in battle at Kārūr.

ŚĀLWA. Name of a country in the west of India, or Rajasthan, also the name of its king.

ŚALYA. King of the Madras, and brother of Mādrī, second wife of Pāndu. In the great war he left the side of the Pāndavas and went over to the Kauravas. He acted as charioteer of Karṇa in the great battle. At the death of Karṇa he succeeded him as general, and commanded the army on the last day of the battle, when he was slain by Yudhishthira.

SĀMA-VEDA. The third Veda. *See* Veda.

SĀMA-VIDHĀNĀ BRĀHMAṆA. The third Brāhmaṇa of the *Sāma-veda,* it has been edited and translated by Burnell.

SĀMAYACHĀRIKA SŪTRAS. Rules for the usages and practices of everyday life. *See* Sūtras.

ŚĀMBA. A son of Krishṇa by Jāmbawati but the *Linga Purāṇa* names Rukmiṇī as his mother. At the swayamvara of Draupadī he carried off that princess, but he was pursued by Duryodhana and his friends and made prisoner. Balarāma undertook to obtain his release, and when that hero thrust his ploughshare under the ramparts of Hastinā-pura and threatened it with ruin, the Kauravas gave up their prisoner, and Bala-rāma took him to Dwārakā, where he lived a dissolute life and scoffed at sacred things. The devotions of the three great sages Viśwāmitra, Dur-vāsas, and Nārada, excited the ridicule of Śāmba and his boon companions. They dressed Śāmba up to represent a woman with child and took him to the sages, inquiring whether he would give birth to a boy or a girl. The sages answered, "This is not a woman, but the son of Krishṇa, and he shall bring forth an iron club which shall destroy the whole race of Yadu, ... and you and all your people shall perish by that club." Śāmba accordingly brought forth an iron club which Ugrasena caused to be pounded and cast into the sea. These ashes produced rushes, and the rushes when gathered turned into clubs, or into reeds which were used as swords. One piece could not be crushed. This was subsequently found in the belly of a fish, and was used to tip an arrow, which was used by the hunter Jaras, who unintentionally killed Krishṇa. Under the curse of Durvāsas, Śāmba became a leper and retired to the Panjāb, where by fasting, penance, and prayer he obtained the favour of Sūrya (the sun), and was cured of his leprosy. He built a temple to the sun on the banks of the Chandrabhāgā (Chināb), and introduced the worship of that luminary.

ŚĀMBA-PURĀṆA. *See* Purāṇa.

ŚAMBARA. In the Vedas, a demon, also called a Dasyu, who fought against King Divodāsa, but was defeated and had his many castles destroyed by Indra. He appears to be a mythical personification of drought, of a kindred character to Vritra, or identical with him. In the Purāṇas a Daitya who carried off Pradyumna and threw him into the sea, but was subsequently slain by him. (*See* Pradyumna.) He was also employed by Hiraṇyakaśipu to destroy Prahlāda.

ŚAMBHU. A name of Śiva; also one of the Rudras.

ŚAMBŪKA. A Śudra, mentioned in the *Raghu-vanśā*, who performed religious austerities and penances improper for a man of his caste, and was consequently killed by Rāma-chandra.

ŚAMĪ. The *Acacia suma*, the wood of which is used for obtaining fire by friction. So Agni, or fire, is called Śamīgarbha, 'having the Śamī for its womb.' It is sometimes personified and worshipped as goddess, Śamīdevī.

SAMPĀTI. A mythical bird who appears in the *Rāmāyaṇa* as son of Garuḍa, and brother of Jaṭāyus. According to another account he was son of Aruṇa and Śyenī. He was the ally of Rāma.

SAMVARAṆA. Son of Riksha, fourth in descent from Ikshwāku, and father of Kuru. According to the *Mahābhārata* he was driven from Hastināpura by the Pānchālas, and forced to take refuge among the thickets of the Indus. When the sage Vaśishtha joined his people and became the priest of Rāja's family, they recovered their country under Kuru.

SAMVARTA. Writer of a Dharma-śāstra or code of law bearing his name.

SAMVAT, SAMVATSARA. 'Year.' The era of Vikramāditya, dating from 57 B.C.

ŚANAIŚ-CHARA. 'Slow-moving.' A name of Śani or Saturn.

SANAKA, SANANDA, SANĀTANA, SANAT-KUMĀRA. The four Kumāras or mind-born sons of Brahmā. Some specify seven. Sanat-kumāra (or Sanat-sujāta) was the most prominent of them. They are also called by the patronymic Vaidhātra. See Kumāra.

SANAT-KUMĀRA PURĀṆA. *See* Purāṇa.

SANDHYĀ. 'Twilight.' It is personified as the daughter of Brahmā and wife of Śiva. In the *Śiva Purāṇa* it is related that she changed herself into a deer when Brahmā attempted to do violence to his daughter. Brahmā then assumed the form of a stag and pursued her through the sky. Śiva saw this, and shot an arrow which cut off the head of the stag. Brahmā then reassumed his own form and paid homage to Śiva. The arrow remains in the sky in the sixth lunar mansion, called Ardrā, and the stag's head remains in the fifth mansion, Mriga-śiras.

SANDHYĀ-BALA. 'Strong in twilight.' Rākshasas and other demons, supposed to be most powerful at twilight.

ŚĀNDILYA. A descendant of Śandila. A particular sage who was connected with the *Chhāndogya Upanishad;* one who wrote a book of Sūtras, one who wrote upon law, and one who was the author of the Bhāgavata heresy: two or more of these may be one and the same person. The Sūtras or aphorisms have been published in the *Bibliotheca Indica*.

SĀNDĪPANI. A master-at-arms who gave instruction to Bala-rāma and Krishṇa.

SANDRACOTTUS. *See* Chandragupta.

SANGĪTA-RATNĀKARA. A work on singing, dancing, and pantomime, written by Śārngi Deva.

SANHITĀ. That portion of a Veda which comprises the hymns.

SANHITOPANISHAD. The eighth Brāhmaṇa of the *Sāma-veda,* where text with a commentary has been published by Burnell.

ŚANI. The planet Saturn. The regent of that planet, represented as a black man in black garments. Śani was a son of the sun and Chhāyā, but another statement is that he was the offspring of Bala-rāma and Revatī. He is also known as Āra, Koṇa, and Kroda, and by the patronymic Śaura. His influence is evil, hence he is called Krūra-driś and Krūra-lochana, 'the evil-eyed one.' He is also Manda, 'the slow;' Pangu, 'the lame;' Śanaiś-chara, 'slow-moving;' Saptārchī, 'seven-rayed;' and Asita, 'the dark.'

SANJAYA. 1. The charioteer of Dhritarāshtra. He was a minister and went as ambassador to the Pāndavas before the great war broke out. He is represented as reciting to Dhritarāshtra the *Bhagavad-gītā*. His patronymic is Gāvalgani, son of Gavalgana. 2. A king of Uja-dattā.

SANJNĀ. 'Conscience.' According to the Purāṇas she was daughter of Viśwa-karma and wife of the sun. She had three children Manu Vaivaswata, Yama, and Yamī (goddess of the Yamunā river). "Unable to endure the fervours of her lord, Sanjnā gave him Chhāyā (shade) as his handmaid, and repaired to the forests to practise devout exercises." The sun beheld her engaged in austerities in the form of a mare, and he approached her as a horse. Hence sprang the two Aświns and

Revanta. Sūrya then took Sanjnā back to his own dwelling, but his effulgence was still so overpowering, that her father, Viśwa-karma, placed the sun upon his lathe, and cut away an eighth part of his brilliance. She is also called Dyumayī, 'the brilliant' and Mahā-vīryā, 'the very powerful'.

ŚANKARA. 'Auspicious.' A name of Śiva in his creative character or as chief of the Rudras.

ŚANKARĀCHĀRYA (Śankara + āchārya). The great religious reformer and teacher of the Vedānta philosophy, who lived in the eighth or ninth century. A native of Kerala or Malabar, he lived a very erratic life, disputing with heretics and popularising the Vedānta philosophy by his preaching and writings wherever he went. His travels extended as far as Kashmīr, and he died at Kedāranāth in the Himālayas at the early age of thirty-two. His learning and sanctity were held in such high esteem and reverence, that he was looked upon as an incarnation of Śiva, and was belived to have the power of working miracles. God Śiva was the special object of his worship, and he was the founder of the great sect of Smārtava Brāhmans, who are very powerful in the south. He established several *maths* or monasteries for the teaching and preservation of his doctrines. Some of these still remain. The chief one is at Śringa-giri or Śringiri, on the edge of the Western Ghats in the Mysore, and it has the supreme control of the Smārtava sect. The writings attributed to him are very numerous, chief among them being his Bhāshyas or commentaries on the Sūtras or aphorisms of Vyāsa, a commentary on the *Bhagavad-gītā,* some commentaries on the upanishads, and the *Ānanda-laharī,* a hymn in praise of Pārvatī, the consort of Śiva.

ŚANKARA-VIJAYA. 'The triumph of Śankara.' A biography of Śankarāchārya relating his controversies with heretic sects and his refutation of their doctrines and superstitions. There is more than one work bearing this name; one by Ānanda Giri, which is published in the

Bibliotheca Indica and another by Mādhavāchārya. The latter is distinguished as the *Sankshepa Śankara-vijaya.*

SANKARSHAṆA. A name of Bala-rāma.

ŚANKHA. Writer of a Dharma-śāstra or law-book bearing his name, he is often coupled with Likhita, and the two seem to have worked together.

SĀNKHĀYANA. 1. Name of a writer who was the author of the *Sānkhāyana Brāhmaṇa* of the *Rig-veda,* and of certain Srauta-sūtras also called by his name 2. He is the oldest known writer on the Ars Erotica, and is author of the work called *Sānkhāyana Kāma-sūtra.*

SĀNKHYA. A school of philosophy. *See* Darśana.

SANKHYA-DARŚANA. Kapila's aphorisms on the Sānkhya philosophy, which have been printed.

SĀNKHYA-KĀRIKĀ. A work on the Sānkhya philosophy, written by Īśwara Krishṇa; translated by Colebrooke and Wilson.

SĀNKHYA-PRAVACHANA. A text-book of the Sānkhya philosophy, said to have been written by Kapila himself.

SĀNKHYA-SĀRA. A work on the Sānkhya philosophy by Vijnāna Bhikshu, edited by Hall in the *Bibliotheca Indica.*

SANNYĀSĪ. A Brāhman in the fourth and last stage of his religious life. (*See* Brāhman.) In the present day the term has a wider meaning, and is applied to various kinds of religious mendicants who wander about and subsist upon alms, most of them in a filthy condition and with very scanty clothing. They are generally devotees of Śiva.

ŚĀNTĀ. Daughter of Daśa-ratha, son of Aja, but adopted by Loma-pāda or Roma-pāda, king of Anga. She was marreid to Rishya-śringa.

ŚĀNTANU. A king of the Lunar race, son of Pratīpa, father of Bhīshma, and in a way the grandfather of Dhritarāshtra and Pāndu. Regarding him it is said, "Every decrepit man whom he touches with his hands becomes young." He was called Satya-vāch, 'speaker of truth,' and was remarkable for his "devotion and charity, modesty, constancy, and resolution."

ŚĀNTI-ŚATAKA. A country of verses on peace of mind. A poem of repute written by Srī Śihlana.

SAPTARSHI (Sapta-rishi). The seven great Rishis. Gotama, Bharadwaja, Vishwamitra, Jamad-agni, Vashistha, Kashyapa, and Atri.

SAPTA-VADHRI. A Vedic Rishi, who says, in a hymn. "Aświns, by your devices sunder the wickerwork for the liberation of the terrified, imploring Rishi Sapta-vadhri." Sapta-vadhri had seven brothers who determined to prevent his having intercourse with his wife. So they shut him up everynight in a large basket, which they locked and sealed, and in the morning they let him out. He prayed to the Aświns, who enabled him to get out of his cage during the night and to return to it at daybreak.

ŚARABHA. 1. A fabulous animal represented as having eight legs and as dwelling in the Himalaya. It is called also Utpādaka and Kunjarārāti. 2. One of Rāma's monkey allies.

ŚARA-BHANGA. A hermit Rāma and Sītā visited the Dandaka forest. On seeing Rāma he declared that his desire had been granted, and that he would depart to the highest heaven. He prepared a fire and entered it. His body was consumed, but there came forth from the fire a beautiful youth, and in this form Śara-bhanga departed to heaven.

ŚĀRADĀ-TILAKA. 1. A mystic poem by Lakshmaṇa. 2. A dramatic monologue by Śankara, not earlier than the twelfth century. 3. Name of a Tantra.

ŚARADWAT. A Rishi said to be the father of Kripā. He is also called Gautama.

SARAMĀ. 1. In the *Rig veda* the dog of Indra and mother of the two dogs with four eyes each Sārameyas, who were the watchdogs of Yama. Saramā is said to have pursued and recovered the cows stolen by the Paṇis, a myth which has been supposed to mean that Saramā is the same as Ushas, the dawn, and that the cows represent the rays of the sun carried away by night. 2.

The wife of Vibhīshaṇa, who attended upon Sītā, and showed her great kindness when she was in Rāvaṇa's captivity. 3. In the *Bhāgavata Purāṇa,* Saramā is one of the daughters of Daksha, and the mother of wild animals.

SĀRAMEYAS. The two children of Saramā, Indra's watchdog; they were the watchdog of Yama, and each had four eyes. They have been compared with the Greek Hermes.

ŚARAṆYŪ. 'The fleet runner.' A daughter of Twashiri. She has been identified with the Greek Erinnys. According to hymn of the *Rig-veda,* "1. Twashtri makes a wedding for his daughter. (Hearing) this, the whole world assembles. The mother of Yama, the wedded wife of the great Vivaswat (the sun), disappeared. 2. They concealed the immortal (bride) from mortals. Making (another) of like appearance, they gave her to Vivaswat. Śaraṇyū bore the two Aświns, and when she had done so she deserted the two twins." In the Nirukta the story is expanded as follows:—"Śaraṇyū, the daughter of Twashtri, bore twins to Vivaswat, the son of aditi. She then substituted for herself another female of similar appearance, and fled in the form of a mare. Vivaswat in like manner assumed the shape of a horse and followed her. From their intercourse sprang two Aswins, while Manu was the offspring of Savarnā (or the female of like appearance.)" The *Brihad-devatā* has another version:—"Twashtri had twin children, (a daughter) Śaraṇyū and (a son) Triśiras. He gave Śaraṇyū in marriage to Vivaswat, to whom she bore Yama and Yamī, who also were twins. Śaraṇyū took the form of a mare and departed. Vivaswat, in ignorance, begot on the female who had left Manu, a royal Rishi, who resembled his father in glory; but discovering that the real Śaraṇyū, Twashtri's daughter, had gone away, Vivaswat followed her quickly, taking the shape of a horse of the same species. Recognising him in that form, she approached him with the desire of sexual connection, which he gratified. In their haste his seed fell on the ground, and she, being desirous of offspring, smelled it. From this act sprang the two Kumāras—Nāsatya and Dasra—who were lauded as Aświns (sprung from a horse)."—*Muir's Texts,* v. 227. See the Purāṇic version under "Sanjnā".

SĀRASWATA. 1. In the *Mahābhārata* the Rishi Sāraswata is represented as being the son of the personified river Saraswatī. During a time of great drought he was fed with fish by his mother, and so was enabled to keep up his knowledge of the Vedas, while other Brāhmaṇas were reduced to utter lack of subsistence so that study was neglected and the Vedas were lost. When the drought was over, the Brāhmans flocked to him for instruction, and 60,000 acquired a knowledge of the Vedas from him. "This legend," says Wilson, "appears to indicate the revival, or, more probably, the introduction of the Hindu ritual by the race of Brāhmans, or the people called Sāraswata," who dwelt near the Saraswatī river. Sāraswata Brāhmans still dwell in the Panjāb, and also in many other parts. 2. The country about the Saraswatī river. 3. A great national division of the Brāhman caste.

SARASWATĪ. 'Watery, elegant.' In the Vedas, Saraswatī is primarily a river, but is celebrated in the hymns both as a river and a deity. The Saraswatī river was one boundary of Brahmāvartta, the home of the early Āryans, and was to them, in all likelihood, a sacred river, as the Ganges has long been to their descendants. As a river goddess, Saraswatī is lauded for the fertilising and purifying power of her waters, and as the bestower of fertility, fatness, and wealth.

SARASWATĪ KĀNTHĀBHARAṆA. A treatise on poetical and rhetorical composition generally ascribed to Rāja Bhoja.

SARAYU. The Sarju river or Gogra.

ŚARMISHṬHĀ. Daughter of Vrishaparvan, the Dānava, second wife of Yayāti and mother of Purū. *See* Devayānī.

ŚĀRNGA. The bow of Krishṇa.

SARVA. A Vedic deity; the destroyer; subsequently a name of Śiva and of one of the Rudras. *See* Rudra.

SARVA-DARŚANA SANGRAHA. A work by Mādhavāchārya dealing with the Darśanas or schools of philosophy, whether orthodox or heretical.

ŚARVARĪ. A woman of low caste, who was very devout and looked for the coming of Rāma until she had grown old. In reward of her piety a sage raised her from her low caste, and when she burnt herself on a funeral pyre. She ascended from the pyre in a chariot to the heaven of Vishṇu.

SARVA-SĀRA. Name of an Upanishad.

ŚAŚĀDA. 'Hare-eater,' a name given to Vikukshi.

ŚAŚĪ, ŚAŚIN. The moon, so called from the marks on the moon being considered to resemble a hare *(Śaśa).*

ŚĀSTRA. 'A rule book, treatise.' Any book of divine or recognised authority, but more especially the law-books.

ŚATA-DHANU. A king who had a virtuous and discreet wife named Śaibyā. They were both worshipper of Vishṇu. One day they met a heretic, while Śata-dhanu conversed with him, the wife "turned away from him and cast her eyes up to the sun". After a time Śata-dhanu died and his wife ascended his funeral pyre. The wife was born again as a princess with a knowledge of her previous existence, but the husband received the form of a dog. She recognised him in this form and placed the bridal garland round his neck. Then she reminded him of his previous existence and of the fault which had caused his degradation. He was greatly humiliated and died from a broken spirit. After that, he was born successively as a jackal, a wolf, a crow, and a peacock. In each form his wife recognised him, reminded him of his sin, and urged him to make efforts for restoration to his former dignity. At length "he was born as the son of a person of distinction," and Śaibyā then elected him groom and they lived happily together." When he died both "ascended beyond the sphere of Indra to the regions where all desires are for ever gratified." "This legend," says Wilson, "is peculiar to the Vishṇu Purāṇa, although the doctrine it inculcates is to be found elsewhere."

ŚATA-DHANWAN, ŚATA-DHANUS. 'Having a hundred bows.' A Yādava and son of Hridika, he killed Satrājit, father of Satya-bhāmā, the wife of Krishṇa, in his sleep, and was himself killed in revenge by Krishṇa.

ŚATA-DRU. 'Flowing in a hundred (channels),' the name of the river Sutlej, the Zaradrus of Ptolemy, the Hesudrus of Pliny.

ŚATA-GHNĪ. 'Slaying hundreds.' A missile used by Krishṇa, it is described in the *Mahābhārata* as a stone set round with iron spikes, but many have supposed it to be a rocket or other fiery weapon.

ŚATA-KRATU. 'The god of hundred rites;' Indra.

ŚATAPATHA-BHĀHMAṆA. A celebrated Brāhmaṇa at tached to the White Yajur-veda, and ascribed to the Rishi Yājnawalkya. Found in two Śākhās, the Mādhyandina and the Kāṇwa, this is the most complete and systematic as well as the most important of all the Brāhmaṇas. It has been edited by Weber.

ŚATA-RŪPĀ. The first woman. According to one account she was the daughter of Brahmā, and from their incestuous intercourse the first Manu, named Swāyambhuva, was born. Another account makes her the wife, not the mother, of Manu. The account given by Manu is that Brahmā divided himself into two parts, male and female, and from them sprang Manu. She is also called Sāvitrī. *See* Virāj and Brahmā.

SATĪ. A daughter of Daksha and wife of Rudra, *i.e.*, Śiva. The *Vishṇu Purāṇa* states that she "abandoned her body in consequence of the anger of Daksha. She then became the daughter of Himavat and Menā; and the divine Bhava again married Umā, who was identical with his (Siva's) former spouse." The authorities generally agree that she died or killed herself on account of the quarrel between her husband and father. *Kāśī Khanda*, a modern work, represents that she entered the fire and became a Satī. *See* Pitha-sthāna.

SATRĀJITA. Son of Nighna. In return for praise rendered to the sun be beheld the luminary in his proper form, and received from him the wonderful Syamantaka gem. He lost the gem, but it was recovered and restored to him by Krishṇa. In return he presented Krishṇa with his daughter Satya-bhāmā. There had been many suitors for this lady's hand, and one of them, named Śata-dhanwan, in revenge for her loss, killed Satrājit and carried off the gem, but he was afterwards killed by Krishṇa.

ŚATRU-GHNA. 'Foe destroyer,' twin-brother of Lakshamaṇ and half-brother of Rāma, in whom an eighth part of the divinity of Vishṇu was incarnate. His wife was Śruta-kīrtti cousin of Sītā. He fought on the side of Rāma and killed the Rākshasa chief Lavaṇa. *See* Daśaratha and Rāma.

SATYA-BHĀMĀ. Daughter of Satrājita and one of the four chief wives of Krishṇa. She had ten sons, Bhānu, Subhānu, Swar-bhānu, Prabhānu, Bhānumat, Chandrabhānu, Brihadbhānu, Atibhānu, Srībhānu, and Pratibhānu. Krishṇa took her with him to heaven, and she induced him to bring away the Pārijāta tree.

SATYA-DHRITI. Son of Śaradwat and grandson of the sage Gautama. According to the *Vishṇu Purāṇa,* he was father by the nymph Urvaśī of Kripa and Kripī.

SĀTYAKI. A kinsman of Krishṇa, who fought on the side of the Pāndavas, and was Krishṇa's charioteer. He assassinated Krita-varma in a drinking bout at Dwārakā, and was himself cut down by the friends of his victim. He is also called Dāruka, Yuyudhāna and Śaineya.

SATYA-LOKA. *See* Loka.

SATYAVĀN. *See* Sāvitrī.

SATYA-VATĪ. 1. Daughter of Uparichara, king of Chedi, by an Apsara named Adrikā, who was condemned to live on earth in the form of a fish. She was mother of Vyāsa by the Rishi Parāśara, and she was also wife of King Śāntanu, mother of Vichitra-vīrya and Chitrāngada, and grandmother of the Kauravas and Pāndavas, the rivals in the great war. The sage Parāśara met her as she was crossing the river Yamunā when she was quite a girl, and the offspring of their illicit intercourse was found on an island (*dwīpa*) in that river, and was hence called Dwaipāyana. (*See* Vyāsa.) She was also called Gandha-kālī, Gandha-vatī, and Kālānganī; and as her mother lived in the form of a fish, she is called Dāsa-nandinī, Dāseyī, Jhajhodarī, and Matsyodarī, 'fish-born.' 2. A daughter of King Gādhi, wife of the Brāhman Richīka, mother of Jamad-agni and grandmother of Paraśu-rāma. She was of the Kuśika race, and is said to have been transformed into the river. *See* Richīka and Viśwāmitra.

SATYA-VRATA. 1. Name of the seventh Manu. 2. A king of the Solar race, descended from Ikshwāku. He was father of Hariś-chandra, and is also named Vedhas and Tri-sanku. According to the *Rāmāyaṇa* he was a pious king, and was desirous of performing a sacrifice by virtue of which he might ascend bodily to heaven. Vaśishtha, his priest, declined to perform it, declaring it impossible. He then applied to Vaśistha's sons, and they condemned him to become a Chandāla. In his distress and degradation he applied to Viśwāmitra, who promised to raise him in that form to heaven. Viśwāmitra's intended sacrifice was strongly resisted by the sons of Vaśishtha, but he reduced them to ashes, and condemned them to be born again as outcasts for seven hundred births. The wrathful sage bore down all other opposition, and Tri-śanku ascended to heaven, where his entry was opposed by Indra and the gods, but Viśwāmitra in a fury declared that he would create "another Indra, or the world should have no Indra at all". The gods were obliged to yield, and it was agreed that Tri-sanku, an immortal, should hang with his head downwards, and shine among some stars newly called into being by Viśwāmitra.

The *Vishṇu Purāṇa* gives a simpler version. While Satya-vrata was a Chandāla, and the famine was raging, he supported Viśwāmitra's family by hanging deer's flesh on a tree on the bank of the Ganges, so that they might obtain food without the degradation of receiving it from a Chandāla. For this charity Viśwāmitra raised him to heaven.

ŚĀTYĀYANA. Name of a Brāhmana.

SATYA-YAUVANA. A certain Vidyā-dhara.

SAUBHA. A magical city, apparently first mentioned in the Yajur-veda. An aerial city belonging to Hariś-chandra, and according to popular belief still visible occasionally. It is called also Kha-pura, Prati-mārgaka, and Tranga. In the *Mahābhārata* an aerial or self-supporting city belonging to the Daityas on the shore of the ocean, protected by the Śālwa king.

SAUBHARI. A devout sage, who, when he was old and emaciated, was inspired with a desire of offspring. he went to King Māndhātri, and demanded one of his fifty daughters. Afraid to refuse, and yet unwilling to endow a daughter upon such a suitor, the king temporised, and endeavoured to evade the request. It was at length settled that, if any one of the daughters should accept him as a bridegroom, the king would consent to the marriage. Saubhari was conducted to the presence of the girls; but on his way he assumed a fair and handsome form, so that all the girls were captivated, and contended with each other to become his wife. It ended by his marrying them all and taking them home. He caused Viśwa-karma to build for each a separate luxuriously furnished palace, where they lived each as having her husband always present with her, and believing that he was devoted to her and her only. He had a hundred and fifty sons whose desires ever expanding, he resolved to devote himself solely to penance and the worship of Vishṇu. Accordingly, he abandoned his children and retired with his wives to the forest. *See* Vishṇu Purāṇa.

SAUDĀSA. Son of King Sudās. Their descendants are all Saudāsas. *See* Kalmāsha-pāda.

SAUNANDA. A club shaped like a pestle, which was one of the weapons of Bala-rāma.

ŚAUNAKA. A sage, the son of Śunaka and grandson of Gritsa-mada, he was the author of the *Brihad-devatā*, an Anukramaṇi, and other works, and he was a teacher of the *Atharvaveda*. Āśwalāyana was his pupil.

SAURA PURĀṆA. *See* Purāṇa.

SAURĀSṬRAS. The people of Surāshtra.

SAUTI. Name of the sage who repeated the *Mahābhārata* to the Rishis in the Naimisha forest.

SAUVĪRAS. A people connected with the Saindhavas or people of Sindh, and probably inhabitants of the western and southern parts of the Panjab.

SĀVARṆA, SĀVARṆI. The eighth Manu. The name is used either alone or in combination for all the succeeding Manus. *See* Manu.

SAVRṆĀ. Wife of the sun. "The female of like appearance," whom Śaraṇyū wife of Vivaswat, substituted for herself when she fled. Manu was the offspring of Savarṇā. This is the version given in the Nirukta. In the *Vishṇu Purāṇa*, Savarṇā is daughter of the ocean, wife of Prāchīnabarhis, and mother of the ten Prachetasas.

SAVITRI. 'Generator.' 1. A name used in the Vedas for the sun. Many hymns are addressed to him, and he is sometimes distinguished from that deity. 2. One of the Ādityas.

SĀVITRĪ. 1. The holy verse of the Veda, commonly called Gāyatrī. 2. A name of Śata-rūpā, the daughter and wife of Brahmā, who is sometimes regarded as a personification of the holy verse. 3. Daughter of king Aśwa-pati, and lover of Satyavān, whom she insisted on marrying, although she was warned by a seer that he had only one year to live. When the fatal day arrived, Satyavān went out to cut wood, and she followed him. There he fell, dying, to the earth, and as she supported him, she saw Yama, king of the dead, who had come for her husband's spirit. Yama carried off the spirit towards the shades, but Sāvitrī followed him. Her devotion pleased Yama, and he offered her any boon except the life of her husband. She extorted three such boons from Yama, but still she followed him, and he was finally constrained to restore her husband to life.

SAVYA-SĀCHIN. 'Who pulls a bow either hand.' A title of Arjuna.

SAYAṆA. Sāyaṇāchārya, the celebrated commentator on the *Rig-veda.* "He was brother of Mādhavācharya, the prime minister of Vīra Bukka Rāya, Rāja of Vijaya-nagara, in the fourteenth century, a munificent patron of Hindu literature. Both the brothers are celebrated as scholars, and many important works are attributed to them; not only scholia on the Sanhitās and Brāhmanas of the Vedas, but original works on grammar and law; the fact, no doubt, being that they availed themselves of those means which their situation and influence secured them, and employed the most learned Brāhmans they could attract to Vijaya-nagara upon the works which bear their name, and to which they also contributed their own labour and learning; their works were, therefore, compiled under peculiar advantages, and are deservedly held in the highest estimation."—*Wilson.*

ŚESHA, ŚESHA-NĀGA. King of the serpent race or Nāgas, and of the infernal regions called Pātāla. A serpent with thousand heads is the couch and canopy of Vishṇu. Sometimes Śesha is represented as supporting the world, and sometimes as upholding the seven Pātālas or hells. Whenever he yawns he causes earthquakes. At the end of each kalpa he vomits venomous fire which destroys all creation. When the gods churned the ocean they made use of Śesha as a great rope. He is represented clothed in purple and wearing a white necklace, holding in one hand a plough and in the other a pestle. He is also called Ananta, 'the endless,' as the symbol of eternity. His wife was named Ananta-śīrshā. He is sometimes distinct from Vāsuki but generally identified with him. In the Purāṇas he is said to be the son of Kaśyapa and Kadru, and according to some authorities he was incarnate in Balarāma. His hood is called Maṇi-dwīpa, 'the island of jewels,' and his palace Maṇibhītti, 'jewel-walled,' or Maṇimandapa, 'jewel palace.'

SETU-BANDHA. 'Rama's bridge.' The line of rocks between the continent and Sri Lanka called in maps "Adam's bridge." It is also known as Samudrāru. There is a poem called Setubandha or Setu-kāvya on the subject of the building of the bridge by Rāma's allies.

SHAD-DARŚANĀ. *See* Darśana.

SHAD-VINŚA. 'Twenty-sixth.' One of the Brāhmanas of the *Sāma-veda.* It is called "the twenty-sixth" because it was added to the *Praudha Brāhmaṇa,* which has twenty-five sections.

SHAṬ-PURA. 'The sixfold city,' or 'the six cities' granted by Brahmā to the Asuras, and of which Nikumbha was king. It was taken by Krishṇa and given to Brahmā-datta, a Brāhman.

SIDDHAS. A class of semi-divine beings of great purity and holiness, who dwell in the regions of the sky between the earth and the sun. They are said to be 88,000 in number.

SIDDHĀNTA. Any scientifc work on astronomy or mathematics.

SIDDHĀNTA KAUMUDĪ. A modern and simplified form of Pāṇini's Grammar by Bhattojī Dīkshita.

SIDDHĀNTA-ŚIROMAṆI. A work on astronomy by Bhāskarāchārya, which has been printed, and has been translated for the *Bibliotheca Indica.*

ŚIKHANDIN, ŚIKHANDINĪ. Śikhandinī is said to have been the daughter of Rāja Drupada, but according to another statement she was one of the two wives whom Bhīshma obtained for his brother Vichitra-vīrya. "She (the widow) perished in the jungle, but before her death she had been assured by Paraśu-rāma that she should become a man in a future birth, and cause the death of Bhīshma, who had been the author of her misfortunes."

Accordingly she was born again as Śikhandin, son of Drupada. Bhīshma fell in battle pierced all over by the arrows of Arjuna, but according to this story the fatal shaft came from the hands of Śikhandin. *See* Ambā.

ŚIKSHĀ. Phonetics; one of the Vedāngas, the science which teaches the proper pronunciation and manner of reciting the Vedas.

ŚILPA-ŚĀSTRA. The science of mechanics, including architecture and any book of treatise thereon.

SINDHU. 1. The river Indus; also the country along that river and the people dwelling in it. From *Sindhu* came the *Hind* of the Arabs, the *Hindoi* or *Indoi* of the Greeks, and our *India*. 2. A river in Mālwa.

SINHALA, SINHALA-DWĪPA. Sri Lanka.

SINHĀSANA DWĀTRINŚAT. The thirty-two stories told by the images which supported the throne of King Vikramāditya. It is the *Singhāsan Battīsī* in Hindustani, and is current in most of the languages of India.

SINHIKĀ. 1. A daughter of Daksha and wife of Kaśyapa; also a daughter of Kaśyapa and wife of Viprachitti. 2. A Rākshasī who tried to swallow Hanumān and make a meal of him. He allowed her to do so and then rent her body to pieces and departed. Her habit was to seize the shadow of the object she wished to devour and so drag the prey into her jaws.

ŚIPRĀ. The river on which the city of Ujjayinī stands.

ŚĪRA-DHWAJA. 'He of the plough-banner,' an epithet for Janaka.

ŚIŚUMĀRA. 'A torpoise.' The planetary sphere, which, as explained by the *Vishṇu Purāṇa,* has the shape of a torpoise, Vishṇu being seated in its heart, and Dhruva or the pole star in its tail. "As Dhruva revolves, it causes the sun, moon, and other planets to turn round also; and the lunar asterisms follow in its circular path, for all the celestial luminaries are, in fact, bound to the polar star by aerial cords."

ŚIŚU-PĀLA. Son of Dama-ghosha, king of Chedi, by Śrutadevī, sister of Vasu-deva. Thus, he was cousin of

Krishṇa, but he was Krishṇa's implacable foe, because Krishṇa had carried off Rukmiṇī, his intended wife. He was slain by Krishṇa at the great sacrifice of Yudhi-shthira in punishment of opprobrious abuse.

ŚIŚUPĀLA-BADHA. 'The death of Śīśu-pāla;' an epic poem by Māgha, in twenty cantos.

SĪTĀ. In the Veda, Sītā is the furrow, or husbandry personified. In the *Rāmāyaṇa,* she is the daughter of Janaka and married to Rāma. She accompanied her husband in the exile but was carried off by Rāvaṇa. Rāma invaded Lanka and killed Rāvaṇa.

When Rāma recovered his wife, he received her coldly, and refused to take her back, for it was hard to believe that she had retained her honour. She asserted her purity in touching language, and resolved to establish it by the ordeal of fire. She entered the flames in the presence of gods and men, but she remained unhurt, and the god of fire brought her forth and placed her in her husband's arms. Notwithstanding this proof of her innocence, jealous thoughts passed through the mind of Rāma, and after he had ascended his ancestral throne at Ayodhyā, his people blamed him for taking back a wife who had been in the captivity of a licentious ravisher. Although she was pregnant, he banished her to the hermitage of Vālmīki, where she gave birth to twin sons, Kuśa and Lava. There she lived till the boys were about fifteen years old. One day they strayed to their father's capital. He recognised and acknowledged them and then recalled Sītā. She returned and publicly declared her innocence. But her heart was deeply wounded. She called upon her mother earth to attest her purity, and it did so. The ground opened, and she was taken back into the source from which she had sprung.

ŚIVA. In Hinduism he is the third chief god with Brahmā and Vishṇu. As Mahākāla, he destroys the universe.

ŚIVA PURĀṆA. *See* Purāṇa.

ŚIVI. Son of Uśīnara, king of the country also called Uśīnara, near Gandhāra. Sage Mārkandeya extols in the

Mahābhārata the great charity and devotion of son. Indra is the shape of a falcon pursued Agni having assumed the form of a pigeon. The pigeon took refuge in the bosom of Śivi, and the falcon would accept nothing from Śivi instead of the pigeon but an equal weight of the king's own flesh. Śivi cut a piece of flesh from his right thigh and placed it in the balance, but the bird was always heavier. He cut again and again, and still the pigeon drew the scale, until the king placed his whole body in the balance. This outweighed the pigeon and the falcon flew away. On another occasion Vishṇu went to Śivi in the form of a Brāhman and demanded food, but would accept no food but Śivi's own son Vrihad-garbha, whom he required Sivi to kill and cook. The king did so, and placed the food before the Brāhman, who then told him to eat it himself. Śivi took up the head and was ready to eat, when the Brāhman stayed his hand, commended his devotion, and restoring the son to life, vanished from sight.

SKAMBHA. 'The supporter.' A name sometimes used in the *Rig-veda* to designate the Supreme Deity. There is considerable doubt and mystery about both this name and deity. "The meaning of the term," says Goldstucker, "is 'the fulcrum,' and it seems to mean the fulcrum of the whole world in all its physical, religious, and other aspects."—*Muir's Texts,* v. 378.

SKANDA. God of war. *See* Kārttikeya.

SKANDA PURĀṆA. "The Skanda Purāṇa is that in which the six-faced deity (Skanda) has related the events of the Tatpurusha Kalpa, enlarged with many tales, and subservient to the duties taught by Maheśwara. It is said to contain 81,800 stanzas: so it is asserted amongst mankind." "It is uniformly agreed," says Wilson, "that the *Skanda Purāṇa,* in a collective form, has no existence; and the fragments, in the shape of Sanhitās, Khandas, and Māhātmyas, which are affirmed in various parts of India to be portions of the Purāṇa. The most celebrated of these portions is the Kāśī Khanda, a very minute description of the temples of Śiva in or adjacent to Vārānasī mixed with directions for worshipping Maheśwara, and a great variety of legends explanatory of its merits and of the holiness of Kāśī. Many of them are puerile and uninteresting, but some of them are of a higher character. There is every reason to believe the greater part of the contents of the Kāśī Khanda anterior to the first attack upon Vārānasī by Mahmūd of Ghazni. The Kāśī Khanda alonc contain 15,000 stanzas. Another considerable work is the Utkala Khanda, giving an account of the holiness of Orissa."

SMĀRTA. Appertaining to the Smriti. The Smārta-sūtras.

SMRITI. Inspiration, as distinguished from Śruti, or direct revelation; what has been remembered and handed down by tradition. In its widest application, the term includes the Vedāngas, the Sūtras, the *Rāmāyaṇa*, the *Mahābhārata*, the Purāṇas, the Dharma-sāstra, especially the works of Manu, Yājnawalkya, and other inspired lawgivers, and the Nīti-śāstras or ethics, but its ordinary application is to the Dharma-śāstras.

SMRITI-CHANDRIKĀ. A treatise on law, according to the Drāvidian or Southern school, by Devana Bhatta.

SOMA. The juice of a milky climbing plant extracted and fermented, forming a beverage offered in libations to the deities, and drunk by the Brāhmans.

SOMADEVA BHATTA. The writer or compiler of the collection of stories called *Kathā-sarit-sāgara*.

SOMAKA. Grandfather of Drupada, who transmitted his name to his descendants.

SOMA-NĀTHA, SOMEŚWARA. 'Lord of the moon.' The name of a celebrated Lingam or emblem of Śiva at the city of Somnāth-pattan in Gujarat. It was destroyed by Mahmūd of Ghaznī.

SOMAPAS. 'Soma-drinkers.' A class of Pitris or manes who drink the soma juice. *See* Pitris.

SOMA-VANŚA. *See* Chandra-vanśa.

ŚRADDHĀ. 1. Faith, personified in the Vedas and lauded in a few hymns. 2. Daughter of the sage Daksha, wife of the god Dharma, and reputed mother of Kāmadeva, the god of love.

ŚRADDHA-DEVA, ŚRĀDDHA-DEVA. Manu is called by the former name in the Brāhmaṇas, and by the latter in the *Mahābhārata*. The latter is commonly applied to Yama.

ŚRAUTA. Belonging to the Śruti. *See* Sūtra and Vedāngas.

ŚRĀVASTĪ. An ancient city which seems to have stood near Faizābād in eastern Uttar Pradesh.

ŚRĪ. 'Fortune, prosperity.' 1. The wife of Vishṇu. 2. An honorific prefix to the names of gods, kings, heroes, and men and books of high estimation.

ŚRĪ BHĀGAVATA. *See* Bhāgavata Purāṇa.

ŚRĪ DĀMA CHARITRA. A modern drama in five acts by Sāma Rāja Dīkshita, on the sudden affluence of Śrī Dāman, a friend of Krishṇa.

ŚRĪ-DHARA SWĀMĪ. Author of several commentaries of repute on the *Bhagavad-gītā, Vishṇu Purāṇa,* etc.

SRĪ HARSHA. A great sceptical philosopher, and author of the poem called Naishadha or Naishadhīya. There were several kings of the name.

SRĪ HARSHA DEVA. A king who was author of the drama *Ratnāvalī*.

ŚRINGA-GIRI. A hill on the edge of the Western Ghāts in Mysore, where there is a *math* or monastic establishment of Brāhmans, said to have been founded by Śankarāchārya.

ŚRINGĀRA TILAKA. 'The mark of love.' A work by Rudra Bhatta on the sentiments and emotions of lovers as exhibited in poetry and the drama.

ŚRINGA-VERA. The modern Sungroor, a town on the left bank of the Ganges and on the frontier of Kosala and the bhīl country. The country around was inhabited by Nishādas or wild tribes, with Guha, the friend of Rāma, as their chief.

ŚRĪ-ŚAILA. The mountain of Śrī, the goddess of fortune. It is a holy place in the south India, near the

Krishṇa, and was formerly a place of great splendour. It retains its sanctity but has lost its grandeur. Also called Śrī-parvata.

ŚRĪ-VATSA. A particular mark, said to be a curl of hair on the breast of Vishṇu or Krishṇa.

ŚRUTA-BODHA. A work on metres attributed to Kāli-dāsa, it has been edited and translated into French by Lancereau.

SRUTA-KĪRTTI. Cousin of Sītā and wife of Satru-ghna.

ŚRUTARSHI. A Rishi who did not receive the Śruti (revelation) direct, but obtained it second-hand from the Vedic Rishis.

ŚRUTI. 'What was heard.' The revealed word. The Mantras and Brāhmaṇas of the Vedas are always included in the term, and the Upanishads are generally classed with them.

STHALĪ-DEVATAS, DEVATĀS. Gods or goddesses of the soil, local deities.

STHĀNU. A name of Śiva.

STHĀPATYA-VEDA. The science of architecture, one of the Upa-vedas.

STHŪṆĀ, STHUṆĀ-KARṆA. A Yaksha who is represented in the *Mahābhārata* to have changed sex for a while with Śikhandinī, daughter of Drupada.

SU-BĀHU. 'Five-armed.' 1. A son of Dhrita-rāshtra and king of Chedi. 2. A son of Śatru-ghna and king of Mathurā.

SU-BALA. 1. A king of Gandhāra, father of Gāndhārī, wife of Dhrita-rāshtra. 2. A mountain in Lankā on which Hanumān alighted after leaping over the channel.

SU-BHADRĀ. Daughter of Vasu-deva, sister of Krishṇa, and wife of Arjuna. Bala-rāma, her elder brother, wished to give her to Dur-yodhana, but Arjuna carried her off from Dwārakā at Krishṇa's suggestion, and Bala-rāma subsequently agreed to their union. She was mother of Abhimanyu. She appears especially as sister of Krishṇa in his form as Jagannātha.

ŚUBHĀNGĪ. 'Fair-limbed.' An epithet of Rati, wife of Kāma, and of Yakshī, wife of Kuvera.

SU-BHĀNU. Son of Krishṇa and Satya-bhāmā.

SU-BODHINĪ. A commentary by Viśweśwara Bhatta on the law-book called Mitāksharā.

SU-BRAHMAṆYA. A name of Kārttikeyā, god of war, used especially in the South.

SU-CHĀRU. A son of Krishṇa and Rukmiṇī.

SU-DARŚANA. The name of Krishṇa's Chakra or discus weapon. *See* Vajra-nābha.

SUDĀS. A king who frequently appears in the *Rig-veda,* and at whose court the rival Rishis Vaśishtha and Viśwāmitra are represented as living. He was famous for his sacrifices.

SU-DESHNA. Son of Krishśa and Rukmiṇī.

ŚU-DESHNĀ. 'Good-looking.' 1. Wife of the Rāja of Virāṭa, the patron of the disguised Pāndavas, and mistress of Draupadī. 2. Also the wife of Bālin.

SU-DHARMĀ, SU-DHARMAN. The hall of Indra, "the unrivalled gem of princely courts," which Krishṇa ordered Indra to resign to Ugrasena, for the assemblage of the race of Yadu. After the death of Krishṇa it was back to Indra's heaven.

ŚŪDRA. The fourth or servile caste. *See* Varṇa.

ŚŪDRAKA. A king who wrote the play in ten acts called *Mrichchhakaṭī,* 'the toy-cart'.

SU-DYUMNA. Son of the Manu Vaivaswata. He was a female, Ilā at his birth but was afterwards changed into a male and called Su-dyumna. Under the curse of Śiva he again became Ilā, who married Budha or Mercury, and was mother of Purū-ravas. By favour of Vishṇu the male form was again recovered, and Su-dyumna became the father of three sons. This legend evidently has reference to the origin of the Lunar race of kings.

SU-GRĪVA. 'Handsome neck.' A monkey king who was dethroned by his brother Bālin. Bālin had been killed, Su-grīva was re-installed by Rāma as king at Kishkindhyā. He, with his advisor Hanumān and their army of monkeys, were the allies of Rāma in his war against Rāvaṇa, in which he was wounded. He is said to have been son of the sun, and so he is called Ravi-nandana. He is described as being grateful, active in aiding his friends, and able to change his form at will. Rumā was his wife.

SUHMA. A country said to be east of Bengal.

ŚUKA-SAPTATI. 'The seventy (tales) of a parrot.' This is the original of the Persian *Tūtī-nāmah* from which the Hindustani *Totā-kahānī* was translated.

ŚUKRA. The planet Venus and its regent. Śukra was son of Bhrigu and priest of Bali and the Daityas (Daitya-guru). He is also called the son of Kavi. His wife's name was Śusumā or Śata-parwā. His daughter Devayānī married Yayāti of the Lunar race, and her husband's infidelity induced Śukra to curse him. Śukra is identified with Uśanas, and is author of a code of law. The *Harivanśa* relates how he went to Śiva and asked for means of protecting the Asuras against the gods, and for achieving his object he performed "a painful rite, imbibing the smoke of chaff with his head downwards for a thousand years." In his absence the gods attacked the Asuras and Vishṇu killed his mother, for which Vishṇu was cursed by Śukra "to be born seven times in the world of men." Śukra restored his mother to life. The gods alarmed at Śukra's penance being accomplished, Indra sent his daughter Jayantī to lure him from it. She waited upon him and soothed him, but he accomplished his patronymic Bhārgava, and also as Bhrigu. He is als Kavi or Kāvya, 'the poet.'

SŪKTA. A Vedic hymn.

SU-MANTRA. The chief consellor of Rāja Daśaratha and friend of Rāma.

SU-MANTU. The collector of the hymns of the *Atharva-veda,* he is said to have been a pupil of Veda Vyāsa, and to have acted under his guidance.

ŚUMBHA and NIŚHUMBHA. Two Asura brothers, who were killed by Durgā. As related in the *Mārkandeya Purāṇa,* these brothers, were votaries of Śiva, and performed severe penance for 5000 years in order to obtain immortality. Śiva refused the boon, and they continued their penance with such increased intensity for 800 years more, that the gods trembled. On the advice of Indra, the god of love, Kāma, went to them with two celestial nymphs, Rambhā and Tilottamā, and they succeeded in seducing the two Asuras and holding them in the toils of sensuality for 5000 years. On recovering from their voluptuous aberrration they drove the nymphs back to paradise and recommenced their penance. At the end of 1000 years Śiva blessed them "that in riches and strength they should excel the gods." In their exaltation they warred against the gods, who, in despair, appealed in succession to Brahmā, Vishṇu, and Siva, but in vain. The latter advised them to apply to Durgā, and they did so. She contrived to engage the Asuras in war, defeated their forces, slew their commanders, Chanda and Munda, and finally killed them. *See* Sunda.

SU-MERU. The mountain Meru, actual or personified.

SU-MITRĀ. Wife of Daśaratha and mother of Lakshmaṇa and Śatru-ghna. *See* Daśaratha.

SU-MUKHA. 'Handsome face.' This epithet is used for Garuḍa and for the son of Garuḍa.

ŚUNAH-ŚEPHAS. The legend of Śunah-śephas, is narrated in the *Aitareya Brāhmaṇa,* King Hariś-chandra, of the race of Ikshwāku, being childless, made a vow that if he obtained a son he would sacrifice him to Varuṇa. A son was born who received the name of Rohita, but the father postponed, under various pretexts, the fulfilment of his vow. When at length he resolved to perform the sacrifice, Rohita refused to be the victim, and went out into the forest, where he lived for six years. He then met a poor Brāhman Rishi called Ajīgartta, who had three sons, and Rohita purchased from Ajīgartta for a hundred cows, the second son, named Śunah-śephas, to be the substitute for himself in the sacrifice. Varuṇa approved of the substitute, and the sacrifice was about to be performed, the father receiving another hundred cows for binding his son to the sacrificial post, and a third hundred for agreeing to slaughter him. Śunah-śephas seved himself by reciting verses in honour of different deities, and was received into the family of Viśwāmitra, who was one of the officiating priests.

The *Rāmāyaṇa* gives a different version of the legend. Ambarīsha, king of Ayodhyā, was performing a sacrifice when Indra carried off the victim. The officiating priest represented that this loss could be atoned for only by the sacrifice of a human victim. The king, after a long search, found a Brāhman Rishi named Rishīka, who had two sons, and the younger, Śunah-śephas, was then sold by his own consent for a hundred thousand cows, ten millions of gold pieces, and heaps of jewels. Śunah-śephas met with his maternal uncle, Viśwāmitra, who taught him two divine verses which he was to repeat when about to be sacrificed. As he was bound at the stake to be immolated, he provided the two gods Indra and Vishṇu with the excellent verses, and Indra, being pleased, bestowed upon him long life. He was afterwards called Deva-rāta, and is said to have become son of Viśwāmitra.

SU-NĀMAN. Son of Ugrasena and brother of Kansa. He was king of the Śūrasenas. When Kansa was overpowered in battle by Krishṇa, Su-nāman went to help him, but was encountered and slain by Bala-rāma.

SU-NANDĀ. A princess of Chedi who befriended Damayantī when she was deserted by her husband.

SUNDA. Sunda and Upasunda, of the *Mahābhārata*, were two Daitya sons of Nisunda, for whose destruction the Apsaras Tilottamā was sent down from heaven. They quarrelled for her, and killed each other. *See* Śumbha.

SU-PARṆAS. 'Fine-winged.' "Being of superhuman character, as Garuḍa, and other birds of equally fanciful description; one of those classes first created by the Brahmādikas, and included in the daily presentation of water to deceased ancestors, etc."— *Wilson*.

SU-PĀRŚWA. A fabulous bird in the *Rāmāyaṇa*. He was son of Sampāti and nephew of Jaṭāyus.

SU-PRIYA. 'Very dear.' Chief of the Gandharvas.

SŪRA. A Yādava king, father of Vasu-deva and Kuntī, and grand-father of Krishṇa, who ruled over the Śurasenas at Mathura.

SURĀ. Wine or spirituous liquor, personified as Surā-devī, a goddess or nymph produced through the churning of the ocean.

SURABHI. The 'cow of plenty,' produced at the churning of the ocean, who granted every desire, and is reverenced as "the fountain of milk and curds." *See* Kāma-dhenu and Nandinī.

SURAS. In the Vedas, a class of beings connected with Sūrya, the sun. The inferior deities who inhabit Swarga; a god in general. According to some, the word is allied to *swarg* heaven;' others think it to have sprung from the derivation assigned to *asura*, and as *a-sura* is said to signify 'not a god,' *sura* has come to mean 'god'.

SU-RASĀ. A Rākshasī, mother of the Nāgas. When Hanumān was on his flight to Lankā against Rāvaṇa, she tried to save her relative by swallowing Hanumān bodily. To avoid this, Hanumān extended his body and continued to do so, while she stretched her mouth till it was a hundred leagues wide. Then he suddenly shrank up to the size of a thumb, darted through her, and came out of her right ear.

ŚŪRASENAS. Name of a people, the Suraseni of Arrian. Their capital was Mathura on the Yamunā, which Manu calls Śūrasena.

ŚŪRPA-NAKHĀ. 'Having nails like winnowing-fans.' Sister of Rāvaṇa, this Rākshasī admired the beauty of Rāma and fell in love with him. When she made advances to Rāma he referred her to Lakshmaṇa, and Lakshmaṇa in like manner sent her back to Rāma. Enraged at this double rejection, she fell upon Sītā, and Rāma was obliged to interfere forcibly for the protection of his wife. He called out to Lakshmaṇa to disfigure the violent Rākshasī, and Lakshmaṇa cut off her nose and ears. She flew to her brothers for revenge, and this brought on the war between Rāma and Rāvaṇa. She described to Rāvaṇa the beauty of Sītā, and instigated him to carry her off. Finally she cursed him just before the engagement in which he was killed.

SŪRYA. The sun or its deity, he is one of the three chief deities in the Vedas, as the great source of light and warmth.

SŪRYA SIDDHĀNTA. A celebrated work on astronomy, said to have been revealed by the sun (Sūrya). It has been edited in the *Bibliotheca Indica* by Hall, and there are other editions. It has been translated by Whitney and Burgess.

SŪRYA-VANŚA. The Solar race. A race or lineage of Kshatriyas which sprang from Ikshwāku, grandson of the sun. Rāma was of this race, and so were many other great kings and heroes. Many Rājputs claim descent from this and the other great lineage, the Lunar race. The Rāma of Udaypur claims to be of the Sūrya-vanśa, and the Jhārejas of Cutch and Sindh assert a descent from the Chandra-vanśa. There were two dynasties of the Solar race. The elder branch, which ruled at Ayodhyā, descended from Ikshwāku through his eldest son, Vikukshi. The other dynasty, ruling at Mithilā, descended from another of Ikshwāku's sons, named Nimi.

SU-ŚARMAN. A king of Tri-gartta, who attacked the Rāja of Virāṭa, and made him prisoner after defeating him, but Bhīma rescued the Rāja and made Su-śarman prisoner.

SUSHENA. 1. A son of Krishṇa and Rukmiṇī. 2. A physician in the army of Rāma, who brought the dead to life and performed other miraculous cures.

ŚUŚHNA. An Asura mentioned in the *Rig-veda* as killed by Indra.

SUŚRUTA. A medical writer whose work was translated into Arabic before the end of the eighth century. There is a Latin translation by Hepler and one in German by Vullers.

SŪTA. 'Charioteer,' a title given to Karna.

SU-TĪKSHNA. A hermit sage who dwelt in the Dandaka forest, and was visited by Rāma and Sītā.

SŪTRA. 'A thread or string.' A rule or aphorism. A verse compared in brief and technical language,—a very favourite form among the Hindus of embodying and transmitting rules There are Sūtras upon almost every subject, but "the Sūtras" generally signify those which are connected with the Vedas the Kalpa Sūtras, relating to ritual; the Grihya Sūtras, to domestic rites; and the Sāmayachārika Sūtras, to conventional usages. The Kalpa Sūtras, having especial reference to the Veda or Śruti, are called Śrauta; the others are classed as Smārta, being derived from the Smriti. The Sūtras generally are anterior to Manu, and are probably as old as the sixth century B.C. Several of them have been published in the *Bibliotheca Indica*.

ŚUTUDRĪ. The river Sutlej.

SU-VAHU. A Rākshasa, son of Tārakā. He was killed by Rāma.

SU-VELA. One of the three peaks of the mountain Trikūṭa, on middle one of which Lankā was built.

SU-YODHANA. 'Fair fighter,' a name of Duryodhana.

SWADHĀ. 'Oblation.' Daughter of Daksha and Prasūti according to one statement, and of Agni according to another, she is connected with the Pitris or manes, and is represented as wife of Kavi or of one class of Pitris, and as mother of others.

SWĀHĀ. 'Offspring.' Daughter of Daksha and Prasūti, she was wife of Vahni or Fire or of Abhimānī, one of the Agnis.

SWA-PHALKA. Husband of Gāndinī and father of Akr^ra, he was a man of great sanctity of character, and "famine, plague, death, and other visitations were unknown", at the place where he dwelt. His presence once brought rain to the kingdom of Kāśī-rāja.

SWAR. *See* Vyāhriti.

SWARGA. The heaven of Indra, the abode of the inferior gods and of beautified mortals, supposed to be situated on mount Meru. It is called also Sairibha, Misrakā-vana, Tāvisha, Tridivam, Tri-pishtapam, and

Ūrdhwa-loka. Names of heaven or paradise in general are also used for it.

SWAR-LOKA. *See* Loka.

SWĀROCHISHA. Name of the second Manu. *See* Manu.

SWASTIKA. A mystical religious mark placed upon persons or things. It is in the form of a Greek cross with the ends bent round.

SWAYAM-BHŪ. 'The self-existent,' a name of Brahmā, the creator.

SWĀYAM-BHUVA. A name of the first Manu.

ŚWETA-DWĪPA. 'The white island or continent.' Colonel Wilford has attempted to identify it with Britain.

ŚWETA-KETU. A sage who, according to the *Mahābhārata,* put a stop to the practice of married women consorting with other men, especially with Brāhmans. His indignation was aroused at seeing a Brāhman take his mother by the hand and invite her to go away with him. The husband saw this, and told his son that there was no ground of offence, for the practice had prevailed from time immemorial. Śweta-ketu would not tolerate it, and introduced the rule by which a wife is forbidden to have intercourse with another man unless specially appointed by her husband.

ŚWETĀSWATARA. An Upanishad attached to the Yajurveda, it is one of the most modern.

ŚYĀLA. 'A brother-in-law.' A Yādava prince who insulted the sage Gārgya, and was the cause of his becoming the father of Kāla-yavana, a great foe of Krishṇa and the Yādava family.

ŚYĀMĀ. 'The black.' A name of Śiva's consort. *See* Devī.

ŚYAMANTAKA. A celebrated gem given by the sun to Satrājita. "It yielded daily eight loads of gold, and dispelled all fear of portents, wild beasts, fire, robbers, and famine." The legend says that though it was an inexhaustible source of good to the virtuous wearer, it was deadly to a wicked one. Satrājita, being afraid that Krishṇa would take it from him, gave it to his own brother, Prasena, but he, being a bad man, was killed by a lion. Jāmbavat, king of the bears, killed the lion and carried off the gem, but Krishṇa, after a long conflict, took it from him, and restored it to Satrājita. Afterwards Satrajita was killed in his sleep by Śat-dhanwan, who carried off the gem. Being pursued by Krishṇa and Bala-rāma, he gave the gem to Akrūra and continued his flight, but he was overtaken and killed by Krishṇa alone. As Krishṇa did not bring back the jewel, Bala-rāma suspected that he had secreted it, and consequently he upbraided him and parted from him, declaring that he would not be imposed upon by perjuries. Akrūra subsequently produced the gem, and it was claimed by Krishṇa, Bala-rāma, and Satyabhāmā. After some contention it was decided that Akrūra should keep it, and so "he moved about like the sun wearing a garland of light".

ŚYĀVĀŚWA. Son of Archanānas, both were Vedic Rishis. In a hymn he says, "Śasīyasī has given me cattle, comprising horses and cows and hundreds of sheep." The story told in explanation is that Archanānas, having seen the daughter of Rāja Rathavīti, asked her in marriage for his son Śyāvāśwa. The king was inclined to consent, but the queen objected that no daughter of their house had ever been given to any one less saintly than a Rishi. To qualify himself Śyāvāśwa engaged in austerities and begged alms. Among others, he begged of Śasīyasī, wife of Rāja Taranta. She took him to her husband, with whose permission she gave him a herd of cattle and costly ornaments. The Rāja also gave him whatever he asked for, and sent him to his younger brother, Purumīlha. On his way he met the Maruts, and lauded them in a hymn, for which they made him a Rishi. He then returned to Rathavīti, and received his daughter as his wife.

T

TAITTIRĪYA. This term is applied to the Sanhitā of the black *Yajur-veda.* (*See* Veda.) It is also applied to a Brāhmaṇa, to an Āraṇyaka, to an Upanishad, and a Prātisākhya of the same Veda. All these have been printed, or are in course of being printed in the *Bibliotheca Indica.*

TAKSHA, TAKSHAKA. Son of Bharata, nephew of Rāma-chandra, the sovereign of Gāndhāra, who resided at and probably founded Taksha-sīlā or Taxila, in the Panjāb.

TAKSHAKA. 'One who cuts off; a carpenter.' A name of Viśwa-karma. A serpent, son of Kadru, and chief of snakes.

TAKSHA-SĪLĀ. A city of the Gāndhāras, situated in the Panjāb. It was the residence of Taksha, son of Bharata and nephew of Rāma-chandra, and perhaps took its name from him. It is the Taxila of Ptolemy and other classical writers. Arrian describes it as "a large and wealthy city, and the most populous between the Indus and Hydaspes." It was three days' journey east of the Indus, and General Cunningham has found its remains at Sāhh-dharī, one mile north-east of Kala-kīsarāī.

TĀLAJANGHA. Son of Jaya-dhwaja, king of Avanti, who belonged to the Haihaya, and is known as the founder of the Tāla-jangha tribe of Haihayas. *See* Haihaya.

TĀLA-KETU. 'Palm-banner.' An appellation of Bhīshma, also of an enemy killed by Krishṇa. Bala-rāma had the synonymous appellation Tāla-dhwaja.

TĀLAM. The throne of Durgā.

TALAVAKĀRA. A name of the Kena Upanishad.

TĀMASA. The fourth Manu. *See* Manu.

TAMASĀ. The river "Tonse," rising in the Riksha mountains, and falling into the Ganges.

TĀMRA-LIPTA. The region immediately west of the Bhāgīrathī—Tamlook, Hijjali, and Midnapore. Its inhabitants are called Tāmra-liptakas.

TĀMRA-PARṆA, TĀMRA-PARṆĪ. Sri Lanka the ancient Taprobane. There was a town in the island that has been called Tāmra-parṇī, on the basis of which the whole island has been called by that name.

TANDU. One of Śiva's attendants. he was skilled in music, and invented the dance called Tāndava. *See* Śiva.

TĀNDYA, TĀNDAKA. The most important of the eight Brāhmanas of the *Sāma-veda*. It has been published in the *Bibliotheca Indica*.

TANTRA. 'Rule, ritual.' The title of a class of religious and magical works, generally of later date than the Purāṇas, and representing a later development of religion, although the worship of the female energy had its origin at an earlier period. The chief peculiarity of the Tantras is the prominence they give to the female energy of the deity, his active nature being personified in the person of his Śakti or wife. There are a few Tantras which make Vishṇu's wife or Rādhā the object of devotion, but the great majority of them are devoted to one of the manifold forms of Devī, the Śakti of Śiva, and they are commonly written in the form of a dialogue between these two deities. Devī, as the Śakti of Śiva, is the especial energy concerned with sexual intercourse and magical powers, and these are the leading topics of the Tantras.

The five Mākāras or five m's are the five requisites for Tantra worship—(1) Madya, wine; (2) Mānsa, flesh; (3) Matsya, fish; (4) Mudrā, parched grain and mystic gesticulations; (5) Maithuna, sexual intercourse. Each Śakti has a twofold nature, white and black, gentle and ferocious. Thus Umā and Gaurī are gentle forms of the Śakti of Śiva, while Durgā and Kālī are fierce forms. The Śāktas or worshippers of the Śaktis are divided into two classes, Dakshiṇāchārīs and Vāmāchārīs, the right-handed and the left handed. The worship fo the right-hand Śāktas is comparatively desent, but that of the left hand is addressed to the fierce forms of the Śaktis, and is most licentious. The female principle is worshipped, not only symbolically, but in the actual woman, and promiscuous intercourse forms part of the orgies. Tantra worship prevails chiefly in Bengal and the Eastern states of India.

TAPAṬĪ. The river Tapti personified as a daughter of the Sun by Chhāyā, she was mother of Kuru by Samvaraṇa.

TĀRĀ. Wife of the monkey king Bālin, and mother of Angada. After the death of Bālin in battle she was taken as wife by his brother, Su-grīva.

TĀRĀ, TĀRAKĀ. Wife of Brihaspati. According to the Purāṇas, Soma, the moon, carried her off, which led to a great war between the gods and the Asuras. Brahmā put an end to the war and restored Tārā, but she was delivered of a child which she declared to be the son of Soma, and it was named Budha. *See* Brihaspati.

TĀRAKA. Son of Vajrānka. A Daitya whose austerities made him formidable to the gods, and for whose destruction Skanda, the god of war, was miraculously born.

TĀRAKĀ. A female Daitya, daughter of the Yaksha Su-ketu or of the demon Sunda, and mother of Mārīcha. She was changed into a Rākshasī by Agastya, and lived in a forest called by her name on the Ganges, opposite the confluence of the Saryu. Viśwāmitra wanted Rāma-chandra to kill her, but he was reluctant to kill a woman. He resolved to deprive her of the power of doing harm, and cut off her two arms. Lakshmaṇa cut off her nose and ears. By the power of sorcery, she assailed Rāma and Lakshmaṇa with a fearful shower of stones, and at the earnest command of Viśwāmitra, the former killed her with an arrow.—*Rāmāyaṇa*.

TĀRAKĀ-MAYA. The war which arose in consequence of Soma, the moon, carried off Tārā, the wife of Brihaspati.

TĀRKSHYA. An ancient mythological personification of the sun in the form of a horse or bird. In later times the name is applied to Garuḍa.

TATWA SAMĀSA. A text-book of the Sānkhya philosophy, attributed to Kapila himself.

TELINGA. The Telugu country, stretching along the coast from Orissa to Tamil Nadu.

TILOTTAMĀ. Name of an Apsara. She was originally a Brāhman female, but for the offence of bathing at an improper season she was condemned to be born as an Apsara, for bringing about destruction of the two demons Sunda and Upasunda.

TIMIN, TIMIN-GILA. The Timin is a large fabulous fish. The Timin-gila, 'swallower of the Timin,' is a still larger one; and there is one yet larger, the Timin-gila-gila or Timi-timin-gila, 'swallower of the Timin-gila.' *Cf.* the Arabic Tinnīn, sea-serpent. It is also called Samudrāru.

TISHYA. The Kali Yuga or fourth age.

TITTIRI. 'A partridge.' An ancient sage who was the pupil of Yāska, and is an authority referred to by Pāṇini. Some attribute *Taittirīya Sanhitā* of the *Yajur-veda* to him. *See* Veda.

TOSALAKA. An athelete and boxer who was killed by Krishṇa in the public arena in the presence of Kansa.

TRAIGARTTAS. The people of Tri-gartta.

TRASADASYU. A royal sage and author of hymns. According to Sāyaṇa, he was son of Purukutsa. When Purukutsa was a prisoner, "his queen propitiated the seven Rishis to obtain a son who might take his father's place. They advised her to worship Indra and Varuṇa, in consequence of which Trasadasyu was born." He was renowned for his generosity. According to the Bhāgavata Purāṇa he was father of Purukutsa.

TRETĀ YUGA. The second age of the world, a period of 1,296,000 years.

TRI-BHUVANA, TRI-LOKA. The three worlds—Swarga, Bhūmi, Pātāla—heaven, earth, and hell.

TRI-DAŚA. 'Three times ten, thirty.' In round numbers, the thirty-three deities—twelve Ādityas, eight Vasus, eleven Rudra, and two Aświns.

TRI-GARTTA. 'The coutry of the three strongholds,' lately identified with the northern hill state of Kotoch, which is still called by the people "the country of

Traigart."—*Wilson*. General Cunningham, however, clearly identifies it with the Jālandhar Doāb and Kāngra.

TRI-JAṬĀ. An amiable Rākshasī who befriended Sītā when she was the captive of Rāvaṇa in (Lanka) Ceylon. She is also called Dharma-jnā.

TRI-KĀNDA ŚESHA. A Sanskrit vocabulary in three chapters, as a supplement to the *Amara-kosha,* which has been printed in India.

TRI-KŪṬA. 'Three peaks.' 1. The mountain on which the city of Lankā was built. 2. A mountain range running south from Meru.

TRI-LOCHANA. 'Three-eyed,' *i.e.,* Śiva. The *Mahābhārata* relates that the third eye burst from Śiva's forehead with a great flame when his wife playfully placed her hands over his eyes after he had been engaged in austerities in the Himālaya. This eye has been very destructive. It reduced Kāma, the god of love, to ashes.

TRI-MŪRTI. 'Triple form.' The Hindu triad. This was foreshadowed in the Vedic association of the three gods Agni, Vāyu, and Sūrya. The triad consists of the gods Brahmā, Śiva, and Vishṇu, the representatives of the creative, destructive, and preservative principles. Brahmā is the embodiment "of the Rajo-guṇa, the quality of passion or desire, by which the world was called into being; Śiva embodies Tamo-guṇa, the attribute of darkness or wrath, and the destructive fire by which the earth is annihilated; and Vishṇu is the embodiment of Satwa-guṇa, or mercy and goodness which has present world. The three exist in one and one in three, as the Veda is divided into three and is yet but one; and they are all Āśrita, or comprehenced within that one being who is Parama or 'supreme,' Guhya or 'secret,' and Sarvātmā, 'the soul of all things'."—*Wilson.*

The *Padma Purāṇa,* a Vaishṇava work gives the supremacy to Vishṇu and says, "In the beginning of creation, the great Vishṇu, desirous of creating the whole world, became threefold: creator, preserver, and destroyer. In order to create this world, the supreme spirit produced from the right side of his body himself as Brahmā; then in order to preserve the world he produced from the left side of his body Vishṇu; and in order to destroy the world he produced from the middle of his body the eternal Śiva. Some worship Brahmā, others Śiva, but Vishṇu, one yet threefold, creates, preserves, and destroys, therefore let the pious make no difference between the three." Tri-mūrti is one body with three heads: in the middle Brahmā, on the right Vishṇu, and on the left Śiva. The worship of Brahmā is almost extinct, but Vishṇu and Śiva receive unbounded adoration from their respective followers, and each is elevated to the dignity of the supreme being.

TRIṆĀVARTTA. A demon who assumed the form of a whirlwind and carried off the infant Krishṇa, but was overpowered and killed by the child.

TRI-PĀDA. 'Three-footed.' Fever personified as having three feet, symbolising the three stages of fever—heat, cold, and sweat.

TRI-PURA. 'Triple city.' 1. According to the *Harivanśa* it was aerial, and was burnt in a war with the gods. 2. A name of the demon Bāṇa, because he received in gift three cities from Śiva, Brahmā, and Vishṇu. He was killed by Śiva. His full name is Tripurāsura and Śiva is known as Tripurāri.

TRI-PURI. The capital city of the Chedis, now traceable on the insignificant village of Tewar, on the banks of the Narmadā.

TRI-ŚANKU. *See* Satya-vrata.

TRI-ŚIRAS. 'Three-headed.' 1. In the Veda, a son of Twashtri; also called Viśwa-rūpa. 2. Fever personified as a demon with three heads, typical of the three stages of heat, cold, and sweating. 3. Kuvera, god of wealth. 4. An Asura killed by Vishṇu. 5. A son or a friend of Rāvaṇa killed by Rāma.

TRI-ŚŪLA. 'A trident.' The trident of Śiva.

TRITA, TRITA ĀPTYA. A minor deity mentioned occasionally in the *Rig-veda*, and generally in some relation to Indra. Thus "Indra broke through the defences of Vala, as did Trita through the coverings (of the well)." In explanation of this and similar allusions, a legend is told by the commentator to the effect, that Ekata, Dwita, and Trita (first, second, and third), were three men produced in water by Agni, for the purpose of rubbing off the remains of an oblation of clarified butter. Agni threw the cinders of the offerings into water, and from them sprang the three brothers, who, from their origin in water (*āp*), were called Āptyas. Trita went one day to draw water from a well and fell into it. The Asuras then heaped coverings over its mouth in one to prevent his getting out, but he broke though them with ease. The *Nīti-manjarī* tells the story differently, Ekata, Dwita, and Trita were travelling in a desert and suffered from thirst. They came to a well from which Trita drew water and gave it to his brothers. In order to appropriate his property the two brothers threw him into the well, placed a cartwheel over it, and there left him. Trita prayed earnestly to the gods, and with their help he escaped.

TRITSUS. A people frequently mentioned in the Veda, who as Sāyaṇa says were "priest who were Vaśishtha's disciples." Vaśishtha himself is said to have belonged to the tribe.

TRI-VEṆĪ. 'The triple braid.' A name of Prayāga. It is so called because the Ganges and Yamuna here unite, and the Saraswatī is supposed to join them through an underground channel.

TRI-VIKRAMA. A name of Vishṇu used in the *Ṛig-veda,* and referring to three steps or paces which he is represented as taking. These steps, according to the opinion of a commentator, are "the three periods of the sun's course,—his rising, culminating, and setting." An old commentator says, "Vishṇu stepped by separate strides over the whole universe. In three places he planted his step, one step on the earth, a second in the atmosphere, and a third in the sky, in the successive forms of Agni, Vāyu, and Sūrya." The great commentator

Sāyaṇa, a comparatively modern writer, understands these steps as being the three steps of Vishnu in the Vāmana or dwarf incarnation, and no doubt that is how this legend seems to have originated.

TRYAMBAKA. 'Three-eyed,' or 'Having three wives or sisters.' 1. A name of Śiva. 2. One of the Rudras. 3. Name of one of the twelve great Lingas.

TRYARUṆA. A king, son of Trivrishan, of the race of Ikshwāku. He was riding in a chariot driven by Vriśa, his Purohita or family priest. The vehicle passed over and killed a Brāhman boy, and a question arose as to who was responsible for the death. The question was referred to an assembly of the Ikshwākus, and they decided it against Vriśa. The purohit by his prayers then restored the boy to life, but remained very angry with them for what he deemed partiality. "Fire henceforth ceased to perform its functions in their dwellings, and the cooking of their food and other offices ceased." The Ikshwākus appeased him and upon his prayers the use of fire was restored to them. This story is told by Sāyaṇa in elucidation of a Vedic allusion, and he quotes the *Śātyāyana Brāhmaṇa* as the authority.

TUKHĀRAS. A northern tribe from whom Tukhāristān obtained its name. They are probably the tribe of Śakas, by whom Bactria was taken from the Greeks. They are also called Tushāras.

TULĀDHĀRA. A very virtuous and and learned trading Vaiśya mentioned in the *Mahābhārata,* to whom Jājali, an arrogant Brāman, was sent by mysterious voice from the sky to wisdom.

TULUNGA. Tuluva, or the country where the Tulu language is spoken, on the western coast south of Goa.

TUMBURU. Name of a Gandharva. *See* Virādha.

TUNDA. A demon slain by Nahusha, the son of Āyus, he had a son named Vitunda, who was killed by Bhagavatī (Durgā).

TURANGA-VAKTRA. 'Horse-faced people.' *See* Kinnaras.

TURUSHKAS. Turks; the people of Turkistan. The Indo-Scythians, who, under Kanishka and other kings of the race, held Northern India.

TURVAŚA, TURVAŚU. Son of Yayāti by Devayānī. He refused to bear the curse of premature decrepitude passed upon his father, and so his father cursed him that his posterity should "not possess dominion." His father gave him a part of his kingdom, but after some generations, his line merged into that of his brother Puru, who bore for a time the curse passed upon his father.

TUSHĀRA. *See* Tukhāra.

TUSHITAS. A gaṇa or class of subordinate deities, thirty-six in number, but sometimes reduced to twelve, and identified with the Ādityas.

TWASHṬRI. In the *Rigveda* this deity is the ideal artist, the divine artisan, the most skilful of workmen, who is versed in all wonderful and admirable contrivances, and corresponds in many respects with Hephaistos and Vulcan. He sharpens and carries the great iron axe, and he forges the thunderbolts of Indra. He is the beautiful, skilful worker, the omniform, the archetype of all forms, the vivifier and the bestower of long life. He imparts generative power and bestows offspring. As the *Śatapatha Brāmaṇa* expresses it, "He has produced and nourishes a great variety of creatures; all worlds (or beings) are his, and are known to him; he has given to heaven and earth and to all things their forms." He created Brahmanaspati above all creatures, and generated Agni along with heaven and earth, the waters and the Bhrigus. He is master of the universe, the first-born protector and leader, and knows the region of the gods. He is associated with the Ribhus, and is represented as sometimes envying and some times admiring their skill. He is represented as being occasionally in a state of hostility with Indra, and he had a son named Viśwa-rūpa (omniform) or Triśiras, who had three heads, six eyes, and three mouths, who was especially obnoxious to Indra, and was slain by him. He had a daughter, Śaraṇyū, who was married to Vivaswat, and she was the mother of the Aświns. In the Purāṇas Twashtri is identified with Viśwakarman, the artisan of the gods, and sometimes also with Prajāpati. One of the Ādityas and one of the Rudras bear this name, as also did a prince descendant of Bharata.

U

UCHCHAIḤ-ŚRAVAS. The model horse. The white horse of Indra, produced at the churning of the ocean. It is fed on ambrosia, and is held to be the king of horses.

UCHCHHISHṬA. The remains of a sacrifice, to which divine powers are ascribed by the *Rigveda*.

UDAYAGIRI PARVATA. The eastern mountain from behind which the sun rises.

UDAYANA. 1. A prince of the Lunar race, and son of Sahasrānīka, who is the hero of a popular story. He was king of Vatsa with Kausambi as the capital. Vāsavadattā, princess of Ujjayinī, saw him in a dream and fell in love with him. He was decoyed to that city, and there kept in captivity by the king, Chandasena; but when he was set at liberty by the minister, he carried off Vāsava-dattā from her father and a rival suitor. 2. A name of Agastya.

UDDHAVA. The friend and counsellor of Krishṇa. According to some he was Krishṇa's cousin, being son of Devabhāga, the brother of Vasu-deva. He was also called Pavanavyādhi.

UDGĀTRI. A priest whose duty it is to chant the prayers or hymns from the Sāma-veda.

UDRANKA. Hariś-chandra's aerial city. *See* Saubha.

UGRA. A name of Rudra, or of one of his manifestations. *See* Rudra.

UGRASENA. A king of Mathurā, husband of Karṇī, and father of Kansa and Devaka. He was deposed by Kansa, but Krishṇa, after killing the latter, restored Ugrasena to the throne. *See* Kansa.

UJJAYANĪ. Ujjain. It was the capital of Vikramāditya and one of the seven sacred cities. Hindu geographers calculate their longitude from it, making it their first meridian.

ULUKA. 'An owl'. Son of Kitava, he was king of a country and people of the same name. He was an ally of the Kauravas, and acted as their envoy to the Pāndavas.

ULŪPĪ. A daughter of Kauravya, Rāja of the Nāgas, with whom Arjuna contracted a kind of marriage. She was nurse to her step-son, Babhru-vāhana, and great influence over him. According to the *Vishṇu Purāṇa* she had a son named Irāvat.

UMĀ. 'Light.' A name of the consort of Śiva. The earliest known mention of the name is in the *Kena Upanishad,* where she appears as a mediatrix between Brahmā and the other gods, and seems to be identified with Vāch. *See* Devī.

UMĀ-PATI. 'Husband of Umā,' that is to say, Śiva.

UPANISHADS. 'Esoteric doctrine.' The third division of the Vedas attached to the Brāhmaṇa portion, and forming part of the Śruti or revealed word. The Upanishads are generally written in prose with interspersed verses, but some are wholly in verse. There are about 150 of these works, probably even more. They are of later date than the Brāhmaṇas but it is thought that the oldest may date as far back as the sixth century B.C. The object of these treatises is to ascertain the mystic sense of the text of the Veda, and so they enter into such abstruse questions as the orgin of the universe, the nature of the deity, the nature of soul, and the connection of mind and matter. Thus they contain the beginnings of that metaphysical inquiry which ended in the full development of Hindu philosophy. The Upanishads have "One remarkable peculiarity, the total absence of any Brahmanical exclusiveness in their doctrine. They are evidently later than the older Sanhitās and Brāhmaṇas, but they breathe an entirely different spirit, a freedom of thought unknown in any earlier work except the *Rig-veda* hymns themselves. The great teachers of the higher knowledge and Brāhmans are continually represented as going to Kshatriya kings to become their pupils."—*Professor Cowell.* The *Rig-veda* has the Upanishad called

Aitareya attached to the *Aitareya Brāhmaṇa*. The *Taittirīya Sanhitā* of the *Yajur* has an Upanishad of the same name. The *Vājasaneyī Sanhitā* has the *Īsa*, and attached to the *Śatapatha Brāhmaṇa* it has the *Brihad Āraṇyaka*, which is the most important of them. The *Sāma-veda* has the *Kena* and *Chhāndogya*. All these have been translated into English. The *Atharva-veda* has the *Katha, Praśna, Mundaka, Māndukya,* and others, altogether fifty-two in number. These are the most important of the Upanishads.

UPAPLAVYA. Matsya, the capital of the king of Virāta.

UPA-PURĀṆAS. Secondary or subordinate Purāṇas. *See* Purāṇa.

UPARICHARA. A Vasu or demigod, who, according to the *Mahābhārata,* became king of Chedi by command of Indra. He had five sons by his wife. He had a son named Matsya (fish), and a daughter, Satya-vatī, who was the mother of Vyāsa by an Apsara, named Adrikā, condemned to live on earth in the form of a fish.

UPA-ŚRUTI. Supernatural voice which is heard at night revealing the secrets of the future.

UPASUNDA. A Daitya, son of Nisunda, brother of Sunda, and father of Mūka.

UPA-VEDAS. Subordinate or inferior Vedas. These are sciences which have no connection whatever with the Śruti or revealed Veda. They are four in number—(1) Āyur-veda, medicine; (2) Gāndharva-veda, music and dancing; (3) Dhanur-veda, archery, military science; (4) Sthāpatya-veda, architecture.

UPENDRA. A title given to Krishṇa by Indra.

URAGAS. The Nāgas or serpents inhabiting Pātāla.

ŪRMILĀ. Daughter of Janaka, sister of Sītā, wife of Lakshmaṇa, and mother of Gandharvī Somadā.

ŪRVA. Father of Richīka and grandfather of Jamadagni.

URVAŚĪ. A celestial nymph, mentioned first in the *Rig-veda*. The sight of her beauty is said to have caused the generation, in a peculiar way, of the sages Agastya and Vasistha by Mitra and Varuṇa. A verse says, "And thou, O Vasishtha, art a son of Mitra and Varuṇa." She roused the anger of these two deities and incurred their curse, through which she came to live upon the earth, and became the wife or mistress of Purūravas. The story of her amour with Purū-ravas is first told in the *Śatapatha Brāhmaṇa*. The loves of Purūravas, the Vikrama or hero, and of Urvaśī, the nymph, are the subject of Kālidāsa's drama called *Vikramorvaśī*. *See* Purūravas.

UŚANAS. 1. The planet Venus or its regent, also called Śukra.

2. An author of a Dharma-śāstra or law-book.

ŪSHĀ. A Daitya princess, daughter of Bāṇa and grand-daughter of Bali, she is called also Prīti-jushā. She fell in love with a prince whom she saw in a dream, and was anxious to know if there were such a person. Her favourite companion, Chitra-lekhā, drew the portraits of many gods and men, but Ūshā's choice fell upon Aniruddha, son of Pradyumna and grandson of Krishṇa. Chitra-lekhā, by her magic power, brought Aniruddha to Ūshā. Her father, on bearing of the youth's being in the palace, endeavoured to kill him, but he defended himself successfully. Bāṇa, however, kept Aniruddha, "binding him in serpent bonds." Krishṇa, Pradyumna, and Bala-rāma went to the rescue; and although Bāṇa was supported by Śiva and by Skanda, god of war, his party was defeated, and Aniruddha was carried back to Dwārakā with his wife Ūshā.

USHAS. The dawn. She is the daughter of heaven and sister of the Ādityas. This is one of the most beautiful myths of the Vedas, and is enveloped in poetry. Ushas is the friend of men, she smiles like a young wife, she is the daughter of the sky, she goes to every house, she thinks of the dwellings of men, she does not despise the small or the great, she brings wealth; she is always the same, immortal, divine, age cannot touch her; she is the young goddess, but she makes men grow old. "All his," adds Max Muller, "may be simply allegorical language. But the transition from Devī, 'the bright,' to

Devī, the goddess, is so easy; the daughter of the sky assumes so readily the same personality which is given to the sky, Dyaus, her father, that we can only guess whether, in every passage, the poet is speaking of a bright apparition or of a bright goddess, of a natural vision or a visible deity." She is called Ahanā and Dyotanā, 'the illumer.'

USHMAPAS. The Pitris or a class of Pitris.

UŚIJ. Mentioned in the *Rig-veda* as the mother of Kakshīvat, she is the female servant of the queen of the Kalinga Rāja. The king desired his queen to submit to the embraces of the sage Dīrgha-tamas, in order that he might beget a son. The queen substituted her bondmaid Uśij. The sage, cognisant of the deception, sanctified Uśij, and a son, Kakshīvat, who, through his affiliation by the king, was a Kshatriya, but, as the son of Dīrgha-tamas, was a Brāhman. This story is told in the *Mahābhārata* and some of the Purāṇas.

UTATHYA. A Brāhman of the race of Angiras, who married Bhadrā, daughter of Soma, a woman of great beauty. The god Varuṇa, who had formerly been enamoured of her, carried her off from Utathya's hermitage, and would not give her up to Nārada, who was sent to bring her back. Utathya, greatly enraged, drank up all the sea, still Varuṇa would not let her go. At the desire of Utathya, the lake of Varuṇa was then dried up and the ocean swept away. The saint then addressed himself to the countries and to the river:—"Saraswatī, disappear into the deserts, and let this land, deserted by thee, become impure." "After the country had become dried up, Varuṇa submitted himself to Utathya and brought back Bhadrā. The sage was pleased to get back his wife, and released both the world and Varuṇa from their sufferings."

UTKALA. The modern Orissa. It gives its name to one of the five northern nations of Bhāhmans. *See* Brāhman.

UTTAMAUJAS. A warrior of great strength, and an ally of the Pāndavas.

UTTĀNA-PAD. 'Outstretched, supine.' In the Vedas, a peculiar creative source from which the earth sprang.

UTTĀNA-PĀDA. A son of Manu and Śata-rūpā. By his wife Su-nritā he had four sons, Dhruva, Kīrtimān, Ayushmān, and Vasu. Some of the Purāṇas gave him another wife, Su-ruchi, and a son, Uttama. *See* Dhruva.

UTTARA (mas.), UTTARĀ (fem.). A son and daughter of the Rāja of Virāta, Uttara was killed in battle by Śalya. The daughter married Abhimanyu, son of Arjuna.

UTTARA-KURU. A region lying far to the north. (*See* Jambu-dwīpa.) (Plural.) The inhabitants of this region.

UTTARA MĪMĀNSĀ. A school of philosophy. *See* Darśana.

UTTARA-NAISHADA-CHARITA. A poem on the life of Nala, king of Nishada, written about the year 1000 A.D. by Śrī Harsha, a celebrated sceptical philosopher. It has been printed in the *Bibliotheca Indica.*

UTTARA-RĀMA-CHARITA. 'The later chronicle of Rāma. A drama by Bhāva-bhūti on the latter part of Rāma's life. The second part of King Rāma, as the *Mahā-vīra-charita* is the first. The drama is based on the Uttara Kānda of the *Rāmāyaṇa,* and quotes two or three verses from that poem. It was probably written about the beginning of the eighth century. It has been translated in blank verse by Wilson, and more literally by Professor C.H. Tawney. There are several editions of the text.

V

VA. A name of Varuṇa; also name of his dwelling.

VĀCH. 'Speech.' In the *Rig-veda*, Vāch appears to be the personification of speech by whom knowledge was communicated to man. Thus she is said to have "entered into the Rishis," and to make whom she loves terrible and intelligent, a priest and a Rishi. She was "generated by the gods," and is called "the divine Vāch," "queen of the gods," and she is described as "the melodious cow who milked forth sustenance and water," "who yields us nourishment and sustenance." The Brāhmaṇas associate her with Prajāpati in the work of creation. In the *Taittirīya Brāhmaṇa* she is called "the mother of the Vedas," and "the wife of Indra, who contains within herself all worlds." In the *Śatapatha Brāhmaṇa* she is called "the mother of the Vedas," and "the wife of Indra, who contains within herself all worlds." In the *Śatapatha Brāhmaṇa* she is represented as entering into a sexual connection with Prajāpati, who, "being desirous of creating, connected himself with various spouses," and among them, "through his mind, with Vāch," from whom "he created the waters;" or, as this last sentence is differently translated, "He created the waters from the world [in the form] of speech (Vāch)."

In the *Atharva-veda* she is identified with Virāj, and is the daughter of Kāma (desire). "That daughter of thine, O Kāma, is called the cow, she whom sages denominate Vāch-virāj."

The *Mahābhārata* also calls her "the mother of the Vedas," and says, "A voice derived from Brahmā entered into the ears of them all; the celestial Saraswatī was then produced from the heavens." Here and "in the later mythology, Saraswatī was identified with Vāch, and became under different names the spouse of Brahmā and the goddess of wisdom and eloquence, and is invoked as a muse," generally under the name of Saraswatī, but sometimes as Vāch.

VĀḌAVA, VĀḌAVĀNALA. The submarine fire which "devours the water of the ocean," causing it to throw off the vapours which are condensed into rain and snow. The word is also written Vaḍava and Baḍava. *See* Aurva.

VĀHANA. 'A vehicle.' Most of the gods are represented as having animals as their vāhanas. Brahmā has the Hansa, swan or goose; Vishṇu has Garuḍa, half eagle, half man; Śiva, the bull Nandi, Indra, an elephant; Yama, a buffalo; Kārttikeya, a peacock; Kāma-deva, the marine monster Makara, or a parrot; Agni, a ram; Varuṇa, a fish; Ganeśa, a rat; Vāyu, an antelope; Śani or Saturn, a vulture; Durgā, a tiger.

VAHNI. Fire.

VĀHUKA. 'Charioteer.' A name and office assumed by Nala in his time of disguise.

VAIBHOJAS. The *Mahābhārata* says, "The descendants of Druhyu are the Vaibhojas." "A people unacquainted with the use of cars or beasts of burden, and who travel on rafts; they have no kings."—*Wilson*.

VAIBHRĀJA. A celestial grove; the grove of the gods on mount Supārśwa, west of Meru.

VAIDARBHA. Belonging to the country of Vidarbha or Birār. The people of that country.

VAIDEHA. Belonging to the country of Videha or Tirhoot, etc. The king or the people of the country. Janaka was called Vaideha and Sītā was Vaidehī.

VAIDYA-NĀTHA. 'Lord of physicians.' A title of Śiva. Name of one of the twelve great Lingas. *See* Linga.

VAIJAYANTA. The palace or the banner of Indra.

VAIJAYANTĪ. 1. The necklace of Vishṇu, composed of five precious gems, pearl, ruby, emerald, sapphire, and diamond, it "is the aggregate of the five elemental rudiments." 2. A law-book current in the south. It is a commentary by Nanda Pandita on the Vishṇu Smriti.

VAIKARTTANA. A name of Karṇa from his putative father, Vikarttana, the sun.

VAIKUNTHA. The paradise of Vishṇu, sometimes described as on Mount Meru, and at others as in the Northern Ocean. It is also called Vaibhra. Vishṇu himself is sometimes designated by this term.

VAINATEYA. A name of Vishnu's bird Garuḍa.

VAIRĀJ. Manu the son of Virāj.

VAIRĀJAS. Semi-divine beings or Manes unconsumable by fire, who dwell in Tapo-loka, butare capable of translation to Satya-loka. The Kāśī-khanda explains this term as the Manes of "ascetics, mendicants, anchorets, and penitents, who have completed a course of rigorous austerities." *See* Pitris.

VAIROCHANA. A name of Bali.

VAIŚĀLĪ. A city founded by Viśāla, son of Triṇabindu, this is "a city of considerable renown in Indian tradition, but its site is a subject of some uncertainty." It was a celebrated place among the Buddhists, and would seem to have been situated on the left bank of the Ganges. General Cunningham places it about 27 miles north of Patna. It is frequently confounded with Viśālā, *i.e.* Ujjayinī.

VAIŚAMPĀYANA. A celebrated sage who was the original teacher of the Black Yajur-veda. He was a pupil of the great Vyāsa, from whom he learned the *Mahābhārata,* which he afterwards recited to King Janamejaya at a festival. The *Harivanśa* is also represented as having been communicated by him.

VAIŚESHIKA. The Atomic school of philosophy. *See* Darśana.

VAIŚRAVAṆA. Patronymic of Kuvera.

VAIŚWĀNARA. A name by which Agni is occasionally known in the *Rig-veda.*

VAIŚYA. The third or trading and agricultural caste. *See* Varṇa.

VAITĀNA SŪTRA. The ritual of the *Atharva-veda.* The text has been published by Dr. Garbe.

VAITARAṆĪ. '(The river) to be crossed,' that is, the river of hell, which must be crossed before the infernal regions can be entered. This river is described as being a trail of blood, ordure, and all sorts of filth. A second river stated by the *Mahābhārata* is in the country of the Kalingas; it must be the river of the same name (vulg. "Byeturnee") somewhat higher up in Cuttack.

VAIVASWATA. Name of the seventh Manu; he was son of Sūrya and father of Ikshwāku, the founder of the Solar race of kings.

VĀJASANEYĪ-SANHITĀ. The body of hymns forming the white Yajur-veda. *See* Veda.

VĀJIN. A priest of the White Yajur-veda.

VAJRA. 1. The thunderbolt of Indra, said to have been made of the bones of the Rishi Dadhīchi. It is a circular weapon, with a hole in the centre, according to some, but others represent it as consisting of two transverse bars.

2. Son of Anirudha. His mother is sometimes said to be Aniruddha's wife Su-bhadrā, and at others the Daitya princess Ūshā. Krishṇa just before his death made him king of the Yādavas at Indra-prastha.

VAJRA-NĀBH. The celebrated Chakra (discus) of Krishna. According to the *Mahābhārata* it was given to him by Agni for his assistance in defeating Indra and burning the Khāndava forest.

VAKA. 'A crane.' A great Asura who lived near the city of Eka-chakrā, and forced the Rāja of the place to send him daily a large quantity of provisions, which he devoured, and not only the provisions, but the men who carried them. Under the directions of Kuntī, her son Bhīma took the provisions, and when the demon struck him, a terrific combat followed; each one tore up trees by the roots and belaboured the other, till Bhīma seized the demon by the legs and tore him asunder. Kuvera is sometimes called by this name.

VĀLA-KHILYAS. 1. Eleven hymns of an apocryphal or peculiar character interpolated in the *Rig-veda*. 2.

"Pigmy sages no bigger than a joint of the thumb, chaste, pious, resplendent as the rays of the sun." So described by the *Vishṇu Purāṇa,* which says that they were brought forth by Samnati (humility), wife of Kratu, and were 60,000 in number. They are able to fly swifter than birds. The *Rig-veda* says that they sprang from the hairs of Prajāpati (Brahmā). They are the guards of the chariot of the sun. They are also called Kharwas. Wilson says "they are not improbably connected with the character of Daumling, Thaumlin, Tamlane, Tom-a-lyn, or Tom Thumb."

VĀLMĪKI. The author of the *Rāmāyaṇa,* which he is said to have "seen". He himself is represented as taking part in some of the scenes he describes. He received the banished Sītā into his hermitage at Chitra-kūta, and educated her twin sons Kuśa and Lava. "Tradition has marked a hill in the district of Banda in U.P. as his abode." The invention of the śloka is attributed to him, but it cannot be his, because the metre is found in the Vedas.

VĀMĀCHĀRĪS. Followers of the left-hand sect. *See* Tantra.

VĀMA-DEVA. 1. A Vedic Rishi, author of many hymns. In one of his hymns he represents himself as speaking before his birth, saying, "Let me not come forth by this path, for it is difficult (of issue): Let me come forth obliquely from the side." Sāyaṇa, the commentator, says in explanation, "The Rishi Vāma-deva, whilst yet in the womb, was reluctant to be born in the usual manner, and resolved to come into the world through his mother's side. Aware of his purpose, the mother prayed to Aditi, who thereupon came with her son Indra to expostulate with the Rishi." [This story accords with that told by the Buddhists about the birth of Buddha.] In the same hymn Vāmadeva says, "In extreme destitution I have cooked the entrails of a dog," and Manu cites this to show that a man is not rendered impure even by eating the flesh of dogs for the preservation of his life. In another hymn he says, "As a hawk I came forth with speed;" and a commentator explains, "Having assumed the form of a hawk, he came forth from the womb by the power of Yoga, for he is considered to have been endowed with divine knowledge from the period of his conception." 2. A Vedic sage mentioned in the *Mahābhārata* as possessor of two horses of marvellous speed called Vāmyas. 3. A name of Śiva; also of one of the Rudra.

VĀMANA. The dwarf incarnation of Vishṇu. *See* Avatāra.

VĀMANA PURĀṆA. "That in which the four-faced Brahmā taught the three objects of existence, as subservient to the greatness of Tri-vikrama (Vishṇu), which treats also of the Śiva kalpa, and which consists of 10,000 stanzas, is called the Vāmana Purāṇa." It contains an account of the dwarf incarnation of Vishṇu, and "extends to about 7000 stanzas, but its contents scarcely establish its claim to the character of a Purāṇa." "It is of a more tolerant character than the (other) Purāṇas, and divides its homage impartially between Śiva and Vishṇu with tolerable impartiality. It has not the air of any antiquity, and its compilation may have amused the leisure of some Brāhman of Benares three or four centuries ago."—*Wilson*.

VĀNA-PRASTHA. 'A dweller in the worlds.' A Brāhman in the third stage of his religious life, passing his time as an anchorite in the woods. *See* Brāhman.

VANA-CHARAS (mas.), VANE-CHARĪS (fem.). Wanderers of the woods.

VANŚA. A race or family. Lists of the Rishis or successive teachers of the Vedas which are found attached to some of the Brāhmaṇas are called Vanśas.

VANŚA-BRĀHMAṆA. The eighth Brāhmaṇa of the Sāma-veda. It has been edited by Burnell.

VAPUSHMAT. A man who killed King Marutta of the Solar race. Dama, son or grandson of Marutta, in retaliation killed Vapushmat. With his blood he made the funeral offerings to the Manes of Marutta, and with the flesh he fed the Brāhmans who were of Rākshasa descent.

VARA-DĀ. 'Bestower of boons.' A name of Devī, also of Saraswatī.

VARĀHA. The boar incarnation of Vishṇu. *See* Avatāra.

VĀRĀHA-KALPA. The present kalpa or year of brahmā. *See* Kalpa.

VARĀHA MIHĪRA. An astronomer who was one of "the nine gems" of the court of Vikramāditya. He was author of Brihat-sanhitā and Brihaj-jātaka. His death is placed in Śaka 509 (A.D. 587).

VARĀHA PURĀṆA. "That in which the glory of the great Varāha is predominant, as it was revealed to Earth by Vishnu, in connexion, wise Munis, with the Mānava kalpa, and which contains 24,000 verses, is called the Varāha Purāṇa;" but this description differs so from the Purāṇa which bears the name in the present day, that Wilson doubts its applying to it. The known work "is narrated by Vishṇu as Varāha, or in the boar incarnation, to the personified Earth. Its extent, however, is not half that specified, little exceeding 10,000 stanzas. It furnishes also itself evidence of the prior currency of some other work similarly denominated." "It may perhaps be referred to the early part of the twelfth century."

VĀRĀṆASĪ. The sacred city of Benares; also called Kāśī.

VĀRAṆĀVATA. The city in which the Pāndavas dwelt in exile.

VARARUCHI. A grammarian who is generally supposed to be one with Kātyāyana. There was another Vararuchi who was one of "the nine gems" at the court of Vikramāditya.

VARDDHA-KSHATRĪ. A patronymic of Jayadratha.

VĀRKSHĪ. Daughter of a sage, who is instanced in the Mahā-bhārata as being a virtuous woman, and wife of ten husbands.

VARṆA. 'Class or caste.' The Chatur-varṇa, or four castes, as found established in the code of Manu, are—

1. Brāhman. The sacerdotal and learned class, the members of which may be, but are not necessarily priests.

2. Kshatriya. The regal and warrior caste.

3. Vaiśya. Trading and agricultural caste.

4. Sūdra. Servile caste, whose duty is to serve the other three.

The first three castes were called *dwi-ja,* 'twice born or regenerate," from their being entitled to investiture with the sacred thread which effects a second birth. The Brāhmans maintain that their caste alone remains, that the other three have been lost or degraded, and it is generally believed that there are no pure Kshatriyas or Vaiśyas existing now. The numerous castes which have sprung up from the intercourse of people of different castes or from other causes are called Varṇa-sankara, 'mixed castes.'

VARSHA. A region. Nine varshas are enumerated as situated between the great mountain ranges of the earth:—(1) Bhārata-varsha, India; (2) Kim-purusha or Kinnara; (3) Hari; (4) Ramyaka; (5) Hiraṇ-maya; (6) Uttara-kuru; (7) Ilāvrita; (8) Bhadrāśwa; (9) Ketu-māla.

VĀRSHṆEYA. A name of Krishṇa as a descendant of Vrishṇi. Name of King Nala's charioteer.

VĀRTTIKAS. Supplementary rules or notes to the grammar of Pāṇini by later grammarians, like Katyāyana, Patanjali etc. Kātyāyana is the chief of these annotators, and is called Vārttika-kāra, 'the annotator.'

VARUṆA. One of the oldest of the Vedic deities, a personification of the all-investing sky, the maker and up-holder of heaven and earth. As such he is king of the universe, king of gods and men, possessor of illimitable knowledge, the supreme deity to whom especial honour is due. He is often associated with Mitra, he being the ruler of the night and Mitra of the day; but his name frequently occurs alone, that of Mitra only seldom. In later times he was chief among the lower celestial deities called Ādityas, and later still he became a sort of Neptune, a god of the seas and rivers, who rides upon the Makara. This character he still retains. His sign is a fish. He is regent of the west quarter and of one of the Nakshatras or lunar mansions.

In the Purāṇas, Varuṇa is sovereign of the waters, and one of his accompaniments is a noose, which the Vedic deity also carried for binding offenders: this is called Nāga-pāśa, Pulakānga, or Viśwa-jit. His favourite resort is Pushpa-giri, 'flower mountain,' and his city Vasudhā-nagara or Sukhā. He also possesses an umbrella impermeable to water, formed of the hood of a cobra, and called Ābhoga. The *Vishṇu Purāṇa* mentions an incident which shows a curious coincidence between Varuṇa and Neptune. At the marriage of the sage Rishīka, Varuṇa supplied him with the thousand fleet white horses which the bride's father had demanded of him.

VARUṆĀĪ, VARUṆĪ. Wife of Varuṇa and goddess of wine. She is said to have sprung from the churning of the ocean. The goddess of wine is also called Madā and Surā.

VASANTA. Spring and its deified personification.

VASANTA-SENĀ. The heroine of the drama called *Mrichchhakatī,* 'the toy cart.'

VĀSAVADATTĀ. A princess of Ujjayinī, who is the heroine of a popular story by Subandhu. The work has been printed by Dr. F. Hall in the *Bibliotheca Indica.* He considers it to have been written early in the seventh century. *See* Udayana.

VAŚISHTHA. 'Most wealthy.' A celebrated Vedic sage to whom many hymns are ascribed. According to Manu he was one of the seven great Rishis and of the ten Prajāpatis. There was a special rivalry between him and the sage Viśwāmitra, who raised himself from the Kshatriya to the Brāhman caste.

VĀSTOSH-PATI. 'House protector.' One of the later gods of the Veda, represented as springing from Brahmā's dalliance with his daughter. He was the protector of sacred rites and guardian of houses.

VASU. The Vasus are a class of deities, eight in

number, chiefly known as attendants upon Indra. They seem to have been in Vedic times personifications of natural phenomena. They are Āpa (water), Dhruva (pole-star), Soma (moon), Dhara (earth), Anila (wind), Anala (fire), Prabhāsa (dawn), and Pratyāsha (light). According to the *Rāmāyaṇa* they were children of Aditi.

VASU-DEVA. Son of Sura, of the Yādava branch of the Lunar race, he was father of Krishṇa, and Kuntī, the mother of the Pāndava princes was his sister. He married seven daughters of Āhuka, and the youngest of them, Devakī, was the mother of Krishṇa. After the death of Krishṇa and Bala-rāma he also died, and four of his wives burnt themselves with his corpse. So says the *Mahābhārata,* but according to the *Vishṇu Purāṇa* he and Devaki and Rohiṇī burnt themselves at Dwārakā. He received the additional name of Ānaka-dundubhi, because the gods, conscious that he was to be the putative father of the divine Krishṇa, sounded the drums of heaven at his birth. He was also called Bhū-kaśyapa and Dundu, 'drum.'

VĀSU-DEVA. A name of Krishṇa, derived from that of his father, Vasu-deva; but as that is incompatible with his claims to divinity, the *Mahābhārata* explains that he is so called "from his dwelling (*vasanāt*) in all beings, from his issuing as a Vasu from a divine womb." The name was assumed by an impostor named Paundraka, who was killed by Krishṇa. *See* Paundraka.

VĀSUKI. King of the Nāgas or serpents who live in Pātāla. He was used by the gods and Asuras for a coil round the mountain Mandara at the churning of the ocean. *See* Śesha.

VASU-SENA. A name of Karṇa.

VĀTA. 'Wind.' Generally the same as Vāyu, but the name is sometimes combined in the Veda with that of Parjanya, and Parjanya-vātā and Vāyu are then mentioned distinctively.

VĀTĀPI. Vātāpi and Ilwala, two Rākshasas, sons either of Hrāda or Viprachitti, they are mentioned in the

Rāmāyaṇa as dwelling in the Dandaka forest. Vātāpi assumed the form of a ram which was offered in sacrifice and afterwards eaten by Brāhmanas. Ilwala then called upon him to come forth, and accordingly he tore his way out of the stomachs of the Brāhmans. He tried the same trick upon Agastya, but that austere sage ate and digested him. Ilwala, as before, called his brother to come forth, and assaulted the sage, who told him that his brother would never return. Then Ilwala was burnt up by fire from the eyes of Agastya. The *Mahābhārata* story varies slightly.

VAṬA-VĀSIN. 'Dwelling in fig-trees' (*vata*). Yakshas.

VATSA, VATSA-RĀJA. King of Vatsa, whose capital was Kauśāmbī. A title of the prince Udayana. There are many persons named Vatsa.

VĀTSYĀYANA. A sage who wrote upon erotic subjects, and was author of the *Kāma-sūtras* and *Nyāya-bhāshya.* He is also called Malla-nāga.

VĀYU. 'Air, wind.' The god of the wind, Eolus. In the Vedas he is often associatd with Indra, and rides in the same car with him, Indra being the charioteer. The chariot has a framework of gold which touches the sky, and is drawn by a thousand horses. There are not many hymns addressed to him. According to the Nirukta there are three gods specially connected with each other. "Agni, whose place is on earth; Vāyu or Indra, whose place is in the air; and Sūrya, whose place is in the heaven." In the hymn Purusha-Sūkta Vāyu is said to have sprung from the breath of Purusha, and in another hymn he is called the son-in-law of Twashtri. He is regent of the north-west quarter, where he dwells.

According to the *Vishṇu Purāna* he is king of the Gandharvas. The *Bhāgavata Purāṇa* relates that the sage Nārada incited the wind to break down the summit of Mount Meru. He raised a terrible storm which lasted for a year, but Vishṇu's bird, Garuḍa, shielded the mountain with his wings, and all the blasts of the wind-god were in vain. Nārada then told him to attack the mountain in Garuḍa's absence. He did so, and breaking off the summit of the mountain, he hurled it into the sea, where it became the island of Lankā (Ceylon).

Vāyu is the reputed father of Bhīma and of Hanuman, and he is said to have made the hundred daughters of King Kuśanābha crooked because they would not comply with his licentious desires, and this gave the name Kanyākubja, 'hump-backed damsel,' to their city.

VĀYU PURĀṆA. 'The Purāṇa in which Vāyu has declared the laws of duty, in connection with the Śweta kalpa, and which comprises the Māhātmya of Rudra, is the *Vāyu Purāṇa;* it contains twenty-four thousand verses." The Purāṇa is divided into four sections, the first beginning with the creation, and the last treating of the ages to come. It is devoted to the praise of Śiva, and is connected with the *Śiva Purāṇa,* for when one of them is given in a list of Purāṇas the other is omitted.

VEDA. Root, *Vid,* 'know.' 'Divine knowledge.' The Vedas are the holy books which are the foundation of the Hindu religion. They consist of hymns written in an old form of Sanskrit and according to the most generally received opinion they were composed between 1500 and 1000 B.C. But there is no direct evidence as to their age, and opinions about it vary considerably. Some scholars have thought that the oldest of the hymns may be carried back a thousand years farther. It seems likely that some of the hymns were composed before the arrival of the Aryan immigrants in India, and there is no doubt that the hymns vary greatly in age and spread over a very considerable period.

There are various statements as to the origin of the Vedas. One is that the hymns emanated like breath from Brahma, the soul of the universe. It is agreed that they were revealed orally to the rishis or sages whose names they bear; and hence the whole body of the Veda is known as Śruti, 'what was heard.'

There are four Vedas: (1) Rig, (2) Yajur, (3) Sāma, (4) Atharva. But the Atharva is of comparatively modern origin. The other three are spoken of by Manu as the "three Vedas," and are said by him to have been "milked out as it were," from fire, air, and the sun. In reality the Rig-veda is the Veda, the original work; for the Yajur and the Sāma are merely different arrangements of its hymns for special purposes.

VEDA-MĀTRI. 'Mother of the Vedas.' The Gāyatrī.

VEDĀNGAS. (Veda + angas.) 'Members of the Veda.' The Shad-angas or six subjects necessary to be studied for the reading understanding, and proper sacrifical employment of the Vedas:—

1. *Sikshā*. Phonetics or pronunciation, embracing accent, quantity, and euphony in general.

2. *Chhandas*. Metre.

3. *Vyākaraṇa*. Grammar. Said to be represented by Pāṇini but rather by older grammars culminating in his great work.

4. *Nirukta*. Etymology or glossary, represented by the glossary of Yāska.

5. *Jyotisha*. Astoronomy. Such knowledge of the heavenly bodies as was necessary for compiling a calendar, fixing the day and hours suitable for the performance of Vedic sacrifices and ceremonies.

6. *Kalpa*. Ceremonial. Rules for applying the Vedas to the performance of sacrifices. These rules are generally written in the form of Sūtras or short aphorisms, and so they are known as the Kalpa-sūtras or Śrauta-sūtras.

VEDĀNTA. The orthodox school of philosophy. *See* Darśana.

VEDĀNTA-PARIBHĀSHĀ. A modern text-book on the Vedānta philosophy.

VEDĀNTA-SĀRA. 'Essence of the Vedānta.' A short popular work on the Vedānta philosophy. It has been translated by Ballantyne, and also by Bohtlingk, Roer, and Frank.

VEDĀNTA-SŪTRA. The aphorisms of Bādarāyaṇa on the Vedānta philosophy. They are commonly called Brahma-sūtras.

VEDĀRTHA-PRAKĀŚA. 'Elucidation of the meaning on the Veda.' This is the name of Sāyaṇa's great commentary on the *Rig-veda.* Also of a commentary on the Taittirīya Sanhitā by Mādhavāchārya.

VEDAVATĪ. The 'vocal daughter' of the Rishi Kuśa-dhwaja, son of Brihaspati. As Rāvaṇa was passing through a forest in the Himālaya he met with Vedavatī, a damsel of great beauty dressed in ascetic garb. He fell in love and tried to win her over. She told him that gods and Gandharvas had sought to woo her, but her father would give her to no one but Vishṇu, whom he desired for his son-in-law. Provoked at this resolution, Śambhu, king of the Daityas, slew her father; but she remained firm to her father's wish, and practised austerities to gain Vishṇu for her spouse. Nothing daunted, Rāvaṇa urgently pressed his suit, and boasted that he was superior to Vishṇu. He then touched her hair with the tip of his finger. This greatly incensed her, and she forthwith cut off her hair, and said she would enter into the fire before his eyes, adding, "Since I have been insulted in the forest by thee who art wicked-hearted, I shall be born again for thy destruction." So she entered the blazing fire, and celestial flowers fell all around. It was she who was born again as Sītā, and was the moving cause of Rāvaṇa's death, though Rāma was the agent.—*Muir's Texts,* ii. 498, iv. 458.

VEDA-VYĀSA. 'The arranger of the Vedas.' *See* Vyāsa.

VEDODAYA. 'Source of the Veda.' An epithet of the sun as the source of the Sāma-veda.

VEGAVAT. 'Swift.' 1. A son of Krishṇa. 2. A Dānava who fought on the side of the Śālwas against Krishṇa, and was killed by Śamba.

VEṆA. Son of Anga, and a descendant of Manu Swāyambhuva. When he became king he issued this proclamation:— "Men must not sacrifice or give gifts or present oblations. Who else but myself is the enjoyer of sacrifices? I am for ever the lord of offerings." The sages remonstrated respectfully with him, but in vain;

they admonished him in stronger terms; but when nothing availed, they slew him with blades of consecrated grass. After his death the sages beheld clouds of dust, and on inquiry found that they arose from bands of men who had taken to plundering because the country was left without a king. As Veṇa was childless, the sages, after consultation, rubbed the thigh (or, according to the Hari-vanśa, the right arm) of the dead king to produce a son. From it there came forth "a man like a charred log, with flat face, and extremely short." The sages told him to sit down (Nishīda). He did so, and thus became a Nishāda, from whom "sprang the Nishādas dwelling in the Vindhya mountains, distinguished by their wicked deeds." The Brāhmans then rubbed the right hand of Vena, and from it "sprang the majestic Prithu, Vena's son, resplendent in body, glowing like the manifested Agni." The above has been told, with little variation, in the *Mahābhārata*, the *Vishṇu* and *Bhāgavata Purāṇas,* and the *Hari-vanśa.* The *Padma Purāṇa* says that Vena began his reign well, but fell into the Jaina heresy. For this the sages pummelled him until the first of the Nishādas came forth from his thigh and Prithu from his right arm. Being freed from sin by the birth of the Nishāda, he retired to a hermitage on the Narmadā, where he engaged in penance. Vishṇu was thus pleased, and granted him the boon of becoming one with himself. *See* Prithi.

VEṆĪ-SANHĀRA. 'The binding of the braid.' A drama by Bhatta Nārāyaṇa. The plot is taken from the *Mahābhārata.* Draupadī, the wife of the Pāndu princes, was dragged by the hair of her head into the hall of the Kauravas by Duh-śāsana, and she vowed that it should remain dishevelled until the insult was avenged. After the death of the Kauravas she again braided her hair. Wilson has given an analysis of the drama. There are several editions of the text.

VENKAṬA, VENKATĀDRI. A hill which was a seat of the worship of Vishṇu, it is the modern Tirupati.

VETĀLA. A ghost or goblin; a spirit who haunts

cemeteries and animates dead bodies.

VETĀLA-PANCHAVINŚATĪ. The twenty-five stories of the Vetāla. It is the *Baitāl Pachīsī* of Hindi, and has been translated into all the languages of India. The work is ascribed to an author named Jambhala-datta.

VETRAVATĪ. The river Betwa, which rises in the Vindhyas and falls into the Yamuna below Kalpi.

VIBHĀNDAKA. Son of Kaśyapa. An ascetic who retired from the world and lived in the forest with his infant son Rishya-śringa. A sage of this name is sometimes classed among the great Rishis.

VIBHĪSHAṆA. 'Terrible.' A younger brother of Rāvaṇa. He, like his brother, propitiated Brahmā, and obtained a boon. His was that he should never commit an unworthy action even in the greatest extremity. He was virtuous, and opposed to the practices of the Rākshasas. This led to a quarrel between him and Rāvaṇa, who kicked him from his seat. He flew off to Kailāsa, and under the advice of Śiva he went and allied himself with Rāma-chandra, who received and embraced him as a friend. After the defeat and death of Rāvaṇa he was raised by Rāma to the throne of Lankā.

VICHITRA-VĪRYA. Name of a king. *See* Mahābhārata.

VIDAGDHA-MĀDHAVA. A drama in seven acts by Rūpa on the loves of Krishṇa and Rādhā, written in 1533 A.D. "It is weak as a drama, and its literary merits are small."

VIDARBHA. Birar, and probably including with it the adjoining district of Beder, which name is apparently a corruption of Vidarbha. Its capital was Kundina-pura, the modern "Kundapur," about forty miles east of Amarāvatī.

VIDDHA-ŚĀLABHANJIKĀ. 'The statues.' A comedy of domestic intrigue by Rāja Śekhara. It was probably written earlier than the tenth century.

VIDEHA. An ancient country, the capital of which was Mithilā. It corresponds with the modern Tirhut or North Bihar.

VIDHĀTRI. 'Creator.' A name of Brahmā, of Vishṇu, and of Viśwa-karmā.

VIDURA. A son of Vyāsa by a Sūdra slave girl, who took the place of his cosort. Vidura was called Kshattri, a term ordinarily applied to the child of a Sūdra father and Brāhman mother. He enjoyed the character of the "wisest of the wise," and gave good advice to both Kauravas and Pāndavas, but in the war he sided with the latter.

VIDŪRA. A mountain in Sri Lanka, probably Adam's peak.

VIDVAN-MODA-TARANGINĪ. 'Fountain of pleasure to the learned.' A philosophical work by Rāma-deva, translated into English by Rāja Kālī Krishṇa.

VIDYĀ-DHARA (mas.), VIDYĀ-DHARĪ (fem.). 'Possessors of knowledge.' A class of inferior deities inhabiting the regions between the earth and sky, and generally of benevolent disposition. They are attendants upon Indra, but they have chiefs and kings of their own, and are represented as intermarrying and having much intercourse with men. They are also called Kāma-rūpin, 'taking shapes at will;' Khechara and Nabhas-chara, 'moving in the air;' Priyam-vada, 'sweet-spoken.'

VIDYĀRAṆYA, VIDYĀRAṆYA-SWĀMĪ. 'Forest of learning.' A title of Mādhavāchārya, as patron of the city of Vidyā-nagara, afterwards altered to Vijaya-nagara, the capital of the last great Hindu dynasty of the Deccan.

VĪJA-GANITA. A work on algebra, translated by Colebrooke and by Strachey, it is a chapter of the work called *Siddhānta-śiromaṇi,* written by Bhāskarāchārya. There are several editions of the text.

VIJAYA-NAGARA. The capital of the last great Hindu dynasty of the south. It was originally called Vidyā-nagara, 'city of learning,' after the great scholar and minister Mādhavāchārya, entitled Vidyāraṇya, 'forest of learning.' But in the days of its glory the Vidyā was altered to Vijaya, 'victory.'

VIJNĀNEŚWARA. Author of the law-book called Mitāksharā.

VIKARṆA. A son of Dhritarāshtra.

VIKRAMĀDITYA. A celebrated Hindu king who reigned at Ujjayinī, he is said to have been the son of a king named Gardabhila. His name has been given to the Samvat era, commencing 57 B.C. He was a great patron of learning, and his court was made illustrious by the Nava-ratna, or nine gems of literature, who flourished there. He is a great hero of romance, and many improbable stories are told of him. His real position is uncertain. He appears to have driven out the Śakas, and to have established his authority over Northern India. He is said to have fallen in battle with his rival Śālivāhana, king of the Deccan, who also has an era called Śaka dating from 78 A.D.

VIKRAMORVAŚĪ. 'The hero and the nymph.' A celebrated drama by Kālidāsa, translated in Wilson's *Hindu Theatre*. There are many editions and translations. *See* Purū-ravas.

VIKUKSHI. A king of the Solar race, who succeeded his father, Ikshwāku. He received the name of Śaśāda, 'hare-eater.' He was sent by his father to hunt and obtain flesh suitable for offerings. Being weary and hungry he ate a hare, and Vaśishtha, the priest, declared that this act had defiled all the food, for what remained was but his leavings.

VIMADA. In the *Rig-veda* it is said the Aświns gave a bride to the youthful Vimada, and the commentator explains that Vimada had won his bride at a swayamvara, but was stopped on the way home by his unsuccessful competitors. The Aświns came to his succour, repulsed the assailants, placed the bride in their chariot, and carried her to the home of the prince.

VINATĀ. A daughter of Daksha, one of the wives of Kaśyapa, and mother of Garuḍa. According to the *Bhāgavata Purāṇa* she was the wife of Tārkshya or Garuḍa.

VINDA. Vinda and Anuvinda were joint kings of Avanti and fought in the great war.

VINDHYA. The mountains which stretch across India, and divide what Manu calls the Madhya-deśa or 'middle land,' the land of the Hindus, from the south, that is, they divide Hindustān from the Deccan. The mountain is personified, and according to a legend he was jealous of the Himālaya, and called upon the sun to revolve round him as he did round Meru. When the sun refused the mountain began to raise its head to obstruct that luminary, and to tower above Himālaya and Meru. The gods invoked the aid of Agastya, the spiritual guide of Vindhya. That sage called upon the mountain to bow down before him, and afford him an easy passage to and from the south. It obeyed, and Agastya passed over. But he never returned, and so the mountain remains in its humbled codition, far inferior to the Himālayas.

VINDHYĀVALĪ. Wife of Bali the Asura.

VINDHYA-VĀSINĪ. 'The dweller in the Vindhyas.' The wife of Śiva. *See* Devī.

VIPĀŚ, VIPĀŚĀ. The river Byās, the Hyphasis or Bibasis of the classical writers. A legend relates that it obtained its name through the sage Vaśishtha, who, wishing to commit suicide, bound his limbs with cords and threw himself into the water. The river, declining to drown him, cast him unbound (*vipāśa*) on its bank.

VIPRACHITTI. Son of Kaśyapa and Danu. He is chief of the Dānavas.

VĪRA-BHADRA. A son or emanation of Śiva, created from his mouth, and having, according to the Vāyu Purāṇa, "a thousand heads, a thousand eyes, a thousand feet, wielding a thousand clubs, a thousand shafts; holding the shell, the discus, the mace, and bearing a blazing bow and battle-axe; fierce and terrific, shining with dreadful splendour, and decorated with the crescent moon; clothed in a tiger's skin, dripping with blood, having a capacious stomach and a vast mouth armed with formidable tusks," etc., etc. The object of his creation was to stop Daksha's sacrifice. He is a special object of worship in the Mahratta country, and there are sculptures of him in the caves of Elephanta and Ellora, where he is represented with eight hands.

VĪRA-CHARITA. A book of tales by Ananta, which describes the feuds between the descendants of Vikramāditya and Śālivāhana.

VIRĀDHA. A horrible man-eating Rākshasa, son of Kāla and Śatahradā. By penance he had obtained from Brahmā the boon of invulnerability. He is described as "being like a mountain peak, a man-eater, loud-voice, hollow-eyed, large mouthed, huge, huge-bellied, horrible, rude, long, deformed, of dreadful aspect, wearing a tiger's skin, dripping with fat, wetted with blood, terrific to all creatures, like death with open mouth, bearing three lions, four tigers, two wolves, ten deer, and the great head of an elephant with the tusks, and smeared with fat, on the point of an iron pike, shouting with a loud voice." Rāma, with Lakshmaṇa and Sītā, encountered him in the Dandaka forest, when he foully abused and taunted the brothers, and seized upon Sītā. The brothers proved with their arrows that he was not invulnerable, but he caught them, threw them over his shoulders, and ran off with them as if they had been children. They broke both his arms, threw him down, beat him with their fists, and dashed him to the earth, but they could not kill him, so they dug a deep hole and buried him alive. After his burial there arose from the earth a beautiful person, who said that he was a Gandharva who had been condemned by Kuvera to assume the shape of a Rākshasa, from which Rāma had enabled him to escape. He was also called Tumburu.

VIRĀJ. Manu thus describes Virāj:—"Having divided his body into two parts, the lord (Brahmā) became with the half a male, and with the (other) half a female; and in her he created Virāj. Know that I (Manu), whom that male Virāj himself created, am the creator of all this world." (*See* Manu.) One passage in the *Rig-veda* says, "From his (Purusha) sprang Virāj, and from Virāj (sprang) Purusha." (*Muir's Texts,* v. 50, 369), as Aditi is said to have sprung from Daksha, and Daksha from Aditi. Virāj, the male half of Brahmā, is supposed to typify all male creatures; and Śata-rūpā, the female half, all female forms.

VĪRA-MITRODAYA. A law-book by Mitra-misra, of authority in the Benares (Varanasi) School. It is in the form of a commentary on the *Mitāksharā*. The text is in print.

VIRĀṬA. A country in the vicinity of the modern Jaipur. The present town of Bairat is 105 miles south of Delhi. Its king was called Rāja of Virāta or Rāja Virāta. It was at his court that the Pāndava princes and Draupadī lived in disguise. They rendered him great services against his enemies, and he fought on their side in the great war and was killed by Droṇa. *See* Matsya.

VIROCHANA. A Dānava, son of Prahlāda, and father of Bali, he is also caled Driśana. When the earth was milked, Virochana acted as the calf of the Asuras. *See* Prithi.

VIRŪPĀKSHA. 'Deformed as to the eyes.' A name of Śiva, who has three eyes. Also one of the Rudras. Also a Dānava, son of Kaśyapa.

VISĀKHA-DATTA. Author of the drama "Mudrārākshasa." He is said to be of royal descent, but his family has not been identified.

VIŚĀLĀ. A name of the city Ujjayinī.

VISHṆU. Root, *vish*, 'to pervade.' The second god of the Hindu triad. In the *Rig-veda* Vishṇu is not in the first rank of gods. He is a manifestation of the solar energy, and is described as striding through the seven regions of the universe in three steps, and enveloping all things with the dust (of his beams). These three steps are explained by commentators as denoting the three manifestations of light—fire, lightning, and the sun; or the three phases of the sun—its rising, culmination, and setting. In the Veda he is occasionally associated with Indra.

The preserving and restoring power Vishṇu has been manifested to the world in a variety of forms called Avatāras, litterally 'descents,' but more intelligibly 'incarnations,' in which a portion of his divine essence was embodied in a human or supernatural form possessed of superhuman powers. All these Avatāras became manifest for correcting some great evil or effecting some great good in the world. The Avatāras are ten in number, but the *Bhāgavata Purāṇa* increases them to twenty-two, and adds that in reality they are innumerable. All the ten Avatāras are honoured, but the seventh and eighth, Rāma and Krishṇa, are honoured as great mortal heroes and receive worship as great gods. Krishṇa is more especially looked upon as a full manifestation of Vishnu, and as one with Vishṇu himself, and he is the object of a widely extended and very popular worship.

VISHṆU. Author of a Dharma-śāstra or law-book.

VISHṆU PURĀṆA. This Purāṇa generally stands third in the lists, and is described as "that in which Parāśara, beginning with the events of the Varāha Kalpa, expounds all duties. is called the Vaishṇava, and the learned know its extent to be 23,000 stanzas." The actual number of stanzas does not amount to 7000.

Wilson, the translator of this Purāṇa, says, "Of the whole series of Purāṇas the Vishnu most closely corresponds to the definition of a Pancha-lakshaṇa Purāṇa, or one which treats of five specified topics (Primary Creation, Secondary Creation, Genealogies of Gods and Patriarchs, Reigns of the Manus, History). It comprehends them all; and although it has infused a portion of extraneous and sectarial matter, it has done so with sobriety and judgement, and has not suffered the fervour of its religious zeal to transport it to very wide deviations from the prescribed path. The legendary tales which it has inserted are few, and are conveniently arranged, so that they do not distract the attention of the compiler from objects of more permanent interest and importance." The whole work has been translated with numerous elucidatory notes by Wilson, and a second edition has been published with additional valuable notes by Dr. F. Hall.

VIŚMĀPANA. 'Astounding.' The aerial city of the

Gandharvas, which appears and disappears at intervals.

VIŚRAVAS. Son of the Prajāpati Pulastya, or, according to a statement of the *Mahābhārata,* a reproduction of half Pulastya himself. By a Brahmanī wife, daughter of the sage Bharadwāja, named Idavidā or Ilavidā, he had a son, Kuvera, the god of wealth. By a Rākshasī named Nikashā or Kaikasī, daughter of Sumāli, he had three sons, Rāvaṇa, Kumbha-karṇa, and Vibhīshaṇa and a daughter named Śūpra-nakhā. The *Vishṇu Purāṇa* substitutes Keśinī for Nikashā. The account given by the *Mahābhārata* is that Pulastya, being offended with Kuvera for his adulation of Brahmā, reproduced half of himself as Viśravas, and Kuvera to recover his favour gave him three Rākshasī handmaids: Pushpotkatā, the mother of Rāvaṇa and Kumbhakarṇa; Mālinī, the mother of Vibhīshana; and Rākā, the mother of Khara and Śūrpa-nakhā.

VIŚWA-DEVAS, VIŚWE-DEVAS. 'All the gods.' In the Vedas they form a class, nine in number. They are addressed in the Veda as "preservers of men, bestowers of rewards." In later times, a class of deities particularly interested in exequial offerings, they are generally said to be ten in number, but the lists vary, both as to the number and the names. The following is one list:—(1) Vasu, (2) Satya, (3) Kratu, (4) Daksha, (5) Kāla, (6) Kāma, (7) Dhriti, (8) Kuru, (9) Purū-ravas, (10) Mādravas. Two others are sometimes added, Rochaka or Lochana and Dhuri or Dhwani. *See Vishṇu Purāṇa,* Hall's edition, vol. iii. pp. 178, 188, 189.

VIŚWA-KARMĀ, VIŚWA-KARMAN. 'Omnificent.' This name seems to have been originally an epithet of any powerful god, as of Indra and Sūrya, but in course of time it came to designate a personification of the creative power. In this character Viśwa-karmā was the great architect of the universe, and is described in two hymns of the *Rig-veda* as the one "all-seeing god, who has on every side eyes, faces, arms, and feet, who, when producing heaven and earth, blows them forth (or shapes them) with his arms and wings; the father, generator, disposer, who knows all worlds, gives the gods their names, and is beyond the comprehension of mortals." In these hymns also he is said to sacrifice himself or to himself, and the Nirukta explains this by a legend which represents that "Viśwa-karmā, son of Bhuvana, first of all offered up all worlds in a Sarva-medha (general sacrifice), and ended by sacrificing himself."

In the Epic and Purāṇic periods Viśwa-karmā is invested with the powers and offices of the Vedic Twashtri, and is sometimes so called. He is not only the great architect, but the general artificer of the gods and maker of their weapons. It was he who made the Agneyastra or "fiery weapon," and it was he who revealed the Sthāpatya-veda, or science of architecture and mechanics. The *Mahābhārata* describes him as "the lord of the arts, executor of a thousand handicrafts, the carpenter of the gods, the fashioner of all ornaments, the most eminent of artisans, who formed the celestial chariots of the deities, on whose craft men subsist, and whom, a great and immortal god, they continually worship."

In the Rāmāyaṇa, Viśwa-karmā is represented as having built the city of Lankā for the Rākshasas, and as having generated the ape Nala, who constructed Rāma's bridge from the continent to Sri Lanka.

VIŚWĀMITRA. A celebrated sage, who was born a Kshatriya, but by intense penance raised himself to the Brāhman caste, and became one of the seven great Rishis. According to the *Rig-veda* he was the son of a king named Kuśika, a descendant of Kuśa, but later authorities make him the son of Gāthin or Gādhi, king of Kanyā-kubja, and a descendant of Puru; so Viśwāmitra is declared in the Hari-vanśa to be "at once a Paurava and a Kauśika" by lineage. According to some, Gādhi was of the Kuśika race, having descended from Kusika. Viśwāmitra is called Gādhi-ja and Gādhi-nandana, 'son of Gādhi.'

The most noteworthy and important feature in the legends of Viśwāmitra is the active and enduring struggle between him and the Brāhman Rishi Vaśishtha, a fact which is frequently alluded to in the *Rig-veda,* and is supposed to typify the connections between the Brāhmans and the Kshatriyas for the superiority. Both these Rishis occupy a prominent position in the *Rig-veda,* Viśwāmitra being the Rishi of the hymns in the third Mandala, which contains the celebrated verse Gāyatrī, and Vaśishtha of those of the seventh. Each of them was at different times the Purohita or family priest of King Su-dās, a position of considerable importance and power, the possession of which emulated even if it did not cause their rivalry.

VIŚWA-RŪPA. 'Wearing all forms, omnipresent, universal; a title of Vishṇu.

VIŚWĀVASU. A chief of the Gandharvas in Indra's heaven.

VIŚWEŚWARA. 'Lord of all.' A name of Śiva. The celebrated Linga or emblem of Siva at Banaras. *See* Linga.

VĪTA-HAVYA. A king of the Haihayas, whose sons attacked and slew all the family of Divodāsa, king of Kāśī. A son, named Pratardana, was subsequently born to Divodāsa, and he attacked the Haihayas and compelled Vīta-havya to fly to the sage Bhrigu for protection. Pratardana pursued him, and demanded that he should be given up. Then "Vita-havya, by the mere word of Bhrigu, became a Brāhman Rishi and an utterer of the Veda" (*Mahābhārata*). His son, Gritsa-mada, was a highly honoured Rishi, and author of several hymns in the *Rig-veda.* He was the founder of the tribe of Haihayas called Vīta-havyas.

VITASTĀ. The classic Hydaspes, the Behat of later days, and the modern Jhelum.

VIVĀDA-BHANGĀRṆAVA. A code of Hindu law according to the Bengal school, composed by Jagannātha Tarkālankāra at the end of the last century. It has been translated by Colebrooke, and is commonly known as *Colebrooke's Digest.*

VIVĀDA-CHANDRA. A law-book of the Benares school by Lakhimā Devī, a learned lady.

VIVĀDA-CHINTĀMAṆI. A law-book of the Mithilā school by Vāchaspati Misra. The text is in print.

VIVĀDA-RATNĀKARA. A law-book of the Benares school by Chandeswara, who lived about 1314 A.D.

VIVĀDA-TĀNDAVA. A law-book of the Benares school by Ratnākara.

VIVASWAT. 'The bright one.' The sun. (*See* Sūrya.) Used sometimes perhaps for the firmament.

VIVINDHAYA. A Dānava killed in battle by Chārudeshna, son of KrishŚa. *See* Mahābhārata.

VOPA-DEVA. A grammarian of great repute, who lived about the thirteenth century A.D. at Deva-giri, and wrote the *Mugdha-bodha*.

VRAJA. A pastoral district about Āgra and Mathurā, where Krishna passed his boyhood with the cowherds.

VRĀTYA. "Persons whom the twice-born beget on women of their own classes, but who omit the prescribed rites and have abandoned the Gāyatrī, are to be designated as Vrātyas."—*Manu.*

VRIDDHA. 'Old,' an epithet frequently found prefixed to the books of ancient writers, and evidently implying that here are one or more versions as Vriddha Manu, Vriddha Hārita. *See* Dharma-śāstra.

VRIHAT-KATHĀ. 'Great story.' A large collection of tales from which the *Kathā-sarit-sāgara* was drawn.

VRIHAT-SANHITĀ. The astronomical work of Varāhamihira.

VRIHAN NĀRADĪYA An Upa-purāṇa. *See* Purāṇa.

VRIHASPATI. *See* Brihaspati.

VRIKODARA. 'Wolf belly.' An epithet of Bhīma.

VRINDĀ-VANA. A wood in the district of Mathurā where Krishṇa passed his youth, under the name of Gopāla, among the cowherds.

VRISHṆI. A descendant of Yadu, and the ancestor from whom Krishṇa got the name Vārshṇeya.

VRISHṆIS, VRISHṆAYAS. The descendants of Vrishṇi,

son of Madhu, whose ancestor was the eldest son of Yadu. Krishṇa belonged to this branch of the Lunar race.

VRITRA. In the Vedas he is the demon of drought and congenial weather, with whom Indra, the god of the firmament, constantly at war, and whom he is constantly overpowering, and releasing the rain. Sometimes called Vritrāsura.

VRITRA-HAN. The slayer of Vritra. A title of Indra.

VYĀDI. An old grammarian and lexicographer, somewhat later in time than Pāṇini. A story in the *Vrihat-kathā* represents him as a contemporary of Vararuchi.

VYĀHRITIS. Three mystical words said by Manu to have been milked from the Vedas by Prajāpati—the word *bhūr*, from the *Rig-veda;* the word *bhuvah*, from the *Yajur-veda;* and the word *swar*, from the *Sāma-veda* (*Manu*, ii. 76). The *Śatapatha Brāhmaṇa* defines them as "three luminous essences" which Prajāpati produced from the Vedas by heating them. "He uttered the word *bhūr*, which became this earth; *bhuvah*, which became this firmament; and *swar* which became that sky." A fourth word, *mahar*, is sometimes added, and is probably intended to represent the *Atharva-veda*. *See* Loka.

VYĀKARAṆA. 'Grammar.' One of the Vedāngas, the science of grammar has been carefully studied among the Hindus from very ancient times, and studied for its own sake as a science rather than as a means of acquiring or regulating language. The grammar of Pāṇini is the oldest of those known to survive, but Pāṇini refers to several grammarians who preceded him. One of them was named Śākatāyana, a portion of whose work is said to have been discovered lately.

VYĀSA. 'An arranger.' This title is common to many old authors and compilers, but it is especially applied to Veda-vyāsa the arranger of the Vedas, who, from the imperishable nature of his work, is also called Śāśwatas, 'the immortal.' The name is given also to the compiler of the *Mahābhārata*, the founder of the Vedānta philosophy, and the arranger of the Purāṇas; all these persons being held to be identical with Veda-vyāsa. But this is impossible, and the attribution of all these works to one person has arisen either from a desire to heighten their antiquity and authority, or from the assumed identity of several different "arrangers".

Veda-vyāsa was the illegitimate son of the Rishi Parāśara and Satyavatī, and the child, who was of a dark colour, was brought forth on an island *(dwīpa)* in the Yamunā. Being illegitimate he was called Kānīna, the 'bastard;' from his complexion he received the name Krishṇa, and from his birthplace he was called Dwaipāyana. His mother afterwards married king Śāntanu, by whom she had two sons. The elder was killed in battle, and the younger, named Vichitra-vīrya, died childless. Krishṇa Dwaipāyana preferred a life of religious retirement, but in accordance with law and at his mother's request, he took the two childless widows of her son, Vichitra-vīrya. By them he had two sons, Dhrita-rāshtra and Pāndu, between whose descendants the great war of the *Mahābhārata* was fought.

The Purāṇas mention no less than twenty-eight Vyāsas, incarnations of Vishṇu or Brahmā, who descended to the earth in different ages to arrange and promulgate the Vedas.

VYAVAHĀRA-CHINTĀMAṆI. A law-book of the Benares school by Vāchaspati Misra.

VYAVAHĀRA-MAYŪKHA. A law-book of the Mahratta school by Nīlakantha Bhatta. Translated by Borrodaile.

VYAVAHĀRA-TATWA. A modern work on law according to the Bengal school by Raghunandana, who is also called Smārta-Bhattāchārya.

Y

YĀDAVA. A descendant of Yadu. The Yādavas were the celebrated race in which Krishṇa was born. At the time of his birth they led a postoral life, but under him they established a kingdom at Dwārakā in Gujarat. All the Yādavas who were present in that city after the death of Krishṇa perished in it when it was submerged in the ocean. Some few were absent, and perpetuated the race, from which many princes and chiefs still claim their descent. The great Rājas of Vijaya-nagara asserted themselves as its representatives. The *Vishṇu Purāṇa* says of this race, "Who shall enumerate the whole of the mighty men of the Yādava race, who were tens of ten thousands and hundreds of hundred thousands in number?"

YADU. Son of King Yayāti of the Lunar race, and founder of the line of the Yādavas in which Krishṇa was born. He refused to bear the curse of decrepitude passed upon his father by the sage Śukra, and in consequence he incurred the paternal curse, "Your posterity shall not possess dominion." Still he received from his father the southern districts of his kingdom, and his posterity prospered.

YĀJA. A Brāhman of great sanctity, who, at the earnest solicitation of King Draupada, performed the sacrifice through which his "alter-born" children, Dhrishta-dyumna and Draupadī, came forth from the sacrificial fire.

YAJNA. 'Sacrifice.' Sacrifice personified in the Purāṇas as son of Ruchi and husband of Dakshinā. He had the head of a deer, and was killed by Vīra-bhadra at Daksha's sacrifice. According to the *Harivanśa* he was raised to the planetary sphere by Brahmā, and made into the constellation Mriga-śiras (deer-head).

YAJNA-DATTA-BADHA. 'The death of Yajna-datta.' An episode of the Rāmāyaṇa, it has been translated into French by Chezy.

YAJNA-PARIBHĀSHĀ. A Sūtra work by Āpastambha.

YAJNA-SENA. A name of Drupada.

YĀJNAWALKYA. A celebrated sage, to whom is attributed the White Yajur-veda, the *Śatapatha Brāhmaṇa*, the *Brihad Āraṇyaka*, and the code of law called *Yājnawalkya Smriti*. He lived before the grammarian Kātyāyana, and was probably later than Manu. At any rate, the code bearing his name is posterior to that of Manu. He was a disciple of Bāshkali, and more particularly of Vaiśampāyana. The *Mahābhārata* makes him present at the Rāja-sūya sacrifice performed by Yudhī-shthira; and according to the *Śatapatha Brāhmaṇa* he flourished at the court of Janaka, king of Videha and father of Sītā. Janaka had long contentions with the Brāhmaṇas, in which he was supported, and probably prompted, by Yājnawalkya. This sage was a dissenter from the religious teaching and practices of his times, and is represented as contending with and silencing Brāhmans at the court of his patron. A Brāhman named Vidagdha Śākalya was his especial adversary, but he vanquished him and cursed him, so that "his head dropped off, and his bones were stolen by robbers." Yājnawalkya is also represented as inculcating the duty and necessity of religious retirement and meditation. Therefore, he is considered as having been the originator of the Yoga doctrine, and to have helped in preparing the world for the preaching of Buddha.

The Smriti, or code of law which bears the name of Yājnawalkya, is posterior to that of Manu, and is more precise and stringent in its provisions. Its authority is inferior only to that of Manu, and as explained and developed by the celebrated commentary *Mitāksharā*, it was in force all over India except in Bengal.

YAJUR or YAJUSH. The second Veda. *See* Veda.

YAKSHAS. A class of supernatural beings attendant on Kuvera, the god of wealth. Authorities differ as to their origin. They have no very special attributes, but they are generally considered as inoffensive, and so are called Punya-janas, 'good people,' but they occasionally appear as imps of evil. It is a Yaksha in whose mouth Kālidāsā placed his poem *Meghadūta* (cloud messenger).

YAKSHA-LOKA. *See* Loka.

YAKSHĪ, YAKSHIṆĪ. 1. A female Yaksha. 2. Wife of Kuvera. 3. A female demon or imp attendant on Durgā.

YAMA. 'Restrainer.' In the Vedas, Yama is god of the dead, with whom the spirits of the departed dwell. He was the son of Vivaswat (the Sun), and had a twin-sister named Yamī or Yamunā. These are by some looked upon as the first human pair, the originators of the race; and there is remarkable hymn, in the form of a dialogue, in which the female urges their cohabitation for the purpose of perpetuating the species.

YAMĪ. The goddess of the yamunā river. Sister of Yama.

YAMUNĀ. The river Jamuna, which rises in a mountain called Kalinda (Sun). The river Yamunā is personified as the daughter of the Sun by his wife Sanjnā. So she was sister of Yama. Bala-rāma, in a state of inebriety, called upon her to come to him that he might bathe, and as she did not heed, he, in a great rage, seized his ploughshare-weapon, dragged her to him and compelled her to follow him wherever he wandered through the wood. The river then assumed a human form and besought his forgiveness, but it took some time before she could appease him. Wilson thinks that "the legend probably alludes to the construction of canals from the Yamuna for the purposes of irrigation." The river is also called Kālindī, from the place of its source, Sūrya-jā, from her father, and Tri-yāmā.

YĀSKA. The author of the Nirukta, Yāska lived before the time of Pānini, who refers to his work, but he was not the first author who wrote a Nirukta. *See* Nirukta.

YAŚODĀ. Wife of the cowherd Nanda, and foster-mother of Krishṇa.

YĀTUS, YĀTU-DHĀNAS. Demons or evil spirits of various forms, as dogs, vultures, hoofed-animals, etc. In ancient times the Yātus or Yātu-dhānas were distinct from the Rākshasas though associated with them, but in the epic poems and Purānas they are identified. Twelve Yātu-dhānas are named in the *Vāyu Purāṇa,* and they are said to have sprung from Kaśyapa and Su-rasā. They are associated with the Dasyus, and are thought to be one of the native races which opposed the progress of the immigrant Āryans.

YAVA-KRĪ, YAVA-KRĪTA. 'Bought with barley.' Son of the sage Bharadwāja, he performed great penances in order to obtain a knowledge of the Vedas without study, and having obtained this and other boons from Indra, he became arrogant and treated other sages with disrespect. He made love to the wife of Parāvasu, son of his father's friend, Raibhya. That sage in his anger performed a sacrifice which brought into being a fearful Rākshasa who killed Yava-krīta at his father's chapel. Bharadwāja, in grief for his son, burnt himself upon the funeral pyre. Before his death he cursed Parāvasu to be the death of his father, Raibhya, and the son killed his father in mistake for an antelope. All three were restored to life by the gods in recompense of the great devotions of Arvāvasu, the other son of Raibhya.—*Mahābhārata.*

YAVANAS. Greeks. The term is found in Pāṇini, who speaks of the writing of the Yavanas. The Purāṇas represent them to be descendants of Turvasu, but they are always associated with the tribes of the north-west frontier, and there can be no doubt that the Macedonian or Bactrian Greeks are the people most usually intended by the term. In the Bactrian Pāli inscriptions of King Priyadarsī the word is contracted to Yona, and the term Yonarāja "is associated with the name of Antiochus, probably Antiochus the Great, the ally of the Indian prince Sophagasenas, about B.C. 210." The Purāṇas characterise them as "wise and eminently brave." They were among the races conquered by King Sagara, and "he made them shave their heads entirely." In a later age they were encountered on the Indus by Pushpamitra, a Mauryan general, who dethroned his master and took the throne. In later times the term has been applied to the Muhammadans.

YAYĀTI. The fifth king of the Lunar race, and son of Nahusha, he had two wives, Devayānī and Śarmishthā, from the former of whom was born Yadu, and from the latter Puru, the respective founders of the two great lines of Yādavas and Pauravas. In all he had five sons, the other three being Druhyu, Turvasu, and Anu. He was a man of amorous disposition, and his infidelity to Devayānī brought upon him the curse of old age and infirmity from her father, Śukra. This curse Śukra consented to transfer to any one of his sons who would consent to bear it. All refused except Puru, who undertook to resign his youth in his father's favour. Yayāti, after a thousand years spent in sensual pleasures, renounced sensuality, restored his vigour to Puru, and made him his successor.

YAYĀTI-CHARITRA. A drama in seven acts on the life of Yayāti, it is attributed to Rudra-deva. The subject is Yayāti's intrigue with Śarmishthā.

YOGA. A school of philosophy. The literal meaning of the word Yoga is 'union' and the context is in union with the all pervading cosmic forces that most of us simply refer to as God. Simply expressed, union with God through knowledge or devotion or meditative exercise or action. The common form of Yoga associated with physical/meditative exercise *i.e.* Hatha Yoga is only one form of Yoga through which this divine union can be attained. The four main forms of Yoga are: Gyan Yoga, Bhakti Yoga, Hatha Yoga and Karma Yoga.

Through these four forms of Yoga an individual can grow spritually, develop a balanced personality and finally merge with the divine. It is often stressed in the scriptures that amongst these four practices, the most supreme form of Yoga is Karma Yoga which is the path of selfless action. However, through a synthesis of these

Yogic practices or through any one practice only an individual can enhance his state of self realization, sharpen his awareness and be truly integrated with the cosmic spirit. *See* Darśana and Yājanawalkya.

YOGA-NIDRĀ. 'The sleep of meditation.' Personified delusion. The great illusory energy of Vishṇu and the illusory power mainifested in Devī as Mahā-māyā, the great illusion.

YOGINĪ. A sorceress. The Yoginīs are eight female demons attendant on Durgā. They are Marjanī, Karpūra-tilakā, Malaya-gandhinī Kaumudikā, Bherundā, Mātālī, Nāyakī, Yayā or Śubhāchāra; and Su-lakshanā, Su-nandā.

YONI. The female organ. Alone, or in combination with the linga, it is an object of worship by the followers of the Śaktis.

YUDHI-SHTHIRA. The eldest of the five Pāndu princes, mythologically the son of Dharma, the god of justice. With the Hindus he is the favourite one of the five brothers, and is represented as a man of calm, passionless judgment, strict veracity, unswerving rectitude, and rigid justice. He was renowned as a ruler and director, but not as a warrior.

YUGA. An age of the world. Each of these ages is preceded by a period called its Sandhyā or twilight, and is followed by another period of equal length called Sandhyānśa, 'portion of twilight,' each being equal to one-tenth of the Yuga. The Yugas are four in number, and their duration is first computer by years of the gods:—

1.	Krita Yuga	4000	
	Sandhyā,	400	
	Sandhyānśa,	400	
		——	4,800
2.	Tretā Yuga,	3000	
	Sandhyā,	300	
	Sandhyānśa,	300	
		——	3,600

3.	Dwāpara Yuga,	2000	
	Sandhyā,	200	
	Sandhyānśa,	200	
		——	2,400
4.	Kali Yuga,	1000	
	Sandhyā,	100	
	Sandhyānśa,	100	
		——	1,200
			——
			12,000

But a year of the gods is equal to 360 years of men, so

4800 x 360 = 1,728,000
3600 x 360 = 1,296,000
2400 x 360 = 864,000
1200 x 360 = 432,000
Total = 4,320,000

years, forming the period called a Mahā-yuga or Manwantara. Two thousand Mahā-yugas or 8,640,000,000 years make a Kalpa or night and a day of Brahmā.

This elaborate and practically boundless system of chronology was invented between the age of the Rig-veda and that of the *Mahābhārata*. No traces of it are to be found in the hymns of the Rig, but it was fully established in the days of the great epic.

YUGAN-DHARA. A city in the Panjāb. A people dwelling there and in the vicinity.

YUVANĀŚWA. A king of the Solar race, father of Māndhātri. A legend represents this son as being conceived by and born of his father.

YUVA-RĀJA. 'Young king.' The heir-apparent to a throne.

YUYUDHĀNA. A name of Sātyaki.

YUYUTSU. A son of Dhrita-rāshtra by a Vāiśya handmaid. On the eve of the great battle he left the side of the Kauravas and joined the Pāndavas. When Yudhi-shthira retired from the world he established Yuyutsu in the kingdom of Indraprastha.

Section Three

Bibliography

Agrawal, P.K., *Goddess in Ancient India*, Atlantic Highlands, Humanities Press, New Jeresy, 1983.

Agrawal, Vasudev S., trans. *Devi Mahatmya: The Glorification of the Great Goddess*, All India Kashiraj Trust, Varanasi, 1963.

Ahmad Aziz, *Studies in Islamic Culture in the Indian Environment*, Clarendon Press, Oxford, 1964.

Ahuja, N.D., *Great Guru Nanak and Muslims*, Chandigarh, 1974.

Allen, Michael, *The Cult of Kumari: Virgin Worship in Nepal*, Tribhuvan University, Kathmandu, 1975.

Altekar, A.S., *The Position of Women in Hindu Civilization from Pre-Historic Times to the Present Day*, Reprint, Motilal Banarasi Das, Delhi, 1956.

Archer, John Clark, *The Sikhs in Relation to Hindus, Muslims, Christians and Ahmadiyas: A Study in Comparative Religion*, Princeton University, New Jeresy, 1946.

Archer, William G., *The Loves of Krishna in Indian Painting and Poetry*, George Allen and Unwin, London, 1957.

Arnold, Edwin, *The Light of Asia*, 1890.

Avasthi, A.B. Lal, *Purana Index*, New Delhi, 1992.

Avasthi, A.B.L., *Studies in Skanda Purana*, New Delhi, 1992.

Aryan, K.C., *The Little Goddesses* (Matrikas), Rekha Prakashan, New Delhi, 1980.

Aufrecht, T. ed. *Aitareya Brahmana*, Bonn, 1869, Tr. A.B. Keith, Cambridge, 1920.

Aiyangar, D. Ramaswami, ed., *Stotras of Vedanta Desika (Stotrani), Sri Vedanta Desika Sampradaya Sabha*, 1973.

Babb, Lawrence A., *The Divine Hierarchy: Popular Hinduism in Central India*, Columbia University Press, New York, 1975.

Babb, Lawrence A., "Marriage and Malevolence: The Uses of Sexual Opposition in a Hindu Partheon", *Ethnology* 9, no 2 (1970): 137-48.

Baijnath, R.B. Lala, *Hinduism—Ancient and Modern*, 1905.

Banerjee, P., *Early Indian Religions*, Delhi, 1973.

Barnett, Lionel, *Hindu Gods and Heroes*, Delhi, 1977.

Barth, Mons. A., *The Religions of India*, 1891.

de Bary, William Theodore, *et. al.*, eds. *Sources of Indian Tradition*, 2 Vols. Edited and revised by A.T. Embree & Stephen Hay for second edition, Columbia University Press, New York, 1958.

Basham, A.L., *The Wonder That was India*, Grove Press, New York, 1954.

Basham, A.L. (ed.), *A Cultural History of India*, Clarendon Press, Oxford, 1975.

Barbour, I. (ed.), *Religion in an Age of Science*, London, 1990.

Barnes, J. ed., *Early Greek Philosophy*, Penguin, 1987.

Beane, Wendell Charles, *Myth, Cult and Symbols in Sakta Hinduism: A Study of the Indian Mother Goddess*, E.J. Brill, Leiden, 1977.

Beswick, *The Hindu Gods*, New Delhi, 1994.

Bhandarkar, O.R. Institute, *The Mahabharata* (critical edition), Vol. I-XXX, 1933-36.

Bharati, Agehananda, *The Tantrik Tradition*, Doubleday, New York, 1965.

Bhattacharya, Deben, trans., *Love Songs of Chandidas*, George Allen and Unwin, London, 1967.

Bhattacharya, Deben, tran., *Love Songs of Vidyapati*, George Allen and Unwin, London, 1963.

Backbarn, Stuart H., and A.K. Ramanujan, eds., *Another Harmony: New Essays on the Folklore of India*, University of California Press, Berkeley, 1986.

Bhattacharya, Narendra Nath, *History of the Sakta Religion*, Munshiram Manoharlal, New Delhi, 1974.

Bhattacharya, Narendra Nath, *History of the Tantrik Religion*, Manohar, New Delhi, 1970.

Bhattacharya, Narendra Nath, *The Indian Mother Goddess*, Manohar, New Delhi, 1977.

Bloomfield, M., *A Vedic Concordance*, Reprinted, Delhi, 1972.

Briffault, Robert, *The Mothers: The Matriarchal Theory of Social Origins*, 3 Vols., Macmillan, New York, 1931.

Brooks, Douglas R., *Auspicious Wisdom: The Texts and Traditions of Srividya Sakta Tantrism in South India*, State University of New York Press, Albany, 1992.

Brown, C. Mackenzie, *God as Mother: A Feminine Theology in India: An Historical and Theological Study of the Brahma Vaivarta Purana*, Claude Stark and Company, Hartford, Vt., 1974.

Brown, C. Mackenzie, *The Triumph of the Goddess: The Canorical Models and Theological Visions of the Devi Bhagavata Purana*, Claude Stark and Company, Hartford, Vt., 1990.

Brown, Robert L., ed. *Ganesh, Studies of an Asian God*, State University of New York Press, 1991.

Buckley, M.J., *At the Origins of Modern Atheism*, Yale University Press, New Haven, 1987.

Carmoly, Denise Lordnar, *Women and World Religions*, 2nd ed. Prentice Hall, 1989.

Chakravarti, Chintakeran, *Tantras: Studies in Their Religion and Literature*, Calcutta, 1972.

Chaudhuri, N.C., *Hinduism: A Religion to Live By*, Oxford University Press, New York, 1979.

Christ, Carol P., "Symbols of Goddess and God in Feminist Theology". In *The Book of the Goddess Past and Present: An Introduction to Her Religion*, edited by Carl Olson, pp. 231-51, Crossroad, New York, 1983.

Chopra, P.N. ed., *India: An Encyclopaedic Survey*, S. Chand, New Delhi, 1984.

Coburn, Thomas C, "The Devi Mahatmya as a Feminist Document", *Journal of Religious Studies* 8, no. 2 (1980): 1-11.

Coburn, Thomas C., *Devi Mahatmya: The Capitalization of the Goddess Tradition*, Motilal Banarsidass, Delhi, 1985.

Coburn, Thomas C., "Encountering the Goddess Notes on a Text, Gender, and Society", *Manishi* no. 80 (January-February 1994): 2:10.

Cole, W. Owen, *The Guru in Sikhism*, Longman & Todd, London, 1982.

Cole, W. Owen, *Sikhism and Its Indian Context, 1469-1708*, D.K. Publishers, New Delhi, 1984.

Conze, Edward, *Buddhism: Its Essence and Development*, Philosophical Library, New York, 1951.

Crooke, William, *The Popular Religion and Folklore of Northern India*, 2 Vols., Reprinted, Delhi, 1968.

Crooke, William, *Tribes and Castes of North Western Provinces and Oudh*, Calcutta, 1896.

Coomaraswamy, Ananda K., *The Dance of Shiva*, Farrar Straus, New York, 1957.

Coomaraswamy, Ananda K., *The Darker Side of Dawn*, Smithsonian Miscellaneous Collections, Vol. 94, no. 1, Washington, D.C., 1935.

Coomaraswamy, Ananda K., *Yaksas*, 2 Vols., 1928 and 1931, reprint Munshiram Manoharlal, New Delhi, 1971.

Dandekar, R.N., *Vedic Bibliography*, Bombay, 1946.

Dard, Dr. Gopal Singh, *Translation of Adi Granth*, 4 Vols., 1940.

Dasgupta, Shashi Bhushan, *Obscure Religious Cults*, 3rd ed., K.L. Mukhopadhyaya, Calcutta, 1962.

Das, Veena, "The Goddess and the Demon—An Analysis of the *Devi Mahatmya, Manushi*, no. 30 (September-October 1985): 28-32.

Davies, B., *Thinking About God*, London, 1987.

Davies, B., *An Introduction to the Philosophy of Religion*, Oxford, 1993.

Davies, B. (ed.), *Philosophy of Religion: A Guide to the Subject*, London, 1988.

De, Sushil Kumar, *Early History of the Vaishnava Faith and Movement in Bengal from Sanskrit and Bengali Sources*, 2nd ed., K.L. Mukhopadhyaya, Calcutta, 1961.

Dikshit, S.K., *The Mother Goddess*.

Dimock, Edward C., Jr., and Denise Levertov, trans., *In Praise of Krishna: Songs from the Bengali*, Doubleday, New York, 1967.

Doniger, Wendy, *Asceticism and Eroticism in the Mythology of Siva*, Oxford University Press, 1973.

Doniger, Wendy, *The Origins of Evil in Hindu Mythology*, University of California Press, Berkeley, 1976.

Doniger, Wendy, *The Rigveda: An Anthology*, Penguin Books, London, 1981.

Doniger, Wendy, trans., *Hindu Myths: A Sourcebook*, Penguin Books, London, 1973.

Doniger, Wendy, trans., with Brian K. Smith, *The Laws of Manu*, Penguin Books, London, 1991.

Dowson, John, *A Classical Dictionary of Hindu Mythology and Religion, Geography, History and Literature,* Rupa & Co., New Delhi, 1991.

Dube, S.C. (ed.), *Tribal Heritage in India,* 4 Vols., Vikas, New Delhi, 1977-1981.

Dubois, Abbe J.A., *A Description of the Character, Manners and Customs of the People of India,* 1862.

Dutt, M.N. (tr.), *Agni Purana,* Calcutta, 1923.

Dutt, Romesh, *The Epic of Ancient India,* 1899.

Easton, Stewart, *The Heritage of the Past,* Rinehart & Company, New York, 1957.

Edwards, Marian and Lewis Spence, *Dictionary of Non-Classical Mythology,* 1913.

Elide, Misacea (ed.), *The Encyclopaedia of Religion,* New York, 1987.

Encyclopaedia of Islam, Luzac & Co., 1913-18.

Farquhar, *A Primer of Hinduism,* 1911.

Farquhar, J.N., *An Outline of the Religious Literature of India,* Reprinted, Delhi, 1967.

Forrest, P., *God Without the Supernatural: A Defence of Scientific Theism,* Cornell University Press, 1996.

Facts, Stephen, *The Aboriginal Tribes of India,* St. Martin's Press, New York, 1973.

Gale, R., *On the Nature and Existence of God,* Cambridge University Press, Cambridge, 1991.

Griffith, Ralph J., *The Ramayan.*

Griffith, Ralph, T.H. (tr.), *The Hymns of the Atharva Veda,* 2 Vols. Reprinted Varanasi, 1962.

Griffith, Ralph, T.H., *The Hymns of the Rigveda,* 2 Vols., Reprinted, Varanasi, 1963.

Gupta, V.P. and Mohini Gupta, *Mother Goddess,* Delhi, 1998.

Gupta, V.P. and Mohini Gupta, *An Encyclopaedia of Punjab's History and Culture,* Delhi, 1998.

Haldane, J.J., *Atheism and Theism*, Blackwell, Oxford, 1996.

Hare, E.M. (tr.), *Auguttara Nikaya*, Vol. III & IV, London, 1932-36.

Hastings, James, *Encyclopaedia of Religion and Ethics*, Edinburgh, 1964.

Hawley, John Stratton and Donna Marie Wulff, *Devi Goddesses of India* (ed.), University of California Press, Berkeley.

Hawley, John Stratton, and Donne Marie Wolff, eds., *The Divine Consort: Radha and the Goddesses of India*, Bacon Press, Boston, 1982.

Hick, J., *An Interpretation of Religion: Human Responses to the Transcendent*, Yale University Press, New Haven, 1989.

Hopkins, Dr. E.W., *The Religions of India*, 1895.

Howall, Dr. Geo, *The Soul of India*, 1913.

Hughes, *Dictionary of Islam*, Rupa & Co., New Delhi, 1988.

Hughes, C.J., *The Nature of God*, Routledge, London, 1995.

Isacco, Enrico, and Anna L., Dallapiccola, *Krishna The Divine Lover: Myth and Legend Through Indian Art*, B.I. Publishers, New Delhi, 1982.

Jacobi, H. ed., *Acaranga Sutra*, London, 1882.

Jaggi, Rattan Singh, *Dasam Granth Parichaya* (Hindi), Delhi, 1990.

Jordan, Michael, *Encyclopaedia of Gods*, London, 1992.

Joshi, L.M., *Studies in the Buddhist Culture of India*, Delhi, 1967.

Kalidasa, *Sakuntala* ed. N.R. Acharya, Bombay, 1947.

Kapoor, A.N. and V.P. Gupta, *A Dictionary of World Religions*, Delhi, 1997.

Kaur, Gurvinder, *The Guru Granth Sahib: Its Physics and Metaphysics*, Delhi, 1981.

Keith, A.B., *Religion and Philosophy of the Vedas and the Upanishads*, 2 Vols., Harvard University Press, 1925.

Kennedy, Col. J., *Hindu Mythology*, 1862.

Lal, K.S., *The Legacy of Muslim Rule in India*, New Delhi, 1992.

Ling, T.O., *The Buddha: Buddhist Civilizations in India*, Tufle Smith, 1974.

Lyall, Sir Alfred, *Asiatic Studies* (2 Vols.), 1897.

MacDonell, A.A., *A History of Sanskrit Literature*, Reprinted, Delhi, 1965.

MacDonell, A.A., and A.B. Keith, *Vedic Index of Names and Subjects*, 2 Vols., Reprinted, Delhi, 1951.

MacDonell, A.A., *Vedic Mythology*.

Maity, P.K., *Historical Studies in the Cult of the Goddess*, Calcutta, 1966.

Mani, Vettam, *Puranic Encyclopaedia*, Motilal Banarsidass, Bunglow Road, Delhi-110007, 1984.

Margaret, Stutley and James Stutley, *A Dictionary of Hinduism 1500 BC-AD 1500*, Routledge and Kegan Paul, London, 1977.

Mazumdar, Subhash, *Who is Who in the Mahabharata*, Bhartiya Vidya Bhawan, Bombay, 1990.

Misra, O.P., *Mother Goddess in Central India*, Agam Kala Prakashan, Delhi, 1985.

Mitchell, Dr. J. Murray, *The Great Religions of India*, 1906.

Mitra, R. ed., *Taittriya Brahmana*, Calcutta, 1870.

Moore, Edward, *The Hindu Pantheon*, Indological Book House, Delhi, 2001.

Muir, Dr. J., *Original Sanskrit Texts,* 1870.

Muller, F. Max, ed. *The Sacred Books of the East,* 50 Vols., 1962-66, Reprint of 1879-1910 edition, Motilal, Delhi.

O'Flaherty, W.D., trans. and ed. *Hindu Myths: A Source Book,* Penguin, 1975.

Oman, Prof. John Campbell, *The Mystics, Ascetics and Saints of India,* 1903.

Pande, G.S., *Studies in the Origins of Buddhism,* Allahabad, 1957.

Pojman, L.P. (ed.), *Philosophy of Religion: An Anthology,* Wordsworth.

Pattanaik, Devdutt, *Shiva: An Introduction,* Mumbai, 1997.

Pupul, Jaykar, *The Earth Mother,* Penguin, 1989.

Ramakrishna Mission, *The Cultural Heritage of India,* 6 Vols., Institute of Culture, Calcutta, 1986.

Robson, Rev. Dr. J., *Hinduism and Christianity,* 1905.

Rhys Davids, T.W., *Vinay Pitak,* Oxford, 1881-85.

Rhys Davids, T.W., *Buddhist India,* London, 1993.

Saletone, R.N., *Encyclopaedia of Indian Culture,* 5 Vols. Sterling, New Delhi.

Singer, M.B. & ed. *Krishna: Myths, Rites and Attitudes,* East-West Centre Press, Honolulu, 1966.

Singh, B., *Burial Practices in Ancient India,* Prithvia Prakashan, Varanasi, 1970.

Singh, Harbans, *The Heritage of the Sikhs,* South Asia Books, Columbia, 1983.

Singh, Khushwant, *A History of the Sikhs,* 2 Vols., Princeton University Press, New Jeresy, 1963-65.

Sivananda, *Lord Siva and His Worship,* The Divine Life Society, Shivanandnagar, Distt. Tehri-Garhwal, India, 1996.

Sivaramamurti, C., *Nataraja in Art, Thought and Literature,* National Museum, New Delhi, 1974.

Swaroopanand, Swami, *Shrimad Bhagvad-Gita*, Advaita Ashram (Publication Department), 5 Dehi Entally Road, Calcutta-700014, 1996.

Swinburne, R., *The Existence of God*, Clarendon Press, Oxford, 1991.

Swinburne, R., *The Christian God*, Clarendon Press, Oxford, 1994.

Taylor, B., *Primitive Culture* (2 Vols.), 1888.

Thomas, P., *Christians and Christianity in India and Pakistan*, Allen & Unwin, London, 1954.

Troisi. J., *Tribal Religion: Religious Beliefs and Practices Among the Santals*, South Asia Books, Columbia, 1979.

Valmiki, *Ramayan*, Critical edition, Raghuvira, Lahore, 1938.

Van Buitenen, J.A.B., and C. Dimmit, trans. and eds., *Classical Hindu Mythology: A Reader in the Sanskrit Puranas*, Temple University Press, Philadelphia, 1977.

Ward, K., *Religion and Revelation: A Theology of Revelation in the World's Religions*, Clarendon Press, Oxford, 1994.

Ward, W. (5th ed.), *A View of the History, Literature and Religion of the Hindus*, 1862.

Williams, Sir Monier, *Religious Thought and Life in India*, 1883.

Williams, Sir, Monier, *Indian Epic Poetry*, 1863.

Williams, Sir Monier, *Indian Wisdom*, (2nd ed.), 1875.

Williams, Sir Monier, *Brahmanism and Hinduism* (3rd ed.), 1887.

Wilkins, *Hindu Mythology* (2nd ed.), 1900.

Wilson, H.H., *Essays on the Religions of the Hindus*, 1862.

Wynn, Mark, *Gods and Goddessess: A Natural Theological Perspective*, 1999.